Uncontrollable Blackness

Justice, Power, and Politics

The Justice, Power, and Politics series publishes new works in history that explore the myriad struggles for justice, battles for power, and shifts in politics that have shaped the United States over time. Through the lenses of justice, power, and politics, the series seeks to broaden scholarly debates about America's past as well as to inform public discussions about its future.

More information on the series, including a complete list of books published, is available at http://justicepowerandpolitics.com/.

Uncontrollable Blackness

African American Men and Criminality in Jim Crow New York

DOUGLAS J. FLOWE

The University of North Carolina Press
Chapel Hill

Set in Adobe Text Pro by Westchester Publishing Services

The University of North Carolina Press has been a member of the
Green Press Initiative since 2003.

Library of Congress Cataloging-in-Publication Data
Names: Flowe, Douglas J., author.
Title: Uncontrollable Blackness : African American Men and Criminality
   in Jim Crow New York / Douglas J. Flowe.
Other titles: Justice, power, and politics. Description: Chapel Hill:
   University of North Carolina Press, [2020] | Series: Justice, power,
   and politics | Includes bibliographical references and index.
Identifiers: LCCN 2019046698 | ISBN 9781469655727 (cloth: alk. paper) |
   ISBN 9781469655734 (paperback: alk. paper) | ISBN 9781469655741 (ebook)
Subjects: LCSH: African American men—New York (State)—New York—
   Social conditions—19th century. | African American men—New York
   (State)—New York—Social conditions—20th century. | Crime and race—
   New York (State)—New York—History. | Men—Identity. | Man-woman
   relationships—Social aspects. | African Americans—Segregation—New York
   (State)—New York. | New York (N.Y.)—Race relations—History.
Classification: LCC E185.86 F585 2020 | DDC 305.38/896073—dc23
LC record available at https://lccn.loc.gov/2019046698

Cover photographs courtesy of the New York State Archives, New York State
Board of Parole, Auburn Prison Division of Parole Case Files, Box 2.

For my parents,
Beatrice Devay Alston
and
Oscar Lee Flowe III

Contents

Illustrations

Acknowledgments

Throughout this project I've looked forward to thanking everyone who has had immeasurable impact on my work and personal and spiritual development over the years. These debts will follow me into the spirit world, as they can never be repaid in this life, but I will do my best through scholarship, teaching, and mentoring, as so many have done for me.

A number of preundergraduate experiences shaped my thoughts about history, social equality, and legal justice. At the American Museum of Natural History, Craig Vitamanti taught me about preservation, display, and presentation of historical material items. As president of the New World Foundation and a close mentor, Colin Greer exhibited how activism and political engagement can dovetail with scholarship to force social change; and others at the foundation, including Minette Coleman, Alta Starr, and Jerome Saunders, accepted me like family. I was extraordinarily lucky to bring history and social activism together in my work for the Greater Birmingham Ministries in Alabama, and to collaborate with Scott Douglas and Mary Johnson. As an undergraduate student at SUNY Geneseo I benefited from numerous mentors. I'm especially grateful for the care, advisorship, and candor of history professor Kathleen Mapes with whom I had the conversation that left me certain of what I wanted to do for the rest of my life. I also received support and advice from others like professors Maria Lima, David Tamarin, and Darrell Norris, all of whom modeled how to employ history to address urgent societal issues.

As a Provost's Fellow I joined the University of Rochester in 2007, a place that provided me with endless opportunities to grow as a scholar. I am appreciative of the generous support of the university's Frederick Douglass Institute, especially the timely care received from Jeffrey Tucker, Ghislaine Radegonde-Eison, and Cilas Kemedjio, and the conference travel funding from the institute. While I served as the Graduate Recruitment and Retention Specialist for the university, the David T. Kearns Center for Leadership and Diversity became my second home on campus. Beth Olivares was not only a great director for the program but a warmhearted friend and ally, and she made sure to teach me a lot about recruiting, supporting, and retaining graduate students from diverse backgrounds. Pia Bunson and Dean Wendi Heinzelman were both great colleagues and advocates at many different points. And, Jarron Decker and Francisco Piña made long, lonely days of recruitment travel into festive occasions when we met on the road.

In Rochester's history department, and outside of it, a number of faculty and staff became official and unofficial tutors and friends, including Jacqueline Rizzo, Joseph Inikori, Dorinda Outram, Richard Kaeuper, Matt Lenoe, John Waters, Dan Borus, Larry Hudson, and Ted Brown. Margarita Guillory graciously served on my dissertation committee and brought her command of history to bear on the project. Valeria-Sinclair Chapman was always there at those crucial moments of grad school when one needs guidance, and she helped my transition from student to faculty by providing the sort of insight necessary to navigate that terrain. I'm appreciative for friendships with Celia Applegate, Victoria Wolcott, and especially Elias Mandala, who treated me like a family member. Countless graduate program colleagues did the same, including Samuel Claussen, Emily Morry, Kira Thurman, Peter and Margaret Sposato, Michael Fisher, Michael Lamb, Mitch Gruber, Michelle Finn, Monique Patenaude, Rich Jurnack, Serenity Sutherland, John Portlock, Craig Nakashian, Dan Franke, Dani Picard, Jeff Ludwig, Jessica DeWitt, Kim Cristal Elliot, Laura Sikes, Marc Jambon, Matt Smalarz, Michael Brown, Jamie Saucier, Jay Learned, Paul Dingman, Amy Arbogast, Sam Huntington, and Tiffany Barber. My graduate advisor, Joan Shelly Rubin, has always been a supreme confidant, counselor, and advocate, applying the perfect mixture of instruction, encouragement, and pressure at all the right moments. I am thankful for the times she trusted my instincts, and for the times she made me reconsider them in her signature patient way. Her guidance and presence during some of the most trying times of my academic career are crucial to the foundation of this work and to the historian I have become.

I am forever bound to a series of organizations and people that have supported me in writing. Although this work is drawn from the theme of my doctoral dissertation, it is almost entirely new text, and writing over the past few years has required much substructure. Through the largesse of the American Culture Studies program at Washington University in St. Louis, I served as the Postdoctoral Fellow of Inequality and Identity from 2014–2016. Iver Bernstein, Maire Murphy, Jennifer Gallinat, Terri Behr, Heidi Aronson Kolk, Michael Allen, Linda Lindsey, and Dave Walsh provided daily support and attentiveness, and a contagiously rigorous and dynamic academic atmosphere that forced intellectual growth. The same can be said of the superb care and provision I received from Wash U's Center for the Humanities as a faculty fellow in the fall of 2018. Jean Allman, Rebecca Wanzo, Barbara Liebmann, Kathleen Fields, and Tila Neguse gave me the time I required and the atmosphere necessary for the sort of concentration that needed to happen. In both places I had a great cohort of fellow scholars, including

Tim Moore, Tabea Linhard, Claire McKinney, Matt Fox-Amato, and Jasmine Mahmoud, whose friendship and collaborative spirits fostered a great work environment.

Acquisition and analysis of the voluminous records at the foundation of this work has also required various forms of assistance. Librarians and archivists at the New York Public Library's Rare Books Division in the Stephen A. Schwarzman building and the Schomburg Center for Research in Black Culture, John Jay College's Lloyd Sealy Library, Columbia's Rare Book and Manuscript Library, and the Library of Congress have openhandedly shared untold numbers of letters, reports, personal papers, trial transcripts, and civic documents with me. I have received even more customized assistance from Jim Folts at the New York State Archives in Albany, and Kenneth Cobb and Rossy Mendez from the New York Municipal Archives. Wash U student and future historian Kayla Smith helped process thousands of pages of prison documents from the State Archives Bedford Hills Women's Reformatory collection, and did so with more detail and efficiency than I could have asked for. I am also indebted to my research assistant Theresa Decicco who accurately and determinedly clinched the last documents I needed to see from the municipal archives in the waning days of writing, just at the right time, and with such grace, patience, and clarity.

I joined Wash U's history department faculty in 2016 and have been overwhelmed by the embarrassment of riches the university and department have given me in terms of resources, personal and academic support, and mentoring. Outside of my department, Gerald Early, Rebecca Wanzo, Michelle Purdy, Lerone Martin, Vernon Mitchell, Diana Hill Mitchell, Jonathan Fenderson, Geoff Ward, Shanti Parikh, Damena Agonafer, John Wingfield, Rafia Zafar, Jean Allman, Rhaisa Williams, John Robinson, Janary Stanton, Barbara Baumgartner, Mary Ann Dzuback, Trevor Sangrey, Yvonne Osei, Linda Nicholson, Lingling Gao-Miles, Pete Benson, Angela Miller, Rudolph Clay, and Gail Boker, among others, have created a warm environment of deep scholarship, camaraderie, and community. Jeffrey McCune has challenged me as a scholar in compelling ways throughout my time at the university and stepped in as an advisor at crucial moments. Adrienne Davis has been the consummate advocate, taking a personal interest in me and my work since my first day on campus, and I am deeply appreciative of her unending encouragement, grace, and friendship.

I could not expect a better set of circumstances or group of colleagues in the history department. In conjunction with the Center for Humanities Faculty Fellowship, I have been allotted an academic leave by the department which amounted to a full year sabbatical to work on this book. Everyone in my department has warmly shown concern for my welfare and work, and extended themselves in various ways of welcome, including Daniel Bornstein, Andrea Friedman, Shefali Chandra, Christine Johnson, Hillel Kieval, Diana Montaño, Tim Parsons, Mark Pegg, Peter Kastor, Elizabeth Borgwart, Steven Miles, Christina Ramos, Iver Bernstein, Sowande' Mustakeem, Margaret Garb, Nancy Reynolds, Lori Watt, Alexandre Dubé, Margaret Williams, Monique Bedasse, Cassie Adcock, David Konig, and Anika Walke. I am particularly beholden to Venus Bivar and Corinna Treitel for care beyond the call of duty. Andrea Friedman has pored over many revisions of the chapters in this book and has accepted me in the department and her home like family. So has Peter Kastor, a king among department chairs, who has helped me transition into the department and do my best work and has consistently been there in the best and most difficult moments with equal enthusiasm and persistence. I am forever thankful. I must also thank Wash U's students for making my first few years of teaching amazing, and for helping me to think about the convergence of gender, criminality, and urban space in new dimensions. Particularly, the students in my American Masculinity course for the past two semesters, who have helped me think through some of the materials for this book.

My gratitude is boundless for the input, reading, and inspiritment liberally applied by a number of colleagues including Kali Gross, Victoria Wolcott, Cheryl Hicks, Leslie Harris, Kenneth Hamilton, Gerald Horne, Krystal Frazier, Nathan Connolly, Kaye Whitehead, Shannon King, Jennifer Fronc, Elizabeth Losh, Walter Greason, Marcia Gumpertz, Brandon Byrd, Kalonji Walton, Marsha Barrett, John Cumbler, Anwar Uhuru, and LaShawn Harris. Elizabeth Hinton's reading of revised pages, stimulating comments, and encouragement were critical at just the right moments in the project. I'm grateful for the insight and rigor both Heather Ann Thompson and Rhonda Williams brought to the work as the editors for the Justice, Power, and Politics series, and also as friends and fellow scholars who have galvanized my work with their own. Everyone at UNC Press has been generous with information and their time. Special thanks to my editor Brandon Proia for bringing great clarity to what might have been an arcane endeavor. He has guided me through the process of publication with the right measurements of persistence, patience, and poise. I am likewise thankful for the suggestions and encouragement of my manuscript readers, both of whom helped make this project what it is. I would also like to thank Michelle Witkowski from Westchester Publishing Services, my proofreader Jessica Ryan, and Matthew White for indexing the manuscript.

I also cannot thank Timothy Gilfoyle enough for painstakingly reading and commenting on the entire manuscript and for his willingness to share his resources, connections, and deep knowledge of New York City to help me on my way. Along with Geoff Ward, Andrea Friedman, Chad Montrie, and Jean Allman, he gave days' worth of attention to the book in a timely workshop that improved my insight into urban crime. I am grateful for Chad Montrie's generosity in reading and rereading my chapters, and for what he has taught me about friendship with his caring and generous nature. Alison Parker likewise has affected my way of thinking about history, not only with her scholarship but as a great friend and cheerleader from my graduate school days forward, and my work has benefited from the influence of her penetrating yet sympathetic handling of historical analysis.

I am unsure how this work would have turned out without the devoted bonds, collaborations, and deep intellectual discourses I have had with a few key colleagues and guides. Sowande' Mustakeem and I have spent many days and nights planning projects, pondering themes related to criminality and gender, and dancing until 4 A.M. Our intellectual symbiosis has nourished this work in many ways, and our friendship has nourished the spirit. It is difficult to describe the effect Iver Bernstein's advice and attention have had on my scholarship, and even more formidable to fathom the impression his own work and our conversations have made on the scholar I have become. His tutelage, provocation, meticulous readings, and faith in my work have pushed me to discover hidden strengths and persuaded me into evermore complex ways of thinking about and writing history. As such, he has been a consummate mentor and advocate who has had clear and untold influence on the direction of my career and the shape and texture of this project. Our late esteemed colleague Margaret Garb has had a similar impact on my development as an early scholar through reading my work, with the example of her own scholarship, and with her sheer presence as an ally and friend. Margaret made me feel welcomed at the university and in her home, and she took the type of interest in my work and well-being that sustained me through the years. She is very sorely missed.

Outside of academia many friends and family have contributed to the life-force that allowed me to do this work. I must thank the Dhamma Visuddhi Vipassana Meditation Center in Menomonie, Wisconsin, and the Dhamma Siri Vipassana Center in Kauffman, Texas, each for the provision of ten days of silence and meditation when I needed it. I have experienced tremendous fellowship and togetherness on a weekly basis, and the occasional rejuvenating retreat, with the members of St. Louis' Center for Pragmatic Buddhism for years. Particularly Aaron Gates, Mary Hammond, Lillith Alexandria, Catherine Harman, Jonathon Edwards, James Owens, Detlef Ritter, Michael Holliday, Reena Chesla, and especially Danielle MacCartney, who has tirelessly overseen the center and shared her wisdom with us. The staff at the Creve Coeur, Missouri, Trader Joes has kept me fed and cheered me on all the way with encouragement and kindness. So has Kyle, my massage therapist, with whom I have had some of the deepest conversations during sessions that made long hours of writing tolerable. Ann Wimsatt and Dave Williams have also fed and heartened me periodically, and I admire their consistent work to create a more equitable St. Louis. Other friends like Saxon Hanwacker, Greg Casseus, Sasha Berry, Tyler Mackie, Angelina Sylvain, Anthony Beasley, and Jerome, Brad, and Kenneth Saunders have always inspired me onward and gave their time in critical ways. This project benefited in many different ways from the help of Tamara Van Loo, including research and archival assistance. Sam Claussen has been a peerless confidant and voice of reason in conversations about culture and history since graduate school. And, Damena Agonafer has been a great champion of my work, including helping me get away from it when needed.

I have been blessed with many supportive relatives including Michael and Carolyn Flowe, Joel Flowe, Roger and Theresa Flowe, Valerie Murphy, Paula Flowe, Donald Lanier, Linda King, June Alston, Joyce Parish, Mark Alston, and John Alston. Special thanks go to Kenneth and Joel Flowe, Julio Hernandez, Robert Lanier, and Elizabeth Lanier. Jim Clemente has inspired my work on criminality with his own and has been a great and affectionate friend and family member for as long as I remember.

My longtime friend Diego Iriarte has appeared at my side through the best and most difficult moments, and he and his wife, Christine Mazzarino, have had an inexpressible impact on this project, not only through the kind of generous support often reserved for family, but by crucially putting me up for weeks at a time while I visited New York City archives. Martin Bildstein has been a similarly exemplary friend giving countless hours to the sort of discourse that sparked ideas and concepts for my work, and with long, off-the-grid trips into the Adirondacks. And my friendship with Jerome Saunders has had an immeasurable impact on my writing, analysis of history, and view of the world. Having access to Jerome's candor, intellect, and profound intuition over the years has made me a better scholar and person. I am supremely grateful for the part he has played in my life. This book has benefited greatly from Victor Farwell's guidance and open-hearted teachings about the tremendous presence and power of those who have come before, and our great bond with the past. He has encouraged me to merge head and heart by summoning the content in the recesses of the spirit. *Uncontrollable Blackness* would be a very different book without his consistent and devoted friendship, instruction, and mentorship. My eternal gratitude.

I am particularly thankful for the patience exhibited by a number of close family members while I worked on this book. It may not have always been clear what I was doing, but you all stood by me. I deeply appreciate the encouragement and love given by my sister Crystal Griffin and my niece Ceilani Griffin. My big brother, Oscar Lee Flowe IV, is embedded in my earliest memories of the world. He is foundational to my understanding of life, and his presence and towering intellect have influenced me beyond expression. This book is certainly better from the long abstract social and metaphysical conversations we have had over the past decades and the commitment to seeing reality for what it is that he instilled in me.

I am eternally grateful for the caring motherhood Pierangela Veneziani has given to our daughter, and for her advice and encouragement over the years. She was the first person to inspire me to go to graduate school and show me what it means to be a scholar and professor. Her hard academic work has become a model for my own. I am likewise grateful for the love and patience of my daughter, Ginger Veneziani Flowe, whom I have kept in my head and heart throughout all of my work and everything I do. Ginger's sense of imagination and determination to understand things and people is inspiring. I can only hope to have made her proud with this book.

No one has inspired my scholarship and life more than my parents, Beatrice Devay Alston and Oscar Lee Flowe III, both of whom suddenly left the physical realm during my work on this project, but their spirits have been ever-present throughout. I hope to have combined my mother's generous, gentle, and forgiving take on the world with my father's incisive sense of objectivity to good effect in my view of the past. Watching how they both graciously navigated the crucibles that both African American men and women face nourished this work from its very roots, and they gave me life in many more ways than the obvious. They were both not only peerless parents but my greatest and closest friends. This work is for them.

It is also dedicated to the men and women in this book and all the ancestors who endured, fought, struggled, and died for respect, power, and peace under bewilderingly taxing and lopsided circumstances of racial inequality and violence. With hope, I have accurately channeled their lives and respectfully honored their perspectives in pursuit of greater understanding of their reality and our own. *Ase!*

Uncontrollable Blackness

Introduction

The Crucible of Black Criminality

There are times when disobedience heals a very ailing part of the self.
It relieves the human spirit's distress at being forced into narrow
boundaries. For the nearly powerless, defying authority is often the
only power available.

—Malidoma Patrice Somé, *Of Water and the Spirit*

Growing up in central Manhattan, Dell Whitehead endured many of the challenges common to black New Yorkers in the first two decades of the twentieth century. Born in 1900 to a black migrant from Virginia and an Irish immigrant mother, Whitehead occupied a three-room flat with both parents and six siblings. Although most of his immediate neighbors were African American, his childhood home on West Forty-Fifth Street sat in a black belt straddled by white ethnic immigrants in the working-class Hell's Kitchen neighborhood.[1] Experiencing poverty and the dislocation of delinquency, Whitehead, with an older brother, faced a four-month commitment in a Catholic protectory for children when they absconded from home in 1910.[2] While away, their father died of complications related to asthma and their mother, dependent upon her husband's earnings as a hotel porter, became a single parent without a source of income.[3]

Whitehead contributed to the support of his family in the ways he could, but the difficulty of securing funds led him to a string of arrests. Shortly after his seventeenth birthday, in 1917, he plead guilty to unlawful entry, garnering an eighteen-month sentence in the New York House of Refuge.[4] After release he was arrested for assault with a deadly weapon in 1919, for robbery in 1922, and for the theft of a taxi cab after colliding with a milk wagon during a chase in 1925. Placed on parole the following year, Whitehead violated the terms of his release only three years later during a stretch of unemployment. According to a report in his arrest file, police apprehended him and his brother-in-law when they "jimmied" the entrance of a women's clothing store and removed $1,000 worth of merchandise, and both went to prison for more than two years.[5] During Whitehead's initial intake examination at Auburn Correctional Facility an interviewer summarized his path to incarceration in blunt terms. "As a result of the unwholesome environment in which he was reared, [he] manifested criminal tendencies in his early years," they wrote. Poverty and "close contact with criminal characters" the interviewer concluded, made him "[give] himself to extreme habits, being intimate with prostitutes and drinking to excess," all of which presumably precipitated his crimes. Whitehead, they determined, was "mentally sluggish and unimaginative," and inherently possessed "tendencies toward incorrigibility."[6]

Whitehead's path to prison displays the contradictions, possibilities, and risks New York presented to African Americans at the turn of the century. The urban industrial North allowed blacks latitudes they rarely found in the South, so they moved to places like New York by the thousands. But surveillance, physical and economic marginalization, and violence narrowed their choices. Whitehead's own inclinations doubtlessly guided his decisions in many ways, but it is also clear his surroundings and his unique positionality as an African American man contributed to his predicament.[7] As part of a cluster of districts in the orbit of central Manhattan's Tenderloin neighborhood, Hell's Kitchen was known for decaying structures, poverty, and crime. Notorious as a commercial sex district, the area featured brothels, gambling dens, and pool halls that drew customers from all over the city. On the same block as the Whitehead home and in the vicinity, sex workers and pleasure-seeking clients mixed with theatergoers, department store shoppers, and office workers in commercial exchange.[8] In 1906, the grisly murder of a "mulatto woman" in a black saloon not far from Whitehead's home shocked the city and solidified the area's bloodcurdling reputation.[9] Hell's Kitchen and the Tenderloin were also the sites of well-known racial clashes. Black residents slowly relocating westward into Whitehead's community in the 1890s met fierce resistance from Irish immigrants and entered into what one paper called a "conflict of the races for the supremacy of the neighborhood."[10] Only months after Whitehead's birth, rioting exploded in the vicinity as Irish residents and police officers attacked African Americans seeking vengeance for the stabbing death of an undercover police detective by a black migrant.[11] Widespread bloodshed visited the section multiple times across the next two decades, including once in 1910 following black heavyweight boxing champion Jack Johnson's victory over white challenger Jim Jeffries. The family experienced their own tragedy in 1925 when a jilted lover murdered one of Whitehead's sisters.[12] In this environment, the place he came of age, he likely found it difficult to avoid the dangers of the neighborhood, the temptations of ill-gotten profits, and the wealth of options for risky amusement and self-indulgence.

In the time between Whitehead's birth and his imprisonment in 1929, New York City changed in reality and imagination for African Americans in many ways.[13] At the turn of the century residents witnessed the emergence of the modern metropolis as the city consolidated with Brooklyn.[14] With more than

3.4 million residents by the release of the 1900 census, only London had more citizens and economic influence.[15] In the wake of the Civil War, Gotham came to represent the triumph of corporate capitalism, and it reshaped American culture into what sociologist David Riesman dubbed "other-directedness." As Americans moved from rural to urban settings, the "inner-direction" of custom, religion, and family surrendered to the commodification of work efficiency, new organizations of time and space, and the confusion of identity with patterns of consumption and social life.[16] Christened "America's metropolis" in 1903 by writer Herbert Croly, New York City made urbanity an American value, and it drew far-flung citizens and immigrants to its streets like a capitalist rite of passage.[17] Wall Street, Broadway, and famed institutions like the Waldorf-Astoria and Carnegie Hall embodied the prosperity of global modern enterprises, symbolism that was not lost on black migrants streaming north over land and sea.[18]

For many blacks, New York offered a form of freedom unavailable elsewhere. Embellished stories from friends and family who migrated before, personal desires for novel experiences, and exploitative labor agents enticed them North.[19] Upon arrival they found the city as exciting as advertised, especially in neighborhoods like the Tenderloin. "There is everything in the Tenderloin [that] there is in the world, and you can get it all if you want," one news writer declared in 1899.[20] In 1900, as President William McKinley won reelection with the help of African American voters, the city's black population reached just over 60,000, and the avenues cutting through black neighborhoods became displays of diversity. The black Tenderloin, and later Harlem, became a pastiche of African diasporic cultures, the air filled with the aromas of Southern and Caribbean cooking and the musical babble of accents and dialects from across the hemisphere and the Atlantic. Blacks ranged widely in the recently consolidated five boroughs, but primarily resided in Manhattan. More than 8 percent of that population, roughly 5,000, hailed from the Caribbean, South America, and Africa.[21] Driven to New York by economic conditions and overcrowding at home, and a desire to forego Southern settlement, Afro-Caribbean immigrants composed more than 10 percent of the city's black population by 1910.[22]

In that same year there were more than 91,000 black residents in the city, the bulk making their way from Southern states like Virginia, North Carolina, and Florida.[23] They flocked to avenues where shirtwaist factories towered over cigar shops, theaters, restaurants, candy stores, and clothiers. They witnessed the rise of skyscrapers, the building of a subway network, the arrival of media empires and avant-garde forms of entertainment such as motion picture studios and theaters, which turned the city into a global citadel for modernism. In the mélange of new modes of expression and immoderation, long-established paradigms of Victorian comportment regarding class, gender, and sexuality dissolved in a deluge of commercialism. However, race complicated the matter. As the frontier of the West closed, urban space became a new frontier for everyone, including African Americans one generation or so removed from bondage. New York presented them with unfamiliar discretion but also new and old obstacles that stunted their imaginations of what was possible. As a result, the city is an important historical realm in which to consider the break between the realities of race and discrimination and the aspirations of black men.[24]

The summary judgment of Whitehead's intake interviewer portraying him as a psychologically defective product of his environment divulges the influence pseudoscientific criminological perspectives had on the fates of black men before and after imprisonment. The American legal system had largely accepted the ideas of criminologists like Italian-born Cesare Lombroso, who saw unlawful tendencies as embedded in physical features. Nineteenth-century classical criminological theory argued everyone had selfish inclinations that could only be controlled by legal restrictions, but Lombroso theorized bodily racial differences made entire sections of society "born criminals." In his 1911 publication, *Criminal Man*, Lombroso claimed lawbreakers carried brutish characteristics such as flattened noses, "the projection of the lower part of the face and jaws . . . found in negroes and animals," and "anomalies in the face, skeleton, and various psychic and sensitive functions" associated with "primitive races."[25] Viewing the body as evidence to discern "criminal types," criminal anthropologists defined non-European features as predictors of crime. Borrowing French criminologist Alphonse Bertillon's system of physical measurements to classify incoming prisoners, American penitentiaries produced painstaking descriptions of the bodies of inmates noting shape, size, and color.[26] All prisoners received such evaluations, but assessors often emphasized African American features that they designated as unevolved.

As an example, when Tyler Summers arrived at Sing Sing prison in 1890, his features noted in the admission register struck a eugenic chord. According to evaluators he had a "large and fair shaped head . . . low down small thin ears wellback [sic] on [his] head," and a "high and round forehead, full over the eyes." They were surprised by his small nose, but observed "sunken cheeks. Full mouth [and] thick lips."[27] Diagnostic summaries often included descriptions of black men as "mentally subnormal," "moron," or "ignorant [and] indolent,"[28] and classified them with terms such as "low negro."[29] African Americans were presumed to be criminals in lay rhetoric and popular culture, but criminologists like Lombroso used pseudoscientific evidence to confirm that presumption. In the words of prominent antivice advocate

Charles Parkhurst, emancipation released blacks from servitude but "change of circumstances is no index of change of character."[30]

As a "mulatto," Whitehead embodied the risk of interracial contact, particularly sex. His interviewer determined his mother was also a "mental defective," and with his father she "never properly supervised [him] or provided . . . adequate moral training." Interracial couples, many believed, were ill-omened from the beginning, likely to produce criminals and destroy the lives of white men and women who indulged. Although Whitehead was "mentally sluggish and unimaginative," his partially white lineage endowed him with "a native shrewdness," the interviewer concluded, a sense of cunning that perhaps made him more dangerous than other black criminals.[31] According to prevailing progressive ways of thinking, Whitehead's very existence indicated the breakdown of social and structural decorum, the type that would inevitably lead to further headaches for society if not discontinued.[32]

Many progressive American reformers also bought into these eugenic characterizations and used them to shape their responses to a seemingly disordered society. As a pervasive cultural phenomenon, the Progressive movement, roughly from 1890 to 1920, included myriad groups across the country deploying various tactics to reform work, health, and living conditions according to their ideas of betterment. Reformers included middle-class men and women, business owners, religious leaders, social scientists, and even law enforcement, government officials, and prison personnel. Although certainly not a monolithic group, progressives generally assumed society could be changed to fit the needs of people in some ways, but also that some people should be formed to fit society. Contemporary criminological science considered heredity to be the primary problem, and African Americans were lowest on the eugenic scale. Southern bondage and white plantation paternalism, the logic went, had moderated black instincts to a tolerable degree, but emancipation turned loose a whirlwind of black perversion, an orgiastic crime spree that would inevitably sweep north. Historian Phillip Bruce propagated this philosophy in *The Plantation Negro as a Freeman*, published in 1889, essentially telling his readers a roiling black menace was soon to arrive in their town, and that the only hope would be the creation of two "social bodies" living "side by side, but without intermingling." Blacks, he held fast, would likely revert to their ancestral condition progressively over the years of freedom to come.[33] Some, like Bruce, believed education, greater freedoms, and lessened racial discrimination did nothing to change black criminal inclinations, and they argued "evil tendencies prevail" in the North "in even greater degree than in the South."[34] While a few could be saved through instruction and emulation of whites, prominent criminological and eugenic theory at the time spelled doom for black men and women living on the margins, and progressive reformers set out to safeguard salvageable whites from hopeless racial others by keeping them apart.[35]

The progressive instinct to segregate ran counter to a current of state desegregation that started in late nineteenth-century New York, but it was supported by local and national de facto Jim Crow policies. The phrase "Jim Crow" came from early nineteenth-century blackface minstrel performer Thomas "Daddy" Rice who played the racist "Jump Jim Crow" character, and the popular expression came to represent the system of separation and control that marginalized blacks in the South by the 1890s.[36] New York City had a deep history of racially biased practices long before and after the 1827 state emancipation of enslaved Africans, including large-scale racial violence like the 1863 draft riots.[37] But statewide education integrated following the Civil War and black men received admission to judicial processes in the same period. The state's Civil Rights Act of 1873 gave black men the right to vote, and laws against unfair housing rates and the abolition of statutes prohibiting interracial marriage followed closely.[38] Likewise, the 1895 Malby Equal Rights Act promised to provide "full and equal accommodations, advantages, facilities, and privileges of [all] places of public accommodation or amusement" to African American New Yorkers.[39] Still, state legislation failed to prevent the continuance of de facto segregation based on the perception of blacks as subservient, undesirable, and dangerous.[40] Black criminals depicted in popular culture congealed white imagination around the obligation of controlling black conduct, and Jim Crow protocols bolstered racial attacks by police and citizens.[41] Nationally, the 1896 passage of the milestone court decision *Plessy v. Ferguson* reinforced apartheid codes ruling it constitutional to provide separate but unequal facilities for blacks and whites.[42] Paying lip-service to black voters during his presidential campaign in 1912 Woodrow Wilson hailed African Americans for their "extraordinary progress toward self-support," which he promised to reward with "absolute fair dealing" if he won the 1913 election.[43] Wilson did win the presidency, but blatantly promoted division and filled some administrative posts with outspoken segregationists.[44] Without real federal intervention, black Americans suffered widespread racial attacks like those of 1919's Red Summer and struggled to make headway in economic, social, and residential realms.[45] Racism may not have been encrypted into law in New York as prominently as in some Southern states, but Jim Crow was alive and well in the city.

Stitched into the progressive pattern of thinking is a paradox. Urban centers did, indeed, need restructuring, particularly in terms of factors that impacted the health, happiness, and behaviors of residents.[46] But as reformers saved some from the city itself, they participated in the reproduction of poverty, crime, and racial antipathy in the lives of others by limiting their movements and closing off crucial avenues of self-determination. They used undercover investigations, intrusive studies, and other sorts of surveillance to push for legislation and policing tactics that yoked blacks in a web of restrictions. Reformers sometimes claimed concern for everyone's safety motivated efforts to segregate housing, saloons, and naked bodies, but one can see the seeds of such separation in the missives of New York City voices that already equated amalgamation with crime in the mid-nineteenth century.[47] Whitehead's intake agent and other commentators on race and crime in the 1920s may have considered themselves more enlightened than their predecessors, but their actions and words conveyed the same racist sentiments. Perceiving diminishing sunlight between the races in New York, they folded segregation into existing reform campaigns and sought to patrol the public and private lives of black men with special vigor.[48] Wielding influence with civic administrations, they enlisted police in the enforcement of unofficial mandates regarding black behavior, and officers used petty arrests, billy clubs, and guns to hold the line.[49] Under the constant threat of surveillance and terrorism, blacks experienced a landscape that reduced their chances of reaching the sort of stability progressives claimed to want for everyone and that men like Whitehead never enjoyed.

Understanding segregation as an impediment to black mobility is critical to comprehending the particular experiences of black men, as it not only evokes real tangible barriers but also psychological ones.[50] At the outset of the century much of American life was about movement as migrants, immigrants, and city dwellers sought social and economic fulfillment and access to the levers of modernity, both of which relocation to novel urban spheres promised.[51] The meaning of such city spaces is created socially, crafted in the minds, actions, and cultures of the people who occupy them.[52] Yet, for African Americans, free motion and spatial occupation had a sordid past and present. In bondage, removing one's own body to another location was illegal, and in the Jim Crow South, measures meant to retain and control black labor often outlawed transplantation. As a result, regional and local movement and the inhabitation of certain spaces could become revolutionary for blacks.

In New York, when men like Whitehead traversed the city, they maneuvered through a minefield of unwelcoming locales, at times resolutely challenging arbitrary boundaries with their very physical presence. Like all men they sought self-renewal, self-reliance, economic abundance, and sexual intimacy or conquest; yet, unlike white men, they confronted obstacles that sometimes froze them in place. Frustrated by white attempts to control them, black men needed to designate zones where they could assemble selfhood and nurture their imaginations away from such oversight. New York City never provided this ideal setting, but neighborhoods like Harlem and an auxiliary black built environment in other parts of the city rendered some retreat. By looking at the lives of men like Whitehead, this study interrogates the fusion of concrete, cultural, and hypothetical arenas with concepts of manhood harbored by black men in order to discern what those spaces and concepts meant to them and how and why they fought for them.

This book focuses on the period from the late nineteenth century to the late Harlem Renaissance in order to foreground the transformation of black lives across a span of starts and stops in racial inclusion. Throughout such setbacks, black New Yorkers advanced from small pockets of community in lower-Manhattan to the black settlement of Harlem, energetically participated in politics, and enacted a cultural rebirth. However, in that time, racial realities changed little, and by the 1930s they sat perched upon a precipice overlooking a decade of economic depression.

Accordingly, this work examines the myriad inescapable hindrances and opposing forces birthed in slavery and continued into the new century that were meant to neuter black men and solidify white supremacy, and it centralizes an inquiry of how those men responded to that cultural physiognomy. What did it mean to African American men to be geographically constrained and economically isolated, and how did they resolve to surmount those obstacles? Can we see extralegal activity and criminalized behavior as radical text, filled with content about the existential dreams, dread, and desires of black men? Did they possibly use illegality as a way to traverse restricted visible and invisible terrain?

This work argues in the affirmative and demonstrates how crime might serve as a site of extraction for men intentionally restricted from normative modes of material acquisition and the construction of masculine identity. Blacks often met violence with violence, and they endeavored to secure themselves from humiliation and death when faced with both. Most men ground out a living through legitimate labor, but a significant subsection found it difficult, or impossible, to subsist or thrive with inconsistent work and low pay. At the same time, dissatisfaction with the work available, and an inclination to partake in the Dionysian pleasures of New York City, inspired actions others deemed unlawful.

Nevertheless, men like Whitehead faced a crucible in public, private, commercial, and leisure spaces that demarcated real and invisible boundaries across the city. They labored as porters, elevator operators, cooks, janitors, and furnace tenders if they were lucky, or gave their bodies to ruthless toil in dangerous construction jobs or heavy labor as longshoremen. They struggled to support families, insert themselves into the city's economic mainframe, and achieve the sort of sexual and material gratification most Americans wished for at the time. Before migrating to Harlem, they inhabited a constellation of black neighborhoods and buildings often imbedded in hostile territory and literally under siege when racial tensions flared. They fought for their lives or the lives of loved ones, and in some cases retaliated against racial violence or initiated it themselves. And in the gale that blustered around them, they sought ways to eat when bread was scarce, methods of securing power when restrained, and performed manhood even when denied its normative properties.

Recovering Black Men through Crime

The stretch of decades between 1890 and 1930 encompass a remarkably formative period in the advent of the black criminal in white imagination and in reality. Unbridled crime waves bedeviled most American cities in the late 1800s, and all ethnicities participated. Yet conversations about black crime often emphasized race while many progressives and criminologists understood white crime through class. The solidification of whiteness as a racial category in this period hinged upon delineating blackness as separate, indelible, and criminal.[53] Long before the "culture of poverty" debate of the 1960s and beyond, the black criminal emerged as a mutant-like creature birthed from black pathology and white anxieties about race.[54] In cities like New York, whites often explained ruinous black communities, street crime, high death rates, and broken families with pseudoscientific missives about black inferiority and dismissed discrimination as a cause altogether.[55] This made overt racism disguisable by a mask of concern about crime, a phenomenon that is also mirrored in the "tough on crime" political rhetoric of the late twentieth century. The racialization of black crime thus justified a panoply of diabolical practices ranging from segregation to the communal and ceremonial dismemberment of black bodies for unsubstantiated accusations.

A cadre of thinkers like Nathaniel Shaler, Herbert Spencer, and Frederick Hoffman disseminated social Darwinist ideas that said blacks were less fit for civilization and would face extinction.[56] Along with progressive reformers and lawmakers, they used anecdotal evidence and statistics on black mortality, crime, and imprisonment to prove it. In his eugenic *Race Traits* publication, Hoffman argued the self-slaughtering nature of black heredity was to blame for racial inequality. An innate vulnerability to disease and criminal tendencies would continue high black mortality rates, and, as a result, the race would eventually disappear, he claimed.[57] A later published treatise on racial extinction by Hoffman's fellow eugenicist, Madison Grant, reasoned that if one race did not drive the other out the two would combine into a "population of race bastards."[58] Preoccupied with the idea of blackness as a death sentence for white civilization, some whites put forward solutions. Tales like Joseph Conrad's *Heart of Darkness* (1899) and Edgar Rice Burroughs's *Tarzan of the Apes* (1912) proposed whites recognize their own primitivism and thereby triumph over those considered lesser, beating them at their own game.[59] Some like Alabama senator John Tyler Morgan presented measures to finance black resettlement in Africa.[60] Many considered the 1896 *Plessy v. Ferguson* ruling of separate but unequal a practicable resolution, while other's wondered how long it would take for perceived evolutionary shortcomings to eliminate blacks from the equation altogether.[61]

Willing to concede that race might be responsible for deviant behavior in some cases, black intellectuals like Kelly Miller and W. E. B. Du Bois rejected purely eugenic arguments.[62] Miller, in a lengthy review of *Race Traits*, considered Hoffman's data questionable and bereft of insight about racism and deprivation.[63] Du Bois likewise found Hoffman's conclusions too general since "we can no more fasten upon the bad as typifying the general tendency than we can upon the good."[64] White social scientist Francis Kellor followed in 1901 with a study she argued disproved claims that biology predicted criminal behavior. She compared detailed measurements of the anatomies of white and black prisoners and found no difference could be discerned between them.[65] Commentators like Miller, Du Bois, and a coterie of white critics like Kellor, seemed to experience a sense of conflict and contradiction—on one hand expressing biased views of the black underclass themselves and on the other urging the scientific community to recognize racial disadvantage.[66] In an 1897 speech commencing the assembly of the American Negro Academy Du Bois betrayed such prejudices citing black "immorality, crime, and laziness" as partly responsible for racial strife, but two years later he made a more radical statement in his seminal *Philadelphia Negro* publication.[67] In it, he characterized crime as "the open rebellion of an individual against his social environment," an insurrection that only racial equality could end.[68] In other words, the problem of African American crime should be addressed by those who understood how racism bred illegality, not those who condemned blacks to extinction. With this in mind, a bifold effort could be made to combat lawlessness while fighting its causes. Black leaders would need to be critical of black offenders while trying to dismantle the crucible they navigated.

Centered on the highly transient period from the Gilded Age to the Great Depression, this study includes the lives of Southern migrant men, but its scope will not be limited to them. Black Caribbean and South American migrants and immigrants, native-born New Yorkers, and men gravitating to the region from other parts of the North and West will be included. Given that blue-collar, unskilled wage laborers and the unemployed more frequently found themselves entangled with the law than middle-class men, and considering that many historians have already told the story of black bourgeois men's efforts to maintain a steady sense of their identity, this study focuses on the lives of the working class.[69] By concentrating on the black proletariat and urban poor, it casts light on an understudied aspect of the perennial struggle for black freedom and the centuries-long project of constructing and fertilizing black manhood, particularly as defined by men whose voices are most muted in history.[70] As such, *Uncontrollable Blackness* centers the motivations and circumstances of men who largely went unnoticed by a white and black elite except in crime reports and efforts to change, suppress, or remove them from view.

With their lives so connected to lovers, wives, and other female family members, a deep analysis of any theme involving black men requires placing them into context with black women. This is crucial not only because of the familial, romantic, physical, and emotional connections between men and women, but also because of the profound ways in which partners impacted the formation of black masculine identity. Romantic others uniquely galvanized black men to survive and thrive, whether with legal or illegal acts, through joy and sorrow. They gave meaning to daily grinding work and every-day defiances and made the hearts of men palpitate out of lust, love, or anger.[71] Women also coveted their own longings for respect, stability, pleasure, and freedom; a fact that kindled the flames of black romance for better or worse. Whether migrants or not, both black men and women were in motion, seeking the power to transcend statuses ascribed by race, class, and gender and looking to achieve new statuses of merit in the urban milieu.[72]

A study spotlighting the early twentieth century places the analytical gaze squarely on a time of great cultural and gender transformations for African Americans that had implications for black manhood.[73] A generation of "new negro" men with ideas about self-defense and black nationalism, returning from battle in World War I with combat skills, and experiencing a cultural, intellectual, and commercial revitalization emerged with self-governance in mind, and many affixed that freedom to their masculinity.[74] They challenged Booker T. Washington's accommodationist stance on securing equal rights, and some responded to the horror of lynching with calls for violence and retribution. A new segment of the black intelligentsia, including W. E. B. Du Bois, believed Washington represented an "old attitude of adjustment and submission" that lacked "true manhood."[75] While out of date Washingtonian conceptions of manhood encouraged conformity, Du Bois and new negroes considered self-assertion the crucial ingredient.[76] That recipe often required the mobility of relocation, especially for those who lived in the South. "The negroes are leaving the South because life to them has been made miserable and unbearable," Adam Clayton Powell told a mass meeting in 1917. "These migrating thousands are not seeking money, but manhood rights."[77] George Henry White confirmed this understanding of migration in blunt terms claiming he left North Carolina with the explicit objective of being "treated like a man."[78]

Although working-class whites dealt with some of the same deprivations that lead to crime as African American men, the men in this study are plainly unique.[79] Unlike white men, black men steered through the obstacles of Jim Crow, pervasive race-based limitations, and the sickening gore of public executions. They came of age while planted in the terra firma of the long New Negro era and sowed seeds of radical political thought in the loam of everyday resistances. While European immigrants proceeded to reap the rewards of a collective sense of whiteness, particularly so after World War I, blacks lacked access to the same tools, spaces, and jobs they relied upon.[80] Whites begrudged black men the ideological, financial, and physical accouterment of manhood, a Machiavellian holdover from the antebellum period. Without economic power, jurisdiction over public space, and domestic latitude, black men often found that race largely rescinded male privilege.[81] Fittingly, efforts to achieve greater levels of citizenship and economic power by black men have historically been conjoined with the project of proving, protecting, and sustaining masculine identity. Most black men existed within a duality; fixed between hopes of submerging in American material and carnal contentment and desires to lead respectable lives in the terms accorded to men.

With this in mind, this study illustrates how black men both accepted and rejected white masculine postures, resisted emasculation, and reproduced their own standards of manhood.[82] They found themselves circumscribed by the vestiges of a white power structure crafted to nullify their assertions of gender and maintain white supremacy. As the perennial antagonist in the theatrical drama of racial anxieties, black male bodies occupied cognitive and ideological space in the American psyche, and they faced uniquely panopticon-like surveillance. Thus, their crimes express a particular rebellious posture absent from the experiences of white men.

Conveying the stress and willfulness working-class black men sometimes expressed through breaking laws and recovering their voices from the early twentieth century is a formidable task. While well-known paper collections and repositories hold in-depth information about the lives of black middle-class men and leaders, first- and secondhand articulations of the perspectives of the marginalized and poor are rare and need to be cobbled together from many sources. Because most of the men in this study did not carry diaries or keep personal paper collections, their voices are mostly lost in the wind and their frames nearly invisible on New York City's streetscape outside of sources critical of their lifestyles and choices. Trial transcripts, district attorney indictment files, probation documents, letters, and interviews, along with investigative reports from progressive organizations bring their sentiments into view. Parole records, clemency applications, and inmate case files are especially helpful since turn-of-the-century efforts to make New York prisons more rehabilitative and less punitive encouraged the gathering of information that would help in the prisoner's personal recovery. Prisons generally kept correspondence items and biographical information in addition to forms on the medical, psychological, labor, and educational lives of inmates. Women's prisons and reformatories kept far more complete records of inmates' histories and correspondence than men's facilities, which helped my analysis. In the process of culling particulars from male inmates' records, I have often used women's prison dockets, not only to understand the lives of women, but to find information about their husbands, fathers, brothers, and sons.[83]

Interpreting these sources can also present significant conundrums. Surrounded by authorities during court room testimony or speaking with prison keepers, parole boards, and chaplains likely altered how subjects represented their own perspectives. Even personal letters written to children, parents, lovers, and prison administrators include phraseology molded by shrewd rhetorical objectives that might skew their meaning. However, all human communication comes with biases and predispositions that require interpretation and analysis, not only the words of arrestees and inmates. Even in these circumstances their statements hold much of their unedited viewpoints. With this in mind, I have attempted to carefully extract the mindsets of early twentieth-century black men and women while taking account of these discrepancies. As historian Kali Gross has suggested, one must withhold judgment about crimes and recognize the nonlinear nature of human behavior driven by financial, emotional, and crucial demands and desires when analyzing these sources.[84] Through the prism of such pragmatism, the objective is not to romanticize or justify the actions of these men. Many committed loathsome crimes that make it difficult to sympathize with their plight. However, the goal is to understand this history and the situations they faced, and to distinguish their part in a broader tapestry of responses to Jim Crow. Retelling their stories is meant to clarify our blurry perspectives of their lives and recognize the cogency behind their decisions and motives, even those that strain comprehension. From instances of bloodshed in concrete arenas, contested public leisure spaces, bordellos, and gambling dens, to the disputed and sometimes grisly terms of black romantic bonds, this work makes clear how the imperatives of forming normative hegemonic motifs of masculinity impregnated the crimes or criminalized behaviors of black men in the early twentieth century. Their sentiments, good, bad, or unbelievable, come through in these documents.

Sociologists have produced much of the twentieth- and twenty-first century academic discussion of black crime, often arguing criminality spawned from inequality not from the inadequacies of a "culture of poverty," as some thinkers suggested in the 1960s.[85] Work by scholars like Richard Majors, Janet Mancini Billson, Elliot Liebow, and Elijah Anderson, in differing ways, engage the question of black manhood and crime with a structural approach, recognizing how despairingly isolated black communities necessitate extralegal innovation.[86] Likewise, critical race theorists like Derrick Bell, in *Race, Racism, and American Law*, and Michelle Alexander in *The New Jim Crow*, have argued for a true evaluation of the part of race in legal processes, and an understanding of how deeply entrenched racial bigotry has entrapped black men into mass incarceration.[87] In the realm of historical work, substantial labor has gone into the political, religious, legal, or outright insurrectionary tactics black men used to navigate racial injustice, notably in the collection of essays, *A Question of Manhood*, edited by Darlene Clark Hine and Earnestine Jenkins.[88] Looking at black masculinity specifically, some historical works, like those by Martin Summers, Angela Hornsby-Gutting, and Daniel P. Black, have focused on middle-class manhood, political constructions of gender, or enslavement.[89]

Such important works have laid a foundation for a fuller telling of the past of black men, but they only tell a part of the story, and largely leave out those seeking rights, subsistence, and individual gain with deliberate illegality. The perspectives of the "talented tenth," race men, and political leaders is well documented, but historians have neglected the viewpoints of working-class men, and how they forged manhood, personal economies, and public and private power by breaking the law. While intellectuals and progressives like W. E. B. Du Bois, Kelly Miller, and Booker T. Washington examined the living conditions of the poor and theorized about their impulses and intentions, their subjects of study made decisions about how to wrestle control over their lives from the grip of critics for complex reasons. Many realized racial discrimination diminished their chances of wielding hegemonic masculine privilege, and in their words and actions their hopes and imagination are discernable. *Uncontrollable Blackness* is meant to merge the historical, theoretical, and sociological, all with the intention of understanding how the history of black men ultimately converges with the present.

In this way, this book innovatively introduces masculinity into historical considerations of race, crime, and the fight for rights and citizenship, and expands the scope of African American gender, legal, urban, and familial history. Recently, a number of historians have reengaged the subject of blacks and the legal system.[90] Khalil Gibran Muhammad's seminal study of the early twentieth-century use of pseudoscience to criminalize African Americans laid a foundation for continued analysis of black crime.[91] Kali Gross and Cheryl Hicks have given particular attention to legal regulation, reform, and womanhood. Hicks's book masterfully combines an analysis of black women's lives, labors, and desires while engaging the superstructure of carceral and progressive surveillance that had a part in shaping their opportunities in New York City.[92] Cynthia Blair, Sarah Haley, and LaShawn Harris have also divulged a history of black women's encounters with the law.[93] However, historians have not considered how black men specifically leveraged illicit activities and violence when confronting endless threats to their bodies and masculine identities. Following the work of scholars such as Roger Lane, who discerned a criminal subculture in late nineteenth-century Philadelphia, my work zooms in on the experiences of men and how gender had a part in producing their perspectives and behaviors.[94] Identifying American impulses of racial control rooted in slavery and displaying blossoms fragrant and full in freedom, I detail how these men coped with a justice system bent against them and how constructs of Jim Crow motivated confrontations with the law. This is a subject that cannot be avoided since America's legal system is still curved by racial bias, and by interrogating black criminality in history, my work grapples with the roots of contemporary issues.

The Crucible

As a subject of analysis, *crime* can denote many things. Some crimes, such as murder, are universally considered wrong, while others break regulatory codes dictated by the priorities of governing bodies and populations.[95] What societies consider *criminal* customarily bespeaks the moral, personal, and financial imperatives of those who have the power to make that specification. In American history, legal codes have rarely reflected the needs of African Americans. Indeed, statutory regulations have frequently been designed to bridge gaps between black agency and the perceived needs of white Americans. As such, a crime can be an action acceptable in one context and prohibited when committed by specific groups. Criminal law can communicate the preferences of dominant groups, and crime can symbolize resistance and protest for those disenfranchised. In his work on homicide, historian Randolph Roth argued killings increased in groups that distrusted state and social hierarchy, lacked identification with their own communities, and discerned few paths to winning respect without violence.[96] Deprived of kinship and patriotism in larger society and legitimate avenues to esteem, some black men committed crimes or violence simply to defend their dignity in a society that wholly denied it.[97]

Throughout this work I consider prominent criminological approaches in my analysis, such as labeling, control, strain, and anomie theories, all of which hypothesize about how society itself generates crime. For example, strain theorists argue that in a society where all institutions (family, education, politics, and law, etc.) are invaded by economic concerns, and personhood is hinged on profit-making, the poor are compelled into criminality in order to exist.[98] With these ideas providing a foundation for the study, I primarily interpret black crime through the lens of "critical" criminological theory that acknowledges how *crime* reflects the power structure of society, and that inequality is at the base of illegality and law enforcement. Critical theory further contends that the innate unevenness of capitalism is sustained by a criminal justice system configured to manage poor and minority offenders and overlook systemic corruption.[99] Willem Bonger in 1916 understood this arguing the "oppressed resort to means . . . which they would otherwise scorn" once they realize their predicament.[100] With race as a major determinant of resource allocation and inclusion for the length of American history, black crime often represented decisions made under duress and habits formed in response to the absurdity of historic injustices.

In order to register the set of actions that placed black men opposite the law, I have defined and classified the legal transgressions discussed by placing them into four categories—subsistence, pleasure, violent, and patriarchal crimes. These divisions sometimes overlap, yet this delineation allows consideration of each as separate phenomena as well as generated by interconnected impulses. I consider subsistence crimes, like larceny and robbery, since they compose the most common and often impromptu ways men attempted to supplement meager incomes and secure funds for exigent needs like food and board. I also examine pleasure crimes such as gambling, illegal alcohol distribution and consumption, and participation in the sex trade as procurers and pimps. Most of the men in this study combined both subsistence and pleasure infractions, particularly in the tenements, pool halls, and saloons that catered to African Americans, whether black owned or not. In these spaces where pleasure and subsistence blended, violence was endemic. Black men navigated both inter- and intraracial clashes and sometimes committed assault and murder out of aggression or self-defense, or in order to maintain their economic status in underground markets. Analysis of violent crime recognizes the hazards they faced, and sometimes created, in public commercial spaces that welcomed them, and it gives voice to those men who used it strategically. Scrutinizing entrepreneurialism, leisure spaces, and intimate relationships, I define the final category of patriarchal crime as actions motivated by struggles against the suppression of normative masculine roles and privileges and the desire to establish or sustain domestic and sexual authority over women. This classification includes legal behaviors effectively criminalized when performed by black men, subsistence crimes motivated by the support of children and intimate others, and abuse, sexual violence, and homicide of partners and other women who refused to conform to patriarchal directives. Focusing on these categories, this study foregrounds the lives of men who felt forced into criminality and those who chose to interact with illicit markets or commit felonies when legal means seemed inadequate for their desires, needs, or identities.

At the center of my analysis is a view of black crime as formulated by interconnected historical factors, trends, and currents flowing through the period of study. As such, this work is intervening on much of the last century of research on African American civil rights, migration, protest, and legal history by observing it through the prism of what I call the *crucible of black criminality*. The *crucible* symbolizes several crucial elements of the American past that I see as criminogenic, all bearing the potential to thrust blacks into circumstances where lawlessness and resistant behaviors fulfilled entrenched human needs and aspirations. Because much of the crucible of black criminality impacted both black men and women, it can be a useful model for understanding black crime in general. However, men and women also had separate concerns. Black women not only dealt with hazards relating to race but also pertaining to womanhood. Undoubtedly, through abuse and sexual exploitation, some black men composed a part of black women's crucible. Black men, alternately, faced unique problems of their own relating to the terms of hegemonic masculinity, containment, and violence. Defined as a harrowing gauntlet, or a situation that compels one to make personal transitions and difficult choices, the crucible charts the historical paradigm that so conspicuously positioned black men in juxtaposition to the American legal schema.

Foundational to the crucible is a history of enslavement and the attending personal, psychological, and spiritual epochal wounds to the bodies, identities, and sexual, marital, and familial bonds of African Americans.[101] Intergenerational trauma and collective memory have the capacity to shape lifeways and affect human interaction and are bequeathed to subsequent generations in cultural production, personal and communal injury, and modes of resistance. This is not to argue, as other scholars have, that enslavement forged pathologies in black culture that led to morally wrong behaviors and crime but to establish a framework for fathoming the formidable centrifugal force of American bondage in determining subsequent race relations, mechanisms of protest, and legal discourse.[102] No study of black criminality can ignore how the violence of forced labor set the standards for continued control after emancipation. Nor can one neglect the role of black bondage in contextualizing black freedom. Physical, rhetorical, and political methods of domination during servitude transmogrified into de facto and de jure efforts to restrict African Americans once freed and continued the dynamic of white authority and black resistance produced by enslavement.[103]

Bondage is even more crucial when considered in terms of violence. White slaveholders maintained the cauldron of slavery with unrelenting severity. In addition to subjection and captivity, everyday discipline and punishment included bodily compulsion, and bondsmen and women inhabited a world mentally and physically delimited by cruelty, terrorism, and rape. The universality of brutality in maintaining black subservience institutionalized racial violence as an apparatus of regulation and shaped policing tactics, law, and surveillance in freedom. Black codes translated salient features of slavery into the management of black labor after emancipation and justified lynching. Throughout the text I have used the term *public racial violence* to connote events that not only happened in public but that had collective implications involving experiential and psychological significance for entire communities, often deliberately advertised as visible expressions of racial authority. The terminology is useful in separating isolated interracial conflicts from those that radiated meaning for all observers. With the violence of servitude transferred to jurisprudential injustices and maintained by state and private public racial violence, self and familial protection and offensive attacks, protestations against unfair labor contracts, and various forms of extralegal sentiments and actions became cogent responses. Violence maintained political disenfranchisement and various other aspects of racial caste meant to leave blacks powerless.[104] Murderousness begets murderousness. As such, public racial violence, particularly when buttressed by legal codification, is criminogenic.

Also at the crux of the crucible of black criminality is an American obsession with hegemonic masculinity and patriarchy, the denial of manhood norms to black men, and popular portrayals of them as weak, criminal, and sexually aggressive. Acknowledging that *gender* refers to culture and an ever-changing process, *Uncontrollable Blackness* explores the points where criminality intersects with the development of manhood for black men.[105] The analysis begins just as one version of manhood withered on the vine and two others blossomed. As the 1800s closed, Victorian-era bromides of self-controlled and virtuous masculinity faded. Men were expected to be self-made and economically successful and still situate themselves in what E. Anthony Rotundo calls "passionate manhood," characterized by strength, aggression, and the construction of identity from consumption and self-expression.[106] Previously questionable masculine instincts, such as avarice, lust, and powerful force, became constituents of manly character in light of the militarism of the Spanish American War and cultural movements that criticized the softness of modern life.[107] Established through persuasion, force, or violence, hegemonic masculinity determines successful manhood, who has access to it, and which versions of manliness are disdained.[108] Thus, the options of subordinated men are dwindled, and their resistance creates physical and ideological sites of contest. Women also bear the brunt as men competing for dominance contort romantic relationships to fit their causes and define their gender by rejection of the norms of the opposite sex.[109] Scholars such as Kali Gross, Cheryl Hicks, and Meda Chesney-Lind demonstrate how patriarchy can be crime-inducing for women in the never-ending threat of male oversight, sexual and physical abuse, and bodily exploitation.[110] For black men, the problems of patriarchy and hegemonic masculinity induced continual tension with white men and a compulsion to recover masculine standing.[111] Pronounced and public reconstructions of white manliness built upon the literal and figurative topography of black bodies as white men attempted to reaffirm their dominion through sexual assault, public racial violence, and lynching. White violations of black women impacted those women most, but the inability to protect wives, daughters, and lovers had repercussions for black men as well and frequently compelled decision-making that could lead to widespread violence against them. In turn, white men inverted the interracial sexual power dynamic by concocting the black rapist and using that mythology to justify crime legislation, lynching, and further black censure.[112] The adoption of masculinity touchstones by black men was also problematic. Paternalism sat at the center of physical and sexual abuse and homicides black men sometimes enacted against black women.[113] Resultantly, American hegemonic white masculinity can be seen as criminogenic as it inspired legal and illegal denunciations of black manhood, encouraged black men to breach racial boundaries when limited by law, and presented brutal patriarchal patterns of behavior for men frustrated by attempts to castrate them.

Maintaining one's masculine identity in the threatening hippodrome of Jim Crow New York City came with intensified economic threats. For Americans, manhood is inseparable from the acquisition of monetary resources, and another constituent of the crucible is capitalism's requirement of material imparity. Critical criminology theorists consider the inequality and deprivation of the poor under capitalism to be fundamental to crime.[114] As historian Tom Sugrue put it, "capitalism generates economic inequality [and] African Americans have disproportionately borne the impact of that inequality."[115] The history of New York includes vast numbers of poor whites;

but for African Americans, legislation supporting race-based segregation, job discrimination, and commercial omission curated black communities into dioramas of economic quarantine.[116] Black leaders, professionals, and individuals sailed against the tide of complete subdual, yet as American work, leisure, and identity-building depended increasingly on participation in the market economy, men and women ostracized from legitimate commercial necessities and indulgences could find themselves on the margins of law. E. Anthony Rotundo summed up the dilemma most men faced in the early twentieth century by writing "now, a man was expected to be jealous of his autonomy and free from reliance on external authority. In this world where a man was supposed to prove his superiority, the urge for dominance was seen as a virtue."[117] New York City saw an increase in the influence and presence of an economic elite in the 1890s, and extreme poverty brushed shoulders with wealth daily.[118] This study questions the force of this transition on African American men and how it may have been criminogenic.

Perhaps most relevant to the crucible of black criminality is the American urge to contain sources of mainstream anxiety and the construction of blackness as a "problem" in white imagination. Many of the country's pivotal racial developments hatched from panic and angst. Whites anxious about emancipation concocted plans to recapture black labor, criminalize black freedom, and disenfranchise black voters. Fears that white manhood would lose hegemony spawned movements of manly vigor and imperialism in the early twentieth century. Grappling with imperatives to renew personhood and masculinity, and control racial others, whites considered blacks an external threat to the national project. Caught in this whirl of historical fragments and bits of cultural substructure, and groaning under the burden of altered gender, economic, and relational priorities, black men and women enacted political protests, migrated, built institutions, and confronted white power in all venues. Swirling cultural change required adaptation and resilience, especially as white hegemonic norms attempted to contain black energies and movements, and restrict pathways to urban consumption and citizenship. In the process of harnessing the energies of the prewar decades and the giddiness of the roaring twenties, whites characterized black men as the poison in the punch.[119] With American anxiety consolidated around the threat of urban diversity in the early twentieth century, black men became the most feared boogie man. Surveillance and efforts to segregate shared spaces and streets engendered the inclination to criminalize black legal behaviors such as occupying public venues, interracial sex and marriage, and the very act of securing the American dream.

White New Yorkers committed to this racial imbalance utilized popular cultural forms to solidify it. Enjoying a surge of popularity in New York in the 1890s, "coon songs" and minstrel shows publicized the fantastical stereotype of the black criminal.[120] Rife with images of black men gambling, stealing watermelons, and wielding razors, ditties like "All Coons Look Alike to Me" and "Little Alabama Coon" presented "negro tastes and ambitions," in the words of one journalist.[121] Storylines depicted blacks as both lazy and murderous, and they mocked black progress, effectively inverting the popular mythology of the "self-made man."[122] Contrary to time-honored allegories of American men, "coons" abandoned family responsibilities, lived off of women they abused, and whiled away their time indulging in pleasures.[123] "Leave Your Razors at the Door" told of razor toting black men frightened to enter a "ragtime reception" without weapons, and the inevitable melee that interrupted their good time.[124] This body of spectacles stitched two sets of assumptions together; first that criminality lied in wait in the black genetic makeup, and second that once let loose from the paternalism of plantation life, blacks strayed morally. In this logic, migration to the electrifying freedom of Northern urban centers signaled the utmost deviation since blacks were unqualified for civil society.[125] The crowd-pleasing ballads gave many white listeners what they wanted; confirmation that inequality and lynching were justified since no blacks were clean-handed.[126] Thus, "coon songs" reconciled prevailing themes of romantically subordinate black slaves and the perceived disorderliness of blacks in cities, and they presented law and order as the only solution.

African Americans also used musical and cultural forms to support their ideological stakes in the race question. Through melodies about loss, triumph, pain, and revenge, black blues music communicated both the trauma of the crucible and the conviction to defy trenchant inequality by any means necessary. It expressed the tenor of black lives in the early twentieth century with popular songs that captured the emotionality and despair caused by a brutal legal system, chain gang labor, and public racial violence. Black listeners and musicians could be forthright about the world they lived in while singing tunes, experience a sense of simultaneity by communicating common sentiments nationwide, and release the pressure of pent up rage.[127] Preceding the popularity of blues, folkloric stories and ballads about black badmen like Stagolee and Devil Winston proliferated, particularly for black Southerners and migrants to the north. Characters like Railroad Bill, who "shot all [the] buttons off the head brakeman's coat,"[128] embodied heroic models of brazeness that many blacks celebrated and used in their own lives to construct identity and physically or symbolically resist white-enacted cruelty. Hard, determined, and willing to die for their dignity or personal gain, these figures therapeutically played out fantasies of retributive violence and self-interest that many blacks savored.[129] Such tales of "crazy" men and women pervaded early twentieth-century blues songs, narratives where subjects struck out against whites in ways that seemed to guarantee death. In one representative song derived from the real story of a black Memphis man who shot two police officers, a black outlaw is hailed as a hero:

> Two-Gun Charlie is a mighty man.
> Mows down 'dem cops wherever he can.
> Got two pistols that sho' am fine.
> Gives 'dem bastards a hot old time.[130]

For men in particular, blues ballads articulated existential dread and the hopes of overcoming it, the pessimism that racial hurdles could be vaulted, and the murderous anger that might result.[131] The musical form can be seen as a collective statement of struggle in the process of comprehending one's freedom on a landscape punctuated by equal measures of unfreedom. Autonomy meant constant negotiation in terms of race and gender with whites and fellow African Americans.

The power dynamics of interracial conflict could be mirrored in intraracial affrays, causing black interactions to sometimes devolve into private or public hostility. In tales of revenge against both blacks and whites, blues singers popularized fantasies of black self-actualization with bloodshed and the seizure of power through sheer force. However, some songs specifically addressed the broader white-controlled world and toyed with the possibilities of uprooting racist structures and resisting the seemingly unstoppable momentum of white supremacy. The badmen in folklore and blues songs were not simply the product of black fancy but had been drawn from real life. The story of Railroad Bill, for instance, came from the life of Alabama turpentine worker Morris Slater who shot an officer and escaped on a train in 1893.[132] As a result of the way art imitated real life, the blues not only served as a cathartic component of black entertainment and storytelling but also as a cultural form animating a guerilla spirit in the minds and bodies of blacks rightfully pessimistic about their prospects under Jim Crow.

Author Richard Wright expressed this rising emotional fantasy of vengeance in his autobiographical work, *Black Boy*. Growing up in the South in the 1920s he witnessed the vehemence of racial violence and lynching. "A dread of white people . . . came to live permanently in my feelings and imagination," he wrote. In one instance Wright lost sleep after hearing the story of a black man murdered by a white mob. Stricken with grief, the man's wife tricked his killers into allowing her to tend to his body just before revealing a shotgun and slaying a few of them. Whether true or not, for Wright the tale was "emotionally true" and he vowed to himself that he would follow the example of the distressed widow if ever he had to. The woman's story provided structure to a sense of helplessness in the face of a relentless threat, and such fantasies, he wrote, became "a moral bulwark that enabled me to feel I was keeping my emotional integrity whole."[133] Real and fictitious small and large-scale black insurrectionists were not simply insane outlaws, it is clear, but powerful representations of restlessness in the face of white supremacy from which blacks might derive a type of spiritual deliverance.

Understanding such insurgent responses to the crucible by black men requires investigation of their lives in a series of spaces where they forged their masculine identity. Like most Americans, black men assembled their gendered status in public, private, commercial, sexual, and material ways, and each chapter examines the realms where this construction took place in mind and body. Normative early twentieth-century manhood required self-governance, authority over private spaces, industrial and capitalist prosperity, and unrestrained expression of sexual dominance. Chapter 1 tracks how unemployment, housing patterns, and race-based limitations framed black life and pushed some to economic and spatial margins. It engages the crucible of public space by examining the cognitive boundaries forged by street surveillance, public racial violence, and police brutality, and how blacks responded to it. Such an inquiry benefits from the sociological framework of "symbolic interactionism," which prioritizes the significance of human interaction, the agency of individuals, and the impact of subjective interpretations of environmental and communal phenomenon.[134] Black men interacted with each other and other New Yorkers in forging the significance of urban space, for better or worse, and this chapter lays a foundation for understanding the role the physical and social landscape played in their decision-making. Chapter 2 analyzes interracial and racially exclusive black saloons and how the vigilant supervision they attracted from law enforcement and progressive reformers had a part in shaping their meaning for black men. The saloon functioned as a relatively hospitable public space of camaraderie, amusement, and economic benefit for them but also as a site of considerable peril. Black men who straddled the law or existed outside of it as proprietors or patrons are foregrounded, and the chapter argues that in those spaces they wished to intermix pleasure and profit with hegemonic constructions of black masculine identity.

The book's remaining chapters demonstrate the significance of illegality as it relates to relationships with women, whether consensual or otherwise. Chapter 3 delineates early twentieth-century contests between black and white men fought on the conceptual terrain of white women's bodies. Using the 1906 abduction and white slavery trial of Roosevelt Sharp, the study connects antiprostitution campaigns in the city to prevailing efforts to prevent interracial sex and marriage. It argues that men like Sharp, involved in the sex trade and married to white women, purposefully upended racial and sexual edicts by consuming and governing white flesh in direct opposition to popular and apparent mandates. Chapter 4 wrestles with the dynamics of gender in another type of control; namely the struggle for patriarchal domestic and sexual authority in black intimate relationships and how crime figured into efforts to manage families both ideologically and economically. The chapter explores a number of trial transcripts and prison case files that illuminate the often unstable and shifting terrain of black intimacy in an urban landscape rife with racial inequalities. Analyzing these documents, I draw out the multiple ways in which crimes of passion and financially motivated felonies connected to the successful and failed efforts of some black men to create sustainable families, households, and relationships. I also give voice to men who explained their crimes with conceptions of manhood and the raw desire to solidify patriarchal hegemony. In some cases, men killed or maimed their partners for infidelity, abandonment, or for disobeying directives about the suitability of social habits and workplaces, and this work argues criminality often sprung from the inner reaches of the politics of black intimacy.

Chapter 5 spreads a somewhat soothing balm on the wounds produced by the previous chapter by appraising the impacts of imprisonment and parole on men and their families and narrating a story of love and devotion that passed through prison walls. When men and women went to prison, loved ones waited on the outside, visited, wrote letters, campaigned for their release, and attempted to improve their homes and lives in anticipation of reunions. Many men linked their ability to improve their own lives after release to the beautiful and affectionate bonds they cultivated with significant others but also framed the fates of wives and lovers in terms of their own masculinity. Utilizing countless letters and prison dockets, this chapter stitches together a narrative of commitment, optimism, and pledges and actions of loyalty that prove how instrumental men believed women to be to their rehabilitation. But diverging desires and conflicting gendered expectations frequently put them at odds in the pursuit of better lives. Viewed together, a tale of dreams, resistance, conflict, and redemption unfolds in these chapters. Obscured by time and voicelessness, and largely edited from the historical record, black men in contention with the law are an important part of American history, and this book prioritizes their circumstances and perspectives.

The fact that manhood occupied the minds of black men confronting the crucible of New York City is discernable from their own words. By revealing a linkage between black masculinity and crime, this work recovers how illegality served deeper individual, familial, communal, and political needs for autonomy and control. It forged patriarchal and fraternal connections, and it satisfied a yearning for expression, carnality, and survival that current liberal discourse of black criminality has not unwaveringly acknowledged. *Uncontrollable Blackness* registers the alluring, and sometimes irresistible, perks that attracted men to commit acts from petty theft to murder. Thieves, robbers, burglars, domestic abusers, and murderers derived pleasure, profit, and power from their actions, all resources they desired not only for simplistic forms of human satisfaction but also to consolidate identities around hegemonic forms of masculinity. In the process, they might engage in horizontal violence, turning what Frantz Fanon called the "aggressiveness sedimented" in the muscles of colonized subjects against their own people.[135] Some developed tough personas for the specific purpose of avoiding the emotions that came with such behaviors and projecting a muscular version of manhood that might sustain the benefits of criminality.[136]

It is at this base level of perseverance at the dawn of modern Northern "free" black politics that we see the existential urgency to declare independence from racialized bourgeois social norms and to imagine and live new kinds of civic engagement. At this nexus, black criminality and expressions of masculinity have always existed in implicit and explicit revolt against American institutions and life, which have attempted to colonize black minds, bodies, and souls to their own purposes. Bearing this in mind, *uncontrollable blackness* as a term both signifies the prodigious challenges and injuries of racism for African Americans and conjures the spirit of insurgency, come hell or high water. It is a declaration of war against the mechanisms of racial oppression and those that maintain them. As James Baldwin put it, in American society the black man has been "forced to snatch his manhood, his identity, out of the fire of human cruelty that rages to destroy it."[137] Extralegal activity might symbolize attempts to prove one's manly worth by seizing the vestiges of virility or flipping the script of racial or sexual domination in the interests of commandeering gendered authority. It might also represent the reclamation of one's person and spirit from the labyrinthine racial politics of the time. Can we see participation in underground economies as fortifying a sense of control and economic power for black men? Did civic surveillance, police brutality, public racial violence, segregation in housing and leisure, and criminal stigmatization foster a sense of isolation, distress, and nihilism that made crime and violence viable remedial options for them? These questions are still crucial to contemporary discourse about black communities and urban structures of power today. In this work, I argue it is impossible to comprehend the interplay of crime, poverty, and police violence in African American communities of the late twentieth and early twenty-first centuries without apprehending the politics of black criminality, protest, and policing in these early years of the formation of black freedom.

Chapter 1

No Sunshine in the City

Crime, Control, and the Cauldron of Public Space

Where does one run to when he's already in the promised land?

—Claude Brown, *Manchild in the Promised Land*

When the country speaks of a "new" Negro . . . it is not really referring to
a change in the Negro . . . but only to a new difficulty in keeping him in his
place, to the fact that it encounters him (again! again!) barring yet another
door to its spiritual and social ease.

—James Baldwin, *The Fire Next Time*

Arriving in New York City in 1880 hoping to apply his training as a black-
smith, South Carolina migrant Jeremiah "Lamplighter" Dunn worked for a
horseshoer in Greenwich Village. Enjoying steady employment for a decade
and a half, he lost his position when the blacksmithing union forced him out
of the trade in 1895. That year, Dunn took a job as a chauffeur for a "million-
aire" in the Hudson Valley north of the city but quit after two years because
"it was too cold up there for me." He then returned to Manhattan to labor in
a series of gambling dens, dancehalls, and saloons in the city's "vice" districts
where he encountered numerous instances of violence.[1] In one incident he
shot two men at his workplace after a dispute. "My life was threatened . . . and
I had to look out for myself," he later recounted. In another, he fired upon an
attacker who impaled him with a butcher knife. When cornered, he reasoned,
"I couldn't go through the wall, [and] I had to defend myself."[2] In yet another
occurrence, muggers cut him "from the top of my head . . . down to the side
of my cheek" in the hallway outside of his flat. "The gas was turned out. . . .
I was knocked down and cut [so] I shot them," he explained.[3] In each of
these circumstances all involved were African American. Presiding judges accepted Dunn's pleas of self-defense and deposed the cases without trial.
His luck changed on August 26, 1900, when a dispute with a group of white
"boys" ended in the death of Jack Brewer. According to the *New York Times*,
while standing in front of a poolroom on the corner of Sixty-Second Street
and Amsterdam Avenue, Lamplighter opened fire on the group for "hurling
epithets" and killed Brewer.[4] After hiding for days he surrendered to police
on August 30 and faced charges for murder.[5]

In the days before Dunn's surrender, the racially mixed blocks of Midtown and the Tenderloin district descended into bedlam as white mobs randomly targeted African Americans. Enraged by Brewer's shooting, one gang set out to annihilate their "share" of the "negro population," smashing the windows of a black occupied tenement and assaulting residents as they fled the building.[6] Pretending to mistake James Arnold for Dunn, another group of white men battered him "shamefully" stopping only when police intervened. Realizing police participated in much of the city's racial violence, Arnold declined medical assistance and retreated.[7] Earlier in the month brawling took place across central Manhattan as white citizens and police responded to the killing of an officer by a black migrant with heinous acts of violence, and those conflicts continued sporadically at the time of Brewer's death.[8] Primed to confront police terrorism by then, blacks resisted arrest and defended themselves. Detained for getting "sassy" with a flatfoot during the fracas, William Hopson fought until beaten unmercifully. George Meyer and six other men attempted to rescue him but were arrested themselves. Meyer fought but failed to escape and reached police headquarters with a fractured skull.[9] Similar violence fanned out into surrounding blocks and collided with scattered battles in other parts of the city. As both disturbances raged, they merged into a constellation of racial skirmishes in Manhattan's most diverse neighborhoods.

Dunn's arrest mostly quieted the fervor, but the shooting and the following turmoil represented the features of a crucible of public space black men encountered in the North at the turn of the century. New York was already unstable terrain for most African Americans, but the new centennial altered their cognitive maps of the city. In-migration and housing discrimination made it so poor blacks and whites lived closely in the Tenderloin, frequented many of the same businesses and leisure spaces, and mingled in commercial, congenial, and intimate ways. Such adjacency made constructive and romantic cross-racial liaisons possible but also bred antipathy and terrorism in moments of tension. The stretch of Amsterdam Avenue near the site of Brewer's shooting typified central Manhattan's racial multiplicity. Describing the neighborhood one witness confirmed "a great many colored people live over there," and on weekend nights they gathered "in crowds walking to and fro . . . mingling with white people."[10] Dunn never admitted to shooting Brewer, but he acknowledged how the racial politics of the neighborhood sparked bloodshed. After surrendering he told officers he hid in fear of the mob, but not out of acknowledgment of guilt. "You know the mob around here," he supplicated, "you know very well what that gang would do" if they found him.[11]

African American Rosanna Weston saw such danger as a child in San Juan Hill noting white areas were "forbidden territory," but "they used to come over on this side [to] fight."[12] One white resident admitted as much. "We used to fight the niggers down on San Juan Hill" without interference from the police, he explained. "[Blacks] never came up [to us], we usually went down there."[13] In this environment, men like Dunn sought equal access to public urban space, and their claims on manhood depended upon it, but white men fought to hem them in. Both committed to maintaining masculine identity and the unfettered access to the city manhood required, they entered into a contest most discernable on the city's pavement. With the state apparatus of the police on the side of whites, black men were harassed, assaulted, and killed with impunity, and such altercations haunted the sidewalks like specters of an eventual race war.[14] Neither Brewer nor a handful of witnesses identified Dunn as the shooter, and a jury dismissed the murder charges in the end, yet the entire affair revealed the streets of New York City as paradoxical spaces of contest and contradiction. White and black working-class citizens often lived together out of necessity or convenience, but racial antipathy might trigger combat that changed the essence of their living circumstances, and the meaning of communal space.

Dunn's experiences also articulate how employment inequity and housing locations affected black men's lives and personal choices. Competition with white immigrants and job discrimination led to reliance on badly paid service work, chronic unemployment, and the inability to consistently support households. It might also encourage or force participation in the drumbeat of illegal transactions in the communities of the Tenderloin. Men like Dunn tried to avoid New York's fickle job market by lodging themselves in a busy nightlife culture, which often fulfilled their desires for self-gratification but submerged them in the dangers associated with pleasure industries. Housing patterns that separated, clustered, or isolated populations reproduced social advantage and disadvantage.[15] As Dunn's robbery and assault in the hallway of his building indicate, one's home could be surrounded by peril. Housing segregation and economic straits made the construction of an exclusive inner-realm challenging and broke down partitions between private and public. High rents obliged the introduction of boarders in many homes, and cramped, unheated, or unpleasant tenements provided skimpy cover from the elements. Furthermore, escape from bad housing, resource gathering, and the sheer desire to socialize or participate in street commerce drew blacks to the sidewalks where they might also take advantage of public amenities they lacked at home.

However, this occupation of space drew the attention of white and black critics. Reformers, police, and white neighbors attempted to control working-class African Americans, and "knickerbockers," middle-class blacks with deep roots in the city, worried poor blacks threatened the relative calm of late nineteenth-century race relations.[16] Racially contiguous housing patterns and rivalries for accommodation additionally determined how clashes played out.[17] Old resentments lived on among neighbors who remained nearby, and when blacks moved into new areas whites formed restrictive covenants, attacked the newcomers, or enlisted police in the fight to preserve exclusivity. Work competition likewise sparked melees. "Do you think you could go near a bricklayer's job?" one black worker scoffed, "They kill you. Those were white man's jobs."[18] Housing and labor lockouts funneled blacks into decaying slums, and white citizens, reformers, and police patrolled the borders of those communities to restrict one's footprint.[19] To such a degree, the places where one lived and made their money remained important, as men like Dunn sought economic and spatial mobility but understood they would have to fight for it.

Such restrictions and violence ran counter to the reasons blacks migrated in the first place. Thousands left the South to escape ruthless sharecropping contracts, Jim Crow codes, and racial violence, and in pursuit of opportunities to reformulate their selfhood while enjoying the modern pleasures of urban living.[20] For blacks, mobility meant freedom, and despite its flaws New York City represented greater liberty.[21] African Americans occupied street space "chewing the fat," or conspicuously "strolling" on avenues in ways that fostered social life and built community.[22] Upon arrival in New York, one male migrant argued "their eyes were opened. They tasted something better."[23] Northern climes were more attractive, another claimed, because "white folks all through the southern states . . . don't want to see you have a good time."[24] As a newcomer in 1899, James Weldon Johnson gaped at the "alluring world" of the Tenderloin with "greatly lessened restraints" than in the South but also "fascinating perils."[25] He later described the exhilaration of disembarking in New York through the eyes of a character in his 1927 semi-autobiographical novel. The protagonist felt "the dread power of the city; the crowds, the lights, the excitement, the gaity [and] my blood ran quicker and I felt that I was just beginning to live."[26] A 1906 survey of 512 black migrants found just over 50 percent moved north for higher wages, but many also cited "better conditions," the desire for travel, and being "tired of the South."[27] In another survey in 1909, others reportedly wanted to "get out and see something of the world."[28] The city offered alluring visual and aural bliss, sex, dancing, and modern excitements that were irresistible to some.[29]

Observing the streets of New York City through a historical periscope, parts of the landscape are obscured by time, but one can still detect insurgent heterogeneous street scenes rife with racial boundaries, some hazy and others clear-cut. African American men navigated the avenues of the urban North often with a sense of dread realizing white violence might interrupt their lives at a moment's notice. Unfinished conflicts often reignited when new disagreements or fistfights arose, small-scale altercations escalated into battles, or encounters with police turned deadly. Attempting to find lawful ways to respond to such disturbances, some blacks relied upon legalistic appeals to reinforce claims on respectability and convince police and civic leaders their rights should be protected. Yet, others, like Jeremiah Dunn, prepared themselves physically and psychically for the violence they expected. This reality made the public realm something different for blacks than for other racial and ethnic groups. While the city's many dangers had consequences for all New Yorkers, stoops, sidewalks, and streets tested the resiliency of black denizens in unique ways. Many sought means to deny complete constraint by committing subsistence and pleasure crimes in alleys, hallways, and rooftops, or taking control of public space through force. Thus, black men faced threats to their corporal existence by innovatively asserting their presence and physically resisting controversial deployments of police power. Deprived of the lawful protections and opportunities enjoyed by white ethnics, and baptized in the blood of frequent attacks, blacks literally fought for their claim on public spaces.

"Bound to Expand or Explode"

In August 1916, nearly fifty black and white reformers and leaders convened at the home of Columbia professor Joel Elias Spingarn in Amenia, New York, for a three-day conference hosted by the National Association for the Advancement of Colored People. In collaboration with W. E. B. Du Bois, Spingarn presumed the bucolic Hudson Valley backdrop would foster harmony among the conferees. Du Bois found the setting especially fitting and therapeutic. Perched upon a ridge he noted the "calm beauty" of it all amid the "rocky uplift of land, the nestle of lake, and the sturdy murmur of brooks and brown rivers."[30] Although special guests like Presidents William Howard Taft and Theodore Roosevelt declined attendance, others such as Mary Church Terrell, Kelly Miller, Fred Moore, and John Hope arrived in droves on a misty chilly morning. "At last," Du Bois wrote of the first day of the conference, "we began to have a rollicking jolly time."[31] For three days visitors attended roundtables on black education and trade schools, industrial opportunity, and disenfranchisement. They heard speeches and enjoyed recreation in the verdant hills surrounding the manor.[32] "We were gloriously fed," Du Bois remembered. "Miraculously steaming and perfectly cooked," magnificent dishes circulated at meal times and "we ate hilariously in the open air." Gorged on sumptuous feasts the participants "swam and rowed and hiked and lingered in the forests and sat upon the hillsides and picked flowers and sang."[33]

In all the saturnalia the guests discussed the problem of race and drew collaborative connections across various organizations all striving for the same causes. Planning the conference in the wake of Booker T. Washington's death in 1915, Du Bois and Spingarn endowed the Amenia gathering with the objective of bridging the gap between warring factions within the movement for black equality; and one resolution of the event was to repeat it annually in order to maintain the partnership. The conference would not reconvene until 1933 because the world had "gone crazy" when America entered World War I in 1917, and the Spingarn home burned to the ground in the same year.[34] Still, Du Bois considered the meeting a success that symbolized a new beginning. "Probably on account of our meeting the Negro race was more united and more ready to meet the problems of the world than it could possibly have been without these beautiful days of understanding," he concluded.[35]

The Amenia conference stood alone in many ways as a gesture of unity meant to close the ideological gaps between an emerging crop of "new negroes" and the preceding generation. It represented the convergence of Washingtonian politics of respectability and accommodationism and developing viewpoints favoring more radical protest. Nevertheless, Du Bois may have overstated its impact on the fate of African Americans in the years that followed. Calling it a "landmark . . . of the way in which the American Negro became a man," he appealed to future historians to remember the event reverently.[36] While many of the participants, including Du Bois, engaged in crucial undertakings to address urgent black issues, their attendance at the Amenia conference simultaneously serves as allegory for the rift that existed between working-class African Americans who preferred more immediate forms of popular protest and the middle-class "talented tenth" that Du Bois often exalted.[37] Members of the caucus in the mountains all wanted respectability, thrift, voting rights, "assertion of our essential manhood," and law enforcement, but only differed on "how to get these things," Du Bois confirmed.[38] The statement acknowledges the variety of viewpoints and exigencies shaping responses to the problem of race in the first decades of the century. Wishing to consolidate Du Boisian and Washingtonian adherents on the subject of racial progress, the conference organizers did not address the perspectives of blue-collar blacks living lives of necessity and survival in racialized slums ninety miles south in New York City. The opulence, pomp, and privilege of the affair contrasted sharply with the economically downtrodden existences of many of the urban blacks whose lives attendees genuinely wished to improve.

One must wonder what perspectives the residents of a black enclave in Manhattan's San Juan Hill neighborhood would have brought to such a gathering if they had attended one. Enjoying a warm night in the summer of 1904 scores of onlookers on West Sixty-Second Street witnessed Joseph Poole's death at the hands of a policeman. According to prosecutors, Officer Frederick Miller "clubbed one man over the head," then "went along the block, ordering people indoors . . . [and] inflicting blows . . . on other colored people."[39] Things became even worse when Poole defended himself and began to wrestle with the officer.[40] Mamie Shaw heard Poole exclaim, "What are you hitting me for? I didn't do anything" and watched the officer knock him to the ground. "And then this policeman drawed [sic] his revolver and shot" while standing over Poole, she remembered.[41] Another observer testified Miller heartlessly "relieved himself" in the lot near where Poole lay dying.[42] In response to the shooting, bystanders erupted with anger. "The people were hollering . . . 'it is a shame to shoot that man after he is down,'" Shaw recounted.[43] Jolted awake by gunfire Sylvia Lewis also witnessed the chaos. She heard someone "saying it is awful for that bastard . . . to kill [him] for nothing," then the sound of bricks landing on the ground near the officer's feet. Incensed, Miller "looked all around" for the person throwing bricks and fired a shot at Lewis's window. She was then "knocked senseless" and when awakened she noticed wounds on her cheek and ear, and blood splattered on her night skirt.[44]

Joseph Poole's death sparked an investigation into Officer Miller and he faced murder charges. During his trial the West Sixty-Second Street residents argued that in addition to murder and assault, he violated their constitutional rights, but the defendant and defense attorneys connected popular interpretations of black public leisure as "disorderly" with the police obligation to protect white citizens. Miller claimed the dispute began as he attempted to disperse "quite a crowd" gathered on the street "shouting, singing, and using indecent language" in front of a "notorious dive."[45] In his version of the story, he shot Poole in self-defense when the throng attacked him, and a procession of white witnesses and police officers corroborated his rendering of events. In the process of portraying Miller as an officer under siege his attorneys exploited prejudices about black neighborhoods by questioning the propriety of carousing on the street in the early morning hours. "Why were those people out in the street, at half past two o'clock in the morning," a defense attorney asked. "[They] were in that evil neighborhood for no good purpose."[46] Counselors also warned that convicting an officer for policing racial margins came with risks. "While you and I are in bed, our houses are protected, and our streets are patrolled . . . [so] your liberty and mine, may remain safe and not harmed." Convicting Miller would give "carte blanche to the negroes . . . to attack the next officer who dares to interfere with their midnight orgies."[47]

However, for Poole and his neighbors, streets, stoops, corners, and alleyways served as critical spaces for relaxation after long days of labor and presented crucial connections to the city.[48] Although his neighbors were enjoying leisure on the street at the time, Poole himself was on duty as a nightwatchman at a construction site when the encounter happened and reportedly refused to leave out of fear he would lose his job. By clearing those spaces as residents used them for work or recreation, Miller and other officers reframed sidewalks as supervised zones, regulated legal and illegal behavior, and altered blacks' understanding of *public*. Nevertheless, the details of the trial forced the jury and the city to confront police brutality writ large. Prosecutors established Miller's history of questionable assaults on other denizens, black and white, a practice many New Yorkers complained of, and the subject of a reform movement at the time. With the tide of public sentiment turned against him, the jury convicted Miller of manslaughter.[49] However, as one prevailing aspect of a crucible blacks faced in Northern public space, police brutality did not end with the novel conviction of one officer.[50]

In the decades before Poole's death, violence and racial terrorism punctuated New York City's historical composition like high notes in an operatic tragedy. For much of the nineteenth century, African Americans inhabited dingy and overcrowded ghettoes hosting a mélange of ethnicities such as the Five Points district, a section of Greenwich Village nicknamed "Little Africa," and parts of Brooklyn.[51] Roaming a street dubbed "Cut-Throat Alley" in 1861, one writer observed "crazy, toppling tenement-houses" filled with "thieves, beggars, prostitutes, old and young, black, white, and gray, huddle[d] together . . . every night in the indiscriminate beastliness of a sty."[52] Most notably, gun-toting hordes protested Civil War conscription by attacking African Americans in July 1863.[53] Already familiar with street violence of the kind, witnesses of the draft riots would see many more attacks. White gangs like the Whyos, the Bottle Alley Gang, and the Big Flat Gang controlled blocks and passageways and thrived because of incompetent or insufficient policing and the displacement of poverty.[54] In the Bowery and the Five Points "it was worth a negro's life to be seen," wrote one black *Times* editorialist. Blacks needed guns for protection as "they were assaulted by roughs . . . dragged to station houses and subjected to further brutality by the police." Even worse, in Brooklyn "pushing them off the sidewalks, killing and throwing them into the river was the common pastime" as "thugs of the white race . . . watched for stray negroes as the sportsman watches for game."[55] The butchery of racial terrorism coupled with muddy, foul, and unsanitary surroundings forced African Americans to wander outward from Five Points.

At the same time, a spike in black numbers quickened by a wave of arrivals from the South made expansion even more urgent. By 1910, Gotham's black numbers topped 91,000 people, most of whom had come from the South, giving New York the second largest black population in the nation, after Washington, D.C. In the next two decades the influx increased by 257 percent, raising the population of blacks to more than 152,000 by 1920, and again to 327,706 by 1930.[56] In addition to the rising tide of Southern migrants, immigrants from the West Indies, South America, and Africa landed daily in seafaring vessels and experienced a "great race-welding," according to writer Alain Locke.[57] Jamaicans, Cubans, Barbadians, and Panamanians, among others, swelled the internationally born share of the black population to 37,000 by 1910. Southern blacks fled disenfranchisement, a white supremacist campaign of lynching and intimidation, and an economic system bent toward recovering slave labor for utilization by the planter class.[58] Likewise, black immigrants often made the trip to escape oppressive economic and cultural situations in their respective countries. Swelling already with immigrants from Europe and other parts of the world, the streets of the Tenderloin undulated with foot traffic, commerce, and rare cultural diffusion.

By 1900, the bulk of black Manhattanites occupied an important node in New York's social, economic, and cultural core that fostered opportunities for population growth but exposed them to added scrutiny and conflict that drove continued movement. Refugees from Southern Manhattan settled into an archipelago of black belts stretching from Greenwich Village to Midtown in the undefined Tenderloin district and San Juan Hill, and newcomers quadrupled the black population of the city.[59] African American institutions such as the Bethel African Methodist Episcopal Church, fraternal organizations, hotels, and the black YMCA flourished alongside entertainment venues that gave a stretch of Fifty-Third Street the moniker "Negro Bohemia."[60] San Juan Hill, which took its name from the famous battle of the Spanish American War, sat north of the Tenderloin between Sixtieth and Sixty-Fourth Streets and became famous for bloody racial skirmishes by 1905.[61] Black housing in these areas primarily existed in pockets surrounded by the homes of Irish, German, and Italian immigrants, a configuration that, in many ways, re-created the tribal tensions of the Five Points.[62] In the pastiche of cultures and races, clashes blazed and gangs continued to flourish. There were the Italian Five Pointers and Sicilian mafia families, the Eastmans led by Jewish tough Monk Eastman, Irish gangs like the Hudson Dusters in Greenwich Village, and Chinese Hip Sings and Tongs in Chinatown, all seeking cash, space, and resources at the same time.[63]

Some blacks moved to Brooklyn and Harlem for better housing and relief from the conflict, yet continued migration soon overwhelmed those communities and pushed settlers into sections of Queens and the Bronx.[64] From Harlem's first black residential outpost on West 134th Street in 1903, blacks radiated outward until they covered forty-eight blocks between 130th and 144th Streets in 1920.[65] In Brooklyn, early black settlers lived in the village of Weeksville, directly east of downtown, and along Fulton and Atlantic Avenues. More than 18,000 African Americans called the borough home by the 1900 census and just over 31,000 by 1920, that community spreading from downtown to Fort Green, Bedford-Stuyvesant, and Vinegar Hill. Likewise, existing black communities in Queens persisted in Flushing and South Jamaica and those communities grew at the turn of the century and onward.[66] In 1910, one census enumerator noted black subway riders disembarked in Midtown less frequently than before. "They're up in that far Harlem country" and elsewhere, he posited.[67] The continual movement of businesses and commerce from Wall Street up the island forced blacks to move North.[68] Even more urgently, the 1900 Tenderloin riot and others that followed set the stage for the early decades of the twentieth century, mimicking a big bang sending black residents scattering to distant corners of the city seeking safer and perhaps more racially exclusive places to live. "Penned in the gangster-ruled blocks of lower Manhattan," Claude McKay mused about this process, "they were bound to expand or explode."[69]

In the middle of small and large explosions in lower Manhattan, and meeting resistance in new neighborhoods, blacks attempted to settle into lives kept precarious by law enforcement. Miller's murder trial demonstrates the depth of the problem of policing. Already menaced by their white neighbors, police brutality represented a seemingly insurmountable hardship for African Americans. New York's bluecoats had a long history of clubbing and shoving pedestrians along streets and sometimes beating suspects to death for small offenses. The city's 1894 Lexow Committee investigation publicized police attacks as an issue that affected all New Yorkers but only resulted in highlighting its impact on "respectable" citizens, and by the time of Poole's murder, that violence had become progressively more racialized.[70] Police connections to the city's dominant Democratic political machine, Tammany Hall, made brutality complaints hard to press, especially for blacks who made up a fraction of the electorate and primarily voted Republican.[71] Wielding influence over local and state governance, law enforcement, courts, and organized crime, Tammany had a part in the hiring of police officers, enticed them to commit election fraud and attack opposition voters, and collected graft from corrupt officials, all of which made the police department a tool worth shielding from criticism.[72] In a number of large-scale conflicts patrolmen fearlessly harmed blacks and refused to safeguard them from white mobs. Although Miller's bloodthirst garnered him a prison sentence, black onlookers understood his conviction to be an anomaly and realized it would not reverse the ethos that animated and protected most policemen. Unpunished violence would continue to interrupt the lives of blacks simply wishing to make their lives in the city.

The conferees at Amenia understood these issues very well, as they certainly not only witnessed racial violence in their respective hometowns but had likely experienced it themselves. Still, their focus on respectability overlooked the urgent needs and desires of the residents of West Sixty-Second Street, whose lives were shaped by toil, penury, and restriction. The conference, which took place a number of years after Poole's death, allegorized a continually growing rift between middle-class and elite blacks and the working class and poor in Northern urban neighborhoods like the Tenderloin, San Juan Hill, and Harlem. Sometimes forced into the street by undesirable housing, or simply utilizing public space for socializing and community-building, the city's poor black residents remained under the same threats that characterized their lives since the end of slavery. Surrounded, as they were, by hazards to their health, happiness, mobility, and lives, New York City became a harsh theater of injustice that seized them in cycles of struggle and, sometimes, defiance. Navigating the city meant finding ways to participate in the economy by any means necessary, acquiring housing meant fighting to defend it, and the simple act of savoring the freedom to occupy public space could mean losing one's life. Du Bois and the Amenia conference-goers recognized the critical issues poor blacks faced, but the symposium simultaneously invokes questions about how middle-class blacks encountered working-class strategies of confronting racial mistreatment. While black progressives and intellectuals sought to make education, hard work, and law enforcement central to the struggle for citizenship rights, they met resistance that reflected the fundamental dilemma of lawfulness for blacks. Dissatisfied with tactics that yielded few immediate results, pressing daily requirements for provision and safety, and the desire to soothe ailing spirits, came first for many.

Health, High Rents, and the Hazard of Housing

Wherever blacks lived, housing remained the most immediate and vital necessity, but segregation and residential reform reduced their likelihood of finding suitable dwellings and created other distinct problems. High rents and poor housing affected peace of mind, well-being, and mortality outcomes and forced African Americans to resort to boarding situations more often than other racial groups. Consequently, crowded homes with thin walls, windows in airshafts, and nosy neighbors had less privacy and fresh air, and tenants relied upon thoroughfares for life and leisure. Some blacks in marginal neighborhoods resented being placed in close proximity to illicit trades, often inside their tenements, which brought on building raids by police and literally or metaphorically flung open the curtains on their lives.[73] Housing discrimination furthermore placed poor blacks and whites into opposition. Before the exodus to Harlem, New York City had not yet developed large black "ghettoes."[74] Census records show racially exclusive buildings and blocks in central Manhattan, but black and white tenements sat side by side.[75] While these housing patterns did not author the drama of race relations, they set the stage for encore performances. Housing also took on political and ideological significance for African Americans. Like others at the time, they were increasingly aware of the impact of surroundings on contemporary notions of morality and health. Through various publications and church discussions, middle-class blacks championed the establishment of successful households and families as indicators of racial progress.[76] One black *Amsterdam News* writer promoted instruction in "natural hygiene, biologic living, and physical culture," as the answer to "highly emotional amusements," alcoholism, poor diets, and "voodoo medicine."[77] If uplift required pure homes, pleasant décor, and the healthful attentive handiwork of a housewife, rancid slums sandwiched between brothels and cabarets spelled calamity for blacks making New York City home.[78]

As early as the 1850s housing studies determined the city's working class inhabited ramshackle, cramped, and disease-ridden tenements, and by the end of the century little had changed. Many buildings reserved for blacks were dark and malodorous, in disrepair, and "as a rule . . . unfit for human habitation," one observer decided.[79] A 1901 investigation by the city's Tenement Commission exposed "dangers from immorality and disease" exacerbated by the lack of "proper bathing facilities, air space, and small parks" between buildings. "Fire[,] . . . overcrowding, foul cellars and courts, and like evils" tormented tenement dwellers the commission determined.[80] In the same year, reformers and muckraking journalists pushed for the formation of a Tenement House Department and the passage of the Tenement House Act, legislation that included upgraded requirements for all new construction. Ironically, the law, which was meant to improve housing for blue-collar tenants, ultimately encouraged developers to build structures with better facilities, outward-facing windows, and indoor bathrooms, but at higher costs to renters. At the same time, the elimination of decaying buildings trimmed the city's existing stock of cheap lodging and deepened issues of overcrowding and dilapidation in what remained.[81] Furthermore, instead of improving low-income housing and addressing negligent landlords, organizations like the Department of Health stopped at the disbursement of condescending guidance on health and cleanliness practices to the poor.[82] Black fraternal organizations such as the Odd Fellows and the Sons of New York offered health and death benefits, social spaces, balls, promenades, and other types of support to their members, but these organizations often catered to bourgeois blacks who had the funds for yearly dues, leaving poor blacks with few services.[83] Shortly after the turn of the century housing in Harlem opened a safety valve for those wishing to escape the Tenderloin and Greenwich Village, and a contingent of middle- and working-class blacks relocated. Although new homes in Harlem allowed expansion into northern Manhattan, they did not solve problems of housing shortages, and they too became filled to overflowing and run down in a few years.[84]

Such movements of African Americans from one section of the city to another invariably elicited feedback, surveillance, and sometimes violence from whites. Objecting to black neighbors, white New Yorkers collectively treated them as one would a pestilence, taking measures to ferret out immorality like an inherent contagion and to quarantine them to certain locations. Fittingly, a panic induced by a number of smallpox cases, reportedly introduced by black migrants, allegorized the racial animus coursing through the veins of the city's social physique at the turn of the century.[85] With outbreaks across the metropolitan area and the discovery of a number of black victims, press reports inculcated the perception blacks posed a pathogenic threat to nearby white residents, employers, and passersby. "Smallpox finds in the system of the colored race a most savored place to revel" and remains longer than "is usual for other patients," one tabloid writer supposed.[86] In a typical case in 1900, smallpox struck a racially mixed section of the Tenderloin claiming twenty-nine victims, and the *Times* attributed the flare up to the arrival of two black men.[87] Seeking to cleanse the city, the Health Department deployed a "disinfecting corps" in "Little Africa," and newspapers reported on their efforts as if relaying the details of an invasion. The "sanitary squad" scrubbed "everything in sight, including droves of curious pickaninnies" and rooted into cellars and homes they deemed in need of cleaning.[88] Cosmetic improvements failed in the face of widescale poverty and dislocation, but the city's racially targeted efforts to eradicate smallpox mirrored militaristic campaigns to preserve separation. Behind the entire premise that African Americans transmitted an emergent plague lay assumptions of racial inferiority that not only rationalized segregation, but justified extraordinary measures for maintaining it.

As blacks sought living space, one might imagine unseen lines of scrimmage drawn across the city's panorama. Concerned about softening racial protocols, New York's white citizens candidly criticized the ebb and flow of blacks and equated their movements with criminality in written appeals to local newspapers and anticrime organizations. One *New York Indicator* writer proposed sending blacks to "some colony in the outskirts of the city" where they would not foul things up for "worthy citizens."[89] In a 1912 letter to the *Times* a white Harlemite wondered the same, asking whether something could be "done to put a restriction on the invasion of the negro." Citing an "enormous colony of them" in a section of Harlem, the disgruntled resident deplored having "to walk out in the driveway because the sidewalk is taken up by these blacks, who haven't either the good grace or manners to move an inch."[90] Under the notion that blacks posed criminal dangers, destroyed property, and lowered housing values, landlords and real estate holders formed racial covenants and campaigned to close all-white neighborhoods off from demographic change.[91] In 1911 a representative of one protective association in Harlem claimed the recent arrival of black families precipitated a decrease of nearly $80,000 in real estate value on one block.[92] Another organization, the Property Owners' Protective Association of Harlem, then pooled resources to purchase property "that seemed in danger of falling into the hands of negroes," pressured real estate brokers to reject black clients, and urged members to commit to selling or renting only to whites. The association also hired private investigators "to watch the negro settlers" and "report any disorder to the police."[93] Although these efforts eventually failed in Harlem, they represented organized resolutions to bridle black movement across city terrain in definite terms.[94]

Aware of the limited options for African American tenants, opportunistic landlords charged them higher rents than whites for distressed and miserably unsanitary housing. Discrimination by some property owners forced blacks into a lopsided supply and demand setting where they competed with other black renters for fewer spots.[95] Searching for a better dwelling in "respectable streets," one black resident in Greenwich Village offered to pay nearly double the rental fees, but "they would not rent . . . to colored people." Even in open housing "we have to pay big rents," she explained. "More than white folks have to pay, and it comes harder on colored people than whites, too."[96] Less than $22 per month in 1919, the average Harlem rent leapt to nearly $42 by 1927, $8 more than typical for other parts of the city.[97] Thus, the rent crisis blacks faced appeared to be a scheme of speculation by greedy real estate agents. Realtors bought buildings currently or previously occupied by whites, minimally refurbished them, increased the rent, and admitted black tenants.[98] If whites remained, they then left those buildings and landlords allowed structures to degenerate, amenities to stall, and pest infestations to flourish.[99] Visiting Harriet Newman's family home in 1917 one parole inspector described it as "very plain and in poor condition" with a low ceiling, few windows, and no running water. "The place was swarming with flies . . . in terrible disorder," and "it seemed almost incredible that people could live in such discomfort."[100] Desperate for better housing, African Americans submitted to steep contracts in such buildings. However, like some comic paradox, inflated rent made living situations less stable, and many sacrificed the food, clothing, and other necessities that might have insulated them from the vagaries of neglected homes in order to meet payments.[101]

To offset the cost of rent, black tenants made space for boarders, which created congested and perilous conditions.[102] Out of twelve black families in a 1905 census enumeration of a stretch of Fifty-Ninth Street, all housed an average of 6.3 boarders. Living with his wife and sister-in-law, minister Elder Bowles welcomed four boarders into his apartment, and Rosa Kincaid and her son supplemented their income from service positions by taking in up to ten lodgers at a time.[103] A study by the Federation of Churches in 1897 discovered subtenants in over 40 percent of black households overall in the city, more than half of whom were unrelated to the head.[104] Likely as a result, by 1925 density in black neighborhoods exceeded that of the rest of Manhattan by more than 113 people per acre, with Harlem thronged beyond others.[105] According to the Bureau of Social Hygiene, the mass of "roomers" formed "a menace to the health and morals" of black communities and households.[106] Besides the discomfort of congestion, opening one's door to outsiders merged public and private in ways that threatened the sanctity and safety of the home.[107] Some lodgers failed to pay rent on time, disturbed the peace and privacy of the original residents, or committed violent or property crimes.[108] Two months into Calvin Scott's board with Isaac and Edna Harris in 1925 he stopped working and began "drinking liquor heavily."[109] Admittedly "out of my mind," over work stress and the Harrises' refusal to loan him money, Scott attempted to burn their house to the ground, but failed.[110] Even worse, lodgers sometimes carried out acts of sexual violence. Eighteen-year-old Sallie Woodward reported being raped by a roommate of her sister in 1911.[111] Likewise, a boarder in Millie Hale's grandmother's home impregnated her three times before her seventeenth birthday and left her to raise the children alone.[112] Although white households also took in supplementary renters, the housing pressures blacks withstood made the admittance of lodgers nearly inevitable. Coerced to compromise their privacy and security by a predatory housing market, they often had no choice but to endure undesirable and occasionally risky living situations.

Tight, unhygienic, and sometimes unheated housing also had implications for the health and comfort of all residents.[113] In 1890, the general death rate for black Manhattanites was 30.27 per 1,000, 36 percent higher than that for whites, and 541 black infants perished before their first birthdays, almost double that of white infants. Tuberculosis posed part of the problem. In the same year 845 blacks succumbed to the disease versus 379 whites, a difference of 122 percent.[114] This disparity only worsened between 1915 and 1928 when black consumption deaths jumped once again from just over 500 to 800, an increase of 60 percent, while whites saw a steep decline.[115] Blacks also died of diseases related to blood circulation, reproductive problems and venereal infections, and homicide. They were 266 percent more likely to face violent death.[116] Maladies associated with malnutrition and exposure contributed to a black mortality rate nearly twice that of whites by the 1920s.[117] This discrepancy illuminates the most salient and corporeal effects of housing segregation. Although pseudoscientific claims erroneously associated high black mortality with weak immune systems, statistics on communicable contaminations directly resulted from living conditions. Blacks with higher wages often had no choice but to live in housing that negatively impacted health, and those with lower wages lacked the resources to mollify their situations with health care, proper nutrition, and amenities. Queens resident Hannah Mott's family suffered many losses resulting from likely preventable health ailments. One child was stillborn, another died of a food-borne bacterial infection, and yet another passed away from tuberculosis.[118] Bronx resident Henry Johnson similarly lost "three or four" children in infancy, and another in an accident at home.[119] Efforts by organizations like the Urban League and the Sub-Committee on the Prevention of Tuberculosis among Negroes to teach proper hygiene and preventative measures had little impact, and the real problems of low wages, poor housing, and malnutrition kept mortality rates high across the time of study.[120]

Where disease thrived, so did illicit trades, and some African Americans complained of the difficulty of avoiding what they considered immoral or threatening to their sensibilities and bodies.[121] Middle- and working-class blacks had a complex relationship that included emulation and engagement but also tension. Critical of the behavior of the poor but hemmed in by urban apartheid, bourgeois blacks often failed to find housing that would cushion them against the severity working-class blacks experienced, or fulfill their desires for reputability.[122] Besides a few elites, even black literati of the Harlem Renaissance, or those Wallace Thurman called the "niggerati," had little choice but to live in tenements overflowing with residents.[123] "Wherever they move," author Claude McKay wrote, "the common people follow and threaten to submerge them."[124] This is not to say only hostility existed between the classes. Black elites often promoted progress through improving the lives of the poor, and commoners not only aspired to upper-class status, but might express pride in the accomplishments of fellow blacks.[125] Still, black traditionalists often wished to change, or at least avoid, the perceived unbecoming conduct of the laboring class and stem the flow of migrants from the South.[126] Sometimes believing their continued success in the North hinged upon the maintenance of respectability and standards that would appeal to white observers, some middle-class blacks chastised poor blacks and migrants and advised them to adjust their behavior or remain in the South. In one prime example, black writer Paul Laurence Dunbar's 1902 novel, *The Sport of the Gods,* narrated a migrant family's decomposition in New York, a story meant to confirm for readers the hazards of the urban North.[127] Away from the paternalism of Southern racial customs and rural work, some believed blacks rendezvoused with dissipation and crime. "What is to be done with them," Dunbar wrote in another publication, to keep "idle, shiftless Negroes . . . from inoculating our civilization with the poison of their lives?"[128] "We are constantly mortified by the conduct of young Negroes," one *Age* article explained. "They block the sidewalks, impede traffic and by their unseemly conduct cause much needless trouble."[129] Such "fifteen-cent gentlemen with two-dollar canes," in the words of Booker T. Washington, sullied the image of respectable blacks and quickened the flames of racial antagonism that combusted in the lives of all black New Yorkers, no matter their status.[130]

Because of this stigmatization, a realtor initially rejected Reverend Hutchens C. Bishop and his wife as tenants although they had a "fairer complexion than most white[s]," the reverend claimed. "The agent came to look upon my references [and] found that I was a colored man," he explained. The couple managed to convince the broker of their respectability and rented the apartment, yet Bishop called attention to the burden housing segregation placed on middle-class blacks. Without such fortune he and his wife would have been forced to live in "a noisy tenement house among a class of people that I do not care to be particularly identified with," he concluded.[131] Such an environment would fail to insulate the respectable from the disreputable and could possibly precipitate a transformation for the worst in those already criminally inclined, it seemed. Conditions migrants settled in were "of such a nature that very frequently the good are made bad and the bad made professional criminals," W. E. B. Du Bois supposed.[132]

Concerned about safety and black racial destiny, middle-class men like Bishop might find themselves in conflicts with their working-class neighbors who had different concepts of propriety. This disjuncture led to the death of black postal clerk James Dunham in 1893. Confronting a group of men gambling near the entrance of his home, Dunham threatened to have them "locked up" if they did not disperse.[133] Resenting his interference, Solomon Harper told Dunham, "You can't rule the lane!" and the dispute turned violent.[134] Harper fled the scene when Dunham got the best of him but later approached him on the street and beat him to death with a brick.[135] The proceedings of Harper's murder trial demarcated a rift existing between segments of the black community. One witness described the gamblers as "fellow[s] that don't work, and don't do nothing but loaf around," while others made Dunham into the aggressor.[136] Some men like Dunham disapproved of how others occupied public space and in attempts to rein in their behavior, they contributed to the surveillance of the working class and unemployed. At the same time, men like Harper, who admitted to partially supporting himself with "cards and horses," objected to unflattering characterizations of their leisure and pushed back on surveillance from blacks as well as whites, sometimes in lethal ways.[137] The tragedy of Dunham's death exemplifies how intraracial tension constrained black lives. Both men reacted to the other out of pride but also out of a desire to control the implementation of public space in their neighborhood and shape it to their respective needs.

Accordingly, seeking stable and sustainable living spaces presented all black New Yorkers with considerable obstacles. Available housing ran the gamut from poor to uninhabitable, often occupied unsafe areas, impelled the sacrifice of privacy for affordability, and kept living situations in constant flux.[138] Men might relocate multiple times a year in an unending effort to set down roots and create a sense of sustainable residency.[139] Some fled rental flats, rooms, and lodging houses when bills piled up or moved from place to place in hopes the next location would be better. In the years between 1925 and 1929 Virginia migrant Harold Murphy lived in a series of furnished rooms across Harlem eventually settling in a "disorderly house" known for gambling and "frequented by persons of loose moral character," as reported by a prison intake official.[140] Rooming in such dreary tenements, crowded in with other boarders and families, and lacking the privacy most adults wished for, men like Murphy could be denied the desired fruits of their labor, and they struggled to create or sustain households of their own. To solve the housing problem, enterprises like the Afro-American Company bought buildings in Harlem and black churches invested in real-estate for black tenants. Formed in 1910, the National Urban League (NUL) established a bureau to help blacks distinguish between "certified" and "suspicious" housing, teach proper sanitation, and instill a sense of community pride with initiatives like the Utopia Neighborhood Club.[141] Nevertheless, housing continued to impair black health and lives, encourage reliance upon streets and commercial spaces like saloons, and frame disputes with white and black neighbors. Homes became metaphors of the false veneer of New York City. Meant to be spaces where one might control one's own destiny, residences presented insistent dilemmas that thwarted the ambitions of black men and women alike.

"Satisfied to Live by Illegitimate Means"

Discrimination in the city's residential arena mimicked that in the economy, and black men languishing from work inequity sometimes turned to illicit trades, theft, and muggings for subsistence and self-gratification.

Twenty-three years old by 1929, Charleston, South Carolina migrant Winston Coburn committed burglary and robbery multiple times across the 1920s. Released on parole from a two-year sentence in 1928, Coburn worked as an elevator operator but lost the position after only three weeks. Reeling from lack of income for months, and likely frustrated by limited options for his livelihood, he burglarized a Harlem residence taking more than $500 worth of jewelry, and police apprehended him while pawning the loot.[142] In his initial prison intake in 1929 he ascribed his actions to the fact he "needed money" between jobs, but another interview told a different story.[143] The examiner characterized Coburn as a "self-indulgent and carefree youth [who is] averse to steady employment and fond of amusement." Coburn, himself, admitted he committed burglaries to acquire "money for theatres and clothing" and to participate in "the recreational life of the city."[144] With lengthy stretches of unemployment on his record, and lacking explanations for his own support, the interviewer assumed Coburn "subsisted on the proceeds of thefts" and robberies, most of which would go unpunished.[145]

A relentless series of challenges obstructed the ambitions of men like Coburn. Like black women, they faced prejudice when looking for work, but with domestic labor in high demand, women had better employment prospects. To fill those jobs, women migrated more frequently, which resulted in asymmetrical male/female populations.[146] Just over 800 black men resided in the city to every 1,000 black women in 1900, a proportion that only leveled slightly by 1910.[147] Consequently, African American women supported themselves more often than white women as many struggled to find financially supportive partners, and men rarely earned the income necessary to act as sole breadwinners, sometimes needing support from women themselves.[148] Black men were generally barred from upper-echelon white-collar jobs and most industrial positions and lacked the political connections that many other ethnicities used to land jobs in public sector services. As a result, they relied mostly upon service or domestic employment as cooks, waiters, shoe-shiners, or hard laborers in construction or in coal yards.[149] However, from 1900 forward, black men steadily lost domestic, unskilled, and service positions to white immigrants.[150] For example, in the first decade of the century, the number of black porters in the city decreased 23 percent from 2,143 to 1,645 as white porters swelled by more than 1,000.[151] Jobs black men previously dominated, such as elevator operators and longshoremen, could be seasonal and were only available as long as whites did not want them.[152] "The ordinary coloured man can't do as much work nor do it as well as the ordinary white man," one employer believed. "The result, is, I don't take coloured men when I can get white men."[153] Seeking employment in 1921, writer Langston Hughes recalled such bigotry when one employer told him "I didn't advertise for no colored boy." "I found it very hard to get work in New York," he wrote. "On many sides, the color line barred your way of making a living."[154] In a survey of 100 black men living in Greenwich Village's "Little Africa" in 1900, 69 percent had jobs in service as waiters, porters, drivers, and day laborers, all positions with long hours, high rates of turnover, and low pay.[155] Blocked from New York's industrial sector and skilled trade unions, they also relied upon positions as janitors and servants but lost ground even in those fields later in the decade.[156] Additionally, education did little to change their lot. In the words of a black student in Brooklyn, "there is nothing better for a colored boy to do if he finishes the course," so he decided to drop out and help support his family with menial labor instead.[157]

Such labor offered little advancement and smothered men in debt and insolvency. The costs of living in New York combined with dead-end occupations made much of the work blacks found seem as exploitative and obligatory as sharecropping. After more than six years of toil in various service positions, Barbados immigrant Frederick Challenor wrote his wife in 1913 to say he was "still trying to find a good janitor's job," the lack of which forced him to borrow money frequently and remain in a cyclical financial deficit.[158] In 1916, black social worker Forrester B. Washington surveyed one hundred black men doing similar work in twenty-five apartment buildings across the city and noted their limited prospects. Most served in ground-level positions, such as doormen or elevator operators, and only 2 percent ascended to the rank of superintendents.[159] Stranded in first-rung occupations, they endured "monotonous, drab, uneventful" toil, and an "extremely morbid and vicious" existence, Washington wrote.[160] The average worker served up to ninety-eight hours, seven days per week, without holidays. Including tips, most made $31 per month, at best 49 percent less than the $60 one study determined necessary for monthly family subsistence.[161] Perhaps fortuitously, the vast majority of men surveyed were single, but necessary per diem expenses quickly depleted meager funds. With lodging rent averaging $6 per month, shelter took up 22 percent of their income, often for a dark, unventilated, shared room. Minus transportation, laundry, clothing, and leisure costs, the report concluded, they had very little left for meals. Washington supposed "the only place where they can skimp being on their food—they do it and menace their health in doing so." Of those men married with children, 62 percent had working spouses with wages on par to their own, and 40 percent kept lodgers in order to pay $18 or more for rent each month.[162]

Under the circumstances, the average worker in Washington's study, and legions of black men with similar work, overhead, and responsibilities, found themselves fiscally immobile and embittered by an economic stonewall. Such a slim margin between subsistence and homelessness might also leave them stressed out and emotionally weary. After laboring alongside New York dockworkers in 1919 novelist Jean Toomer wrote "such things only dwarf the soul, weaken the body, dull the mind and prohibit fruitful activity."[163] "I hated such work from my birth," W. E. B. Du Bois commented in his 1920 autobiography. After a stint as a server, he claimed he audaciously "disowned menial service for me and my people."[164] Unlike Du Bois, most black men had little choice but to withstand undesirable occupations or change positions. Having trouble finding a good paying job, one man claimed he switched jobs frequently out of optimism. "I always felt that there was a better position somewhere in the big city for me," he told an interviewer.[165] For others, the rat race proved too taxing and they withdrew from the legal market altogether. In addition to a short time running an elevator, Winston Coburn reported only one other four-month-long job on his record, an indication he remained unemployed for the bulk of seven years.[166]

Expressing frustration with work options and an appetite for modern diversions, Coburn's crimes articulate the proclivities of men who chose subsistence crime over thankless labor and economic entrapment. Idle often for weeks or months, they might steal or commit robberies out of desperation or opportunism.[167] Chronically unemployed, Wiley Lawrence lived rent-free in "various basements and pool rooms" and intermittently slept on the street for seven years after migrating to New York City in 1919.[168] In the next decade police arrested Lawrence more than eleven times for charges including robbery and grand larceny, and he received a lengthy prison sentence for picking a subway passenger's pockets in 1929. In an interview with an officer on admission to Auburn prison, Lawrence confessed to resorting to theft "as a means of subsistence" when joblessness made him desperate. Condemning him as a "vagrant" who has "no desire to work" an interviewer at Auburn noted he seemed "satisfied to live by illegitimate means."[169] Starvation and homelessness pushed John Green to commit robbery after only four days in the city. Accompanied by a friend he entered a delicatessen with a revolver, ordered the clerk to give him "a small quantity of groceries," and fled. Once caught Green admitted to supporting himself with "small robberies" including four in New York and many others in Philadelphia before he relocated.[170] Muggings and burglaries could be lucrative, sometimes yielding hundreds, if not thousands, of dollars, when successful. In 1917, William Burgess and Allen Hicks burglarized two apartments removing $4,092 worth of property including jewelry, silverware, expensive clothing, and an opera glass.[171] Burgess and Hicks went to prison for their crimes, but their case indicates how some took risks to alleviate financial strains and obtain access to goods and services otherwise unavailable. It also shows how alluring such thefts and burglaries could be. With many African American men making less than $30 per month, such rich takes represented more than a decade's worth of salary and provisions.

Wallace Jenkins (pseud.), an inmate at Auburn prison, arrested for blackmail in 1914. Courtesy of New York State Archives and Records Administration, Albany, New York (Inmate #35321, Series B0082).

Considering the possibilities of crime, it is unsurprising many black men chose to forgo inhumane, fruitless labor for vocations in the underground economy. For men overcome by the economic sea of New York City and dreaming of sailing on its crests, the bonds of legality tended to loosen. Often unable to envision their desired lives within the rule of law and the stricture of bourgeois benchmarks of reputability, some men interwove fantastical ambitions with the odds of making a profit on the streets. The Clearing House numbers operation perfectly illustrates how illicit commerce and black imagination dovetailed. Bettors aimed to hit a three-digit random number with a 600:1 pay off, a far-fetched proposition that left few with significant windfalls.[172] Such gambling rackets provided capital where there otherwise would be very little.[173] Millions of paper slips circulated in Harlem and San Juan Hill providing cashflow for lucky winners, "runners," and numbers kings and queens.[174] Collectors went door to door, picked up wagers on the street, and earned a 20 percent brokerage from all bets, often clearing up to $50 per day.[175] When successful, they dressed finely and commanded respect on the streets, while numbers controllers floated by in chauffeured vehicles.[176] Beginning as a porter, Danish West Indies immigrant Casper Holstein amassed

Casper Holstein in *Opportunity Magazine* after donating $1,000 for the Holstein prizes in the annual writer's contest, 1926. Schomburg Center for Research in Black Culture, Photographs and Prints Division, New York, New York.

more than $500,000 from the action by the late 1920s. As a gambling czar he kept his flash to a minimum but trickled capital into Harlem by giving gifts to children during holidays and donating to newspapers, schools, and Marcus Garvey's Black Star Shipping line. Kidnapped and extorted in 1928, Holstein's empire crumbled and he did a stint in prison a few years later, but he furnished a compelling model for black collective deliverance through unlawful means like gambling.[177] Although the chances of winning remained slim, the prospect of relieving the burdens of city life, if even momentarily, attracted players like a snake charmer. Claire M. Halley's 1927 *Amsterdam News* published anecdote, entitled "Fickle Lady Luck," depicted a "dandy" named "Sweet Cider," who also started out as a porter, but through the magic of numbers he could be found strutting from a luxury motorcar in a pearl-gray suit with a fedora hat, suede gloves, patent leather shoes, and an ebony cane. "Sweet Cider didn't believe in working, so he . . . let the numbers play for him" and with each win he acquired more material luxuries, which he considered further "proof of his importance."[178] Like Holstein, Cider's luck eventually ran out, but both of their stories paraphrased the fantasies of many black New Yorkers reconciled with the truth of their situation. There were few ways of transcending the privations they faced, and underground markets and crime had to be considered as viable options.

Seeking the worldly and emotive benefits of alternative industries, some men leveraged urban space to their advantage in crimes that had the capacity to reformulate their relationships with the public world. Numbers runners used packed sidewalks to cover their business as they collected bets and communed with clientele.[179] In many cases, defendants admitted to committing crimes in hallways, alleyways, and rooftops, or remote locations recognizing those locales limited the view of witnesses and police. Roofs turned to spaces of relative safety where gambling, violence, and robberies happened or where men might attack police with projectiles to protest controversial arrests down below and fade into apartments before capture. Playing craps with a group of men on a roof, Roscoe Byrd alleged one player took his money and disappeared while the others threatened to toss him to the ground if he tried to follow.[180] Unused passageways and secluded streets harbored crimes against unwary individuals. Before their arrest in 1921, Jacob Jameson and an accomplice made a habit of hiring taxis, taking them to isolated locations, and sticking them up.[181] When two men robbed a Japanese tourist in the same year they dragged him into a vestibule on West Ninety-Ninth Street, climbed to the roof after stripping him of his belongings, and escaped across a number of buildings before descending to Columbus Avenue away from the scene of the crime.[182] Crowds and activity made busy strips like Columbus ripe for pursuits like car theft, pickpocketing, purse snatching, and swindling. When Gregory Brown spirited away a Harlem woman's handbag on a busy section of 148th Street, he hid in a basement and threw the spoils into a storeroom to escape detection.[183] Rebecca Wheeler lost $196 dollars in a "leather-dropping" scam where two men promised her profits if she made change for a fake $500 bill found in a planted pocketbook. In the end, the men ran off with Wheeler's money and left her with the counterfeit cash.[184] All of these cases represent moments when men embedded in clandestine street commerce used the anonymity and invisibility of blighted racialized spaces in order to grasp the reins of economic and spatial power, if only briefly. Although much of the city's structures curved against the interests of black men, those who sought alternative pathways to sources of remuneration frequently designed systems to turn the city's landscape, crowds, and blind spots into personal assets.

In the dusk of economic dislocation, lawlessness illuminates the deeper experiential meaning of job insecurity for black men in New York City. Most apparently, unequal access to wages meant unequal consumer power and severance from resources in a city built on economic exchange. Racially rigged competition with whites led to "occupational eviction" and brief or scattered work histories.[185] After migrating from Crescent City, Florida, in 1907, Jacob

Jameson wandered from job to job working as a bell hop, a cigar maker, a waiter, and a theater porter within a short time.[186] Harry Robinson left his job as a building porter "on his own accord," and tried his luck first pressing clothes, then maintaining buildings for a real estate agent until "business depression" eliminated his position in 1928.[187] Some found consistent work, particularly with the help of organizations like the National Urban League, but most never emerged from the rhythmic cycle of meager jobs, unemployment, and penury.[188] As such, work inequity wrought material, cognitive, and emotional delimitations that suspended aspirations in a web of restrictions. Wage earning and masculine identity maneuvered lockstep in the early twentieth-century social world since money meant autonomy and control of the "world of men."[189] Actively closed off from legitimate livelihoods, black men may have felt emasculated by a public renunciation of their roles as breadwinners, belittled by financial straits, and exasperated by the inability to savor legal pleasures. Reaching the city in 1903 with his wife Mary, Harry Rock found he could not "get one cent ahead," and after less than a year he was "crazy to get in the country away from this old New York," his wife wrote a relative. "He hates it here."[190]

Precarious work, therefore, had broad implications for African American men that went beyond economic and material deprivation. Job insecurity led to housing insecurity, and for some, underground markets and crime were the answer to unsettled living situations. Yet time on the streets and participation in public illicit trades had existential impacts on their health and freedom and made the already treacherous streets of New York even more hazardous. Thus, labor discrimination bolstered spatial segregation in a unique way. With their wages suppressed, black men often could not afford better housing or to take part in countless facets of New York's glittery self-indulgence, whether they were admitted or not. With "open and easy downward roads" before them, one pastor reasoned, "you would wonder that so many have been able to resist" the temptations of the city.[191] Discovering legitimate avenues to achieve status partially roadblocked, quick proceeds from crime could be a cathartic release in a world composed of threats to livelihood and masculinity.

"Police in a Fight with 1,000 Negroes"

In August 1900 black migrant Arthur Harris killed undercover police officer Robert Thorpe for assaulting him and his common-law wife, May Enoch, triggering one of the largest conflicts in New York City history. Harris fled the city, but white citizens and police marauded through the Tenderloin assaulting every black person they encountered.[192] Newspapers reported that police ignored the violence or joined in emphatically since they felt "vindictive against colored people generally."[193] Mobs surrounded blacks, ripped them from moving streetcars, and assaulted them on the sidewalks. Police arrested and abused them at a local station house where nearby residents reported hearing agonizing cries throughout the night.[194] "It is a common thing to hear coming from the 37th Street station," one observer noted, but on this day, it was exceptional.[195] Subsequent testimony from black witnesses and victims like Chester Smith revealed a bitter night of terror that imprinted the memories of black New Yorkers from then forward:

> I saw a crowd . . . composed mostly of police officers and children. Some one in the crowd said, "There is a nigger!" pointing at me. . . . Somebody threw a brick at me, which struck me in the back, and then one of the policemen came up to me and struck me in the left eye with his club. . . . I then ran into the saloon. . . . One of the policemen ran in after me, and told me . . . that the mob had dispersed [but] I saw that they were still waiting outside. I said to the officer . . . "No, sir, I can't go out there; they'll kill me." The policeman then lifted me from the ground and threw me through the swinging door into the street. The glass in the door was broken, and I fell on my hands and knees. The policemen and the mob then began beating me, the policemen beating me with their clubs.[196]

As the fighting continued over a number of days, black residents of the Tenderloin formed the Citizens' Protective League (CPL) to punish assailants and follow through on indictments of police.[197] The CPL immediately requested the mayor's attention to the subject in a letter demanding "common justice." "We by no means condone the crime of Harris," they reasoned, but it "does not justify the policemen in their savage and indiscriminate attack upon innocent and helpless people."[198] With the help of attorney Frank Moss, known critic of police violence and the director of the Society for the Prevention of Crime, the CPL attempted to sue the city on behalf of black victims, but to no avail. The organization's efforts had little effect on the overall problem and some African Americans purchased revolvers at hardware stores and pawnshops and defended themselves.[199] Seen purchasing a large arsenal of weapons, one black bartender threatened: "I understand they're knocking down negroes 'round here. The first man tries it on me gets this," he proclaimed while brandishing a gun. Angry that officers participated in the riot, others showered patrol cops with garbage, bricks, and bottles from rooftops and windows. Continuing even after Harris's arrest, intermittent violence resulted in at least two deaths and scores of injuries.[200]

Far from an isolated event, the Tenderloin uproar erected physical and psychological boundaries for African Americans across the city and spelled out directives about the regulation of sidewalks and the management of black bodies. Journalists, police, and reformers considered men like Harris menacing to whites, particularly white women, and sought ways to control their conduct. However, black women would not receive such safeguarding. Officer Thorpe likely mistook Enoch for a sex worker when he mistreated her on the street, and in trying to protect her, Harris brought down conflagration on the entire community. Station house mutilation and tortuous interrogations reinforced the power police wielded on the street. Black arrestees complained of receiving "third degree" tactics, an array of brutal methods meant to force confessions to crimes they may or may not have committed.[201] Suspects were beaten and disfigured, deprived of sleep and food, and psychologically tormented into admitting guilt, a process the *Amsterdam News* called an "indoor lynching."[202] In one case, officers arrested a witness of police brutality right after his testimony ended, reportedly thrashed him in custody, and singed his hands and legs with lit cigars.[203]

The Tenderloin episode likewise tells the story of how blacks rebuked these cruelties with outright counteroffensives. Countless newspaper stories recount how African Americans submerged in the features of the crucible fought back.[204] Black men like Harris might react in the heat of the moment when threatened, and groups of blacks vehemently contested unjust detainment or brutality. In 1907, a mob of black Harlemites slashed and kicked one policeman nearly to death for "butting in" on their affairs, and nearly one thousand onlookers "gathered to give battle" when other police interfered, as one paper told it. The fighting "was fast and furious" with blacks attacking police with "rocks, bottles, and whatever else they could lay hands on."[205] Such fighting ultimately spawned from a struggle for space and the power to determine appropriate public customs, and blacks who challenged whites in the streets contributed to a communal and popular culture of resistance and self-defense.

African American antipathy toward authority also grew from the fact police did little to prevent crimes against them.[206] Robberies, burglaries, and shootings impacted their sense of safety in their own communities, and a complex and often violent relationship with law enforcement left them without much recourse when lobbying for protection. No black officers walked beats in Manhattan until 1911 when the appointment of Samuel Battle broke the trend.[207] With the bulk of police derived from Irish Catholic heritage, the heat of street rivalries rose into the ranks of local departments. Patrolmen cleared streets with clubs and petty arrests and investigated white complaints or murders but often ignored misdeeds that affected blacks. In a 1915 inquiry into public agencies, social workers quoted police who said they "considered the colored people worthless, and it was 'useless to bother with them.' So long as they did not murder each other [police] 'let them do as they pleased'" to one another.[208] The lack of authentic policing had real consequences for black citizens. Theft, robbery, rape, and violence made their homes feel unsafe, and the streets dangerous and impassable. With rampant burglary in his building, one man resorted to pawning his "best clothes" during the week and retrieving them on Saturdays in order to keep them safe.[209] The state of disquiet likely elevated for the black residents of West Twenty-Ninth Street in December 1904 when Sterling Green shot his wife and brother at his home, fatally wounded another man on the street, and randomly fired upon police officers before they stopped him.[210] "I don' like New York," one woman told interviewers, "it's too wicked! People is too wil'! They is full o' hell!"[211]

Police unwillingness to stop or fully investigate property or violent crimes against blacks exposed their blatant indifference to the safety of black residents, which reinforced the distrust African Americans held for law enforcement. The 1915 sociological study into public agencies also revealed that blacks accustomed to injustice in court were "panic stricken" when coming in contact with the law, and they often withdrew complaints "against one another" to avoid proceedings. When they did complain, very little happened. Noting fights and "all manner of indecencies" happening without police interference, three black mothers demanded help, but police treated them "as though they themselves were the offenders," the study showed.[212] Corruption and graft only made matters worse. As nerve centers of lawlessness, brothels, gambling dens, and illegal saloons padded the pockets of beat cops and captains with bribes for protection. Black cop Samuel Battle recalled running afoul of his fellow officers involved in "graft and things of that kind" when he raided a saloon secured by kickbacks as a rookie. "I didn't know what I was doing, I guess," he commented sarcastically, "I thought it was honest and honorable to do your work correctly."[213] In city lore, the Tenderloin took its name from a corrupt police captain who considered the underworld his personal piggy bank, one that financed the purchase of choice cuts of meat.[214] It was also a licentiously fitting name for a district well known for commercial sex that needed police insurance in order to function. Unconcerned with the deleterious effects of vice on the black Tenderloin and Harlem, lawmen profiting from clandestine markets had little incentive to regulate them.[215] This combination of factors converted black districts into illegal green zones where pleasure-seeking whites might "slum" for an evening before retreating to safer ground.

While neglecting the overall security of blacks, police used vague legal classifications for petty arrests, harassment, and ill-treatment in attempts to control black behavior and protect whites. As a result, black pedestrians thought carefully about how they traversed the city. In 1916, officers detained one black man for wandering into a neighborhood on West Twenty-Fourth Street because, they claimed, "there [are] no colored people living in there."[216] Across a five-year period, Wiley Lawrence endured confinement for "disorderly conduct" a total of eight times, in most cases for ostensibly legal behaviors such as loitering, but also for gambling and "singing in the street."[217] Facing comparable blockades Hattie Pierce avoided the streets almost entirely. "When it comes to the night," she explained, "I [haven't] been out of my house in a month almost, in no way, shape or form, not even the day time. I can't even walk the street, the cops are hounding me day and night, picking me up and taking me to the station house."[218] In his 1931 memoir, former police captain Cornelius Willemse confessed to openly attacking black men on the street for loitering during his early years as a beat cop. On one occasion he threatened a group with "skull trouble" for occupying a Sixth Avenue corner, and when they refused to leave he sprang into action, leaving them bruised and bleeding on the ground. When the men lodged a complaint about the attack at the station house, Willemse received the reassurance of his superiors that their grievances would not stick. His sergeant gave him a "broad wink" and, within earshot of the complainants, told him to place them all under arrest; a move that made them flee the building. Willemse considered the entire episode enlightening and informative for a young officer learning the ropes of sidewalk maintenance. Such brutality could be justified, the sergeant reasoned, if the officer made "a collar" since "you can always use force to overcome unlawful resistance" to arrest.[219] Accordingly, many police had the authority to maim lingerers if they only threatened them with detainment on trumped up allegations.

Magistrate court documents from one Manhattan district in 1901 reveal large numbers of African Americans jailed on such nebulous charges. Out of 514 blacks confined from the district that year, men made up the large majority, and 296 faced charges for vagrancy, intoxication, and disorderly conduct. Arrests ramped up in warmer months when discomfort from heat or the desire to socialize drove slumdwellers into the avenues. In the first three months of 1901 police arrested sixty blacks for disorderly conduct and related charges, but the number increased by 68 percent to 101 in the summer months as they enforced unofficial edicts regulating the usage of public space.[220] After one such capture of more than thirty black men accused of "lounging about the corners" and harassing "young white girls," a magistrate praised police for "keep[ing] the streets clear of objectionable persons, so that respectable persons could walk unmolested."[221]

Legal codes and middle-class or religious rules about sexual correctness composed another baited trap on the moral landscape of the city. Queer black men faced heightened scrutiny as police collared them for being visible on streets and charged them with "degenerate disorderly conduct," a kind of persecution their neighbors sometimes helped along.[222] During his early days in New York, author Wallace Thurman had an experience that illustrates the targeting of black homosexual men. When he accepted $2 for sex with a man in a public restroom, two undercover police appeared and arrested him. While in jail Thurman requested monetary aid to pay his fine from friend and fellow author, Arna Bontemps, who in turn elicited the help of a minister. Realizing Thurman wished for privacy, the minister himself demanded a "pound of flesh to keep silence," a request Thurman outright rejected.[223] Outside of the threat of arrest, Thurman's ordeal reveals how and why gay social life often remained hidden. Like other queer men, he worried about being discovered since prevailing rules of decorum condemned homosexuality, and press agents published the details of men arrested for "degeneracy."[224] Yet, drag queens, "fairies," and lesbians received a higher level of acceptance in black communities like Harlem than in other parts of the city and composed part of a vibrant nightlife and performance culture relished by people of all sexual orientations. Working-class blacks likely understood queer men and women made New York City home for the same reasons as other migrants, relating to economics, and freedom, and savored the anonymity that might allow their full sexual expression.[225] Often resigned to black and tan saloons, cabarets, or even restrooms, the crucible of public space had added meaning to queer men. Twentieth-century changes in sexuality invited them out into the open to some extent, but the white and black middle class and police simultaneously sought to suppress them.

Painfully familiar with the misery of custom-fit regulation and surveillance, and often unwilling to hobble slowly in the skintight shackles of the crucible of public space, many African American men at the turn of the century and after were primed to resist by an emerging aesthetic of outright rebellion. Whether figurative, cultural, economic, or literal revolt, a generation of "new negroes" submerged themselves in the waters of resistance, bathing in the warmth of the possibilities of personal and collective growth. Urban, more educated than their parents, and often trained militarily, many blacks reared in the aftermath of the 1896 *Plessy v. Ferguson* Supreme Court decision that bolstered Jim Crow, sought to protect flesh, bone, and identity in the only ways left.[226] Following the violence in the Tenderloin, black *New York Age* editor, T. Thomas Fortune, told an audience that blacks should "get at the throats of the white men . . . [to] protect ourselves, and if need be die" in self-defense.[227] When a group of New Yorkers formed the National Association for the Advancement of Colored People (NAACP) in the summer of 1910 it signaled the city's new pivotal position in the larger strategy for black rights nationally. With leaders like W. E. B Du Bois, Ida B. Wells, and black minister William Henry Brooks, the NAACP put forward a stratagem that included boycotts, legal advocacy, and self-defense.[228] Through the organization's *Crisis* magazine, Du Bois railed heartily against lynching and engaged in what one scholar called "militant journalism."[229] For some, the relatively tame efforts of the NAACP were not urgent enough. Radical orator and organizer Hubert Harrison, or "Black Socrates," gave thunderous black nationalist speeches on the corners of Harlem and, after the 1917 racial pogroms in East St. Louis, Illinois, he told blacks they should arm themselves and fight.[230] Jamaican-born Marcus Garvey openly promoted black separatism and pushed self-defense to Harlem audiences, exclaiming that black folks would never gain freedom "by praying for it."[231] And writers and musicians, like Claude McKay, in his famous "If We Must Die" poem and singer Josie Miles in "Mad Mama Blues," elevated ideas of violently upending racial hierarchies until those sentiments suffused the lives of new negroes.[232] In one line of Miles's song she wails:

> I took my big Winchester, down off the shelf
> I took my big Winchester, down off the shelf
> When I get through shootin', there won't be nobody left.[233]

Blacks were in the process of dispensing with "implied inferiority" and envisioning their own "spiritual emancipation," author Alain Locke wrote in 1925.[234] Casting off metaphysical chains, they sometimes fought their white neighbors when violence arose, attacked police officers en masse or individually, and in some instances died while rebelling against systematic and public racial attacks.[235] Most notably, they defended themselves fiercely nationwide during the bloodshed of the Red Summer of 1919 when whites attacked African Americans in multiple cities across the country.[236] The new negro "differs radically from the timorous, docile negro of the past," one *Independent* writer crooned, because "when he's hit, he hits back."[237]

Respectability certainly obliged blacks to live within the confines of the law and to therefore advocate for legal redress in the wake of racial attacks. Yet the question remained: How would one endure attacks so frequent and bloody when the prospects for legal protection remained slim? While whites initiated most racial disturbances in the first two decades of the twentieth century, many also occurred when blacks refused to live within the parameters designated for their life, leisure, and labor, and when they acted to reconfigure those boundaries in ways that suited their needs. Hence, across the long New Negro era, blacks encountered a crucible that challenged their very existence in the avenues of New York City, one that required a reassessment of their values and beliefs about respectability and law.

———

Viewing early twentieth-century housing, work, policing, and public racial violence from the angle presented here, it is natural to interpret these forces as thoroughly asphyxiating to the dreams and life expectancies of African American men. Just like black women, they interfaced with an urban landscape that rejected their participation outside of systems that exploited them, and they could be circumscribed to the point of immobility. City officials and police used law to minimize the impact of blacks on white's prerogatives, narrowing their options to protect themselves and making police power an arm of the city's racial politics.[238] However, blacks found ways to confront these barriers either directly or indirectly. Because the legal system upheld all facets of the crucible of public space, those determined to undermine them often broke the law. Black men seeking unsegregated housing had to fight to maintain residence, and seeking better jobs stoked contention with whites who sometimes took their frustrations out on blacks. The inability to upgrade one's occupation might then produce the impulse to steal, rob, or enter into the steady stream of illicit trading likely found nearby. Bad housing and social needs spurred street usage and exposed black leisure to dangerous scrutiny, and emerging radical ideologies inspired African Americans to fight back. Ultimately, the crucible of New York's exciting and opportunity-laden panorama coerced black men to decide whether or not to break the law in order to seize the modern moment or to survive. Some deliberately chose criminality and retaliatory violence, and others simply found themselves in lawless territory by default while resisting complete annihilation.

The bloodshed, chaos, and uncertainty characterizing the racial skirmishes of the early twentieth century set the stage for confrontations that had ramifications for black manhood throughout the time of study. Believing black bodies disrupted modernity, whites often criminalized black men who jubilated in claims to urban life but simultaneously excluded them from the "wholesome leisure time activities" to be found in the city.[239] With inspections and aggression, reformers and police redefined "public" as regulated, and the threat of arrest hovered above all black street gatherings. The events surrounding the Tenderloin riots and Frederick Miller's brutality trial represent moments of simultaneity when blacks realized New York City was not what they hoped it would be. For some measure of safety, they formed black enclaves, opened their own institutions, and frequented black-owned and -operated leisure spaces in order to escape the crucible of public space, at least for the moment.

Chapter 2

Sex, Blood, Guns, and Gambling

Pleasure, Profit, and Peril in New York City's Black Saloons

I'm de rough stuff of dark-town alley,
I'm de man dey hates to see.
I'm de rough stuff of dis alley,
But de womens all falls for me.
Lawd, Lawd, how dey hates me!
Lawd, Lawd, how dey swear!
Lawd, Lawd, how dey hates me!
Lawd, Lawd, what-a mo' do I care?

—Black folklore ballad

The social treatment accorded even the most successful Negroes proved
that one needed, in order to be free, something more than a bank account.
One needed a handle, a lever, a means of inspiring fear.

—James Baldwin, *The Fire Next Time*

In May 1903 a grim and bloody conflict in a mixed-race saloon left two white
police officers dead and one severely injured, all at the hands of a black waiter.
Donning plainclothes the three officers had just attended the annual police
parade and decided to continue the festivities at the Lenox Hotel saloon
when the encounter happened. "Drinking all night," witnesses claimed, they
"picked a fight" with Jim Singleton, their African American server. In the
thick of a loud quarrel, the officers "beat him so unmercifully" with the butts
of their guns that "blood streamed down his face and neck." Enraged, Singleton "began blazing away" with a revolver as the officers scrambled out of
the building and onto the pavement. His shots killed two of the men instantly
and gravely wounded the third before a local patrolman tackled him. Onlookers witnessed a grisly scene in front of the saloon where two officers bled to
death on the sidewalk and another stumbled up the avenue and collapsed.
A gang of white men formed nearby and demands for vengeance could be
heard above the din of shocked bystanders, but police carted their captive
away before any more violence took place. Badly beaten and wounded himself, Singleton reportedly had "nothing to say," about the incident upon arrival

at the station house, "except that he was defending himself" when he shot those police officers.[1]

Imbedded in the disturbing spectacle of violence at the Lenox Hotel saloon was a duplicitous representation of racial conflict and cohabitation. Men of all races gravitated to public houses for drinks and to socialize, and as a result of the teeming, claustrophobic dimensions of working-class neighborhoods, complete separation ranged from impractical to impossible. To anti-alcohol and temperance organizations already critical of saloons as "foes of social progress," racial difference only exacerbated their damnation.[2] For proponents of segregation and moral reformers, the officers' deaths represented the miscalculation of interracial closeness which inevitably led to lawlessness and turmoil.[3] Progressive antivice organizations and police officials worked to keep saloons and other leisure establishments segregated in order to avoid such events, not because of their own racial antipathy, they argued unconvincingly.[4] Around the turn of the century, New York legislation like the 1895 Malby Equal Rights Act made racial discrimination in commercial accommodations illegal, but many restaurants, bars, and other venues ignored the law by overcharging black drinkers or violently barring them, and courts failed to uphold the mandate in legal claims.[5]

White patrons themselves might also reinforce the color line, particularly in saloons with clientele from specific ethnicities that wished to keep those spaces for themselves.[6] In one newsworthy episode in 1917, a large-scale deadly conflict in Midtown's San Juan Hill district ignited when a black patron in a white saloon protested an extortionate price for a drink. Although the would-be customer was in the company of a white friend, a number of men harassed and assaulted him until he left and then pursued him into a black saloon where a group of black patrons defended him.[7] Such street-level rivalries reflected and reinforced civic rhetoric about the hazy racial guidelines governing the city's cosmos of consumable pleasures. Proprietor associations openly opposed the Malby law, and progressive reformers pushed to resegregate saloons with meticulous investigations and threats of closure. However, the proclivities of patrons of drinking dens, pool rooms, and cabarets ranged beyond the boundaries of touchstone racial norms and conflicts. Despite some rollicking battles and antagonism, working-class whites and blacks often chose to spend free time together and forged economic, material, and sexual bonds in commercial spaces. Bearing this duality in mind, the storminess on the night after the police parade parodied the love/hate relationship between white and black New Yorkers in the dim recesses of taprooms and nightclubs. That quickly, tension might break an unspoken temporary cease-fire and reopen the clumsily dressed wounds that had little time to heal since the last spasm of violence. In one horrifying moment, the realities of Jim Crow shattered a relatively peaceful multiracial setting and disrupted the lives of everyone involved.

Suspended by the racial tensions of New York's nightlife, black men in need of venues for relaxation and work were often relegated to emergent red light districts and hangouts like the Lenox, and critical observers reinterpreted their presence in ways that isolated them as malefactors. In the aftermath of the shooting, newspapers portrayed Singleton as a "bad negro" and inoculated his persona with the malady associated with mixed dives.[8] Situated in the Tenderloin's "Minettas" district, an area "infested" with "the worst colored criminals in the city," the Lenox allowed blacks and whites to mingle in immoral and adulterous ways, according to journalists.[9] Arrested and released only weeks before for "conducting a disorderly house" in the Lenox, Singleton seemed to characterize the prevalent figure of the black tough, a contentious personage composed of real and fictitious accounts of the lives of black men.[10] For many white critics, the whole situation confirmed popular misgivings about interracial black and tan saloons in the worst way. But for Singleton, the shooting doubtlessly carried spatial, economic, and juridical meaning in addition to the immediate need to protect his body from further harm. Fifty years old at the time, he had been imprisoned twice since 1877. Once for five years related to an assault on a police captain, during which he was shot in the neck, and again for robbery in 1883, a charge that committed him to Sing Sing prison for fifteen years.[11] Discharged on parole in 1898 and maintaining a job, Singleton likely understood the harassment of the police as a threat to his freedom. Emblazoned with the mark of criminality, labor in a saloon might have been the easiest to acquire, and being rejected from many other public and commercial spaces, the Lenox may have existed as a crucial point of entry into the social and economic life of the city for him. Burdened with financial and behavioral parole requirements, the unwelcomed quarrel presaged reversals of his momentum since release. Hoping to enjoy the male-centered pleasures of the saloon and the earnings of legitimate work in peace, it is clear Singleton also shot those policemen for imperiling his progress, publicly insulting his dignity, and testing his manhood.

For marginalized black working-class men like Singleton seeking cash, contentment, and self-respect, saloons appear as material and architectural sites of potential power. Enclosed from public view, and away from police-patrolled avenues, exclusively black or black and tan spots represented racial nether regions of fellowship where these men might hold sway. In the actual and metaphorical shade saloons provided against the city lights and the radiant glare of civic superintendence, they performed "hidden transcripts," the assortment of routine, and often covert, resistances oppressed groups use to subvert unequal power systems.[12] Situated in these realms, some black men participated in activities and aspects of cultural consciousness that fostered conviviality and allowed the reclamation of their bodies from the drudgery of ruthless, badly paid labor.[13] They engaged in pastimes, political discourse,[14] camaraderie, and sexual encounters that affirmed their claim on masculinity, and, to some extent, they deliberately avoided the censorious gaze of emissaries of New York's legal and social structures. In these complex forums of exchange, work and pleasure intermingled in more fulfilling ways than in normal toil. Men like Singleton made money as waiters, bartenders, and bouncers, or hustled cash by gambling, mugging, prizefighting, or taking part in the sex trade as pimps.[15] As a result, liquor rooms emerge as more than sites of relaxation and consumption. They were also links to legitimate and illegitimate resources, and ideal spaces in which to shape one's masculine status. It is clear that black men encountered challenges from progressive investigators and white patrons in mixed-race saloons, but exclusively black dives might grant them time to unload the albatross of racial politics and exercise their claim on manhood away from white men.[16] For those beleaguered by torrents of violence and police brutality that limited their cognitive scope of the city, predominantly black saloons became internalized, semi-private spaces that served them in ways the integrated commercial realm failed to.[17] Black-owned saloons also symbolized collective economic gain for the individual and the community, as some black keepers gave charitably to race enterprises and causes.[18] As such, black drinking and entertainment venues enacted a symbiosis between patrons and keepers, both supplying the other with the critical ability to imagine themselves outside of the cauldron of the public world.

This chapter foregrounds preprohibition black nightlife in the first two decades of the century and the early years of the 1920s for temporal and analytical reasons. Most historical studies of early twentieth-century American saloons have focused on white ethnic immigrants and neglected the full experience of African Americans.[19] Zeroing in on this period centers a nascent moment in black men's saloon patronage before white-owned prohibition-era speakeasies overran Harlem in the mid-1920s. A 1928 investigation by one antivice organization concluded whites owned 95 percent of Harlem's bars by then, all of which offered a "convenient place . . . to go on a moral vacation" for whites from other parts of the city.[20] Black saloon usage preceding this demographic switch emerges more fully by focusing on drinking spots before the decided black migration to Harlem. This is not to say slumming only took place during the Prohibition era. White New Yorkers had descended upon poor and racialized communities for the scenery, sex, and inebriants since the early nineteenth century, and by 1900 black and tans existed in many parts of the city.[21] As a result, interracial hangouts flourished even before the triumph of the temperance movement, but they were more likely to have black owners. This detail is important in view of the function those haunts performed in the lives of men pushed to the margins of legality. In a realm forged by black men for black men, they might employ assorted tactics, including violence, to delineate their own spaces and reinforce their masculine identities in ways white-owned Prohibition-era speakeasies and cabarets prevented.

Drenched in décor and symbolism invoking the lore of American manhood, black saloons likewise nourished a seedling spirit of nonconformity to systemic legal and de facto emasculation. Just as violence initiated by whites erected psychological and physical boundaries for black men, in turn, those men might use terroristic methods in an ongoing contest with police, white toughs, or other blacks who threatened them or challenged their authority. In the process, it is clear, some willfully adopted popular stereotypes of black criminality in order to reformulate public or commercial space to their advantage and customize the meaning of those spaces in the minds of other men. Thus, in the period from the 1890s until the early years of Prohibition, the black tough character evolved in the melodrama of New York's collective fantasy. Black blues musicians crooned about bandits and heartless killers who chose to fight and die before conforming to white rule, and writers and other producers of culture expressed black daydreams of criminal profit and retribution. Simultaneously, the notion of the black criminal became a chimera cultivated in the fertile grounds of white horror and fascination as whites simultaneously rejected African Americans and paid to view or indulge in their nightlife culture. However, in this early era of black saloons, certain establishments and neighborhoods remained closed to slummers, and some men may have deliberately embodied the chimera of the black tough, and relished the psychological and spatial power it afforded them, even among other blacks. Toughs purposely or serendipitously cultivated personas seemingly morally and personally unreachable to the rest of civilization, as if emerging from a place incomprehensible to others. They therefore substantiated claims to space and displayed their inherent difference with violence and symbols meant to fabricate what sociologist Jack Katz calls the "impenetrable self," or the ability "not to give up, and not to give in."[22]

After taking the lives of two police officers and wounding another, Jim Singleton personified this specter for police and possibly others. When he arrived at police headquarters crowds of angry whites thronged the building, but black admirers brought him a basket of fruit in solidarity.[23] The assistant district attorney in his case did not recommend an indictment because evidence showed Singleton shot only once the officers nearly took his life, and a grand jury dismissed the homicide cases.[24] However, as one police captain later indicated, before release "he'd learned how the police treat tough guys" in the station house. Angry about his acquittal, patrolmen kept Singleton in their sights, one sergeant noting that "every bad man . . . thinks he's a hero," and now others were "out to knock off a cop."[25] Only days after Singleton's release, the same officer who responded during the fatal encounter arrested him again on the sidewalk in front of the Lenox and charged him with disorderly conduct. According to the patrolman, he found Singleton "strutting up and down" like "king of the coons [with] a bunch of niggers" at his side. They heckled the officer as he passed shouting, "the niggers have a chance now," he relayed, and their fearlessness made him "tired." "They are chesty down there now," after the high-profile exoneration, he noted, and when he ordered Singleton to leave the area he refused. "I arrested the most notorious of the lot," the officer explained, and while searching Singleton he discovered "a big thirty-eight-calibre gun in his pocket all ready for business."[26]

Pleasure

The seduction of early twentieth-century saloons was undeniable. Both furtive and thrilling, in many ways, they epitomized the alluring lights and shadows of New York City. Cash exchange mingled with the expectation of pleasure and excitement, yet the enclosed space and darkness might offer anonymity; a fact that afforded a tinge of danger and wonder. Respectable wandered into the grasp of disreputable, as music, food, whiskey, and burlesque spectacles drew people of all walks of life like a siren song. Oftentimes hidden around corners, in alleyways, disguised as flats in brownstones, or below street view and recessed into the gloom under buildings, dives turned pedestrians into clandestine revelers in mysterious realms. Men contrived manly identity from saloons and reinforced those identities through relationships with other men, making the barroom into a site where modern manhood reformulated in commercial, personal, and public ways.[27] They swarmed into saloons for the free lunches that came with 5 cent beers, sometimes gorging on crackers, cheese, roast beef, pork, liverwurst, loaves of bread, and pickles.[28] Regularly occupying rooming houses and lodging situations, men often lacked leisure spaces in their domiciles, and saloons became their living rooms.[29] Some doubled as policy shops, where throngs gathered to bet on numbers, or pool rooms where men watched or wagered on billiards or card games like faro and poker.[30] Others indulged patrons in interracial cabaret performances and a brassy cosmopolitan clientele that mimicked New York's diversity.[31] Many establishments encouraged illicit sex, skirted excise regulations on alcohol, and payed police to turn a blind eye on all the debauchery. These places also served as hot spots for men connected to the city's rougher undercurrents. Pickpockets, bookies, flesh-peddlers, scam artists,

and robbers operated out of the plethora of drinking spots scattered throughout the city, or settled into dingy booths to make connections with other
hustlers for future endeavors.[32] Gin mills likewise embodied a sense of class
binarism; working-class bars sometimes catered to the tastes of bourgeois
New Yorkers, and even lounges considered respectable might have a seedy
underbelly. Fundamentally, these places blurred the boundaries between
respectable and criminal, especially garish nightclubs where middle-class
whites and blacks mingled with pimps, cocaine dealers, and desperados.[33]

Saloons comprised only one aspect of a broader emerging unisex realm of
public enjoyment at the turn of the century that allowed the consumption of
the products of various cultures and ethnicities, but filtered the participants
in terms of race. Black New Yorkers at the time typically occupied New York's
heart of entertainment in Midtown, Greenwich Village, and the Tenderloin
but struggled to be included. In 1895 Oscar Hammerstein's Olympia Music
Hall sprang up on Broadway in Times Square surrounded by glittering mar-
quees and minstrel show advertisements, and music outfits like Tin Pan
Alley and the New York Phonograph Company not only produced black
ragtime music but also racist coon songs that depicted hideous black stereotypes. French, German, and Jewish lobster palaces and oyster bars competed for diners amid movie theaters and crowded dancehalls, and patrons
spilled onto sidewalks seeking places to drink and be merry.[34] Drawn to the
avant-garde enjoyments and technologies of the modern city, black men
found many spaces like theaters, nickelodeons, and cinemas frequently
banned or isolated them in segregated sections, and social venues for white
patrons barred them altogether.[35] White men and women frequented black
and tan saloons seeking working-class nightlife or jazz music, but African
Americans were seldomly granted such consideration in white hangouts.
Nonsegregated saloons ran counter to the heterosocial nature of America's
"new mass culture," one that accepted a mélange of genders and European
ethnicities but depended upon the omission of blackness and the delineation of public as "white."[36]

Facing exclusion from the gaiety, black men sculpted spaces they could
control and freed themselves from the urban crucible on a nightly basis. Like
all Americans, they turned to various forms of consumption to build identity near the turn of the century, and they claimed arenas where they might
develop a sense of entitlement, commercial self-determination, and pleasurable self-indulgence.[37] Since police and corrupt politicians often allowed
illicit markets to flourish in black communities, black men had unique access to them.[38] In darkly lit, rum-soaked interiors they dipped into a reser-
voir of cash fed by legal and illegal trades.[39] As an alternative to the drudgery
available in domestic and service positions, entertainment venues invoked

novel experiences and portended spatial mobility, increased pay, and the prospect of controlling one's own labor. With the objective of avoiding seemingly meaningless and low-paid toil, black men relished access to trades that combined income with bliss and allowed a measure of independence they rarely acquired from other work. They savored the chance to manage their bodies and time when engaged in amusement-based vocations, dancing, gambling, and drinking.[40] Brothels and bars furnished a homosocial environment within which one could relax, find sympathetic ears for complaints about the vagaries of family life and labor, talk about sports, listen to ragtime music, play games, and have sexual encounters.[41] Considering common early twentieth-century associations between manhood and consumption, coupling work and leisure in a world of diversion proved attractive for many black men.

Such a merger of bliss and income might grant them the emotional and material benefits that broader American culture associated with masculine vigor. As Victorian-era protocols of manly decorum faded, new imperatives of commercial participation replaced them. A nineteenth-century ethos of work and production gave way to a consumer orientation, one that prioritized the use of public and recreational spaces, creating bodily markers of masculinity, and amassing material items through individual earnings.[42] In this context, a study of saloons and cabarets sheds light on the implications of such spheres for black men as built environments. Observing such places himself, sociologist William H. Jones considered cabarets provinces "where original nature can be freed" and "improper conduct becomes conventionalized."[43] Both enchanted and disquieted by the surroundings, a tabloid reporter described such a scene during a visit to a "negro cabaret" in 1922. In a "long, low-ceilinged" basement that "reeked heavy of stale tobacco smoke" he witnessed the dynamism of a "crowd of negroes." The clientele, composed mostly of "big brawny" off-duty longshoremen, huddled into the bar for pork sandwiches and the gaudy exhibition of a tireless female dancer.[44] Mass-distribution of goods and the depersonalization of labor at the time increasingly compelled American men to fashion their identities with similar manly leisure. For black men, black-only saloons appear as locales somewhat abstract from the exposure of sidewalks and streets, as retreats where they might assess the precise meaning of their own demands and obligations without white maintenance.[45] They might also feel empowered in interracial black and tans, where white patrons sometimes deferred to them. Understandably, the materiality of saloons may have provided masculine attributes and references in spades, and psychologically they became vital alternative public dimensions with the capacity to alter one's place in a hierarchy of men.

Black men also had practical reasons for frequenting their favorite raths-keller. Saloons were important refuges from inadequate housing and provided various services from bathing and exercise, to postal delivery and political networking.[46] Proprietors sometimes linked habitués with political platforms and business contacts, or might issue loans and give other sorts of timely support.[47] Ike Hines ran an exemplary black and tan in the Tenderloin occupying a three-story building with a chop suey restaurant in the basement. Serving many theater performers, the club had a parlor with tables, a piano, and a buffet on the main floor, space for rehearsal above, and Hines's apartment on the top level.[48] Black actors, boxers, celebrities, and noteworthy guests like Frederick Douglass came to hear bands play and see dancers shimmy to syncopated tunes.[49] In addition to cashing checks for regulars, keeping credit accounts, and disbursing loans and charity, keepers like Hines connected customers to municipal bureaucracies by trickling political party money into their pockets in exchange for votes.[50] Making up only a small portion of the city's electorate, black men did not receive this sort of inducement as often as white men, but some black saloonkeepers still linked patrons to the Democratically led Tammany Hall or the Republican Party in significant ways. In 1904, Charles William Anderson organized the Colored Republican Club in a black enclave on West Fifty-Third Street, an institution that doubled as a social drinking space and political pipeline. In addition to an assembly suite, the club had a poolroom, a lounge, a room to play cards, and a stage for weekly performances by black entertainers.[51] Through his connections to state leaders like then Governor Theodore Roosevelt, Anderson channeled political patronage to blacks including some cash and modest post office positions.[52] Club owners like Hines and Anderson may have had profit and personal prestige in mind, but they administered meaningful benefits to black men who lacked them elsewhere. With admittance to the wider extravaganza of New York's offerings spotty at best, black men greatly valued venues tailor-made for their civic and social presence.

However, these spaces could not escape surveillance by reformers, law enforcers, and concerned citizens who considered saloonkeepers herdsmen of miscreants and outlaws. Alcohol consumption rose sharply in the first decade of the century. In the 1880s Americans consumed nearly a half-million gallons of beer but by 1910 the number of gallons swelled to more than two million.[53] Groups like the Anti-Saloon League, which opened its New York City offices in 1899, sought to completely end the booze-fueled party, but for many critics of American drinking culture, alcohol itself was not the problem.[54] Innocent men, they argued, could be harmed by the environment of a saloon or might change for the worse since they certainly came into contact with thugs and prostitutes eager to entice them into gambling and sex. Teetotalers saw saloons as hellholes sending men down an inferno of alcoholism, pauperism, and domestic violence, and worried those men would drag their families down with themselves. To saloon critic John Marshall Barker, the author of the definitive 1905 book *The Saloon Problem and Social Reform*, liquor rooms wrecked "personal self-respect," menaced the institution of the family, and hobbled the development of a "good society" overall.[55] Political and cultural sabotage might brew in their shaded innards and, for those restless about civic crooks feeding from the teat of forbidden enterprises, drink clubs were the nexus of city corruption. "If American people do not control it," Theodore Roosevelt wrote as New York City Commissioner before the turn of the century, "it will control them."[56] Most assuredly, these uncontrolled places became more dangerous when filled with African American men and women, many believed. As the 1893-formed Committee of Fifty put forward in its 1905 published diatribe against saloons, "a Negro" drinker was far more "apt to commit some impulsive crime than a white man."[57]

Investigations by organizations like the Committee of Fourteen (COF) illuminate how race figured into their open condemnation of saloons and the push to segregate or close them.[58] As one of the most visible and prolific progressive organizations, the COF sat within a robust coterie that included the Society for the Prevention of Crime and the City Vigilance League, groups already working against prostitution, gambling, and alcohol, and critical of interracial hangouts.[59] Formed in 1905, the COF deployed agents to investigate saloons and dives considered problematic, observed the behavior of patrons, and sometimes invented moralistic or legal infractions outright.[60] Investigators took detailed notes of nights spent carousing, drinking, and interacting with sex workers, and regularly stopped just short of committing crimes themselves. A series of reports from the Tenderloin and Harlem convey confusion, allure, and outrage about the fleshly, multiracial qualities of the frenetic scenes agents entered. Visiting the popular Marshall's bar in 1910, one detective noted tables filled with interracial couples sharing drinks and warbling raunchy ballads. "The girls began singing very low songs . . . [and] raised their skirts so high, their person could be seen," he wrote, noting Marshall's "is a meeting place for white women and their colored lovers."[61] Surveillance in 1913 yielded tales of "mixed couples" using obscene language in the Ebling saloon on Thirtieth Street and confirmed one "white woman lives with her negro escort." Later, a "negress" solicited the inspector and "proposed that I go in [a] hallway and have a good time" for 25 cents. After declining the offer, he watched the same woman take another white man into a passageway guarded by "two negro pimps."[62]

In their mission, the COF also culled the complaints of anonymous citizens, landlords, and business managers who worried about decorum and safety in their neighborhoods and responded in kind. Dreading plunging property values and upset over the loss of lessees, the white owner of a Harlem tenement lodged a grievance against a nearby saloon for raising the crime rate. The place "harbors the worst element possible," he wrote, and made it so white men in the vicinity had been repeatedly mugged by "colored streetwalkers." Requesting the saloon serve its last beer as soon as possible, the letter-writer asked to remain anonymous. "If they should discover me, it would most likely lead to bodily injury."[63] A representative for the famous Twenty-Ninth Street Gilsey House Hotel likewise denounced nearby saloons tarnishing the aristocratic ambience in the vicinity. One tavern especially disconcerted the complainant since it catered to white women "that live with niggers [and] they have niggers upstairs that entertain [them]," he wrote.[64]

Digging into these establishments the COF unearthed perceived sexual misdeeds they feared bled into the streets and into the families of men and women who frequented saloons; yet, in the process, they betrayed racist philosophies about interracial socializing by most passionately attacking black and tans. Reports make clear COF sleuths and leadership wished to redeem whites gone astray, but at the same time they further isolated black patrons and relegated them to the pile of the condemned. Investigators described African Americans as inseparable from the environmental hazards of vice and humanized whites perceived to be tossed in the waves of black depravity. With this mindset, leadership directed saloonkeepers to segregate their clientele or lobbied to close their businesses, and often ignored all-black saloons; an oversight they attributed to insufficient numbers of black investigators. Targeting racial intermixing ultimately encouraged black drinkers to patronize exclusively black bars and cajoled black saloonkeepers to exclude whites from their establishments. Armed with salacious details and complaints, COF management coaxed police to shutter black and tans and pressured brewers to pull their products from saloons that refused to submit.[65] In this way, the COF and its sister organizations added yet another antagonist to a scene already rife with uncertainty. White and black leisure came with the usual drama, but progressive reformers aimed to cleave them apart and close the curtains on encore performances.

Racially biased critiques of mixed leisure from the COF and concerned individuals raises questions about how to interpret the enchantment whites held for black and tans. On one hand, when living close together black and white neighbors sometimes formed relationships organically out of convenience or desire, frequented the same places, and imbibed from the same

A Black-and-Tan Dive in "Little Africa" (Broome Street), Richard Hoe Lawrence and Henry Granger Piffard (1842–1910) for Jacob August Riis (1849–1914). Museum of the City of New York, 90. 13. 1. 166.

taps. On the other hand, the practice of slumming expressed a different, more voyeuristic purpose. When groups of middle-class whites caravaned to black locales, they participated in a popular culture that leered at representations of black criminals, sentimentalized black life in the Old South, and consolidated whiteness around vivid images depicting racial difference. Attempting to address the growing presence of blacks in the city, producers of coon songs, minstrel shows, and plays fostered fantasies of obedient plantation "darkies," tales and imagery that soothed latent white desires that blacks return to an imagined docility.[66] Idealized Southern narratives fed an attraction to a racialized nightlife that afforded moments of escapism for curious white slummers. British travel writer Stephen Graham captured this flight of fancy best when characterizing visits to black saloons as trips to the old plantation South with "wisps of cotton blowing about." Inside, one experienced a "Southern night" with a "group of Negroes . . . singing a Dixie song" and taking on the personas of slaves and children, Graham wrote. But outside, the blare of modernity continued "persistently, regularly, like a pulse."[67]

The simultaneous condemnation and fetishization of black saloons by progressives and slummers reveals a sense of duplicity. In the waters of New York's nightlife, white regard for African Americans emerges as a double-headed leviathan; one head strongly repudiating black citizens and the other lusting after black culture and bodies. The whole behemoth swam in a current of antimodernism, flowing from suspicions that an overcivilized modern life had begun to dissolve American character, weaken autonomy, and wash away individuals' sense of truth and existence.[68] Antimodernism constituted a reaction to the hysterical unreality of technologies and luxuries, and the displacement of physical, spiritual, and familial customs of self-reliance by dependence upon urban services and amenities. As the familiar bases for establishing personhood disappeared and were replaced by urban intemperance, some Americans sought ways to return to old customs, even if only superficially. Reformers and slummers existed on either end of a spectrum of engagement with African Americans, but both came to the table out of the same dissatisfaction with modernity. Antimodernist thought championed primal pursuits as spiritually and physically reconstructive, since the immoderation of middle-class city life withdrew urbanites further and further from the natural human state. When whites descended into black and tans for jazz, dancing, and eroticism, they often sought escape from the detached apathy of material progress into the abandon of "negro vogue" authenticity.[69] Critics of modern life also understood cities as crime-filled and unhealthy, and they promoted either departing for the countryside or fixing urban ills. As such, when bourgeois firebrands condemned mixed bars, they did so out of fear the cask of novel interracial thrills might tip over and splash into their own lives. Thus, both slummers and reformers contributed to pervasive early twentieth-century sentiments of antimodernism that came to life across all aspects of American culture. Blacks, it seemed, were concurrently primitive vestiges of a simpler time, and overly modern harbingers of the doom of a strange new urbanity.

That doom might come, some worried, in the physical altercations and murders that resulted from interracial closeness, particularly when alcohol uncorked racial antipathy and the lurking bloodthirst of black men. In his 1906 memoir former police commissioner William McAdoo described "Tenderloin type negro[es]" as the source of such conflicts. "The male species," he wrote, "is the over-dressed flashy-bejewelled [sic] loafer, gambler . . . generally carrying, in addition to the indispensable revolver, a razor." Once "in pursuit of plunder, or out for revenge . . . they use both weapons with deadly effect," and in the process degraded conditions for respectable residents and preyed upon the virtue of white women. When the afternoon sun lit the dingy streets of the Tenderloin "they can be seen sunning themselves in front of their favorite saloons and gambling-houses, like snakes coming out of their holes." The insurgent attitude of this criminal type made segregation essential. "They are impudent and arrogant in their manner and will block the sidewalks until white women have to go around to get past."[70] Telling white Brooklynites to avoid the Tenderloin altogether, one Brooklyn paper claimed drunk murderous black men acted as if "that part of town belongs to [them], and white people have had much to suffer" at their hands."[71]

McAdoo's comments and that of the Brooklyn journalist reflected popular racism at the time but also charted the factual contestation of urban space between white and black citizens, one that caused warfare on the streets and in saloons. In one example, visiting white Virginian Wendell Stokes stabbed black saloon worker Monte James to death when he tried to eject him from the barroom. Before dying, James told police Stokes "was drinking pretty smart" so bartenders cut him off and James then walked him to the door. As they left, Stokes "stabbed me . . . in the left side," he told investigators.[72] Stokes claimed James robbed and assaulted him before the attack but lacking evidence he received a nine-year prison sentence. However, his punishment would be revoked shortly when prominent Virginians lobbied for his release using language similar to McAdoo about black men in New York.[73] According to one recommender, James's death was "justifiable homicide" since the "burly negro . . . tried to rob" Stokes. The writer additionally argued the prisoner "was forced . . . to kill [James]," considering his "resentment at being put out of the place by a negro." Claiming Stokes would have faced no jail time if the incident took place in the South, he asked the governor to recognize racial customs and fix the situation. "From what I have seen of the black element there, [the courts] should not only have discharged [Stokes], but paid him well for his work."[74]

The social and visible arrangement of saloons, and the inclination of men to regulate them, made them sites of contestation in terms of gender as well as race. As a number of historians have argued, urban spaces gained meaning from the actions of those that lived in them. Barrooms merged material indulgence with a physical structure that condensed masculine symbology into the architecture.[75] Men dominated the space bodily and ideologically, and literally relegated women to rear rooms and side entrances, and sometimes barred them altogether. Like their white counterparts, they frequently approved of the presence of women for entertainment, companionship, and sometimes paid sex, but bristled or reacted violently when wives, daughters, and significant others breached the limits of their versions of respectability by drinking, carousing, and joining in late-night revelries.[76] Hoping to consolidate and control patriarchal relationships with women and exercise some measure of domestic authority, black men might quantify the success of their households by considering the propriety of the behavior of black women. This inclination reflected broader trends in the evolution of gender norms. Early twentieth-century American men often considered new liberties women took in the realms of commercial consumption and sexuality to be threats to their prospects of cementing their own masculinity around the cocoon of family life. As such, black men hoping to bolster their manhood in saloons sometimes wished to regulate the intimate access women had to the same spaces.

Ella Burns's singing gig in Goldgraben's cabaret made her husband Jackson Burns homicidal. Returning from a navy deployment in 1919, Jackson discovered Ella interned in a prison hospital where she was being treated for syphilis. Convinced the disease proved she had been unfaithful or resorted to prostitution in his absence, Jackson tried to end her employment at the bar, reconstruct their household using his version of "respectability," and secure his wife in the domestic sphere. However, their reunion was short-lived. As soon as she recovered from her illness, Ella ended their relationship and resumed her position at the saloon. To rein her in Jackson instructed her to quit, telling her to "leave that place or else she would be carried out."[77] He also implored her employer to fire his wife because "[he] was capable of taking care of her, and didn't want her in the place." A musician himself, he likely plied his trade in saloons as well but understood the threat her career posed to his sexual and domestic authority. Frustrated by Ella's intransigence and believing he had no further recourse, he approached her while she performed and fired a revolver at her head, hitting her once. Ella survived the injury but as Jackson fled he killed a pursuing police officer and faced charges for murder and assault.[78]

Burns's testimony during his trial clarifies his motivations for attacking his wife and also contextualizes the sentiments of other men who committed similar acts of violence against women. Seizing upon common masculinist anxieties about women's commercial and sexual freedoms, he claimed Ella's actions drove him insane and he sought sympathy from the jury. Attempting to reassemble his marriage, he told them, he struggled with the insecurity and embarrassment of Ella's profession as they traversed their community as a couple. "Even when we were going to church," Jackson explained, "she wouldn't be respected by the people around." Men called her by suggestive nicknames such as "'blondy' and 'Frenchy,' and [other] remarks like that were made on the street." Goldgraben's clientele, it seemed, felt a sense of propriety over his wife because of her erotic performances. "They would say, 'you don't know us on the street now, but you are all very lovely, when you are getting our nickels and dimes around on the floor." Jackson believed the establishment of a household supported primarily by his own earnings, and possibly supplemented by more appropriate labor for Ella, would solve their marital disputes. "I told her she could . . . work anywhere else she wanted," he told the jury, "except that place, [somewhere] that was a respectable place." In an effort to prove his worth, he claimed he "did all I could do for her, and I put up everything, every cent that I could . . . to make home pleasant," but it was not enough.[79] Whether jurists empathized or not, there was the matter of the dead police officer to settle. The jury found Jackson guilty of second-degree murder and gave him a sentence of twenty years to life in prison.[80]

Ella's dissent with her husband highlights the greater rivalry between men and women engaged in the commercial economy of New York City and working to fulfill their unique aspirations with the tools the city afforded. Rather than conforming to preserve her marriage, Ella retained the autonomy and consumer power gained in her husband's absence. "She said that she was going to continue in [Goldgraben's]," Jackson recalled, "because I wouldn't give her what she wanted." Beyond the material insufficiency of her husband's wages she furthermore objected to the limitations of his version of domesticity and respectability. Believing he wanted her to "be sitting around in the house, with a knitting needle, and not go any place," she chose her own vocation and self-sufficiency over the bonds of matrimony. Jackson's attempt on her life conveys the perspective of some working-class black men when it came to gender. In his case, violence against his wife not only represented annoyance with her obstinacy, but publicly flaunted dominion over his household and her body, and advertised an inclination to use lethal force against those who challenged his authority. He also expressed unwillingness to allow her to put her body on display in public and plainly stated his claim on the space of saloons when he may not have had such prerogative in other realms. Undoubtedly, race was not the only set of politics men wished to escape when situated in leisure. Jackson also hoped to avoid the sort of criticism he might endure from other black men if his wife forsook the terms of respectability. While men welcomed women in limited and self-indulgent capacities, an explicit need to maintain those sites for themselves and control intimate partners sometimes generated profound hostility.[81] Saloon patronage allowed men to conceptualize their manhood in opposition to womanhood, embedding themselves in a homosocial space traditionally forbidden for women and conducive to manly activities.[82] For black working-class men, saloons stimulated a sort of passionate manly self-expression that lack of money and segregation from other forms of amusement often disallowed elsewhere.[83]

Queer black men also resorted to sexually flexible black lounges and clubs that provided a measure of cover, away from police and critics.[84] White queer men gathered at Turkish and Russian bath houses, restaurants, YMCA residential hotels, and "comfort stations," but for gay African American men, many of these spaces were off-limits, and they in turn made black and tans into sites of unfettered self-expression and sexual freedom.[85] Working-class African Americans were largely openminded about homosexuality and in many cases, otherwise heterosexual men had sex with self-described "fairies" dressed in women's garb simply because of their availability in saloons. The sexual politics of the time allowed such lovemaking without one's own manhood coming into question, if only one remained in control of the intercourse and did not allow penetration of themselves.[86] This is not to say that men who identified as "fairies" did not often suffer scorn and beatings in the masculinized scope of saloons. Progressively into the 1900s Freudian psychology and biological research began to peg men with male sexual partners as "homosexual," "inverts," or pathologically ill since they often lacked emerging physical and cultural markers of masculinity, and working-class men were not exempt from these viewpoints.[87] Still, queer men became far more visible in New York's nightlife into the 1920s when they attended drag shows at speakeasies and cabarets in Harlem, openly dressed as female impersonators, and held masquerade events like the Hamilton Lodge's "Faggot's Ball."[88] An *Amsterdam News* report on one such event in 1929 shows the level of acceptance and mockery queer men experienced in public by then. Three thousand "normal ones . . . looked on in mirth at the girlish antics of the other 2,000, whose acts certainly class them as subnormal, or, in the language of the street, 'fairies.'"[89]

No matter their sexuality, the surveillance, criticism, and legal action black men received not only artificially forced separation between white and black pleasure-seekers, but also marginalized black saloonkeepers out of areas deemed reputable. Letters written to the COF by one police inspector about the problems of racially mixed drinking dives reveal how police and progressives colluded to quarantine black leisure. In a 1916 letter Inspector John Daly alerted COF leadership to the efforts of a "colored man" they had recently ousted to reopen his business elsewhere. Worried about the presence of a black saloon in the new location, Daly requested that the COF stop him once more. "I hope you will be able to block him at this place also," Daly wrote. "Tell [him] that Jersey City would be a good place to open." In a subsequent letter, Daly more specifically cited race as a concern. Referring to three previously shuttered black bars he asked the COF to prevent their reopening in the multiracial San Juan Hill neighborhood. Closing these places "has made an almost entirely new neighborhood down in that locality. . . . Conditions are so much improved, that the good residents there are endeavoring to bring about a change in the name." The area would take "a great step backward," he suggested, if the COF could not stop the opening of more black saloons. "No matter what kind of agreement they make" with the COF, Daly argued, "they cannot exist unless they sell to negro women," a state of business he believed inevitably led to problems.[90]

Perhaps because of the evaluation of progressive reformers and civic personnel like Daly, and the overhead and licensing fees that placed one in debt to breweries, many black men opened saloons illegally. A 1910 grand jury investigation reported at least ten black-run speakeasies between Twenty-Sixth and Fifty-Eighth Streets alone, yet the records of the National Negro Business League officially enumerated only five a year earlier. This discrepancy may divulge the large number of illegitimate barrooms, many of which proprietors camouflaged as other businesses. Although the business league record shows so few saloons it reports more than twenty-six black-owned restaurants and lunch counters, seventeen hotels and lodging houses, and ten billiard rooms, all of which may have also functioned as saloons.[91] When unable to imbed drinking dens in lawful enterprises, some black men sold liquor in apartments and abandoned structures throughout the city, kept an exclusive clientele, and bribed officers to allow operation. According to the *Times*, "two enterprising colored men bought a keg of beer" and dispensed it in a makeshift speakeasy in a cellar in 1895.[92] In another case, the owners of a Harlem liquor store illegally dispensed spirits to "colored loafers" and tenants in an adjacent building through a hole in the wall.[93] Short-lived and unstable, these sorts of establishments permitted black men and women to benefit from a profitable demand for libations and social life while usually avoiding the probe of inspectors for some time. More so than legal saloons, illegal drinking arrangements might bring raids, but until then, they fulfilled a deep desire to splurge and party. And, for entrepreneurs with very little capital, they opened up an entire array of profitmaking opportunities.

Black rent parties, or "chittlin' struts," brought commercial pleasures into the home and boosted household economies for the hosts in the same way illegal taprooms did. Some tenants threw rent parties to earn money when coffers ran low, and others turned gatherings into continuous business ventures. Unlike public saloons and jook joints, "rent shouts" needed little overhead and avoided most legal oversight, but still featured gambling, dancing, alcohol, and music.[94] As white New Yorkers increasingly patronized black and tans, rent parties also gave blacks a refuge from slummers who made institutions like the Cotton Club into "a Jim Crow club for gangsters and monied whites," in the words of writer Langston Hughes. White club owners shunned most black patronage "unless you were a celebrity," but welcomed white strangers to ogle those blacks they admitted "like amusing animals in a zoo."[95]

Rent parties thus multiplied not only to make ends meet for cash-strapped tenants but "to have a get-together of one's own, where you could do the black bottom [dance] with no stranger behind you trying to do it, too." They operated late and catered to the specific tastes and budgets of guests. Hughes considered parties he attended "more amusing than any night club" with "awful bootleg whisky and good fried fish or steaming chitterling[s] . . . sold at very low prices."[96] In the process, rent parties, like makeshift saloons, linked blacks to the commercialized pleasure industry on their own terms and created private spaces for black merrymakers weary of other options.

Jaded by investigations and supervision, black legal and illegal saloon proprietors sometimes took measures to conceal their businesses and deny white patrons. Entrances might be complex, requiring visitors to convince inquisitive doormen to open bolted doors or making them ramble through curtains in basements, apartments, or hallways.[97] One investigator noted the byzantine entrance of Connors Café forced entrants through a private building's dark hallway and "the whole premise has the appearance of being closed." Barron Wilkins's place a few doors down had a "doorman [and] lookout constantly on the job" who kept the door bolted at all times.[98] Suspicious or unknown white guests might never make it inside. COF agent David Oppenheim reported rejection at the door of an all-black saloon when the porter told him "we don't let white men in here unless we know them."[99] Barred from another popular club, an investigator recalled seeing white men refused at the door while black customers were "served whatever they would order." One white man said he "did not mind drinking with Negroes, but the manager said he could not be served," the agent observed before going home himself.[100]

In the rejection of white patrons we see how black saloonkeepers understood their businesses as delicately balanced on the scales of New York's scene of amusement. Managing both the mixed nature of nightlife and the critical glare of progressives could be taxing and injurious to one's profitability. Self-segregation might help avoid prying eyes, but it lowered a business's bottom line by reducing its share of the commerce in the vicinity. Nevertheless, it is obvious barring whites may have served an emotive function for black men. Emissaries of progressive organizations brought New York City's white power structure into the guarded space of the saloon. If black patrons and keepers imagined a sense of safety in liquor cellars, rebuffing all unknown whites was an attempt to plant physical barriers between raucous, smoke-filled dens of self-expression and those who wished to audit them. In addition, there were also psychological barriers that made some black saloons unlikely to receive white guests. Tabloids advertised black crime emphatically in daily reports and editorial displays, and some places lived up to the hype.

Profit

Barron Wilkins's experiences as a saloon and cabaret owner in New York City both typified and wildly departed from those of other black entrepreneurs in many ways. With business savvy and perseverance, he acquired the sort of wealth and consumption habits many black men sought when starting their own enterprises. Born in Portsmouth, Virginia, in 1865, just as slavery ended, Wilkins and his family moved to Washington, D.C., when he was still a child.[101] Like other black migrants, he left in search of work and enterprise in the mid-1890s. Through toil in a number of service industries in various cities, he saved enough money to invest his earnings in a venture in New York City. Realizing saloons were "the most prosperous business," he bought a small commercial space on Thirty-Fifth Street in the Tenderloin and transformed it into what one journalist called "the biggest money maker for its size" in the city.[102] With those profits he opened a number of others including the famous Barron's Exclusive Club on 134th Street in Harlem in 1903, a spot that attracted a "large number of white patrons" and became known as "one of the best cabarets in the city," according to the *Times*.[103] Looking back on his employment by Wilkins, composer Duke Ellington remembered "big spenders, gamblers, sportsmen, and women, all at the peak of their various professions" in the Harlem cabaret.[104] Wilkins was thrust into the limelight in 1910 when famed pugilist Jack Johnson rented luxury space in the upper floors of his Tenderloin establishment. He remained in the press as a prominent figure in the black community and the city from then on with members from the black Knights of Pythias and Booker T. Washington's National Negro Business League among the clientele.[105] Harlemites praised his charity, investment in black businesses, and respectability, but they also celebrated his success. His brother Leroy Wilkins also ran a popular saloon in Harlem that added to the cachet of their name. Barron Wilkins and his young wife, Caroline Sparrow, formed a flashy, powerful couple, both appearing in newspapers and gossip features. One column cheered Barron's "distinctions and quiet suavity" and his ability to "swing votes" among African Americans.[106] Another described Caroline as "daring, beautiful, vivacious and bewitching," and an "accomplished musician and trained nurse." Their home on West 134th Street, a conversion of three apartments above Wilkins's swanky uptown nightspot, was "one of the most lavishly furnished apartments" in Harlem, and when tired of the city the couple escaped to a summer cottage in New Jersey.[107] As a pioneer among black businessmen, part owner of the Negro League's Brooklyn Black Sox, and an active figure in city politics, Wilkins came to be considered "Harlem's richest man" by the 1920s in the estimates of some observers.[108]

Portrait of Harlem, New York, businessman, nightclub owner, and black baseball club financier Barron Wilkins, 1906. Schomburg Center for Research in Black Culture, Photographs and Prints Division.

Wealth and apparent respectability did little to secure Wilkins from the same scrutiny other black saloon proprietors experienced, nor did it keep him from breaking the law. In some cases, overzealous agents condemned his establishments for allowing interracial contact, and in others he defied injunctions that controlled saloon activities and liquor sales in order to placate the desires of his diverse clientele. The COF time and again infiltrated Wilkins's taprooms and cabarets and reported on activity they considered violations of civic mandates and their own codes of decency. Visiting Wilkins's Harlem business covertly in the fall of 1912, one investigator observed a crowd of well-dressed black patrons mingling with "quite a few white women," a number of whom seemed to be "in their natural element."[109] Large paintings of nude women emphasized the wanton nature of one of his places for one sleuth, as did the "nice looking brown-skinned girls" singing pornographic songs with a two-piece orchestra.[110] Another investigator told of the difficulty of gaining entrance and detailed the interactions of white and black patrons who mingled and danced together in a crowded room. One white woman traveled in a group of black women, and another sat fondling and kissing a black man.

While there, the investigator also met a woman-friend of the bartender who "was willing to go out and go to bed for a dollar."[111]

With such evidence of unseemliness in Wilkins's lounges across some years, the COF pressured police to raid his businesses. In 1910 officers interrupted poker, craps, and race betting operations in one of his bars in a sweep of raids in the Tenderloin.[112] A 1915 raid sent slummers, including "richly dressed" white women wearing "fortunes in jewelry," scattering from Harlem back downtown, and Wilkins to the jailhouse.[113] He made headlines again in 1917 when he arranged a meeting with sex workers for undercover agents in one of his bars, and again in 1922 when police charged him with operating after legal hours.[114] For these infractions, the police commissioner stationed uniformed agents inside Wilkins's Harlem place for a stretch in 1917, which seriously impacted profits.[115] With his alleged legal infractions well known, he gathered detractors who saw his operations as deleterious to the city and the black community. Black social and uplift workers criticized his barrooms as "one big obstruction to the moral betterment" of Harlem in a 1924 editorial.[116]

Wilkins's fortunes show how commercial trades figured into the ambitions of black men, but his legal troubles illuminate the impact critics had on their chances of survival and the difficulties of straddling both respectability and illegality. Saloonkeeping provided a way for men to escape the devaluation of their labor and break away from wage earning altogether.[117] Opening a business could be an aspirational goal for the potential profits but might also connect them to a sympathetic community of other men, foster their control over a social space, and cultivate links to underground markets that presented avenues for further economic growth. However, constant superintendence made operating a saloon perilous and complicated. Surveillance and intimidation tactics applied by progressives and civic leaders had far-reaching effects on black proprietors. Lacking the capital Wilkins began with, most opened bars using the "tied saloon" system where breweries advanced the licensing and bonding fees, often as high as $3,000 combined, and in exchange they received an exclusive supply deal. When investigators discovered desegregated crowds like those in Wilkins's businesses, COF leaders pressured brewers to discontinue supply or revoke liquor licenses in order to coerce compliance or force offenders out of business. Beer makers often complied realizing their cooperation in cleaning up the saloons they supplied might count in their favor with increasingly vocal prohibitionists.[118]

On the other hand, corrupt police and politicians might allow legal violations for a fee. The powerful Tammany Hall, the Democratic political machine that often ran New York's government, had a symbiotic relationship with crime, many charged. Gangs not only aided in getting votes for the

Democrats, but also lined the pockets of politicians with graft.[119] Yet, by allowing prostitution, gambling, and illegal saloons to flourish, Tammany Hall officials saw themselves as placating a lascivious working-class public who had a right to blow off steam when not laboring.[120] Potential keepers of illicit saloons, poker rooms, and bordellos lobbied permission from appropriate Tammany Hall district captains, who then collaborated with police to determine the price of protection. The bill could be steep, but it bought a level of impunity that enabled saloonkeepers to cater to diverse clients.[121] In a 1916 letter to the city police inspector, COF executive secretary Walter G. Hooke told of officers who recently removed an investigator from a section of Harlem at the request of a black bar owner.[122] For such protection, J. W. Connors paid $75 per month, and Leroy Wilkins admitted to paying $60 for "the privilege of running a saloon any way he pleased." But Wilkins's testimony in a corruption trial against one police inspector revealed more complex reasoning. Wilkins claimed he had no choice but to pay for protection because no matter the condition of his place the police "could easily frame him up and put him out of business," if he did not pay. "To pay was the easiest way" to run his business, he confirmed.[123]

James Marshall's struggle with the COF is an excellent example of the balance one needed to walk the tightrope between reputability and profit. Occupying adjacent four-story brownstones and a basement at 129 West Fifty-Third Street, Marshall's served dinners with musical acts, and gussied-up blacks and whites mingled with celebrities like entertainers Cole and Johnson, Jim Europe, and Aida Overton.[124] Black vaudevillians Bert Williams and George Walker set up shop there in 1897 making it a headquarters for the artistic expression of black men.[125] The saloon contained handsome suites on upper floors, a cellar for performances, and a fancy dining room on the first floor, which was one of a few such restaurants that allowed blacks entry.[126] "White women" who sought "colored lovers" frequented, according to James Weldon Johnson. Along with other places in the area, Marshall's impacted the way blacks saw the city and created a new "fashionable way of life" for them. The sight "of well-dressed colored men and women lounging and chatting in the parlors, loitering over their coffee and cigarettes while they talked or listened to the music, was unprecedented," Johnson explained.[127] But, for the COF, Marshall's was just another black and tan, and they took action when probes discovered it stayed "open nearly all night" with "white women and colored men" engaging in "most questionable orgies and revels."[128]

In 1912 Marshall complained about what he considered unfair assessments of his business and requested help from Fred R. Moore, the editor of the black owned *New York Age*. Moore wrote a letter to the COF on Marshall's behalf stating: "I have been in his place about eight times [and] I observed nothing out of the way." Acting as an intermediary and purveyor of the COF's ethics, Moore continued, "I have been careful to impress upon him what he is required to do; and the things that the Committee stands for. . . . I can see no reason why he shouldn't have his license."[129] Regular attendee W. E. B. Du Bois also found Marshall's to be respectably run, and he challenged the COF on their attempts to shut it down. Marshall's, he wrote, was "about the only place where a colored man downtown can be decently accommodated." The response Du Bois received further clarifies how race infused the motives of groups like the COF. "If [Marshall's] could be conducted for either your race or mine, [it] undoubtedly would not be objectionable," the COF's general secretary replied, but "it has that unfortunate mixing of the races which . . . always means danger." When Du Bois threatened to enact a lawsuit with support from the National Association for the Advancement of Colored People, the COF acquiesced, but their efforts continued against Marshall's and other saloons.[130] With such backing, James Marshall ignored the COF's requests, and they pressured his supplier to "find a new and more trustworthy representative" of their product.[131] Checking in on the brewer's progress in ousting Marshall in 1918, COF leadership suggested other methods for terminating his agreement, including demanding any back payments be paid in full immediately. If that did not work, they proposed stopping the supply of beer, reporting him to the Board of Trade, and informing the city's Excise Commission of his liquor violations. By the time of this correspondence the COF had been working to revamp the saloon for almost a decade, and Marshall had been navigating their criticism with varying levels of success for that long.[132]

For many black saloon proprietors like James Marshall, COF meddling aggravated existing challenges to their profitability and made it hard to keep their clientele. Hoping to stave off constant threats to his own business, proprietor William Banks penned numerous letters to the COF from 1908 to 1918 promising a list of concessions, but yearly examinations determined he failed to meet the organization's standards. For instance, one 1911 investigation noted white women in the basement, a "fat man who was extremely vulgar in his contortions [and] actions," and rooms that "can be hired for immoral purposes."[133] Another inspection a year later determined the same rathskeller to be designated for "white men to meet colored women" and detailed the comings and goings of white and black women presumed to be sex workers.[134] In response, COF officers issued citations instructing Banks to alter the space to fit their notions of decorum and to keep white and black patrons apart. In 1908, Committee Secretary Thomas H. Reed told Banks to discontinue his dancehall, move the billiards tables and piano out of the basement, and bar women he knew to be sex workers.[135] Banks accepted the COF's rules but enforcing racial separation was impractical, and making the space racially exclusive proved uneconomical for him. Because black barrooms usually sat in the middle of interracial entertainment districts, barring or restricting whites drastically diminished earning potential, and most black proprietors walked a demanding gauntlet to please customers and the COF at the same time. Segregating leisure spaces also likely placed proprietors into a logistical nightmare. Stories of racial violence in the early twentieth century often make it difficult to conceptualize how white and black pleasure-seekers sought each other's company, but investigations reveal how they caroused, drank, laughed, and had intimate and erotic experiences together. Lodging an arbitrary unseen barrier between the sexes and races would have been next to impossible for businessmen who had any hopes of turning a profit. When black proprietors did ban white customers, they very often made exceptions for whites they knew personally, but turning away men and women because of their race unnaturally capped their potential returns.

COF incursions into black saloons therefore represented metaphorical tentacles from the bourgeois public world that invaded watering holes black men envisioned as self-sustaining and discreet. Like working-class whites, black saloonkeepers and patrons benefited from the arrangement and material structure of saloons as exclusive, dark, and removed from view in myriad ways; yet covert inspections disemboweled those semiprivate spaces and spilled their innards into the spotlight of white criticism. Following COF orders to dismantle those havens could be costly, sometimes including major spatial modifications pertaining to furniture, décor, and construction. Performing such renovations to meet COF conditions, Leroy Wilkins "expended thousands of dollars . . . only to have my money tied up seemingly with no chance whatever" of pleasing the committee.[136] Aware of a similar strain on his earnings, William Banks composed a strongly worded four-page letter to COF secretary Walter G. Hooke in 1910. "This business, as you know, is one that the patrons themselves make or mar," he argued. "Unless I cater to their wishes I cannot survive." He also framed his objections to the COF's constant intrusions as a transgression against his manhood. "I do not want merely to exist I want to live and if the signing of that agreement is to furnish the former and not the latter then I decline to live up to it. No man, with a particle of manhood, binds himself and remains bound when he finds those bonds are detrimental to his best interests both morally and financially," he concluded.[137] Nevertheless, Banks remained a target of the COF and eventually of the police when in 1916 his bar appeared on a list of "places where thieves and prostitutes congregated."[138] In the early fall of that year an officer captured him in the act of illegally serving alcohol on Sunday and arrested him for violation of liquor tax laws.[139]

As black business leaders, brothers Barron and Leroy Wilkins likewise invoked their claims to manhood when faced with interference by the COF. In a 1912 letter, Barron implored the organization to consider the importance of self-government for black liquor dealers. Requesting a postponement of judgment on his business, he argued it would be unmanly to accept their restrictions rather than make the changes on his own. "I want to show you that I am a man of my word, and that I want to do what is right" without being forced, "[and] run my place right because all the other colored places seem to follow me and I am honestly interested in raising the tone of these places." Wilkins set his appeal in a frame of independence, collective resolution, and leadership. The disciplinary nature of the COF's ultimatums controverted the statement of racial advancement black businessmen made through their own enterprise, he asserted. "I want to show the white people that we colored men are capable of running clean business places as well as anybody else. And if I can keep straight the others are sure to follow suit." Edicts from the COF, he reasoned, impaired his ability to be a leader in his own fraternity of saloon-keepers. "I was just getting ready to prepare a letter pamphlet on what not to do, and what to do, to distribute among us but if you make me sign a paper it will have a tendency to greatly reduce the good it might accomplish," he maintained. "They probably wouldn't pay much attention to it under those circumstances."[140] Leroy Wilkins staked his own claim to manhood in a similarly commanding letter to the COF in 1915. "[I] believe in being a man among men but, in this deal I am satisfied I am not being treated the least fair," he told them.[141]

By challenging the COF the Wilkins brothers expected to secure their businesses from the fluctuations that came with restricting clientele and censoring their behavior, but they also objected to external oversight that hampered manly self-determination for themselves and their fellowship of black businessmen. They saw COF dictums as an appendage of other forces they likely encountered throughout their lives. As migrants from Virginia, like other black men, they doubtlessly endured incalculable challenges to their manhood and presumed their entrepreneurial success and reputation would grant them the respect and sovereignty they deserved. They also may have believed their rights as businessowners would be honored more consistently in the North than in the South. Hence, their letters express the common frustration black men felt when realizing racial perceptions would undermine hard-earned autonomy, no matter their status or location.

Such lopsided scrutiny fostered real criminal activity, some liquor dealers argued, by forcing black saloons underground. When caught in the scopes of organizations like the COF and effectively labeled as disorderly and immoral, drink purveyors could be typecast in a way that obviated efforts to remain respectable. According to the black-published *Amsterdam News*, the COF made "microscopic investigation[s]" of black saloons but "left practically untouched the protected flocks of white places" all over the city. "Discrimination . . . breeds distrust and rebellion and a determined effort to do clandestinely what would otherwise have been done with more restriction and safety."[142] Black liquor dealers also worried COF condemnation was part of a white plot to continue to control booze sales in black neighborhoods and force out black keepers. Leroy Wilkins accused the COF of such motives in a 1915 letter to Walter G. Hooke. Although whites already owned the bulk of saloons in Harlem, "seemingly, ninety-nine per cent of the complaints . . . are made against Colored Liquor Dealers," he wrote. Complaints, he contended, did not come from Harlem residents but from white competitors who wished to "monopolize all the Colored trade and close ALL the Colored places."[143] In 1911 Barron and Leroy Wilkins along with a coterie of others formed the Negro Liquor Dealer's Association of Greater New York in order to govern themselves and resist white business encroachment. At the association's first meeting, Royal Café proprietor John W. Connor ascribed the loss of business to white bars to the bad reputations of some black places. By agreeing upon regulations across all represented establishments, the members intended to remove the stigma of black saloons as "dens of vice" and to consistently project decency. They agreed to improve the conditions within their own control and reduce the incidence of drunkenness by refusing drinks to patrons in a besotted state. Correspondingly, they hoped that by maintaining racial separation they would win the favor of the COF and thereby attract black patrons away from their white competitors.[144] However, racial separation proved to be unrealistic in the frantic nightlife of Harlem and Midtown, and records indicate most popular black nightclubs remained integrated into the 1920s.[145]

As members of the Negro Liquor Dealer's Association, William Banks and both Wilkins brothers eventually gave in to the COF and wrote multiple letters that demonstrate the power the organization's leaders had over black operations. In one 1913 letter Banks promised never to permit dancing or unaccompanied women after "7 o'clock at night" and not to employ entertainment without consulting the COF beforehand since previous acts had been deemed salacious.[146] "We will not allow colored men accompanied by white women nor colored women accompanied by white men to our premises at any time," Banks reassured a year later in 1914. "Nor will we permit colored men with white women or colored women with white men to be in the same party or parties or at the same tables or to mingle in any way in my premises."[147] In the same manner, Barron Wilkins promised to conduct his business as a "bona fide saloon," remove the cabaret performances, and restrict access to unaccompanied women.[148] Leroy Wilkins additionally pledged to disallow "vulgar or suggestive songs" or "anything that will be regarded as indecent."[149] Subsequent investigations cited all men for violations, but their ostensibly honest attempts to comply are telling. Committee evaluation had the potential to disrupt, alter, or even end black businesses, and their probes could cut deeply into revenue. Banks, Marshall, and the Wilkins brothers understood the pitfalls of hostile surveillance and resisted in the ways they could. Yet ultimately, the interventions of progressive groups, police departments, and concerned politicians affected their ability to sustain legal saloons. Hobbled by the conservative principles of bourgeois observers, black saloons either struggled to survive, found innovative ways to avoid supervision, or made themselves racially exclusive in order to lessen the scrutiny they received.

By 1916, after a decade of investigations, COF management believed their pressure campaign to be a bittersweet success. An annual report from that year celebrated the removal of many interracial bars from the Tenderloin, but lamented their relocation in Harlem and the Bronx.[150] According to an earlier report, black "cheap houses" and places "whose chief attraction was perversion" predominated in Midtown in 1905, and the streets were "patrolled by hundreds of women." Although progress was slow because of "the cry of race prejudice," by 1914 swaths of "negro places" had closed on Twenty-Eighth Street and Thirty-Fifth Street, and the COF had changed the conditions of the one remaining sex resort on Thirty-Seventh Street.[151] A year later that area had been "practically cleaned up" of black sex workers with no further problems, they reported.[152] Their efforts had worked, although imperfectly, and more work was needed.

In the midst of such challenges to his livelihood, Barron Wilkins died in a shootout with a gambler and "dope fiend" in front of his Harlem club in 1924. His assailant claimed Wilkins had threatened his life over a bootlegging debt, but black Harlemites mourned Wilkins's death as they would a celebrity and remembered him as generous and honorable.[153] Newspaper readers marveled at his bestowal of businesses, furniture, automobiles, jewelry, real estate, and investment securities to his wife and family, totaling more than $125,000.[154] Reverend Adam Clayton Powell preached at his funeral and black leaders like Fred Moore, and white politicians like James Joseph Hines, acted as pallbearers in a procession attended by 70,000 onlookers.[155] The contradictions of Wilkins's career and funeral symbolize the dualism he and other black men often embodied. Steeped in the world of commercial nightlife, they adhered to imperatives to maintain respectability; yet they nurtured ambitions and desires that compelled them outside of legal boundaries. Like other entrepreneurs, Wilkins ostensibly allowed the sex trade to flourish in his clubs, but he reportedly barred his wife from entering the premises.[156] Progressive organizations and police made this polarity unavoidable by magnifying the faults of black-run enterprises, intervening in their affairs, and sometimes effectively criminalizing otherwise legal behaviors. Wilkins's death near the doorway of his business materialized another substantial mortal vulnerability of the smoke-filled and gaudy nightlife of black hangouts. Notwithstanding biased examinations, like other places where alcohol converged with leisure, gambling, and sex, black saloons produced the usual dangers. Brazen murders like the one that ended Wilkins's run as an entertainment tycoon happened regularly, eliciting outrage from black and white observers and making evenings out perilous for those who patronized and owned New York's black saloons.

Peril

Making his way between a number of black saloons in Brooklyn on a partly cloudy Sunday evening, COF investigator Reverend William S. Rainsford mentally catalogued the unique perils those places produced.[157] Surveying a row of barrooms on Brooklyn's Myrtle Avenue he noted one "full of tough niggers" with a back room that was "pretty rank at times."[158] Little more than a block away he encountered a scene that curdled his blood and forced him to flee for his safety. The saloon at 173 Myrtle Avenue was "rotten" in his perspective. "This is a dangerous 5¢ whiskey place [with] a bad gang of niggers. [It] is not safe," Rainsford wrote. Alarmed by the setting he quickly "beat it out of there" before there could be trouble.[159] During meticulous searches for violations white investigators like Rainsford sometimes feared for their lives, considering black dives to be hair-raising localities forming the crux of a larger orbit of vice. In their descriptions they often regarded black regulars as inseparable from the dingy built environment and betrayed prejudices about the ways working-class blacks spent their free time. In another report, Rainsford condemned what he called a "filthy nigger joint" for the squalor he discovered therein, adding it "should be closed for sanitation purposes."[160] Despite his biases, the frightening accounts COF personnel received from Rainsford is strikingly telling. Although some whites had the inclination and courage to cross taboo racial boundaries, many shuddered at the thought. The strip of Myrtle Avenue bars most likely harbored a number of illicit trades common to urban saloons in general, but Rainsford's missives make it apparent how dives that served black men loomed as restricted no-go zones in the psyche of some white New Yorkers.

Essays written by white investigative journalists and news writers elucidate the dissemination of perspectives like Rainsford's into New York's popular press and how the exploits of black men formed cognitive horizons for whites, in some cases. Venturing into black districts of the Tenderloin for thrilling reports, journalists hunted for engrossing particulars and advertised fearsome exaggerations about those communities.[161] To novelist Stephen Crane, the exploits of black toughs made black districts seem forbidden. "Even a policeman in chase of a criminal would probably shy away instead of pursuing him into the [Minettas]," Crane imagined of a notorious section of Greenwich Village. Characters such as a man dubbed "Bloodthirsty" disturbed him the most. "Large and very hideous" with a "rolling eye that shows white at the wrong time," Bloodthirsty infamously employed "the wide lightening sweep of his razor" to underline tales of past fights and victories.[162] Attorney Frank Moss contributed his own chilling sketches in 1897 with phantasmagorical descriptions of the Minettas neighborhood as dangerous and disembodied from the rest of the city. The "streets . . . lead everywhere and nowhere," and "a depraved, quarrelsome and criminal colony of negroes" made it "practically closed to travel," he wrote.[163]

A year earlier, in 1896, the *Times* declared a "miniature race war" in a popular Minettas restaurant, instigated by black gang members trying to oust white patrons. While the men celebrated the New Year with noisemakers, some diners asked them to quiet down and the conflict began. "We blowed our horns just to show them who we was," one of the men later stated, "and then they got mad at us [because] ladies was eating. They wasn't colored ladies so we blowed again." When the manager attempted to force the merrymakers out they wrecked the restaurant by throwing platters, food, and condiments, and "went for every white man in the place" to chants of "kill the white trash" from onlookers, according to the *Times*.[164] "White folks had to give way to blacks," a *Sun* writer proclaimed in 1916. Police battled with "drunken negroes" nightly, and white men who wandered into the neighborhood needed to be rescued by police "who sailed into the negroes splitting heads everywhere." In one comical sequence of events in 1916, word got around that Minettas' inhabitants threatened to assault Mayor John Purroy Mitchel if he ever stepped foot in the area. To prove a point, Mitchel visited the district surrounded by "husky policemen—known as 'nigger cops'" who cleared the street as he rambled through.[165] To police captain Cornelius Willemse, Minetta Lane was a place where even a cop strode with muscles tense and "where his hand clutches his nightstick grimly."[166] These exaggerated reports reproduced a trendy impression of black New Yorkers and crafted those notions at the same time. Some white ethnic enclaves in Manhattan had comparably iniquitous reputations, but racial bias made neighborhoods like the Minettas seem even more remote, alien, and hazardous in popular imagination. With these grisly descriptions, columnists sketched the contours of the color line in wide strokes around blacks and advised white readers to keep away, thereby reinforcing the rationale that leisure spaces should be segregated.[167]

In spite of their sensationalism and bigotry, these portrayals held some truth. The one-sided racially biased nature of investigative reports does not obscure real concerns about safety in black neighborhoods. Toughs like "Bloodthirsty" not only affected the white imagination but also very realistically impacted black residents of all classes as they went about their lives and had ramifications on their feelings of security in their own neighborhoods. Concerned about safety in the Minettas, Bettie Watts relocated in order to escape neighbors who "drank beer, played music, danced, and caroused" excessively outside. "The crowd in the yard was so rough that I couldn't stay there," she explained.[168] Shelton Pierce likewise worried about run-ins with gangs on Minetta Lane and traveled longer routes on streets he deemed safer to avoid the area. Pierce also admitted to carrying a revolver when he was "around that neighborhood and . . . had a little money on me."[169] Seeing saloons as part of the problem, one *New York Age* writer vehemently renounced the "dens of vice and crime" that "are sapping the life out of young men and women" in black neighborhoods. "In sections where good people ought to feel at peace, there they find the greatest shame," he presumed.[170]

The reality of black crime inspires questions about the possible expediency of existing on the other side of law and the conceivable benefits of cultivating a persona as a "tough" through violence and terrorism. The obvious benefits of participating in illegal markets abound. Gambling, pimping, selling illicit substances, robbery, and theft produced quick material proceeds and instantly augmented consumer power. However, some men clearly hoped to reap the multidimensional psychic and spatial rewards of establishing a reputation for violence that might counter the topographical constraints they experienced in a largely white-controlled public. They also leveraged observable behavioral tropes of power and domination in order to safeguard their dignity against white and black offenders alike. With the development of an aggressive and threatening persona, black toughs installed cognitive and emotional boundaries in the minds of others and garnered individual and cultural dividends. Black gangs and organized crime syndicates used intimidation and notoriety to secure territory and control the flow of capital, and individuals likewise amassed their own sense of power through public conquests.[171] Considering the importance of the saloon in the formation of a public sphere for black men, drinking dens become paradoxical sites, endowed with a sense of duality that many urban forces pressured black men to take on themselves. They often harbored desires for respectable work, patriarchal households, and the trappings of middle-class lives like most other American men, but a pervasively unequal racial paradigm drove them to make hard decisions regarding their relationships with the law. Some took the challenge willingly and indulged in the real and metaphysical revenue they received. Under such circumstances, the choice to manipulate legality in beneficial ways seems not only logical but crucial to the formation of one's identity. Pressed to the wall economically, policed, censured, and labeled criminal, choosing to embrace an outlaw status might have cathartic results.

In a landscape rife with threats made-to-measure for one's intersectionality, forming and maintaining identity might require openly protecting honor and demanding respect from opposers. Drinking in a predominantly white saloon in 1899 Jesse Witt made such demands when he overheard a white patron announce that "every nigger in Georgia ought to be lynched" in response to some political question. "Then and there and with all the vigor he had," the *New York Times* later reported, Witt "endeavored to annihilate such portion of the white race as happened to be present." Finding himself outnumbered he left the saloon only to return shortly with a razor. "Breaking into the barroom like an angry bull, he began to slash right and left," as drinkers fled in fear, the *Times* continued. Before he left, Witt managed to injure a number of patrons, including one man he cut across the torso and another whose fingers he nearly severed. However, while fleeing the scene he was cornered by a mob and badly beaten before police intervened. In police custody Witt showed no remorse for his actions but reportedly only "expressed regret that the men he had injured would not die."[172] Whether or not this story is entirely accurate, the tabloid depiction of Witt's attempt to "defend his race" highlights a popular portrayal of the black "tough." As mentioned in chapter 1, white citizens, civic reformers, and police attempted to restrict black behavior and movements in ways that presaged or enacted larger racial clashes. In response, African American men like Witt sometimes lashed out when they deemed it necessary to defend their dignity and bodies from white urbanites or resist police brutality.

The life and death of Wesley "Gold Tooth Tacks" Maxwell clarifies how some men may have leveraged the perception or reality of black crime to portray themselves as toughs and employ that persona as an asset. During the trial for his murder, witnesses characterized Maxwell as a menacing gun-carrying pimp, and officers described him as "very stocky built" and a "good physical man" with a reputation as a "cop fighter."[173] Allen Clay testified Maxwell terrified everyone in the area of William Banks's saloon daily, boasted of his physical prowess and violent exploits, and showed off a revolver. He was a "regular bully," Clay swore, and he "talked with a good deal of swagger and bravado" about how hard he could "hit a man and kill him and so on." Intoxicated and "acting fierce" in the saloon, Clay claimed, Maxwell went about "bulldozing everybody" and keeping the "whole crowd terrorized" on the day he died. That morning Maxwell stole one of Clay's cuff buttons and rebuffed his protests by declaring: "I guess I will kill myself a nigger to-day."[174] Maxwell "always had a bad reputation ever since I knew him . . . [for] fighting and cutting and shooting, and carrying on," Clay recalled. Other witnesses remembered seeing Maxwell assault patrons and strip them of cash, but he was most notorious for fatal confrontations with whites and convictions for violence and robberies on both sides of the racial divide.[175]

On the day he died Maxwell had a fateful run-in with Clinton Branch. Formerly friends and roommates with the deceased, Branch endured countless abuses, thefts, and threats throughout the years and maintained that he shot Maxwell in self-defense. "I was afraid of him," he explained in court. "I always used to let him take my money and use it," but "I knew he was a bad man [and] a bully . . . everyone who knows him will tell you that." On the night in question Maxwell snatched a one-dollar bill from Branch during a card game and remarked, "I just like to make myself a bad fellow," according to witnesses. Maxwell further humiliated Branch by searching his pockets for money and calling him "vile names" in front of other patrons. Branch complied because "[Maxwell] liked to have his way in everything, and would get [mad] at anybody who didn't let him have it." After leaving the saloon to avoid more trouble, Branch ran into Maxwell in front of the establishment on the street later on. Facing more threats during this second encounter he shot Maxwell in the heart and turned himself in to police.[176]

Even before his murder trial newspapers represented Branch as a cold-hearted killer. "Without much parley," the *Times* raved, "[Branch] walked up to [Maxwell], put the muzzle of his revolver against [his] breast, and fired." Standing with the gun clutched in his hand defiantly when police arrived, Branch shouted, "What are you butting in for?" and threatened the officers in the newspaper's version of events. They described Branch then relishing his outlaw persona as police led him to a Tenderloin station house. Along the pathway "colored men and women stood . . . gaping at the prisoner . . . who, with his brown derby tipped back on his head . . . seemingly enjoy[ed] the notoriety which his crime had brought him. He beamed on the crowds as he passed, and smiled at the audible comments on the shooting."[177] The likely more accurate narrative of Maxwell's life and death related by witnesses during the trial against Branch raises questions about how crime figured into the lives and identities of some black men and reveals the sort of trepidation their actions may have engendered in public psychology. As mentioned, saloons provided most black men with legal and illegal sources of income and places for recreation in an alternative public space they felt more welcomed in. Nevertheless, it also functioned as a pivot point for the lifestyles of men like Maxwell who engaged in violent acts meant to bolster their reputations and elicit monetary rewards.[178] Likely because of the perception Branch himself was a tough, a jury rejected his claim of self-defense and convicted him of manslaughter.[179]

All the same, as a historical moment, Branch's actions believably reflected real fear for his life since, like other men, he navigated the perils that came with the pleasures of drinking spots. In his testimony, he told of how Maxwell threatened him for refusing to subsidize gambling losses the day before the shooting, and on the following afternoon he learned Maxwell planned to kill him.[180] Shaken up and concerned for his safety, Branch bought the murder weapon at a pawn shop and carried it until their final encounter. It is telling Branch did not seek police help but instead believed the only way to deal with Maxwell was through his own self-defense.[181] Likely skeptical that police would protect him, he also surely worried that involving authorities would only enrage his antagonist. Once he understood Maxwell meant to harm him, he had the option of avoiding him, especially since he planned to leave the city for seasonal work in a matter of days. Still, he frequented his usual haunts and armed himself in case of trouble, actions that register his own determination to steadfastly occupy the space of the saloon regardless of an imminent threat. By shooting Maxwell to death, Branch himself physically and spiritually embodied the iconography of the black tough, and possibly reaped recognition and esteem from onlookers with knowledge of the demeanor of the departed. Although he was not the hardened assassin newspapers depicted him as, he still may have relished his role as the victor momentarily when he ended Maxwell's reign of terror in a public forum and walked away triumphant, albeit escorted by police.

The ultimate meanings of the conflict between Wesley Maxwell and Clinton Branch, and the actions of men like Jesse Witt and Jim Singleton when coming across contempt from white saloon patrons, may not be fully discernable, but it is clear they all lashed out for reasons relating to respect and the need to maintain their dignity and control over spaces endowed with significance for their manhood. Branch's response to Maxwell appears to be defensive in nature, but he also acted out of an unwillingness to ignore humiliation and threats, and an aversion to backing down or retreating. Although Witt and Singleton attacked white men for racist remarks and abuse, and Maxwell terrorized blacks for personal gain, all used aggressive measures to command public space and similarly risked their lives and freedom to enforce unspoken customs about race and masculinity. Singleton, most astonishingly, publicly upended legal and racial hierarchies by killing police officers and not only living, but remaining free to continue the battle. After his 1903 disorderly conduct arrest he continued working as a waiter, possibly at the Lenox, and he later appears in a 1910 census boarding in a brownstone in Greenwich

Village and employed as a store manager.[182] All of these men, purposely or not, contributed to the formation of invisible barriers in the minds of other citizens and forged a sense of exclusivity in black communities while deliberately reinforcing their own racial or masculine identities. Many black toughs gained reputations for fearlessness in the face of white sovereignty by responding to public racial violence with violence and disrupting the rules of racial decorum like Witt and Singleton did. They thereby had a part in altering the psychological landscape for whites in ways that policing, surveillance, and mob offensives did for African Americans. The awe they might inspire in the imaginations of those who wished to immobilize and neuter them, had the capacity to grant them a fleeting but robust sense of amnesty to the crucibles they faced. Yet it should not be dismissed that the actions of men like Maxwell simultaneously impacted the physical safety and imaginations of blacks in similar ways. Such bullying thereby formed one aspect of the crucible of black criminality for men like Clinton Branch, who felt they had no choice but to become "tough" themselves in order to survive men like Maxwell.

––––––––

Considering the stories of these men, the spectrum of the issues they faced, and the possible benefits of exclusively black leisure establishments, we can see the saloon as a complex debated site ripe with implications for masculinity. Recovering these instances of camaraderie, bravado, brusqueness, and indelicacy in the hypermasculinized locales black men utilized for life and recreation is crucial to understanding their lives in New York City, overall. By appraising the capacity of counterauthoritarian lifestyles to construct identity and form resistance, it is possible to retrieve and reproduce the ways criminality bolstered concepts of virility. We can begin to discern the possible purpose of crime in managing profound personal, familial, and collective imperatives while seeking a sense of self-governance in legally restricted spaces, and in seizing financial, patriarchal, and masculine control over one's life, work, and family. Looking closely at the lives of black saloon patrons and owners, and examining their fears and aspirations as they played out in illegal acts, or other behaviors later criminalized by progressive and civic reformers, it is intuitive to fasten their mundane, urgent, and long-term needs to their choices. Growing into a significant portion of the city's population in the early twentieth century, black men felt increasingly hemmed in by restrictions placed on their mental and physical maps of the built environment and found themselves in constant tension with the regulatory bondage of bourgeois societal conventions. At this junction between freedom and the heavy limitations produced by white disapproval, notions of manhood struggled to thrive. Although Wesley Maxwell menaced the people in his community, he also represented the existential frustration and dissatisfaction some men experienced when largely excluded from many aspects of the economy, and his behavior illuminates the tactics some chose to give themselves marginal advantages.

The setting of Maxwell's last day is also important. As the center of public life for many black men, saloons rivaled fraternal clubs, churches, and workplaces as the most important spaces for the formation and maintenance of identity. Instances of violence in black and desegregated saloons existed within a kaleidoscope of responses to life in Jim Crow New York City. Facing the challenges of fast-shifting terrains, quickly changing standards of morality and legality, and a barrage of edicts meant to reshape their priorities to fit white middle-class ethics, black men often found themselves at odds with the law and hindered by regulations. The deprivation caused by joblessness and isolation further deepened the need to find alternative means of expressing and maintaining a steady sense of one's manhood and impunity. Black saloons did not remove these threats and permanently solve the problems of unemployment, but for many they became the backdrop in a theater of masculine codes of behavior, and constantly contested spaces where black men had some leverage, and a chance to define themselves and their ideas of manliness.

Chapter 3

White Women Forced to Live in Negro Dives

Roosevelt Sharp's Abduction Trial and the Contested Terrain of White Women's Bodies

He simply wishes to make it possible for a man to be
both a Negro and an American.

—W. E. B. Du Bois, *The Souls of Black Folks*

On March 21, 1906, Helen Watts, a white woman, nervously testified in New York City's General Sessions Court and detailed her alleged abduction and sexual enslavement by Roosevelt Sharp, a black resident of the Tenderloin. According to Watts she lost her wits while drinking in a saloon and woke up someplace else. "I don't remember being taken out," she explained, "but when I came to my senses I was in [Sharp's] house."[1] Stripped of her clothing and disoriented, Watts charged Sharp threatened violence if she refused intercourse with clients, exclusively African American men. "I was kept there against my will; I fought strongly every time and when I did I was beaten" by Sharp.[2] Visibly shaken and rocking anxiously on the stand, she described months of involuntary sex so frequent it made her sick.[3] Another woman, Caroline Kelly, followed with testimony that echoed Watts's indictments of the man who sat only a short distance away from both women in the courtroom. Each gave their statements quietly and forthrightly yet broke down and cried several times under the defendant's watchful glare, according to press outlets. One *New York Times* article reported Sharp seemed to hypnotize the women with an intransigent stare "that more than once had a perceptible effect." Nevertheless, each woman described periodic brutalities, padlocked doors and windows in the defendant's house, and being kept in an "unbroken state of intoxication" at his command. Accused of controlling a "syndicate of disorderly houses" and imprisoning women for several years, Sharp regarded the courtroom defiantly, "his smoke-colored face looking as if it had been cut out of iron, [with] his arms crossed over his chest" in anger.[4]

Sharp's trial gave progressives and police leaders the opportunity to try a case of "white slavery," a charge that assumed black and immigrant men frequently snatched white women from theaters, dancehalls, and saloons and forced them into sex work.[5] Progressive antiprostitution groups bent on proving the existence of white slave rings understood such a racially charged case would do the trick.[6] Headlines about compulsory sex work made Sharp's trial highly visible. So did stories claiming police discovered networks of resorts peddling the flesh of captured white women in the area. Although Sharp apparently had an exploitative relationship with the women in his house, prosecutors needed to prove he kept them against their will in order to convict him of abduction and connect his activities to a citywide conglomerate of slavers. Apart from emancipating women currently in bondage, legal efforts against men like Sharp provided ideological satisfaction for whites mortified by the contemporary vogue of racial and sexual politics in commercial sex districts. Refocusing on involuntary sexual servitude curved public attention away from the role of urban class inequality in driving women to sex work, and angled it toward the danger autonomous and pleasure-seeking women attracted to themselves.[7] As a result, some scholars have argued, white slavery claims also functioned as a way to continue gender inequality by reinforcing the logic of women's domesticity and scaring them back into the kitchen.[8] In other words, white slavery claims served the double-purpose of criminalizing black men with the audacity to indulge in consensual or illicit interracial sex, and refuting the personal and bodily freedoms unattached working-class white women asserted.

Noting that chivalrous protection came with notions of masculine ownership of women, Georgia reformer Rebbeca Latimer Felton criticized the sorts of inequalities, abuse, and rape white women befell at the hands of white men. In her 1930 book on white women of Georgia she argued courts should be the ones to protect them, not individuals or mobs.[9] Women, like men, had begun trending away from the asceticism of Victorianism toward the self-gratification and consumption of the twentieth century, and new pleasure venues facilitated the breakdown of traditional courtship arrangements.[10] Women who participated in the "treating system," or the practice of fulfilling men's expectations of closeness or sex in exchange for a night of fun, rebuked customs that prohibited premarital sex and shook up previous gender norms.[11] For those worried about this disruption of habit, convicting Sharp would verify white prostitutes only seldomly engaged in sex with black men by choice. Such a reallocation of the meaning of interracial eroticism might negate white/black lust and romance and effectively criminalize it. Teetering on the edge of delirium, many white observers expected the trial to bring to light the innards of a smutty flesh market, shine sanitizing sunlight into the crevices of slums, taprooms, and brothels, and ultimately root out black men traversing the forbidden terrain of white womanhood.[12] A strain in antebellum thought about sexuality, morality, and prostitution characterized white women as "fallen women" forced into villainy by an amoral world.[13] Films such as *Tenderloin at Night* (1899) and *Traffic in Souls* (1913) conveyed this perspective in vivid celluloid images in the very same dark theaters girls purportedly disappeared from.[14] Regarding such a dangerous world, white slavery advocates promoted two inherent goals: the condemnation of black men as sexual deviants and rapists, and the redemption of white women from "fallen," unprotected statuses. They also left black women out of the equation and in the process confirmed their vulnerable standing.[15]

As a historical moment, the Sharp trial embodies broader debates about gender and race going on nationally in the early twentieth century. It sat within a decade of more stringent classifications of blackness, and the solidification of racial categories around color in new laws against interracial sex and marriage, nativist immigration policies, and lynching.[16] Turn-of-the-century pseudoscientific theories on black heredity pegged African Americans as controlled by sexuality. Discounting the fact most black men lynched for rape never received trial, Father Thomas F. Price, a Catholic Priest, blamed it on inherent sensuality. While they were well aware of the "swift and terrible punishment" that would surely come, he argued black men's sexual desire overpowered their logic since they were more likely to commit rape than white men. It was not because of discrimination that lynchings happened daily, according to Price, but due to the "sunken condition of those men."[17] In 1906, President Theodore Roosevelt agreed when he told Congress "the greatest existing cause of lynching is the perpetration, especially by black men, of the hideous crime of rape."[18]

In the two decades before World War I, many American cities and states passed laws to deal with sex slavery, and the 1910 federal White Slave Traffic Act, or the Mann Act, which outlawed the interstate transport of women for "immoral purposes," netted more than 8,000 offenders.[19] The ensuing vice campaigns played a part in reinforcing existing racial boundaries, and in defining sexual perimeters around white women.[20] White New Yorkers used investigations, legislation, and violence in an effort to prevent interracial sex before it got out of their control. At the time, they witnessed the loosening of Victorian conduct and the advent of a heterosocial public culture, one that included a contingent of single white working women. While African Americans challenged racial customs through social and political means as "new negroes," white women took advantage of reorganized family, labor, and spatial imperatives and reimagined themselves as "new women," free to engage in the public realm.[21] Rather than performing their duties of birthing babies and making households, these women were indulging in "viciousness, coldness, and shallow-heartedness" in the words of President Roosevelt in 1905.[22] For proponents of segregation, the trial of Roosevelt Sharp emphasized the liabilities of a hybridized society and conjured imagery of kidnapping and interracial rape. Plump with carnal details, it hung heavy on the limbs of

New York's tree of sexual politics and burst into a flaming jubilee before it hit the ground.[23] As an alleged abductor, Sharp appeared to flip the script of racial domination, alternatively casting himself as slave driver and consumer of white flesh. Whether the abduction charge was true or not, he had already inverted American historical racial precedents by claiming sexual authority over the bodies of white women. In the process of addressing interracial sex, progressives and law enforcers forged another aspect of the crucible of black criminality. They targeted black men for ostensibly legal sexual interaction and singled them out as sole offenders in an interracial sex trade. Whether consciously or not, men like Sharp challenged this crucible in legal and illegal ways.

Sharp's trial also coincided with weighty changes in ideas about white masculinity. Nineteenth-century conceptions of American manhood centered on production and restraint, but the new century ushered in novel concepts of manliness focused on consumption, bodily development, and primitivism.[24] Experiencing a "crisis," white men resented the freedoms of "new women," large-scale immigration, and the erosion of racial customs.[25] Through various "mechanisms of masculinization," they campaigned for the restoration of white male power in realms where they perceived they had lost it.[26] White supremacist political and ideological prophets championed a martial, vigorous form of white manhood predicated on sport, dominance in the home, the idealization of an antimodern "strenuous" natural life, and the reinforcement of superiority through conquest of lesser races.[27] Harboring antimodernist notions of primal manliness, white men superimposed their own dreaded inadequacies on black men and indulged in a form of self-hatred; one they expressed by corraling and sometimes destroying black bodies in public.

White men feared a low-white birth rate and the loss of control over white women would sap their racial power, and they believed they had to intervene. Good wives and good mothers were essential to the advancement of white material and artistic brilliance, in Theodore Roosevelt's words, since those women performed the "greatest duty" of bearing and raising healthy children numerous enough "that the race shall increase."[28] As a scapegoat, white men produced the stereotype of the "black brute," one most graphically sketched in the 1915 film, *The Birth of a Nation*.[29] The brute symbolized their fear of losing property, political and economic control, and dominion over white women's bodies—pure and fertile wellsprings of white progeny. Sex between white women and black men seemed to pose an existential threat by producing black offspring from white wombs and negating the reproduction of white men and women. As New York City lawyer Madison Grant put it in his popular eugenic book, "the cross between a white man and a Negro is a Negro."[30] In other words, the very existence of black men held up a mirror reflecting the distorted, unsure countenance of white manhood, and inter-racial sex, in theory and in the flesh, forced some sort of reckoning. Resent-ing their own likeness in the looking glass, white men redoubled the rhetoric and violence maintaining Jim Crow, and one of their greatest directives in-volved preventing reproduction between black men and white women. Thus, men of both races entered into a literal and figurative battle of masculinities—one that frequently took place across the material and fictive terrain of white women's bodies.[31] Sharp's alleged actions signified a defeat for white men in this theater of war. Real or imagined narratives of black on white rape not only foreshadowed plot twists leading to tragic endings, they were cataclysmic in their own right and upended fantasies of white mascu-line sexual conquest. Thus, white slavery became an appendage on a larger anatomy of white violence against black men, one that reinterpreted inter-racial sex and prostitution as rape and white genocide, which justified any means of retaliation.

Interracial sensuality and the sex trade also clearly had meaning for Sharp himself. Characterized as a "mulatto" with gray eyes and a nose that was "not very flat" in a prison record for an earlier offense, he may have imagined him-self as straddling racial identities.[32] Whether he considered interracial sex a direct assault on white masculinity or not, it likely signaled a reclamation of his own manhood in the face of arbitrary racial limits. The denial of eroti-cism with an entire segment of the opposite sex symbolized yet another method of excluding black men from full global realization of the early twentieth-century masculine form. Whether fetishized or not, white women, after all, were still women, and still sometimes sought or opened themselves to the advances of black men. As white men strove to fulfill all of the require-ments of manhood by making white women off-limits to blacks, cross-racial intimacy may have had revolutionary meaning for men like Sharp.

Aware of the rules he violated, Sharp may have also considered the sex trade an opportunity for freedom from the economic, ideological, and phys-ical limitations of life in New York. Historians have argued African Ameri-can women sometimes chose prostitution not simply to earn money for necessities but to circumvent the strictures of family and marriage require-ments and to plug into a world of consumption and leisure.[33] Leeching the profits from the sale of women's bodies might have played a similar role for black men. Sharp witnessed his own father reap the socioeconomic benefits of brothel work by transgressing racial and sexual rules and challenging white authority in the 1880s, and he inherited his reputation when he started his own enterprises at the end of the century. Well known to the police, he had gambling-houses, dance palaces, and bars in Minetta Lane, near Thompson Street, and in Greenwich Village, and he had likely spent years forming and protecting his corner of the underworld; the loss of which was economically devastating.[34] Garnering visible measures of success by the time of his arrest, Sharp may have seen his business as a confirmation of his manhood that allowed him to vault over the obstacles placed in his path by the racial politics of the city.

The Battleground of White Womanhood

Nearly twenty years before Sharp's white slavery trial, the *Evening World* published an exposé on prostitution in "the vilest house in town," a Grand Street dive owned by his father, also named Roosevelt Sharp. The senior Sharp, the writer explained, was a "copper skinned negro" with "high cheek-bones, piercing, cruel-looking black eyes, and a black mustache." The article instructed visitors to the "mysterious looking saloon" to keep to themselves, hide valuables, and disregard the interracial nature of nighttime celebrations. "Express no surprise at the number of white women and preponderance of blacks, and be careful not to speak to any of these women unless they speak to you first, for the blacks are very jealous and the white women like to lash them into fury sometimes." Known for "cruelty" himself, Sharp senior ran a sex market out of his club. "It is said that no woman whom [Sharp] wants to keep has ever been able to escape from his clutches." Worth more than $100,000, he made his money "trafficking in white women for the amusement of his colored patrons," the *World* reported. Dispensing especially strong beer and whiskey that caused "pandemonium" among regulars, Sharp had two other establishments in the area that the journalist assumed kept him flush with cash. "The old man is a dressy negro, wears a magnificent diamond horse-shoe pin in his scarf, a stud of value in his shirt, and a gold stop-watch worth several hundreds of dollars." Shrouded in mystery and notoriety, his Grand Street nightclub became a hangout for "young bucks in gorgeous raiment and flash jewelry" nightly swaggering "into the foul-smelling, low-ceilinged barroom."[35]

Sharp senior apparently protected his trade by mostly barring white men and bribing police, but his businesses had their share of trouble. In 1879 three men refused to pay their bill in one of his dives and forced him into a fracas which involved police officers.[36] Only days before, a more serious incident took place in another bar that brought citywide attention. Police alleged a black patron killed the white wife of a prominent businessman and Sharp dumped her body into a mass grave.[37] Known for exaggerating descriptions of black crime, the *National Police Gazette* declared her death the result of the company she kept, and brutality by her "Negro Master." A jury later ruled the death due to alcoholism and pneumonia, but the tragedy only added to a list of questions about Sharp's saloons.[38] The owner himself had been arrested multiple times for liquor violations and selling sex. An 1884 raid on his Coney Island resort, the Virginia House, sent him to jail with "a number of white women."[39] Even worse, in 1889 police arrested his son, Sharp Jr., for stabbing a patron in one of the elder Sharp's saloons.[40] The man survived the attack but the younger Sharp received a sentence of three years in Sing Sing prison, and the judge presiding over his hearing called his father's place "a trap" for women.[41] Sharp Jr. received discharge in 1892 and likely reentered the sex and liquor trade immediately after release. In 1900 he informed census-takers he made his living from "liquor" while a 1905 census classified him as the owner of a livery stable.[42] By the end of the century he married his father's former business partner, Jennie Allen, described by journalists as a "comely white woman," and he opened his own saloon, brothel, and horse gambling operations in the Tenderloin.[43]

As the heir to his father's racket and infamy, Sharp entered a swiftly growing and changing sex industry; one that included interracial prostitution, particularly in clusters on the extremities of the Tenderloin's commercial sex district. Around 1900, most black brothels lined the blocks between Eighth and Ninth Avenues in the Thirties and Forties, but they could also be found elsewhere in Harlem, on a stretch of Seventh Avenue dubbed "African Broadway," or in Greenwich Village near Cornelia Street. Enterprises swelled not only from the demand of a multiplying population but also as an inadvertent byproduct of antivice measures. The 1896 Raines Law limited the sale of alcohol on Sundays to hotels and restaurants. In an attempt to circumvent that restriction, some saloon owners applied for hotel licenses and created makeshift sleeping quarters in storage rooms, or legitimately remodeled into hotels. At the same time, antiprostitution efforts closed many of the city's massage parlors and bordellos where sex workers conducted business and forced them into the streets, tenements, and saloons all over the city.[44] A collaborative relationship resulted between proprietors and women operating out of their barrooms and private quarters. The women increased the sale of alcohol by inducing men to purchase drinks, and they paid a small fee for the use of the saloon's newly available bedrooms with their clients.[45] Noting this arrangement, one inspector for the reform group, the Committee of Fourteen (COF), condemned Percy Brown's Lenox Avenue place, known not only for prostitution but also as a dispensary of cocaine and opium. An investigation by the National League for the Protection of Colored Women discovered Brown's black pianist himself was a pimp who had "several white girls in the street getting money for him."[46] Another place, the Buckingham Café, similarly lived up to a reputation as a hang-out for "colored pimps and crooks." And a block and a half away, the St. Douglas Club catered to black and white hustlers who lured young female factory workers there for "the most outrageous affairs against all laws of decency," the report concluded.[47]

Hence, Sharp's abduction trial did not materialize solely out of the imaginations of white progressives. Sex work and the businesses surrounding it provided a lucrative underground economy for men and women disenchanted with the vagaries of wage labor or suffering from chronic unemployment. Although reformers overemphasized their participation, some men did in fact act as procurers of clients for women and attempt to live off the proceeds of their sexual labor. New York City experienced real increases in the number of sex workers in the early twentieth century, and some were in fact abductees traded like cattle and shipped to other regions of the country. To be certain, the sex industry likely grew as a result of exponential increases in the city's population, and compulsory sex work never reached the pandemic proportions reformers feared.[48] Still, growing pains from demographic and gender transitions in the city and changes in the nature of prostitution prompted valid inquiry into the roles men played. In the years before Sharp's arrest, men had wrestled the bulk of control over the trade from women as they entered the masculinized space of saloons.[49] Without the protection of the brothels of the nineteenth century, women could be recruited and victimized by pimps, "cadets," and saloonkeepers who acted as their protectors and employed connections to local police and politicians to secure their businesses from the law.

Sharp likely labored to procure customers for the women in his house in a similar way, but in proving abduction, prosecutors had their work cut out for them. By the time of the trial, sexual experiences unthinkable in the South happened with regularity in the North. White slavery reformers either missed or ignored the fact that many white women chose to be sex workers on their own, solicited black men openly, and considered prostitution an unremarkable aspect of a life they had chosen. Although some women arrived at sex work out of desperation or coercion, others entered the trade out of attraction to the lifestyle or through social connections and worked with their networks to recruit newcomers.[50] In contrast to bringing in between $6 and $12 per week in domestic and manufacturing positions, women might make up to $50 a night as streetwalkers.[51] Thus, many white women chose to intertwine their lives with New York's racially diverse commercial sex scene, a fact that was inconvenient to the progressive mission of saving them. Although black men understood the risk of lovemaking with white women, the lines blurred in a gaudy, titillating nightlife where those same women very often purposely submerged themselves and sought contact with black men.[52]

As white slavery discourse sought to reaffirm the value of the bodies of white women like Helen Watts and Caroline Kelly, it also highlighted the critical, xenophobic, and voyeuristic regard many whites held for black women.[53] During and after bondage, whites justified the sexual exploitation of black women through stereotypes that depicted them as seductive and sexually available, and in emancipation the white imagination birthed her male counterpart, the black rapist.[54] In an example of how this operated in New York, one COF report cast white prostitutes as inactively placed "into colored people's company" by men but did not give the same benefit of doubt to black women. "Colored women street walkers," the report deduced, openly haunted a corner on West Twenty-Sixth Street, willingly sold their bodies, and choreographed robberies.[55] White antiprostitution campaigners felt less sympathy for "the vicious and drunken colored woman" than her "white sister." According to Police Commissioner William McAdoo, black women were more "likely to use a weapon freely, and not a few of them carry revolvers and razors." In his 1906 memoir he recalled a "band of colored women who prey[ed] on white men" and made the streets dangerous.[56] Black women would not be included in the white slavery rescue attempt since they were culpable in their own tumble to rock bottom, and their perceived conduct and lack of inhibitions made it so they could not be saved. But it is clear that while robbery, theft, assault, and paid sex were rampant in the whisky soaked and smoky rooms of bars in the Tenderloin, black women were certainly not the only female culprits.

The way police and press handled the death of a black woman in 1896 exemplified this spirit of inequality. Police discovered a "ghastly bundle" containing the dismembered body of twenty-year-old black migrant Mary Martin in the Tenderloin's red-light district, but her case commanded less press attention than Sharp's alleged misgivings a decade later. However, in an effort to identify the body, police put her remains on display in a Tenderloin station house, garnering a circus of interest. "White people," the *Times* reported, "entered [the station] and left giggling," some "brought babes in arms to look at the dead," and children attempted to sneak in without parents, but "the colored people behaved better."[57] The profane exhibition of Martin's corpse, under the auspices of police work, epitomizes profound disregard for the black female personage that penetrated to the core of New York City's public, institutional, and legal structure. While anti-white slavery progressives canonized white womanhood as the theoretical linchpin of civilization, they abandoned black women to the gusts of an unpredictable urban climate.

This perception simply reflected a historic emphasis white society placed on white womanhood over that of other women. During slavery, white men designed social codes relating to interracial sex to preserve the racial distinctions defining the system and to safeguard their own control over white and black bodies.[58] They designated black men's sexuality for the fertilization of black wombs in the breeding of human property, and they themselves violently appropriated black women's bodies, and sometimes those of black men, for erotic conquest.[59] Whereas both white and black male access to black women replenished the material wealth of the plantation through procreation, white men saw sex between those same black men and white women as an apocalyptic threat. Late nineteenth-century political, economic, and spatial changes invoked this threat anew as African Americans increasingly shed the exploitation of plantation life and sharecropping. In freedom they discarded the white male economic/reproductive model to forge their own versions of manhood, womanhood, and sexuality, and white working-class women began to do the same. In this new cosmos of sensuality, white male attempts to wrestle control of all bodies black and white ran the gamut from legislative and political responses, to lynching and rape.[60] Just like those forms of terrorism, white slavery allegations against men like Sharp expressed dismay about both the social and physical mobility of blacks and the emergence of white women from the cocoon of white patriarchy.

Anticipating white women's pupal stage of independence, white men attempted to prevent it from the dawn of emancipation. The Ku Klux Klan (KKK) drafted all white men in a war to protect their women from black men they presumed would seek vengeance once free, and they made the preservation of female purity a call to arms.[61] The end of slavery had swept up a whirlwind of sexual tension that clung to politically significant physical and economic changes.[62] Abolition simultaneously withdrew black women from the sexual control of white men and gesticulated toward future intercourse between black men and white women. Klan indoctrination depicted white women as sexually inert, making all black/white intimacy and marriage seem like rape, and nullifying the possibility of consensual sex.[63] Rape was not as rampant as white men feared, but the rhetoric of groups like the KKK had a deeper meaning. Black men expressing their sexual urges across the color line symbolically threatened white supremacy since white women represented the ultimate racial boundary line white men could hold.[64] Although many white men were literally concerned about the loss of sexual dominance over white women, the mandate to prevent their despoilment boiled down to a scramble to retain racial power. Terrorism, lynching, bodily mutilation, and castration publicly distilled that racial power into a heady moonshine imbibed by onlookers in all parts of the country.

For whites the intoxicating power of public racial violence reinforced asymmetrical racial norms. For African Americans, homicidal spectacles acted as embankments in a battle for their basic humanity. Common conversations about race in the 1880s explained lynching as the only mechanism able to defend white women from the weaponized sexuality of the black rapist.

Crowds of white men would avenge such assaults in public to advertise the punishment to would-be rapists and in order to participate in the ritualistic reclamation of masculine power from the alleged despoiler in a scene of flames, smoke, and blood.[65] Consuming the flesh of black men in view of the world was meant to communicate the strength of white manhood and demonstrate its importance in an alleged contest between savagery and civilization.[66] Although the first rise of the Klan collapsed in the 1870s, their ideas about whiteness, manhood, and sexuality continued into the twentieth century.[67] White men the country over privileged white women as bulwarks of civilization while making them hostages to their own purposes of retaining racial privileges and hegemonic masculinity.

These men responded to a roiling sea of changes they were nearly helpless to govern. At the turn of the century, the practices of urban working-class women, particularly those enthralled by the epicurean nature of public pastimes, disrupted the remodeling project of white manhood. Around 1900 those women began to attend social clubs without escorts or chaperones, cavorted with single men to racy music, and performed modish dance moves that mimicked sexual intercourse.[68] The fact that black musicians not only composed but played much of the music that fueled the party only made matters worse. The limb-raising and body-convulsing melodies were not coon songs meant to reaffirm whiteness, but black produced pieces with themes that captured the bodily freedom of a black working class. What happened when white women danced themselves into this ambush? They might trade extramarital sex for fun soirees, lounge in black and tans, and give themselves to black men for lust, love, or money; actions that belied the myth of white women's nonsexuality and imperiled theories of white superiority. White slavery germinated in this atmosphere.[69] The perception of the black rapist was therefore an important part of the reaffirmation of white manhood in the post-emancipation South and slowly trickled into Northern phraseology near the end of the nineteenth century, around the time the white slavery scare came to the fore.[70]

As policyspeak for the sexual enslavement of otherwise virtuous white women, the deployment of the term *white slavery* in Sharp's eventual abduction trial and otherwise changed the meaning of interracial sex.[71] Late nineteenth-century advocates for women's health and morality considered prostitutes unredeemables who had chosen immoral lives; but by the 1900s, many of New York's reformers emphasized the involvement of black and immigrant men and reimagined white women as victims.[72] In his memoir, *A Cop Remembers*, police captain Cornelius W. Willemse recalled a number of immigrant women snatched from their point of debarkation at New York's Castle Garden's immigration receiving facility. Men promising jobs and security plied "hundreds upon hundreds of young girls fresh from the towns and villages of Europe" and abducted them, he cautioned.[73] Writer George Kibbe Turner best described the underlying rationale for white slavery legislation: "The chastity of women is at the foundation of Anglo-Saxon society. Our laws are based upon it . . . nothing could be more menacing to a civilization than the sale of this as a commodity."[74]

Intent on reestablishing the victimhood of white sex workers and emphasizing the role of black men, secretary of the New York Probation and Protective Association, Maude Miner, published *Slavery of Prostitution* in 1916.[75] In the study, Miner described an interstate white slave traffic system that transformed seemingly safe interactions with men in cafes, clubs, and amusement parks into traps where women could be persuaded or strong-armed into sex slavery. Out of 471 night court defendants surveyed, most of whom were white, she cited 304 who said they were coerced into sex work. The women complained of exploitative arrangements and the difficulty of resisting pressures and directives, particularly under the influence of liquor. Many were "seduced" by charismatic admirers, others tricked by strangers, and still more "forced, assaulted, or drugged" in places "managed and patronized principally by colored men," she concluded.[76] If alcohol blunted their faculties, cocaine, she worried, would loosen their morals, compromise their sanity, and condemn them to harlotry.[77] Rose Schafer had saved money and wore "swell clothes and . . . di'monds" until she acquired a cocaine habit. "She's crazy when the dope is in her," another respondent commented on Schafer, "they say she is living now with a colored feller."[78] Miner worried more women like Schafer would become intoxicated by the noisy drug and alcohol filled black and tan clubs scattered around the Tenderloin and other parts of Manhattan, and that they would stay there. In such places teenaged girls "were seen . . . singing and dancing in the most indecent manner with colored men" who had purposely doped them up. "Some [men] dispensed cocaine . . . and gave [it] to young girls for the first time."[79]

To be sure, men involved with sex work frequently coerced and exploited women, but the focus Miner and others put on color illustrates one of the problems with the city's antivice campaign. It is evident Miner, like most progressives, worked to improve people's lives and sincerely cared about the young women in her charge. But unfortunately, for Miner and others, humanizing white women caught in the rapture of nightlife depended upon dehumanizing black men and women. Miner and other progressives portrayed white women as nonactors in prostitution and reimagined black men as unemotional sportsmen. In the same year as Sharp's abduction trial, William McAdoo railed against black pimps in his memoir. In his estimation, they slept all day, prowled the streets at night, and had "one or more unfortunate women in their train whose earnings from a life of shame they appropriate."[80] The White Slave Traffic Act grew from such an uneven perception of the sex trade and allowed prosecutors to single-out men as executors of an international slave exchange that vice reformer Clifford G. Roe called "infinitely more inhuman than the black slave traffic."[81]

Miner and McAdoo's obsession with race reveals how white slavery advocates ultimately attempted to limit white and black sexual contact, whether forced or not. By removing the agency of white women from the equation, and foregrounding racial others in a market that included everyone, they redefined interracial sex as vice and rape, and therefore bolstered legal and illegal efforts to prevent it. The difference in black and white perceptions of interracial saloons, like James Marshall's Café, illustrates this impulse. According to James Weldon Johnson, black and white entertainers visited Marshall's nightly, and most blacks considered it respectable, including *New York Age* editor Fred Moore, who vouched for Marshall with the COF.[82] Where Johnson saw a trendy rendezvous, the COF saw a place where "colored cadets and procurers" met "their white women."[83] Make no mistake, blacks themselves certainly complained about places they considered disreputable. Consider a 1911 *Age* article that condemned "buffet flats, thrones of lewdness and castles of drunkenness," and directed readers to "look to the good, quiet, decent element in our churches and homes" for moral standards.[84] Still, forced to dualistically straddle the line between vice and respectability because of segregated housing patterns, blacks like Johnson, Marshall, and Moore often understood law-abiding citizens sought good times in mixed bars, not just pimps and crooks. Thus, white and black onlookers interpreted the meaning of multiracial leisure differently according to their positionality in the city's nightlife, and this rift in judgment aided in the construction of a white slavery crisis. As Johnson and Moore realized, nocturnal merrymaking was far more complex and mosaic than critical reformers wished to admit. The tilted perspectives of white slavery crusaders revealed a cartoonishly partisan impression of interracial sex, one that condemned even authentic sexual connections as illicit and forced. In reality, cross-racial eroticism happened primarily because blacks and whites had desires that ignored racial politics. In the minds of most black and tan frequenters, the race of other patrons did not make or mar their experiences. Black men and white women mingled out of choice, natural inclination, or because of sexual attraction, far abstract from the panic of moralistic segregationist views.

The COF's point of view dominated public conversation about vice in the years before and after Sharp's trial and molded the rhetoric of white slavery. Brothels, pimps, and saloon and hotel managers at the time administered a carnal market that raked in up to $20 million per year and yielded a tide of profits to police and political leaders as protection fees. With graft and bribery well known among New York reformers, antivice and white slavery campaigns condemned law enforcement for allowing it.[85] Most remarkably, in *McClure's* magazine writer George Kibbe Turner's 1909 article, *The Daughters of the Poor*, he designated New York as "the leader of the world in this class of enterprise" and primarily blamed Jewish immigrants and the political engine of Tammany Hall for recruitment and "shipments of women to the four corners of the earth."[86] Affronted by the accusation of corruption, Tammany leadership chose philanthropist John D. Rockefeller Jr. to lead an investigation in hopes he would expeditiously absolve the organization of wrongdoing before the next election.[87]

The Rockefeller grand jury tried dozens of cases over a six-month period.[88] In one suit, prosecutors charged Belinda Moss, an African American woman, with keeping and selling white women.[89] Arresting officers and investigators portrayed Moss as a seductress and kidnapper, and her purported captives as "girls," but they turned out to be experienced sex workers in their mid-twenties, and the abduction case collapsed.[90] Nevertheless, Moss received a five-year prison sentence, a punishment that represented an "important accomplishment in the progress of our larger undertaking" to prosecutors.[91] Embedded in the larger trial, Moss's case contributed to a psychological racial division forming at the turn of the century. As legislation, like the 1895 Malby Law, made systematic segregation illegal in New York, it failed to stop it in practice. As mentioned earlier, increases in racial hostility and a decline of racial tolerance accompanied the expansion of black migration in the first few decades of the twentieth century, and statewide legislation reflected this change. Following suit, New York City reformers sought to pass a state bill prohibiting interracial marriage in 1910. Awkwardly titled the Act to Amend Domestic Relations Law, in Relation to Miscegenation, the statute aimed to prevent future weddings and nullify existing marriages. Although it never passed, coupled with the Rockefeller Grand Jury trial it represented a larger movement to restrict black and white physical intimacy in the state and to legally target men and women like Moss and Sharp who crossed the color line.

Because of Tammany Hall's known collection of payoffs from commercial sex, some openly questioned the sincerity of the grand jury they organized.[92] But Rockefeller took his job seriously, even donating $250,000 of his own money to fund the investigations once civic coffers dried up.[93] The jury collected testimony from informants in order to prove or disprove the existence of white slavery syndicates but they did not receive a definitive answer. In testimony, George Kibbe Turner backtracked and denied the existence of an international syndicate but confirmed some people owned numerous houses of prostitution, sometimes colluded with other houses, and Tammany Hall protected their businesses "in every way they possibly could."[94] Telling of his own investigations, United States Immigration Commission member Jeremiah Jenks agreed, confirming "a few cases where girls have been compelled against their will" but argued they were usually "there of their own accord" and had "no special desire to leave that business."[95] Ultimately, the trial ended the tug of war between enthusiasts and moderates concluding the truth of the matter was more complex than both imagined. The eventual report established that "trafficking in the bodies of women does exist, and is carried on by individuals, acting for their own individual benefit," rather than a worldwide network headquartered in New York City.[96] This verdict recognized sexual exploitation as a humanitarian crisis supported by police corruption. Armed with such information, Rockefeller organized the Bureau of Social Hygiene to continue his investigation outside of the panic-stricken formula of white slavery, but in the "spirit of scientific inquiry."[97]

Although the grand jury failed to identify sex-slaving cabals of immigrant men and African Americans, it exposed the vital organs animating the white slavery furor.[98] Just like campaigns to control public space and commercial venues like saloons, policing of racial and sexual perimeters constructed physical and mental limitations for African Americans. Legislators, columnists, concerned citizens, and religious or moral demagogues continued to inculcate film noir–esque stories of white women consumed by the urban milieu. In the first two decades of the century, most states passed their own laws against forced sex work signaling the omnipresent concern that modern racial and social configurations would endanger white women.[99] The focus on forced sex grew from intense anxieties about the changes wrought by urban growth. Women had burst forth from the confines of domestic spaces into burgeoning cities, spaces rampant with crime and health hazards, and increasingly inhabited by people from diverse ethnic, racial, and religious backgrounds. These narratives were adaptable enough to be used against a litany of progressive targets including the travails of overconsumption, police corruption that allowed vice to flourish, large-scale immigration, and racial integration. Conservative white slavery crusaders emphasized restrictions on immigration, temperance, and segregation, while liberals believed the answers came in the form of women's rights and other reforms that supported healthy, purified, female-centered households. Thus, progressives involved in the movement ranged widely from the Women's Christian Temperance Union to the Ku Klux Klan.[100]

Historians have questioned the veracity of white slavery claims and proffered arguments explaining them as a response to the changes urbanity made to middle- and working-class comportment.[101] But it is clear white slavery rhetoric was also shaped by the stake white men had in retaining patriarchy and masculine primacy for themselves in an American pantheon of "manhoods." A broader anti-miscegenation fight, which included white slavery campaigns, considered sexual partitioning existentially vital. As middle-class white men employed presuppositions about racial dominance to remake themselves as powerful men, any theory that torpedoed legitimate interracial sex served their purposes. By pushing for white slavery legislation, they not only sought to prohibit sex slavery but to legally remove the threat of interracial sex. Black men were not the only targets of progressive scrutiny on the subject, but mythologies of black rapists drove the discussion in rare ways. Although white women composed much of the movement's leadership, it coincided with a number of events and public discourses that showcased the hypersensitive nature of white revisions in terms of masculinity and the significance white men placed on their rights and obligations to stand between black men and white women by any means necessary.

"To My Mind, He Did the Manly Thing"

The proceedings of Sharp's 1906 trial and the popular press around it contributed to the discourse about interracial contact in the years that followed. One highly publicized event took place in a primarily white neighborhood of the Upper West Side in March 1911. German immigrant Albert Ulrich and his companion Lola told police he and a group of men chased an African American man who was causing trouble in their building. Lingering on the sidewalk and in the vestibule suspiciously, the man smiled and allegedly addressed Lola as "sweetheart" as she returned from a walk.[102] She quickly informed Albert, and when he came to the door of the flat he found "the negro . . . with his hand on the door knob and his eye at the keyhole." "He struck me on the jaw" and fled the building, Ulrich recounted. "We clinched and staggered . . . fell, and he hit his head on a hydrant. Then he got away."[103] Ulrich told authorities he and some "friends" then gave chase and caught the man, who they then handed over to police to have him arrested for unlawful entry and assault.[104] Investigators believed Ulrich's version of the story until the black man they had detained revealed his identity. "This man is mistaken," he explained. "I am Booker T. Washington." Once identified, the Tuskegee educator told a different story than the one given by Ulrich. While attempting to determine the door number of a friend in the building, he regarded a woman politely as she passed him, and seconds later, "the door of the house suddenly opened and a man without a collar and with whisky on his breath came out and smashed me on the head," Washington told.[105] As he ran from the scene, a group of men beat him and then informed police he insulted Lola. Anxious about publicity, Washington minimized his injuries stating he was "not really hurt at all." All the same, the *Washington Post* reported "two lacerations of the scalp, each about 4 inches long" and wounds and bruises on his head and body that required medical treatment.[106]

Beyond the shock blacks expressed about the incident, Booker T. Washington's attack and arrest invoked a national media circus and a discussion about interracial contact, public racial violence, and black self-defense. Because of Washington's status as a respected bellwether in racial politics, the incident elicited responses from white and black leaders, educators, and journalists who condemned his attackers.[107] Most responders wanted to illuminate the absurd inner mechanics of such incidents. The *Afro-American* pointed out how openly it signaled that despite character or social standing, "a colored man . . . is regarded simply as a negro, a creature whose lot must be unwarranted abuse whenever a white person's interests conflict."[108] "Had this been any other Negro the world could not have been made to believe other than that he was a thief, robber or rapist," a *Charleston Messenger* writer agreed.[109] White women "have done the eagle scream before," another editorialist wrote, "and the poor Negro who should happen to be under the sound of her gloats would swing from a tree before she could finish."[110] Washington's highest profile endorsement came from President William H. Taft who ascribed the attack to "insane suspicion or viciousness" and put his support behind the educator.[111] Some black leaders recognized the irony of the incident as an opportunity to criticize everyday episodes of persecution that never made the news. "Nothing since the emancipation would so tend to help the negro race or bring it closer together than this very thing," Adam Clayton Powell, pastor of the Abyssinian Baptist Church in Harlem, told his congregation.[112] Ulrich had either made a mistake that revealed common racial prejudices, or worse, he invented a story to justify tormenting an innocent man, a narrative that would have remained unquestioned if not for Washington's fame. While a faction of onlookers like Powell believed the event might reveal the folly of jumping to conclusions about black men, others were less optimistic. Fighting back, for some, was the only solution. Arguing the occasion strengthened the logic of martial responses to white violence, the black *Rochester Sentinel* invoked a Rooseveltian masculine trope suggesting, "a big stick would have been very appropriate in the hands of Mr. Washington." Such self-defense would "have lesson" and "such brutal assaults by white trash will not happen."[113] Upsetting as it was, the melee that had sent the most famous black leader in the country to the hospital had the wattage to cast light on the thousands of black men beaten, hung, and dismembered under similarly fishy circumstances.

For Washington, however, the attack created quandaries that compelled him to confront his own ideologies. As an educator and famed orator at the time, he famously recommended that blacks be patient in the fight for civil rights, obey the law, and use industry, thrift, and perseverance to win a place in American society, not protest or brazen challenges to white authority.[114] He was still the same man who, at the 1895 Cotton States Exposition held in Atlanta, Georgia, declared in front of a white and black audience that "agitation of questions of social equality is the extremest [sic] folly."[115] With that speech he amassed the trust and confidence of whites nationally, including President Grover Cleveland who christened him a "new hope" for African Americans. His fame drew charity and endorsements for his Tuskegee ventures and locked in valuable white political sponsorship.[116] However, within a few days after his attack, he had unwillingly become the center of a radical conversation about black citizenship that in many ways challenged his accommodationist stance on racial progress. Specifically, the whole ordeal lampooned his belief that if blacks cultivated respectable, industrious personas, they would avoid the wrath of white police and even citizens.[117] Educated, dressed decorously, and regarding those he encountered politely, even Washington, himself, had been beaten, dragged through the streets, and arrested. "The incident is . . . proof that the great 'Wizard of Tuskegee' deals in false logic by advising the colored people to tamely submit to all kinds of brutal treatment," a typical article in a black publication criticized.[118] If Washington was not immune to the illness of racial violence, what chance did working-class black men have to inoculate themselves? Washington understood prosecuting Ulrich might jeopardize his manicured image with his white constituency. If he "exerted his great influence to 'persecute' a white man," one black *Charleston Advocate* editorialist argued, "the work of a lifetime would be seriously threatened."[119] Reports of a Tennessee-based fund to aid Ulrich's defense confirmed the portent of a Southern backlash nearly a week after the incident occurred.[120]

Washington likely considered these factors before dropping the charges of assault against his attacker. "I believe that Mr. Ulrich was justified in attacking not only me but any other man under similar circumstances," he told newspapers. If Ulrich believed Lola to be in danger Washington thought he "was perfectly justified in attacking me. No man could have done otherwise under the circumstances. . . . To my mind, he did the manly thing."[121] Likely inadvertently, Washington's capitulation squandered an opportunity to advertise the blood-soaked history of racial violence that he himself had just experienced, and add his own voice to the antilynching movement. By invoking Ulrich's manhood in his statement, he reinforced mandates of white men to protect white women from black men and justified violence to that end

regardless of the facts in the matter. His statement also legitimized predatory conceptions of black masculinity and presumptions about the dangers
of racial closeness, both of which white supremacists believed validated unpunished bloodshed and lynching.[122] In spite of his concession, Washington cooperated with prosecutors in testimony, but Ulrich's eventual
acquittal confirmed how closely his experience mirrored that of other black
men. Observers like Adam Clayton Powell had hopes of advancing civil rights
and antilynching agendas by contrasting Washington's prestige with Ulrich's
inhumanity, but the episode ultimately honored the obligation of white men
to regulate racial and sexual boundaries in ways that violated the rights and
bodies of black men.[123] In a letter to a friend later in the year Washington admitted he was "in a rather collapsed condition" from "his unfortunate experience in New York," a state of dejection some observers claimed he never
escaped before his death in 1915.[124]

The politics surrounding the assault on Washington echoed tensions attending prizefighter Jack Johnson's victory over white boxer Jim Jefferies in
Reno, Nevada, in July 1910. The fighter publicly embarrassed white men by
winning the heavyweight championship in 1908 and then defeating Jefferies
who came forward to reclaim it. Minutes after the bout ended fighting erupted
from coast to coast. Committed, as they were, to privileging white manhood
over others, champions of white supremacy considered Johnson's victory an
existential threat and quite literally meant to set the record straight with violence in the streets. Simultaneously, many blacks caught in spasms of revelry
defended themselves and in some cases provoked fights.[125] Black men and
women across the country delighted in the fight's result, collected thousands
of dollars from good bets, and tormented whites when they could.[126] However,
white men enacted most of the violence. In Houston, Texas, a white trolley
passenger slashed the throat of a black rider when he "jeeringly proclaimed
Johnson's victory," and in many major cities hundreds of attacks and fights
ended with similar bloodshed. Some of the worst fighting took place in
Manhattan where white gangs attacked "whatever negroes" they found and
set fire to an occupied black tenement.[127] "More than three thousand whites
gathered, and all the negroes that appeared were kicked and beaten, some
of them into insensibility," the *Times* reported.[128] With eighteen deaths and
countless injuries nationwide by the end of the conflict, the fight riots represented a moment of national simultaneity when simmering rivalries in the
realm of masculinity between black and white men boiled over.[129]

The fighting happened in the heat of the moment between men on either
side of a smoldering racial divide, sparked in part because of Johnson's opulent representation of black manhood and undisguised sexual relationships with white women.[130] As a celebrity prizefighter, Johnson existed in a

culture that formulated masculine power with bodily, economic, and sexual indicators, and his imposing physique, triumph over Jefferies, and open erotic conquests wreaked havoc with racial presuppositions of white supremacy.[131] He publicly provoked detractors by sheathing his penis in gauze to emphasize its visual size in his trunks during fights, flaunting his wealth, and deliberately challenging segregation customs and laws.[132] Touring the country in the aftermath of the prizefight, he arrived in New York City accompanied by a large entourage including a number of white mistresses and his wife Etta Duryea, also a white woman.[133] Johnson and Duryea traveled in luxury, lugging servants and valets, trunks, three cars, and stylish European clothing.[134] Reaching the city just as the Rockefeller Grand Jury submitted its findings, Johnson experienced heightened scrutiny from police but also invited trouble on his own flouting laws in ways that signaled his freedom from white authority and emphasized his status as affluent and autonomous. Twice within a week cops arrested him; once for reckless driving and again for obstructing traffic with a badly parked vehicle, charges he believed indicated they were "out to get" him.[135] A string of other arrests involved speeding infractions, run-ins with white men, and the assault of a white burlesque actress who refused his advances.[136] Nevertheless, he proceeded to bolster his persona as a specimen of superior masculinity and to make comparisons between himself and Jefferies that had implications for all white men. Donning a lustrous blue robe and a belt decorated with "the Stars and Stripes," Johnson gave a week-long boxing exhibition at Brooklyn's Hammerstein Theater where he emphasized his dominance in the ring with speeches and the carnivalesque display of his body. "[Jefferies] did all he could to win a fair battle, and took his defeat in a manly way," Johnson told his audience on the first night of performance. "[He] appeared to be at his best in the fourth round, but that was because I was resting," he quipped.[137] Adding insult to injury, while in Brooklyn he made news when he viewed the fight film at another theater along with his wife who "chuckled with delight every time the [film] showed him landing a telling blow on the white man," the *Times* reported.[138]

Johnson's self-indulgent victory lap through New York City and continued disregard for racial customs and laws received criticism from white and black commentators, but for different reasons. For white men Johnson materialized what they feared most since emancipation; that black men, once given the chance, might successfully compete on the playing field of American manhood and win the attention of white women. The boxer's skylarking and lawlessness seemed to confirm such suspicions. A writer for the Texan *Beaumont Journal* recommended a "dose of Southern 'hospitality'" to rein him in, and Governor Cole Blease of South Carolina framed Johnson's interracial marriage as a failure of white society. "If we cannot protect our white

Heavyweight boxing champion Jack Johnson, 1911. Schomburg Center for Research in Black Culture, Photographs and Prints Division.

women from black fiends," Blease told his constituents, "where is our boasted civilization?"[139] In order to spare white men the repeated humiliation of Jefferies's defeat, a number of cities and towns banned Johnson's appearances, fight films, and vaudeville acts under the pretense of preventing further violence.[140]

Some members of the black community also spoke out with honest concern about Johnson's impact on race relations and criticism of his relationships with white women.[141] The fighter boldly declared his preference for white women believing them to be more submissive than black women and more likely to "spoil" a man and "pamper his ego."[142] The black-run *Philadelphia Tribune* satirically reported him "Dangerously Ill" with "White Fever," and other commenters, like Adam Clayton Powell, resented Johnson's lust for white women as a betrayal since it not only stirred up racial hatred but also perpetuated stereotypes of black men.[143] "We in this country would be better off if Jack Johnson would quit the United States, burning the bridges as he leaves," one black reporter wrote.[144] Booker T. Washington weighed in as well, claiming Johnson lacked "mental and spiritual development," and as a result deliberately used his power and money to "injure" his own people. "A man with muscle minus brains is a useless creature," he concluded.[145] Always primed to return a jab, Johnson responded by undermining Washington's image as respectable. "I never got caught in the wrong flat," he retorted, "I never got beat up because I looked in the wrong keyhole."[146]

Remarks by Johnson's critics reveal the tension he provoked around the subject of manhood and sex across the color line, yet the exchange with Washington illustrates two opposing methods of confronting injunctions on interracial contact. When caught in the ideological dilemma presented by the brawl with Albert Ulrich, Washington invoked Ulrich's manhood and duty to protect his wife as a way to extinguish the flames of racial enmity, at least on the side of whites. On the other hand, Johnson breathed life into that wildfire by trouncing white opponents and unashamedly claiming control over white women's bodies. Similarly aware of the possible consequences of upsetting the racial order, they both made diverging decisions about how to comport themselves and, as a result, had two very distinct outcomes. Emasculated but still intact, Washington continued his career mostly uninterrupted, and less than a month following the incident he purchased a large summer home estate overlooking Long Island Sound in Huntington, New York.[147] But Johnson continued to force his sexuality into public view and suffered greatly for it. After years of infidelity and abuse at her husband's hand, his first wife committed suicide in 1911, and he married another white woman, Lucille Cameron, in 1912.[148] In the same year Johnson faced indictment and eventually incarceration when charged with violating the White Slave Traffic Act.[149] With the spotlight of racial politics squarely on him, he had traveled with a prostitute, Belle Schreiber, and his detractors prosecuted him for the newly minted crime of transporting a woman across state lines for "unlawful sexual intercourse."[150] Many black observers viewed the whole episode as evidence of racial prejudice, including one *Chicago Defender* writer who called it an attempt to discredit Johnson since Jim Jeffries "failed to kill him" in the ring. White men had "flooded" the country with "mulattoes" during slavery, but made it a "crime against nature for a negro to marry a white woman by her own consent," he proclaimed.[151] Certainly guilty of that crime and sentenced to one year in prison, Johnson fled for France where he lived for seven years, but returned to serve his sentence in 1920, after which he never regained his title. The high-flying boxer, it seemed, had played with fire and become consumed by the flames.

From the whole Jack Johnson affair, a number of realities materialized. The conflicts that followed the bout in 1910 and his eventual imprisonment symbolized a collective effort by white men to deal with the growing threat of black men, one they believed progressively appeared in Johnson's defiant form. Vigilance would be required, as well as the adoption of an indomitable Southern-styled racial antipathy that gave no quarter to such antics.[152] Southern whites not only expressed contempt for Johnson's conduct but also annoyance with white Northerners for allowing it. As if to actualize this condescension, less than a month after the Johnson-Jeffries fight the *Times* reported a brawl in the subway between a "small white man from Texas" and "a negro nearly twice his size." After noticing the black man leering at white women and loudly claiming he could "whip any man" on the train "Jack Johnson style,'" the Texan "thumped the negro until his arms got tired." To the cheers and approval of white onlookers he told reporters, "I wouldn't have had to whip that coon in Texas because we have the Jim Crow law down there. I don't see how you New Yorkers get along without it."[153] The *Times*'s acceptance of this unsubtle critique of Northern social climes clarifies a change in the racial weather of cities like New York as migration darkened their populations. Taking a cue from their Southern brothers, white men in the North would need to stand firmly in the gap between black men and white women, implementing Jim Crow more strongly in the process. Johnson's persecution through the White Slave Traffic Act publicly fortified an existing social, sexual, and gender structure that revolved around white men as protectors and conquerors, and it effectively unstitched the ragged seam between the maintenance of hegemonic white manhood and federal law.[154]

In the midst of conversations about white slavery, white men collectively avenged Jim Jefferies's defeat through manipulative legislation that effectively outlawed Johnson's legal relationships and marriages. They thereby somewhat expunged his victory and punished him for all to see. Johnson had upped the ante on a national stage, and his circumstances presented a set of contrasting instructions. For black men he not only provided a model of repudiating the sexual politics white men largely espoused but also was an example of the potential results. White men, alternately, learned that legislation would support one of the basic tenets of their claims to virility, and they further entrenched themselves in antimiscegenation doctrines. The well-publicized cases of both Johnson and Washington only tell part of the story. Lacking the influence, resources, and support they both possessed, men like Roosevelt Sharp faced scrutiny from watchful neighbors, police officials, progressive groups, and investigative reporters as they conspired to demonstrate the consequences of interracial sexual impropriety on a local level. Sharp's trial in some ways set the stage for how New York City and

America would handle Washington's assault case and the hysterics surrounding Johnson nearly four years later. As a microcosm of the emotionalism attending both later media spectacles, the 1906 abduction case articulated the same festering sentiments of racial control and segregation, and raised questions about the possibilities for the legal codification of rules against interracial sex.

"I Run This Place to Suit Myself"

The vocations of both Sharp Jr. and his father invoke the reality of black male involvement in the sex trade, a market rife with exploitation of vulnerable women. As part of a larger network of unlawful enterprises, sexual commerce gave black men like the Sharps access to better dividends than they could expect from domestic and service labor, but it also made them likely to forge lopsided, abusive sexual relationships. Although white slavery–obsessed reformers amplified claims of sexual enslavement for rhetorical purposes, a minority of women were truly compelled into the trade by crooked labor agents who tricked them into employment contracts in brothels and sometimes exploitative friends, lovers, and husbands.[155] Arrested for prostitution in 1923, South Carolina migrant Celia Greensmith gave a telling explanation for her entrance into the industry. While living in a rooming house in Harlem and working as a janitor, she became involved with a man who "got influence over her" and forced her to sell her body, she told an intake agent at Bedford Hills Reformatory.[156] Santo Domingo immigrant Dottie Gray had an even more jarring experience claiming to have been "abducted" and "detained" for sex work by two strange men.[157] Although white women endured similar pressures and abuse, racial bias made black women most visible to law enforcement, more likely to be convicted, and less likely to receive resources that might prevent recidivism after release.[158] Accompanied by self-described "commission man" Charles Edgar in 1917, both Effie Baker and Ruby Wilcox offered sex to undercover detectives, and all were arrested.[159] Police originally planned to send the women to the Florence Crittenton Mission, a reform home for sex workers, but "as they were colored girls," one report confirms, they could not receive such consideration.[160] A magistrate charged Edgar with violation of white slavery laws and held the women as witnesses in his case, but after refusing to testify against Edgar, Baker and Wilcox did time in Bedford Hills.[161] Ranging from landlords of rooming houses and proprietors of saloons that catered to prostitution, to part time participants supplementing low wages as bus boys and elevator operators, men like Edgar might see the sex trade as an irresistibly profitable alternative occupation. The involvement of men in sex work also represented one extreme on a continuum of predatory sexual practices that plagued the nation in the early twentieth century. Harassment, coercion, molestation, and rape often affected the lives of black women who had very little recourse to protect themselves.[162] While it is true black men and women often acted autonomously in sexual commerce, both seeking thrills, pleasures, and profits, an uneven power dynamic commonly governed those relationships at best, and in the worst cases, men literally subjugated women for their own gain.

The reality of sexual profiteering in New York converged with fantasies of a hypothetical army of black abductors to frame Sharp as guilty before the formal proceedings of the abduction trial. Newspaper outlets sensationalized his contact with white women and conjured stories of murder and additional abductions. The *Times* made Sharp's interracial marriage and his business liaison with a white woman common knowledge, insisting he regularly traded women like livestock across state lines.[163] Sharp owned a dancehall on West Thirtieth Street, and another on Minetta Lane, deep in the black section of the Tenderloin, both of which he may have kept secure by prohibiting white men as patrons, journalists theorized.[164] Referring to one of these places, tabloids reported a story of two women murdered by Sharp for refusing "to endure any longer the life imposed on them." In that narrative, he then handed them over to a "negro physician" who doctored false death certificates, and a black undertaker who plopped them into a common grave in a "negro cemetery."[165] Sharp managed to remain free so long, another journalist charged, only because he "caused complainants against him to disappear" in a similar manner. According to the *New-York Tribune* a police investigation into the "mysterious disappearance" of one of Sharp's former "slaves" discovered he had likely killed her after she escaped and became a witness for the police.[166] Daily paper writers also lashed out at corrupt police with weak memories who they believed helped men like Sharp elude arrest for a number of years.[167] Although unsubstantiated, such scathing press stories played with racial stereotypes that primed the public to consider Sharp guilty before he had a chance to defend himself in court.

The heavy weight of early twentieth-century racial and sexual politics came to bear on the trial once the testimony of the main witnesses began in March 1906. White women believed to have been drugged, captured, and raped sat in juxtaposition to a black man who, for many observers, personified an existential threat to civil and social order. As a central figure in the case, Helen Watts alleged Sharp forced her to copulate with "four or five negroes a night" for one dollar each and the customers became so frequent she complained of being too sick to work. "I cohabited with so many men," Watts testified, "I could not stand any longer." The prosecution also argued the defendant kept all of the women in the house intoxicated to preserve compliance, took away their clothing, and chained and padlocked all windows and doors.[168] Watts and Caroline Kelly both gave graphic descriptions of beatings, and Watts emphasized one instance when Sharp punched out several of her teeth for refusing a customer.[169] Allegations that the women had been "licked" for slight infractions upset the jury most. After hearing testimony from multiple police officers that authenticated accusations about the condition of Sharp's house, the division between those who questioned Watts's and Kelly's credibility as disreputable women, and those who sympathized, began to close.[170]

The public nature of Sharp's abduction trial broadcasted tales of interracial sex, kidnap, and rape into the city's popular consciousness, all tragedies New Yorkers already worried about. Seemingly hoodwinked by black men and pitifully abused, Sharp's white accusers embodied the archetype of fallen women ensnared in the traps produced by modern urban life, a narrative universalized in early twentieth-century novels and films. Like the lead character in Stephen Crane's *Maggie: A Girl of the Streets*, whose life is destroyed by lecherous men, the emotional pleas of the plaintiffs drew the sympathy of the jury and the observing public.[171] But Sharp's defense attorneys questioned the women's positionality in the raucous nightlife of the Tenderloin and leveraged moralistic directives for womanly decorum to instill doubt about their true relationships with the defendant. In order to prove their arrangement with Sharp was consensual, attorneys depicted Helen Watts and her coplaintiffs as degenerates. She was not a captive, they contended, but had in fact turned to prostitution on her own long before the purported abduction, and once arrested in the raid on Sharp's house, she waited a number of days before notifying police she was a prisoner.[172] In her testimony Watts admitted she in fact escaped the house on two occasions but never left the area or sought help. Instead, she drank in a nearby saloon and was subsequently "driven" back to the house by one of Sharp's henchman.[173] "That woman is bad enough," on her own, one defense attorney judged, and she only accused Sharp of abduction out of "fear of prosecution" and because of pressures placed on her by "missionaries" who hoped to prove the existence of a white slave market.[174] The attorney also informed jurors Watts had been a known sex worker before her time at Sharp's house, "the most heinous and disgusting offense that woman or man can ever be charged with." Married to a "good and respectable" man, she voluntarily left her husband "to lead a life of degradation" and settled for "colored men . . . because she could not get any white man to go with her."[175] If Watts willingly lived in a community primarily inhabited by African Americans before her alleged kidnapping, the attorneys implied, she may be beyond sympathy and rehabilitation.

Determined to speak for himself, Sharp testified in an attempt to clear the cloud of prejudice the media bombshell shrouded him in. His testimony rested on disrupting the choreographed script of the trial that articulated two prevalent ideas at the foundation of the abduction charge; first, that black men involved in the city's commercial sex market were invariably rapists, and second, that white women could somehow emerge from New York's sooty, inebriated culture of hedonism clean-handed. While speaking to the jury he framed himself as the manager of a rooming house with very little control over the actions of his tenants, all of whom were "supposed to be married."[176] He was not a pimp but a businessman who, in the spirit of American capitalism, sought self-sufficiency through various ventures including games of chance, renting rooms, and profit-making leisure enterprises. Without evidence of steady employment for many years, Sharp claimed he had supported himself as a billiard parlor keeper and sometimes by gambling on race horses up until his arrest, but never did he run a "disorderly house."[177]

In his version of events, Sharp had come into contact with Helen Watts during the summer of 1899 while she lived in a "house of ill repute" not far from his own dive, where she "prostituted her body" in a largely black section of Greenwich Village.[178] By her own actions she carried a reputation as a "bad woman," fallen because of an inclination to binge on bad whisky and gratify animalistic urges.[179] "[I've] never taken her into [my] house in my natural life," he protested. Instead, she later came to rent a room in his place at 14 Cornelia Street and he collected rent of $4 a week from her, as he did from other tenants.[180] Sharp also denied keeping the women's clothing, forcing alcohol consumption, and barring the exit, and took the time to emphasize that he "never laid my hands on the [women] in that house." Both Watts and Kelly came and went freely, and in one instance, because of drunken disturbances and disputes with other tenants he "put [Watts] out" himself. "I don't know what you would have to do to keep her from drinking liquor . . . every man she brought in there had a bottle of whisky and she was drunk all the time," he claimed. Moreover, he would not have forced his tenants to drink, he argued, because he didn't "approve of no woman drinking." He could not have kept shanghaied women in secrecy for so long under the watchful eyes of police, he reasoned, noting there was an officer stationed at the door for over a year, an arrangement some police precincts had with known brothels or troublesome saloons.[181] The way Sharp told the story, Watts and Kelly may have sold their bodies in his home, but certainly without his help. "They went out into the street and where they got [men] from, I don't know."[182]

With two other men as witnesses for the defense by the end of the trial there was a reasonable doubt about Sharp's guilt. Even though much of the evidence proved he did in fact run a brothel, the abduction charge remained questionable throughout the case. Regardless of the evidence that Watts and Kelly willingly engaged in prostitution, the jury found Sharp guilty and he received a twenty-year prison sentence.[183] Upon hearing the verdict Sharp remained emotionless and cold-blooded, at least visibly. "[He] showed the same stony-faced indifference to the proceedings that characterized him through the trial," the *Times* reported. "Not a muscle in his face moved when he heard the sentence that confined him within prison walls for the greater part, if not all, of his life." Instead, in defiance, Sharp silently regarded the court with an angry glare. The judge met Sharp's stare with a bitter reference to retributive public justice. "If you lived in some States . . . you may be sure that the slow administration of criminal justice would never have been allowed in your case." "[Sharp] did not appear to mind the remarks of the court in the least" and left the room without reaction, according to the *Tribune*.[184]

Newspapers hailed Sharp's conviction as a victory for progressive efforts against vice, prostitution, and white slavery, and as a test case that set a precedent for how these matters should be handled in the future. For many observers, the convicted black abductor epitomized the problem of black and white sex and proved black men planned to contest racial restrictions on the physical and conceptual terrain of white women's bodies. For African American men, Sharp's conviction confirmed that black men who dared to cross the color line, especially within the context of New York's flourishing sex industry, could be considered rapists or kidnappers, and even consensual interpersonal experiences might count against them. Viewed as naturally depraved, African Americans bore the brunt of all of the probes into the interracial sex trade and whites involved in sex work with black men and women received a different kind of scrutiny that depicted them as forced or circumstantially involved.

Imbedded in a history of unfair imprisonments and lynchings for imagined sexual assaults, Sharp's trial makes plain the specious employment of the term *white slavery*, its versatile usage in trials addressing interracial sex, and how it came to signal inescapable guilt for blacks. The sex trade was egregiously exploitative for white and black women alike, and it is clear Sharp ruthlessly abused and took advantage of the women in his house. Yet, it is also evident in some cases, black men like Sharp and white women cooperated in brothels, saloons, massage parlors, and "disorderly" tenement buildings in consensual sex and business, no matter which way the dynamic of power tilted. It is also very likely those same men and women entered the game for some of the same reasons; just like black women they each had their own aspects of economic bias and employment restriction to overcome, and profit from illicit sex was easily available. Undoubtedly, sex work represented a plausible alternative industry for many New Yorkers in the early 1900s; but for black men, engaging with white women arbitrarily added a level of complexity and scrutiny others did not experience. In a time of transforming ideas of race and gender, discourse on white slavery designated black brothel keepers as unremitting threats to ideals of both white womanhood and manhood.

Diverging reactions from the black community signified two meanings of Sharp's predicament, but also common disquiet about such striking demonstrations of black crime. Concerned about black morality and collective racial destiny, some celebrated Sharp's arrest, but feared it publicized harmful stereotypes of black men and threatened to raise the city's collective blood pressure. Stories of sex slavery, waylaid white girls, and buried cadavers could be injurious to the black community since such tales, whether true or fictitious, had invoked white lust for black blood in the past. "Respectable negroes have no sympathy for Sharp," one reverend proclaimed, "no man in many years has so embittered the public against the negroes in this city." Even respectable citizens would "have to pay the penalty" for his crimes.[185] On the other hand, blacks involved with the sex trade themselves regretted the attention placed on their businesses and resented the interference of progressives. The Sharp case affected the operations of other saloons and brothels as police then raided dozens of places in the vicinity of Cornelia Street, and many denkeepers moved their businesses elsewhere.[186] Hattie Ross, the black missionary worker who discovered Sharp's brothel and brought the case to the district attorney in the first place, received death threats but vowed to die "stirring up dirt."[187] Hence, for black New Yorkers the entire affair was cringeworthy and unpleasant. Whether they believed the accusations of kidnap or not, the glaring nature of the court hearings reflected an unkind light on the whole black metropolis.

Still, the menace interracial sex caused white men, and the possible gratification men like Sharp derived from it, makes sense given the long history between the two. In creating the "black brute," white men had exaggerated black sexual prowess in order to emphasize a supposed animalistic nature, and at the same time attempted to neuter black men. It only seems natural some men like Jack Johnson and Roosevelt Sharp would come to consider their sexuality as weaponized when directed at white women, the very female bodies white men intended to preserve for themselves. In many ways, New York's sex trade at once embodied the distorted sexual, racial, and gendered politics of American slavery, and a reimagining of those dynamics in the urban twentieth century. Black men might invert centuries worth of custom, economic deprivation, and racial and sexual violence simply by taking command of white women's bodies.

———

Roosevelt Sharp's trial also furnishes an opportunity to think about black criminality in the complex way in which it happened; framed by a legal and social system shaped by white supremacy, but also often performed by black men and women who rejected the discriminatory, duplicitous, and constantly shifting terms of legality. Sharp's lifestyle that eventually led to his imprisonment sat at the intersection of his identity as a man, the strictures of his life as an African American, and his yearning to reconcile the two. As such, we can understand his actions and inevitable fate as the result of both his context in a city that sought to demonize him and his own agency in the matter. Like many other black men, Sharp likely entered the sex trade in order to create a financial situation that seemed impossible through legitimate means. On one hand, the inconclusive nature of the trial suggests he may have been falsely accused of abduction and sex slavery. On the other hand, Sharp likely understood the legal, social, and racial implications of his business, yet still took the risk of straddling racial boundaries as he did. Like his father before him, he was likely tantalized by the opportunities for entrepreneurialism, and the sensual, corporeal, and financial benefits of running his own enterprise, and by supervising the bodies of white women he deliberately conquered forbidden territory. He may have also believed that police protection and an all-black clientele would save him from such scrutiny and indictment. During the raid on his home, Sharp confronted undercover police with a biting rebuke when they showed their shields and demanded entrance. "I run this place to suit myself," he told them. "What is more you can never get me right because I only cater to colored people."[188] In the process of catering to his fellow African Americans, he committed crimes, but the district attorney may have exaggerated his part in the broader trade, and popular racial conceptions of white slavery and the nature of interracial prostitution scripted him as solely culpable.

It would be inaccurate to portray Sharp as a victim in this case since he engaged in sexually exploitative, physically violent, and illegal actions. Yet it's clear his likely erroneous conviction for abduction conjoined racial bias with the administration of legal justice in shaping popular perspectives of the features of black masculinity. Years after the white slavery scare ended, the New York Police Department itself called it a "hoax" in one annual report claiming it appealed to "morbid imaginations" that brought fraudulent cases to court. "It is safe to conclude the white slave does not exist, if, in fact, she ever did" the report pronounced.[189] A study commissioned by Rockefeller's Bureau of Social Hygiene in 1917 surveyed 15,000 confirmed sex workers, the majority of whom were white, and determined very few claimed to have been forced into their labor. Instead, most cited family issues, abuse, alcoholism, poverty, and thrill-seeking. As one woman in the study put it, "I loved the excitement and a good time, easy money and good clothes."[190] Yet, the tune sung by witnesses in Sharp's trial harmonized with the music both Booker T.

Washington and Jack Johnson faced when caught in the reticulation of drag-nets policing interracial contact around the turn of the century. Like both of those more famous figures, whites sketched Sharp as a representation of black surrender on the battleground of miscegenation. Seizing upon the characterization of black men as rapists popularized in contemporary cultural production, they legally reinterpreted them as criminal when in romantic or cooperative arrangements with white women. Still, men like Sharp who consciously crossed these boundaries also tell us another grim story. Controlling women's bodies, whether white or black, was often connected to attempts to remake themselves as men. Just as it did in Sharp's case, the search for patriarchal authority and hegemonic masculinity sometimes had disastrously toxic results.

Chapter 4

To Let Her Know That She Did Me Wrong

Illegality, Domestic Authority, and the
Politics of Black Intimacy

Dupree was a bandit,
He was brave an' bol',
He stole that diamon' ring
For some of Betty's jelly roll.

—African American Folk Song

Now I got the crazy blues,
Since my baby went away,
I ain't got no time to lose,
I must find him today.

Now the doctor's gonna do all that he can,
But what you're gonna need is an undertaker man,
I ain't had nothin' but bad news,
Now I got the crazy blues.

—Mamie Smith, *Crazy Blues* (1920)

In 1904 thirty-nine-year-old Virginia native Ida Snow faced trial for the murder of her husband, Elton Snow. By the time of her hearing, her brother, Walter Reed, had already received a twenty-year sentence for confessing to the killing, but prosecutors alleged Ida's involvement. As she told the story, she arrived in New York City in 1898 with her teenage daughter and adopted infant son, rented a house in the Tenderloin, and took on lodgers in order to meet the $75 monthly payment. Married to Elton in 1900, she was happy "only for a short while," but before long, her husband, who traveled for work as a train porter, began to complain about her renters. "When he married me I had my house full of lodgers," Ida later explained in court, and "most of them was men lodgers. [Elton] said that he was out on the road [a lot] and he would not stand for so many men to be in the house."[1] Those demands initiated a series of quarrels that lasted "all the way along" until his eventual death. Once he found a job that did not require travel, Elton implored Ida to "put these men out [and] run the house as he instructed me to," she admitted.[2] However, the bulk of the tension stemmed from her refusals to loan him money to kick off a business enterprise, and from his accusations she had been unfaithful. Requesting $500 to invest in a saloon with entrepreneur Barron Wilkins, Elton warned he would shoot Ida if she did not consent and give up the cash. "You are going to keep fooling with me until I blow your damn brains out," he reportedly told her. He later used the same language while holding her at gunpoint in an attempt to compel an admission of infidelity. In the face of such intimidation, Ida dismissed his orders, had him arrested, and forced him out of her house. Yet, her husband's scare tactics continued once they reunited, and her brother took notice. As Elton arrived home one evening, Reed attacked him with an axe and left his body lying on the street in front of Ida's home. "After [he] threatened your life," Reed later told his sister, "I was sure he was going to kill you [so] I did it first."[3]

A more complex story emerged from the testimonies of boarders, neighbors, and police in Ida's trial, and questions arose about the nature of her business and her relationship with Elton. Witnesses claimed she ran a brothel and an informal saloon out of her home. One neighbor observed "white women go in, followed by colored men," regularly, and a police officer assigned to watch the house reported "colored women . . . soliciting men" on the sidewalk out front. As stated by a tenant, the couple's conflict started because Elton wanted his wife "to live private with him [and] give up her business," but she would not consent. In order to force her hand, he notified authorities about her brothel, invited them to inspect the place, and even abused and terrorized her. Angered by her husband, Ida asked one boarder to find someone to kill him, and another remembered her making an offer of $400 to anybody willing to "get him out of the way." Finding no recourse to handle Elton among her tenants, Ida wired money to her brother and asked him to come to New York and protect her, according to one male renter. "I didn't pay no attention to it all, because women talk so much that they don't know what they are talking about, half the time," he explained in court.[4] However, prosecutors argued Ida meant every word of her threat against her husband's life. With such testimonial evidence, they convinced a jury the defendant put her brother up to the task, and she was remanded to Auburn prison for manslaughter in 1905.[5]

The antagonism between the Snows and the tragic outcome of their relationship reveal a pattern of negotiation and interdependence between black men and women in the early twentieth century and signify how both might conceptualize the meaning of marriage differently. Although most couples aspired to stable unions and households, diverging desires and conflicting gendered expectations sometimes put them at odds. Urban blacks like Elton and Ida had options largely foreign to previous generations, and in migration they had access to a world of modern commerce that altered the parameters of all relationships, including wedlock. Some men saw their own prerogatives in this new culture as essential to their livelihood and manhood but believed women's business and personal aspirations threatened both.[6] Elton might have adhered to prevailing middle-class notions of patriarchy, which required restrictions on female conduct and mandated women's commitment to domesticity. For him, that commitment likely meant he had a responsibility to support and protect a respectable household and ultimately control his wife sexually. Black reformers engaged in projects of racial uplift likewise advocated such an ordered existence through educating homemakers on maintaining moral purity. While reformers' opinions on domestic responsibility ranged broadly, many of them placed the onus on black women and doled out directives on constructing a female-centered nonpublic sphere.[7] Such doctrinaire moralizing made the family a pivotal space for the generation of individual authority for men in the chaos of modernity, and it rendered a clean household with a dutiful wife into a diorama displaying normative masculine achievement.[8]

In his attempts to create his own business and control Ida, Elton meant to curate that display in their home, but he clearly perceived her preferences for illicit work as dynamite in the architecture of his manhood.[9] Many black men believed spouses should prioritize the home instead of paid work, forgo most commercial pleasures, and certainly refrain from sex work; an arrangement only possible through relationship synergy and enough income to subsidize one's household. Ida's ability to eclipse Elton's earnings and her dealings with other men plunged them into a tug of war, and her husband struggled to gain command in the same way many other men did; by trying to overcome his own economic shortcomings, and ultimately, abusing and threatening her. Although he disapproved of her trade, the proceedings of the trial indicate he only publicly condemned it once he suspected her of infidelity. This might be due to the fact he benefitted greatly from her business and reaped the rewards of consumer power and stability it provided them as a couple. Yet, as their marriage came apart, he hoped a change in the financial dynamic would mend their romance, and he regarded the end of Ida's business, and the beginning of his own, as the only salvation for his ailing sense of patriarchy. If sidewalks and saloons could be invaded and controlled by whites, men like Elton wanted to bolster their own sense of masculinity by claiming dominion over their home life, at the very least. Elton's eagerness to manage his household and guide his wife's conduct was not uncommon among American men at the time, but his actions demonstrate a deep sense of frustration and resentment they might experience when facing what seemed like impossible odds.

Despite the cause of the Snows' struggles, Elton's money troubles and abuse of his wife illustrate the profound economic difficulties black men encountered when supporting their households and the extreme measures they might take to keep afloat. Since emancipation, African Americans made every effort to create strong families and home lives under the weight of persistent racial inequality. Hardships securing and maintaining housing, poor job prospects, and the complex menagerie of issues stemming from migration and segregation, fractured living situations regularly.[10] Men stitched their wages together with toil in various labor positions but usually failed to earn enough to keep their partners from needing to make their own money. At this crossroads of priorities and inadequacy, some committed crimes that might bridge the gap. Disheartened, perhaps, by budgetary pitfalls and self-governing partners, they committed what I call *patriarchal crimes*—theft or robbery meant to cement their command of women and homes, or acts of violence against women who would not conform to their versions of commitment. When normative modes of behavior and labor failed to produce the private lives they wanted, such crimes might seem unavoidable. With this in mind we can see a clear reciprocity between illegality and the construction of black families through notions of black manhood. Paradoxically, the men in this study might use crime and murder to produce home lives they considered respectable.[11] The historical record does not firmly divulge the truth of what happened between Elton and Ida Snow, but it communicates the restlessness and angst instilled in black relationships by the converging features of the crucible, already discussed in previous chapters. Thus, through a crucible of domestic space and black intimacy, we witness the confluence of crime and household maintenance, and the resolution of men to affirm birthrights to masculinity on the physical, sexual, and figurative topography of black womanhood.

Ida's determination to run her business against her husband's wishes clarifies how determined many black women were to avoid such deployment of their bodies and lives and to design their own versions of decency.[12] While women like Ida sought marriage and male companionship, some also rejected patriarchal arrangements rife with constraints that mimicked the boundaries of respectability they navigated in public. Just like men, changing gender norms and sexual protocols, mechanized wage labor, expanded patterns of consumption, and commercialized mass media reshaped women's lives and expectations for self-realization and freedom.[13] Job insecurity also put certain types of economic engagement out of reach. Although black women often secured work easier than black men, they mostly found back-breaking domestic labor, low pay, and the usual dangers of mistreatment and sexual assault that came with those positions.[14] They were also saddled with the responsibilities of rearing children, whether their own or those of neighbors and family members, often alone.[15] In order to relish New York City's diversions, they might turn to sex work or other trades that allowed greater profits and maximized control over their own bodies. Not all black women chose the same occupation and recourse Ida adopted, but her choices represent one extreme on a spectrum of behaviors that signaled independence from authoritarian mates and the manifestations of racial inequality. She refused to subsidize Elton's attempts to redesign their lives in terms of his own domestic vision, especially considering the independence she enjoyed before their marriage. "When my husband married me all he had to do was hang up his hat," she told the jury in her trial, "he never bought nothing in my house. My things were my own."[16] Even after Elton's fortunes changed for the better he still did not support her. Through her own enterprises, it is clear, Ida yearned for self-determination within and outside the boundaries of the domestic sphere.

The troubled waters that engulfed both Elton and Ida makes clear how patriarchy can be seen as criminogenic for both men and women.[17] As historian Cheryl Hicks has argued, black women's difficulties primarily stemmed from the disparity between the lives they anticipated and the limitations they faced, not necessarily from intrinsic flaws on their part.[18] As black men struggled with their own predicaments, they sometimes formed a part of the crucible of criminality for those women through physical harm, abandonment, and exploitation of many sorts. As a fitting example, Olivia Copeland set fire to her husband's house in 1929 after years of infidelity and abuse. "I was in very poor health," she later told prison officials, "and in a depressed condition, brought on by my husband['s] cruel treatment."[19] While Copeland ultimately held responsibility for her own choices, she understood her actions as the byproduct of the sort of debasement many other women also suffered. Discord over finances, gender roles, unfaithfulness, and sex increased the chances women would experience desertion and betrayal, domestic violence, or outright homicide. Patriarchy was also crime-inducing for black men who lived in a world that rarely allowed them to seize the tools necessary to meet the standards, requirements, and expectations others had for them or that they placed upon themselves. Badgered by the features of Jim Crow, the pretenses of respectability took a back seat for those who shaped their opinions of propriety with lifestyles that provided relief and a piece of the urban pie. In short, the politics of black intimacy occasionally led to brushes with the law, and romantic connections with women might frame notions of manhood for men who sought power in those relationships, especially when they lacked it elsewhere.

Good Wives, Racial Destiny, and the
Redemption of Black Manhood

In the summer of 1898 more than four-hundred black progressive reformers, scholars, and activists convened for the second Hampton Negro Conference in Virginia to discuss issues relating to black industry, mortality, and womanhood, among others. Framed by the blue arc of the Chesapeake Bay, conference-goers were "charmed by the beauty of the place," according to one account.[20] Among the "strong, earnest and . . . beautiful faces gathered there" was a cohort of black New Yorkers including T. Thomas Fortune, Reverend H. C. Bishop, and Victoria Earle Matthews.[21] On the second day of the gathering, a number of speakers tackled the subjects of women's work, education, and domestic economy with Matthews as a highlight. She delivered a stirring speech on the dangers black women faced in New York City, especially those without husbands. Flocking to Northern cities they inevitably became brokenhearted, "disgraced young creature[s]" from whom "sin-stained years of city life," took every chance of "innocent happiness," she told an audience. Degrading labor, material indulgences, and schemes to funnel them into sex work made their protection urgent.[22] Hampton Institute principal Hollis Burke Frissell followed with an appeal to enact this protection by promoting trades among young men who might be supportive husbands and teaching "young women the art of home making."[23] Prioritizing subjects like black business and labor, schooling, religion, "personal purity," and patriotism, organizers argued the "progressive sprit of the Negro himself" would permit blacks to join "civilization according to the measure of their merit."[24] Combining Matthews's and Frissell's lectures with others on behaviors and work appropriate for women, the conference committee drew up a resolution to organize associations that would instill principles of social virtue, domestic economy, and "all that goes to purify, sweeten, and adorn the home."[25]

The Hampton conference represented a stream of black progressive energy devoted to the improvement of African American life through promoting strong, sustainable families.[26] They believed wholeheartedly that, in the words of one *Independent* writer, "[a] race never rises in integrity above the morality and virtue" of its mothers.[27] Supposing, as they did, that durable unions would breed healthy, moral, and intelligent children that might lead the race to an optimistic future, many of the conferees hinged black racial destiny on the womb, bosom, and uprightness of black women. A malleable and multifaceted concept, "racial destiny" encapsulated a number of objectives, all meant to allow African Americans to be self-sufficient and make progress. Carried in the hearts of black men and women since emancipation, it instilled personal, economic, and political speech and actions with a sense of collective purpose.[28] Regarding the destiny of working-class black men and women, black progressives sought to topple issues associated with poverty, vice, and abandonment, and in their places erect nuclear families defined by middle-class standards. Through marriage and the domestic authority of black men, activists hoped to bring about racial equality.[29] In her 1892 book, *A Voice from the South*, black author and socialist speaker Anna Julia Cooper forcefully advocated for the manly protection of black women, who she considered indispensable to black advancement. "That large, bright, promising fatally beautiful class that stand shivering like a delicate plantlet before the fury of tempestuous elements," she wrote, needed safeguarding from strong brothers and fathers as "the foundation stones of our future as a race."[30]

Merely months before the conference, Victoria Earle Matthews herself had begun efforts to these ends in New York City.[31] By establishing the White Rose Mission Society in February 1898, she endeavored to safeguard "respectable self-supporting colored girls" and "meet the needs of families" with training and guidance.[32] Having been deprived of such direction and modesty historically and powerless to nurture their own families at times during slavery, black women now had the responsibility of creating homes thrust upon them. Ill-prepared for the vicissitudes of family maintenance, they would need instruction in homemaking if they were to meet the challenge, since, in Matthews's reckoning, household building was most important in the "awakening" of black women.[33] Continuing its operation well into the twentieth century, the mission not only housed at-risk migrant women, but also provided help finding appropriate work, domestic training, and classes on cooking, sewing, thrift, and parenting.[34] In the form of the White Rose, Matthews actualized some of the precepts of racial destiny discourse which, among other things, considered competent residential stewardship the fulcrum of racial advancement and placed the burden to produce it squarely on black women's shoulders. However, this did not absolve men of their responsibilities. According to *Colored American* writer Euphemia Kirk, their failure to be a source of strength for black women in molding the fate of African Americans would be treasonous.[35] Men would need to avoid vices, treat their partners with respect, and meet the challenges of winning bread in order for women to assume their righteous roles.

Black progressives' aspirations for fruitful marriages demonstrate how powerful a role matrimony played in black imagination about the future. In bondage and emancipation in the nineteenth century, wedlock took many forms, including legal and nonlegal arrangements, and in marriage blacks hoped to secure themselves from the capriciousness of unfreedom. Because slaveholders had the power to end relationships either by edict or separation, the very act of forming marital bonds involved risk.[36] Even in Northern urban centers slave family and marriage life were stunted. Many bondspeople in New York never married because of the demands of servitude, a lack of space for families to thrive, and an imbalance in the female/male ratio that made women the majority. Married black men often lived away from their wives and children, and even when they all lived together, white owners wielded influence that negated men's authority. In this configuration, women assumed the bulk of family responsibilities, and men lost touch with their obligations as fathers and husbands.[37]

Emancipation brought unfamiliar challenges as marriage became morally and sometimes legally required; yet many blacks saw the option to marry and form families as an integral privilege of their new liberty.[38] For working-class blacks affected by sexual and physical assault, white surveillance, and legal and de facto injunctions in public, forging intimate bonds allowed the construction of private lives that had implications for one's identity in terms of gender and citizenship. Marriage also endowed their lives with romantic and loving bonds that symbolically and legally confirmed their personhood.[39] Nevertheless, blacks underwent the same transformations in the institution of marriage the rest of the country experienced from the early nineteenth century until its end, including increased rates of dissolution and divorce. As early as the 1850s, New York's black leaders used the pulpit and press outlets like the *Colored American* to argue that adoption of white middle-class conduct would lead to respectability and equal rights. Many advocated for a commonplace separation of gender roles and spheres; one that relegated women to domesticity and left worldly affairs of industry, politics, and public life to men.[40] This arrangement would protect women who could then make good homes, and it would inspire men to be moral and supportive, like men should be.

Feminine conservation by black men would be crucial since black women had been denied the safety accorded to white women up until the new century.[41] With their wombs monetized and their sexuality regarded as accessible to all men in slavery, they were refused the benefits of "true womanhood," a state defined by womanly virtue and docility, and in which women might experience protection and wield influence domestically and otherwise.[42] Without similar safeguarding, whites considered their bodies publicly available for abuse, display, or sexual satisfaction. Black men sought to protect black women from such exploitation, but in the process, sometimes treated them as their own property.[43]

In various writings, prominent black author and activist W. E. B. Du Bois conjoined the sexual and bodily fate of black women to the project of reconstructing, defending, and proclaiming black manhood. The very act of controlling and underwriting a household with a forceful model of masculinity as its fulcrum expressed a redemptive form of virility, in his mind. He implored black men to protect "the honor of your wives, [and the] chastity of your daughters," not only for the well-being of women, but for the sake of maintaining their own autonomy as men. Keeping women chaste or faithful meant shielding them from the sexual assault, racial insults, and desecration they endured in public from other men and from harmful influences on their conduct. The black man's burden was effectively the heavy weight of "a mass of corruption from white adulterers, threatening almost the obliteration of the Negro home." Strong husbands and fathers would begin to undo the legacy of debasement and rape black women withstood in slavery. In doing so, they would likewise heal the emasculating wounds men suffered as they watched black women serve white slaveholding men, raise his children, and "at his behest [lay] low to his lust."[44]

This history was due for rectification by twentieth-century black men, Du Bois argued, and unbounded black women directly threatened the project of black uplift.[45] The sheer acts of partying, dancing, drinking, and living independently interrupted the development of powerful and sustainable forms of manhood. This was particularly urgent in the swirl of temptations and opportunities for pleasurable consumption and sex in the varied heterosocial spaces of cities. Indeed, black female bodies became stages upon which dramas of black manhood could be played out, and uncooperative women might doom men, and their race, to subservience. In laying out a path to racial conservation Du Bois bestowed the duty of curating women's moral dioramas and reducing "the vast army of black prostitutes" on black men.[46] Their failure would simply restart the generational cycle of black criminality and degradation; steeped in the conditions of marginalized black communities, immoral mothers would raise immoral children. "What else is there for her to do but sink to the level of her environment and produce recruits for the Tenderloin," Victoria Earle Matthews asked in an 1897 letter to the *Sun*.[47]

White reformers also saw female purity as central to answering the "negro question," but their perspectives reveal racist and classist thinking, and betray other motives. As chapter 3 shows, white progressives chiefly approached white women they considered "fallen" with benevolence and rehabilitation, but often addressed black women with moral panic and attempts to control them. White prostitutes might be pulled from the snares of white slavers, but black women needed to be saved from their own "inefficiency and desire to avoid hard work," in social reformer and activist Francis Kellor's words. With such biases, Kellor established the Association for the Protection of Colored Women in 1905, an organization meant to intercept incoming black women migrants before they found themselves in brothels.[48] In *Outlook* writer Eleanor Tayleur's 1904 article on "social and moral decadence," she likewise cautioned readers about a "dark, helpless, hopeless mass," of black women leading "lawless and purposeless lives" on city streets. In Tayleur's estimation, the abolition of slavery and subsequent migration north harmed black women most since they removed those women from plantations and white patriarchy, depriving them of "food and warmth and privacy." If black men could not provide the same, black women urbanites would harm themselves, and injure their race in the process.[49] For those who accepted popular beliefs of black inferiority, the need for domestic stability in black households presented a social paradox. How would black women remain intact outside of the patriarchal protection of either white masters or black men? Likewise, how would men play their patriarchal roles in securing new generations of women from downfall if raised by decadent women? The success of both of these imperatives depended upon the viability of the other. Putting the bigoted nature of Tayleur's assumptions aside, her comments reveal a plot to manipulate black men and women into a form of self-policing that might ease perceived burdens on the rest of society. Minus plantation control, Tayleur, and writers of a similar ilk, clearly hoped domestic life would serve the same purpose.[50]

The interpretation of black women's bodies as material sites of masculine renewal was not only a pipedream of white progressives and black elites but also motivated some blue-collar African American men. Most black relationships were instigated by sincere sexual and emotional bonds, but securing women in a relatively safe private realm sometimes appeared as a solution to the insecurities and assaults black men experienced in public. They might wish to confirm their identities as men with the sort of respectable domiciles hegemonic masculinity required. Regardless of their own behaviors in leisure, work, and public, they commonly imagined women as their moral personas. Although they understood ideologues promoting racial uplift criticized their lifestyles, black men accepted some of the precepts of respectability. After all, organizations like the White Rose Mission sought to assist them in acquiring the touchstones of modern family living and keeping domestic authority, and they had their own deeply rooted concepts of tradition and propriety to uphold.[51] Still, while reformers made plans for black lives, working-class black men might reject certain aspects of the class-laden philosophies of domestic purity and salvage whatever parts made sense for them.[52] Messy contradictions and individual desires broke down clichés of family and order in real life since women rarely conformed to popular bourgeois ideals of womanhood, and men frequently could not meet middle-class standards of provision. While determining their own rules of propriety, working-class blacks might interchangeably seek the symbols of respectability and discard them when necessary.[53]

"Because Nothing Looks Sweeter Than Your Freedom"

In order to fully understand disagreements over autonomy and domestic authority between black men and women, it is necessary to delineate the expectations women had for their own lives. Many women pursued strong unions with stable partners and healthy families, but the disputes, abandonment, and abuse that sometimes fractured their households and their appetites for independence made it so some shunned the whole enchilada of marriage and parenting, just like some men did. After her arrest for prostitution, Honey Huffman told intake agents at the upstate Bedford Hills Reformatory that she left her husband "once in a while" to go on a "spree."[54] Another woman cited her need to find excitement before marriage, since she had not "seen much of life yet" but had "an intense curiosity to see all of it."[55] Maureen Robinson plainly declared her opinion that marriage was not a necessity. "Some people get along better when they are not married," she told interviewers at Bedford.[56]

When necessary or favorable, other women left children with parents or siblings temporarily or relinquished their parental duties altogether seeking flexibility.[57] In a 1926 study of single black mothers at a local women's hospital one woman admitted to feeling no responsibility to her child when she placed him in a boarding home, and she planned to have him adopted.[58] Expecting no help from the father of her child, a sixteen-year-old Barbadian immigrant, identified only as Hester M., expressed similar feelings. She went to work for a family outside of the city but, according to her employer, she "neglected her baby . . . seemed to hate it," and began "staying out at night and leaving the child alone." Terminated from that position due to the baby's cries, Hester relocated to New York City and continued to disregard her child because she "meant to have a good time while she was still young." Tragically, her baby died after only six months and Hester's family lost contact with her from then forward. Such carelessness was a rare occurrence, but Hester's case, and those of others, illustrates a robust desire for freedom that many black women carried with them through the crucible of New York City. The vast majority of black women cherished their children and loved their spouses, and they did their best to provide devotion and care no matter their circumstances. But many still craved the freedom that domestic life repressed, and with or without the assistance of co-parents and mates, some women found motherhood unbearable.[59]

These women's ambivalence about matrimony and motherhood reflects broader cultural post-Victorian-era strains at the turn of the century. Intellectuals, reformers, and individual women had begun to rebuke the limitations of domesticity in calls for gender equality and in the lives they lived, particularly in cities.[60] Female inclusion in popular dance halls, consumer products advertised to unmarried women, and movies and stars like Joan Crawford and Madge Bellamy promoted new womanhood defined by independence and a "cult of beauty."[61] From 1900 to 1930 the proportion of women workers rose nationally from 20 percent to more than 25 percent, and the percentage of women who continued to work after marriage nearly doubled. Although most of these jobs were menial service endeavors, this upward trend signaled ongoing revisions in the domestic sphere.[62] The age of marriage steadily dropped across the decades, but divorce rates rose from one in twenty-one marriages in 1880 to one in seven by 1924. Many factors precipitated these changes including the necessities of urban life, mounting secularization in American culture, and the demands of World War I, but the progressively dynamic nature of women's habits clearly played a part.[63] Women, like men, thought differently about the meanings of marriage and sexuality in the new century. For many, betrothal no longer beckoned them into a life of servitude, and sex was no longer a chore to slake masculine carnal thirsts, but both invited women to seek personal fulfillment and physical gratification for themselves. Radical versions of womanhood emanated from New York's bourgeoise bohemian scene, like that in sections of Greenwich Village, particularly in the 1910s and 1920s when white and black feminists and intellectuals embraced sexual indulgence as a key to women's liberation.[64] Indeed, when white women entered politics as reformers and suffrage activists or poured into avenues searching for work and pleasure, black women did the same.[65]

Nevertheless, like many other parts of their lives, challenging domesticity was more complex for black women than for their white counterparts. Seizing new freedoms opened previously closed doors that led to varying measures of self-determination but also presented new problems that were less acute for other women. Engaging the subject of women's emancipation from chauvinism in a 1902 publication, Friedrich Engels applied conflict theory, the argument that society is a struggle between the powerful and powerless, to household maintenance. "The modern monogamous family is founded on the open or disguised domestic slavery of women," making the man the "bourgeois, [and] the woman represents the proletariat," he wrote. This unit broke down when women entered public life and modes of production on equal footing with men.[66] Engels and his adherents understood work as another key to women's deliverance from objectification but did not fully account for black women's intersectionality. Relegated to grinding, thankless labor and unprotected by custom or law from exploitation, assault, and rape, sexual freedom and employment rarely afforded them the carte blanche many activists imagined. Race dismantled the privileges of "true womanhood" and blocked upward economic paths, and the plight of their husbands, fathers, and suitors often hindered their progress through normative modes and mechanisms.

For New York's black women, patriarchy often dissolved whether they challenged it or not. Higher rates of employment among married African American women than white women made black households more egalitarian in some ways, but couples sometimes desired the benefits of separate gender-specific roles, and some women sought the protection and support of faithful husbands for their own desires or for the welfare of their families. Furthermore, wage-earning did not always eliminate repressive relationships with men.[67] Understanding the complexity of the issue, Anna Julia Cooper argued black women's family responsibilities appeared to be multifold since they often lacked the ability to choose to live as a housewife and had to straddle both public and domestic life out of necessity.[68] For Cooper, forsaking domestic roles completely could not be the answer to the problems black women faced, but neither would outright submission to men. Working-class black women also grasped this conundrum and often seized the benefits of "new womanhood" in the ways they could. Real liberation remained a distant destination for most women in the early twentieth century, but for African American women, the path was strewn with tailor-made obstacles.

For some women who chose to forego marriage and tend to themselves, sex work could be an attractive alternative to fruitless drudgery. Domestic servants often lived-in with their employers and remained on duty until late, and women with their own families to care for might never see the end of their toil. The work was hard and included a litany of service tasks, perennially low-pay, long hours, and an environment dependent upon the whims of their employer. In search of greater pay or fleeing unreasonable responsibilities and sometimes sexual abuse, black women changed positions frequently or found other ways to make money.[69] While some entered prostitution to make up for lost wages while sick or unemployed, others simply cited desire for "money and pleasure," the ability to purchase clothes and attend movies, and the option to live on their own.[70] They conducted business singly from tenement rooms or with madams and pimps in brownstone bordellos, and they made more money than they might expect as domestic workers but rarely made the sorts of profits white women collected in high-class brothels.[71]

Consider the strategies Lizzie Pickett used to circumvent the limitations wrought by poorly paid labor, marriage, and parenthood after moving to New York City. Born in Farmville, Virginia, she left school at nine years old in 1897 and labored on a plantation for $3 per month. In 1902, after years of farm work, she joined her brother in New York in search of better opportunities. Pickett roomed with him for a short time but then lived on her own and worked as a doctor's assistant making $5 per week; a dramatic improvement over her previous wages. However, she left that position and a subsequent job when she decided she "didn't feel like working anymore." Likely discouraged by available job prospects in the North she returned to her family's home in Virginia in 1908 but left for New York City once again after two years, this time traveling with her significant other and leaving behind a small child. Determined to make her move permanent, Pickett did housework and laundry, but her wages never exceeded $6 per week and she continued to terminate positions out of aversion to the labor. With more time out of work she made a living through sex work, a vocation that led to a series of legal problems. Police arrested her multiple times for disorderly conduct, assault, theft, and public intoxication. In a 1917 interview Pickett informed an agent at Bedford Hills Reformatory she "could have found work at any time" but disliked the drudgery and preferred prostitution.[72] Having trouble keeping employed himself, her common-law husband reportedly lived off of Pickett's earnings.[73] Considering she had the potential to earn up to "$4 from every man," prostitution made other types of labor seem unbearable.[74] After years of trying to make a life for herself in New York City on pennies, Pickett found a way to escape the loop of inadequate wages, albeit one that jeopardized her freedom.

Washington, D.C., native Ruby Wilcox similarly claimed her independence by entering the sex trade. After a few "troublesome" episodes with theft and delinquency, and a stint in the House of Mercy for "disreputable" women, Wilcox's adoptive mother moved her to White Plains, north of New York City. The move caused trouble in their relationship and she soon absconded back to Manhattan to live with a male partner.[75] Speaking about life at home she later told interviewers at the Bedford Hills Reformatory "every girl should have enjoyment," but when living with her mother, she "just didn't feel satisfied." According to Wilcox, her mother was "too strict to live" with, their home in White Plains was lonely, and "the theatres were so far off that [she] could not stand it."[76] Like many other women Wilcox saw her ability to earn her own money as deliverance from familial obligations, and she hinged this liberty on her capacity to enjoy the pleasures available in the city. In addition to participating in the leisure economy, buying groceries, managing their own living space, and designing the features of their lives appealed to many married and unmarried black women. Those with spouses often sought jobs with or without their husband's consent, and unmarried women sometimes found their work aspirations clashed with desires to find and keep male companionship. Either way, women distinctly connected work with freedom and attempted to consolidate their sense of personhood with the imperatives of survival. Accordingly, both Lizzie Pickett and Ruby Wilcox represent black women in constant motion as they departed from middle- and working-class respectability norms and public decorum, and attempted to fulfill their needs and personal desires outside of the bonds of marriage.

Like black men, women like Pickett and Wilcox existed in a region of duality, both hoping for the stability of middle-class respectability and rejecting the limitations it placed on their lives. Barred from writing an admirer while at Bedford Hills, Pickett realized she would likely lose contact with him, but she did not mind. "I can easily find someone else when I get out," she told intake officers.[77] Her flightiness, whether real or demonstrative, represents the true sentiments of many black women coming to terms with the nature of their lives at the time. Although they sought marriages and long-term relationships, like men they often savored the personal license urban culture provided and actively celebrated it. They campaigned for the protections, devotion, and respect attached to normative femininity but might still reject the yokes of domesticity and respectability when they strangled their freedoms and placed the glittery, modern excitements of New York City out of reach. Consequently, black men who wished to bolster their own sense of identity by containing feminine energies and bodies within the boundaries of the domestic sphere often faced an impossible task. Some women indulged in the bliss and revelry of formal and informal public economies, frequented saloons, smoked, danced, gambled, and made money on the streets alongside men. They furthermore made their claim on urban space into a boon by participating in licit and illicit leisure, seeking sexual, sensory, and consumptive pleasure in ways that suited their needs, desires, and fantasies, and straightforwardly challenged the constraints of family life and gender.[78]

Nevertheless, for many women, marriage represented its own sort of freedom. Some desired nuclear family arrangements, calm and clean homes for their children, and the ability to become housewives and shed miserable backbreaking domestic work.[79] Ideally, conjugal unions might also afford independence from parents, consumer power otherwise unreachable, the protection of husbands, and stability in the uncertainty of urban living. For twenty-nine-year-old Victoria Winters the domestic archetype became reality, yet she was discontent with her spouse's tight spending habits. An interviewer from the Bedford Hills Laboratory of Social Hygiene described her as an energetic housewife with "good morals," yet she had an inclination for material possessions that exceeded her husband's financial capacity. Winters kept her employment against her spouse's wishes because she liked "pretty clothes," enjoyed setting an "expensive table and is satisfied only with the best of everything." Although she felt the need to supplement the family's income with her own, she still praised her partner for his ability to keep a "beautiful home" and a "nice bank account," and for his ambitious nature. "He is well educated, an electrician by trade," and with his income he always sought to "excel [and] make a little better showing than his neighbors."[80] From Winters's example it is clear, even when coming together with similar desires of familial backing and companionship, and when actualizing those goals, black men and women encountered conflicting aspirations. These oft-times opposing urges created imbalances with the capacity to reshape intimate relationships around tensions that destabilized households or outright dismantled them. Lacking the resources for such consumption, most black women could only aspire to the stability Winters relished, and they found themselves facing demanding or dangerous situations.

Discord in couples often resulted from "marital role frustration" created by the discrepancy between expectations and the capacities and inclinations of one's partner to fulfill them, and domestic abuse sometimes accompanied these divergences.[81] Black women valued living on their own terms but sometimes found themselves in challenging positions at the confluence of freedom and necessity. For seven months, Ruby Wilcox lived with her "consort" who earned up to $20 per week and with their combined wages they "lived very well," she explained in a statement. Unfortunately, things took a turn for the worse when he slashed her wrist during an argument about alleged infidelity. Grieving their broken relationship and hurt physically and emotionally, she went to live with a friend while she recovered. Disenchanted by low-paying wage labor and unfavorable working conditions, she once again resorted to sex work to finance frequent trips to dance clubs, "moving picture shows," and theaters. Between living spaces, undercover police arrested her for prostitution and once convicted she went to Bedford Hills Reformatory for an indefinite sentence.[82] Although Wilcox had the agency to make her own decisions, part of her troubles stemmed from the abuse she received and the whirlwind it caused in her life. Most assuredly, women like Wilcox understood it was possible to combine their own autonomy with a positive, nurturing, and long-lasting intimate partnership. Unfortunately, romance too frequently included distinct tensions driven by money, distrust, jealousy, and gender inequality that might dislodge women from whatever progress they had achieved.

Marital strife had the capacity to drive other types of illegal behaviors like grand larceny, especially by women left by men to raise children on their own.[83] Millie Hale had complex relationships with the fathers of her children that exemplified the varied negotiated aspects of black intimacy as it relates to support and extralegal means of subsistence. Molested and impregnated two times as a teenager by Gerald Sykes, one of her grandmother's boarders, Hale lived with him as "man and wife" for four years, but frequent quarrels eventually caused them to part. In Sykes's perspective, their relationship ended because Hale refused to leave her familial home so they could create their own household. She also ignored their children and spent time "out with other men," which made him "so disgusted" he had to leave her. In Hale's account, they separated when she discovered Sykes "was going around with other women." Slighted by his infidelity, she married John Hunt "without much thought" because she "wanted to show [Sykes] that she was not dependent upon him." A professional thief himself, Hunt cared for Hale, her two previous children, and their infant child for one year until a lengthy prison sentence removed him from the picture. This turn of events left Hale with three children and nearly no support from their fathers. Sykes sometimes gave her "a few dollars a week," but never consistently kept up payments, or visited his children.[84]

Without assistance, Hale occupied nine separate domestic work positions between 1908 and 1917 and frequently abandoned her work because of the demands of child care or the desire for better compensation. Feeling pressured to improve her situation she committed grand larceny, which threw her life into a tailspin. She subsequently admitted to giving in to the impulse to steal a diamond pendant from the home of her employer in the midst of destitution. She reasoned she needed the money to send to her husband in jail and "her grandmother had to have more money to run the house" they lived in. While incarcerated she changed her mind about marriage and once on parole refused her husband's inquiries about her whereabouts. Recently freed from prison himself, Hale suspected him of adultery and intended to end their marriage.[85]

Whether alone by choice or abandoned by male partners, single mothers like Hale improvised to make ends meet. Facing marginalization in their public and private lives, they often made choices dictated by strained relationships and monetary and material deprivations. Still, their struggles reveal great determination not to be tossed about by the currents that surged around them. Returning to freedom as a parolee, Hale attempted to find work and remain independent from Hunt, but in her letters to her parole officer she complained of the cost of living in New York City and questioned how she could start over and survive without her husband's assistance. "I have to begin at the bottom and start up and you know with the high cost of living I wouldn't even try to buy . . . anything really." With this in mind she grappled with the idea of returning to Hunt and asked her parole officer for advice on the matter. "Don't you think I am justified in wanting a divorce from him," she wrote. "Why should I endanger myself with him now especially when he is running around . . . with all sorts of women?" She then revealed the aggressive tone of conversations about loyalty and separation that frequently led to instances of intimate violence and murder. "He has told people that if I don't go back to him 'I'll know what will happen,'" she wrote. "If he attempts to bother me somebody is going to get hurt . . . pretty bad and that somebody is [my] husband."[86]

These women's stories epitomize the sort of strain unstable finances and illegitimate methods of building capital placed upon romantic unions, and they show how for some black women, black men might compose a part of the crucible of black criminality. Illegal activities meant to balance budgets ran the risk of fundamentally altering the tenor of their lives or ending them. Women appreciated the support they received, yet bristled at infidelity, undue demands, abandonment and poor care, and domestic abuse. The majority of black women sought intimate connections and regularly gave up aspects of their independence to forge deep bonds with men, but they also found contentment in configuring lives beyond the limits of romantic partnerships. Patriarchal directives, mistreatment, and desertion of women and children might place them in circumstances where sex work or theft was the only option. Confronting their own crucibles and navigating the labyrinthine politics of intimate relationships with black women, black men understood the obligations they would need to live up to if they had hopes of attracting or holding on to partners. In addition to black women's expectations, they had their own outlooks for themselves, and standards, commitments, and requirements that were difficult to meet. At this intersection of expectancy, unpredictability, and restriction, some men embraced risky actions that, if successful, promised some breathing room.

"She Will Be Well Taken Care of and Given a Good Home"

Nineteenth-century notions of manhood assumed men existed on an equal playing field outside of physical, heredity, or class distinctions. All men had the capacity to compete, the idea went, if only they took control of their passions and industriously pursued their own liberty through work, accumulated material items and wealth, and served the interests of their families.[87] While this ethos carried into the twentieth century, ever-shifting patterns in gender, labor, and social life opened some new avenues of success and closed others for all men. As early as 1871, social scientist Samuel Eliot questioned the efficacy of traditional manhood roles in a modern wage labor urban society, and whether or not they were still feasible. "To put a man upon wages, is to put him in the position of a dependent," Eliot wrote, "the longer he holds the position . . . the less opportunities he has for self control or the higher business faculties, the less of a man . . . he becomes."[88] By the turn of the century, changing work, life, and leisure customs in increasingly industrial cities and the steady bend of gender norms forged what some historians have called a "crisis in manhood."[89] Machinery, mass production, and other technological advances distanced the average laborer from the means and purpose of production, making work into soulless tedium. As artisans, skilled craftsmen, and subsistence farmers became laborers, they seemed to forfeit control of their industry and ambition to a series of foremen and managers. With work no longer offering a sturdy platform on which to form one's identity, men increasingly sought character and status in leisure and with their families. However, for African American men squeezed out of lucrative jobs and under siege in public and in leisure, struggling to maintain their households meant notions of manhood might seem out of reach in yet another way.[90]

In the domestic and public realms, most early twentieth-century American men benchmarked manliness on the assertion of control over women's bodies and their ability to financially care for them to some extent; but for black men, the gap between their wages and male-headed households had a part in determining the terms of their relationships with women. If new modes of mass production ruptured prevailing notions of white manhood at the time, being left out of most industrial labor presented even more troubling and distinct issues of identity and gender for black men. Whether native to the North or South they experienced trenchant material and spatial restrictions that infringed upon the development of hegemonic masculinity; a condition measured by unfettered access to public space and the touchstone of feminine domesticity at the time. Yet, in order to command a patriarchal household, black men needed to acquire sustainable employment and wages that allowed the types of consumption popularly associated with sustenance. "Very seldom is even the skilled black man paid wages sufficient for the care of a wife and the support of a home," Victoria Earle Matthews wrote in a letter to the *Sun*. "The woman is expected to help him take care of herself."[91] An imbalance in the availability of jobs for black women and men further intensified problems of gender. Significantly more women migrated North than men as a result of better work prospects, and asymmetry produced lopsided households where men more frequently struggled to contribute financially. The noticeably unequal presence of black men and women in New York and diminished employment prospects for men heightened their sense of inadequacy and ramped up tensions in romantic relationships around money, familial control, and domesticity.[92]

Unpredictable job recruitment patterns affected the fortunes of migrants' entire families, regularly forcing multiple household members to seek incomes on their own. Left without other means of survival, lacking health care and social security nets, financial disruptions from illnesses proved disastrous for already shaky career prospects. Suffering from a long-term illness, John Walker managed to make money from "anything he could find . . .

principally as a waiter," as an assistant to a lawyer and a doctor, and "little jobs of moving occasionally." During stretches of unemployment he helped with chores around the house as he recovered, and his inability to hold a job drove his wife and sister-in-law to find work. To make ends meet, both women "did housework sometimes, and sewed," averaging earnings of $6 a week.[93] Either way, men like Walker were determined to put up money for themselves and their families and were willing to take whatever sort of post they could find. Holding onto work required flexibility and perseverance, but job prospects remained bleak and kept households in flux.

Similarly strained, Clifton Jones robbed and killed a well-known white cosmopolite, Charles W. Roxbury, in 1903. Suffering from economic straits for some time with his common-law wife, Liddy Wells, Jones committed the crime out of frustration about his inability to support her.[94] In the years before the murder he drove a coal truck, tended horses at various stables, and worked seasonally with the Barnum & Bailey Circus to make ends meet. Lacking consistent income, Jones improvised his earnings by pawning stolen items when he could. Although Wells was officially married to another man, she shared an apartment with Jones for more than a year when a miscarriage left her ill and unable to work. The couple's rent, as well as bills for clothing and furniture, was weeks behind, and Wells later described their home as largely empty since most of their belongings had been pawned or dispossessed. Worried about their dire circumstances, Jones told Wells he would either solve their money trouble or they would go their separate ways. After selling Roxbury's possessions at a pawn shop he delivered the profits to Wells in hopes it would somewhat alleviate their financial burdens.[95] However, police discovered his identity from the shop proprietor, and Jones was arrested and easily convicted of first-degree murder. Men like Jones frequently experienced the same sort of pressure to create economically solvent households as their white counterparts, but more prevalent job insecurity, discrimination, and low wages meant they regularly missed their mark.[96] Black men likely faced what criminologist David Greenberg called "masculine status anxiety," stemming from fear they may never reach the benchmarks of the customary masculine role.[97] Desperate to gain his footing on the unsure landscape of New York's commercial economy, Jones risked everything to meet the commitment he made to Wells and control their life together.

Jones's actions uncover the irony of patriarchal crimes. Some men who committed extralegal acts often did so for the specific purpose of creating traditional patriarchal nuclear families and circumventing the many factors hampering familial formation and stability in the first place. Navigating the fast-shifting topography of New York City and encountering varying degrees of scarcity, they hoped illegal methods of producing income would eventually bring about reputable circumstances. Criminal actions distinctly defined as unacceptable by white and black progressives alike played a more complicated role for those affected by urban, legal, and cultural designs that impeded their visions of the future. While white and black progressives criticized theft, promiscuity, and nontraditional households, working-class black men and women fashioned their own versions of propriety using the tactics, resources, and relationships that were available, even when failure might be tragically deconstructive. Thus, crimes meant to shield marriages and family units from external intrusion, and allow men to look after female partners, might also have the capacity to end things altogether. Men committed subsistence crimes for many reasons, but Clifton Jones's attempt to keep his relationship with Wells alive with robbery and murder illustrates how some might consider such illegality their only hope of constructing hegemonic, supportive masculine identities and actualizing middle-class versions of domestic authority.

Ultimately, a sense of instability is apparent in the family composition of some black New Yorkers, one that is evidently linked to the varying challenges black men and women faced, separately and together. The relationships between all of the couples in this study can only be fully understood in light of the historical factors of the crucible of black criminality. Historic violence and sexual violations of black bodies, and the economic, spatial, and legal limitations outlined in previous chapters accumulated in a way that stressed both men and women when making their homes and tending to themselves and others. For black men specifically, work discrimination and occupational eviction closed routes to economic solvency, leaving them with an uphill losing battle to fight, and sometimes their families disintegrated as a result, or they drifted apart over time.

Although census records show that between 1905 and 1925 the typical black family had two parents and a male listed as the head of the household in San Juan Hill and the Tenderloin, the census does not tell the entire story, nor can it indicate how those families functioned, and how long they remained intact.[98] In reality, there were significant disparities in the abilities of black men to consolidate households versus their white counterparts, and financial troubles endangered black living situations, even those headed by a male breadwinner. Regardless of the large number of male-headed family units, most flats also housed vast numbers of male lodgers, some of whom lived away from their own children. A great many African American women found in New York State prison records reported raising their children by themselves, a fact that indicates how the loss of partners might force women outside of the law.[99]

Hoping to settle down with the father of her expected child in Virginia, Miriam M. faced blunt rejection. When her paramour learned of her pregnancy he told her he was "too ambitious to cumber himself with the care of a family," and he left for New York City looking for work and to be with another woman.[100] Some men left women with their children because of previous relationships. In a survey of ten black mothers interned at Bedford Hills Reformatory and Auburn women's prison between 1900 and 1927, all but one reported being abandoned by their children's fathers,[101] including Gertrude Harper who gagged her newborn child, "threw it in a pail," and buried it alive when deserted.[102] Ruth Reed's 1926 sociological research on unmarried black mothers in the city determined only half were in committed relationships with their children's fathers.[103] Out of 231 fathers in the study, sixty-one were already married to other women when their children arrived.[104] Working-class African Americans aspired to faithful unions and marriages, but household composition and management presented challenges that required gargantuan efforts to overcome.[105] Many black women never took on the role of housewives but instead contributed to finances or cobbled them together alone and looked to their broader communities for the kind of care typically expected from husbands.[106]

For the many couples that remained together, black men's economic difficulties and the ongoing demand for domestic labor placed black women in a position to provide more often than other women. Although the majority of women migrants were of typical age for marriage, many struggled to find reliable mates. In the last decade of the nineteenth century, only 810 black men resided in New York City for every 1,000 black women, a number that only increased slightly to 850 by 1910. In that year, more than 50 percent of married black women contributed to household income, compared to German women at 30 percent, Italian women at 36 percent, and Irish at 5 percent.[107] In a 1911 study suffragist journalist Mary White Ovington delineated the stark differences between the lives of black working-class women and their white counterparts by looking at their respective love interests. In a white section of the Greenpoint neighborhood in Brooklyn, she saw consistent factory work and livable wages for men as the basis for male-headed nuclear families and stay-at-home mothers. Inversely, unstable employment for black men greatly impacted the security of black marriages and intimate bonds, since women were forced to work.[108] As a result, many women either lived with family, earned their own keep, assisted companions in meeting rent and food bills, or supported men outright. Arrestee Lulu Simpson claimed she paid the expenses of her lover, Jasper Gross, who "would remain in the bed most of the day" while she did domestic labor outside of the home. This arrangement continued until after a quarrel when she told him to leave. Angered, Gross kept the key to the flat and during one visit he stabbed Simpson.[109]

Most men did not resort to such exploitative and murderous behavior, but social scientists and critical observers emphasized incidents of violence and freeloading to condemn jobless black men. Columbia researcher William Fielding Ogburn accounted for these episodes by arguing blacks "revert toward the animal" with "elementary instinctive response[s] to stimuli," even in family arrangements. As a result, "a great amount of non-legal marriages . . . easily made and easily broken" abounded in their communities, in his study.[110] John Clyde, one of Ogburn's colleagues, argued this happened because of inherent "looseness about sexual relations," family desertion, and a "general lack of feeling of responsibility in the homes" of blacks.[111] Those men who remained, Mary White Ovington wrote in 1911, often sponged from women who kept them "in polished boots, fashionable coats, and well-creased trousers."[112] She described a black section of San Juan Hill as inhabited by industrious women feeding and housing themselves and their families, and mostly idle men subsisting from the largesse of lovers and wives, and lounging on corners "in as dandified dress as their women at the washtubs could get for them." Stemming from this lack of responsibility on the part of men, black women's experiences of matrimony remained far more open and changeable, she believed. In other words, lacking the interdependence engendered by male support, black families were more susceptible to division and decomposition. Domestic labor gave married black women mobility that forced interaction with a diverse cross-section of the urban population but afforded them only "few hours to give to [their] children." Such maneuverability changed the nature of wedlock to a different sort of commitment. For women in particular, when a man "turn[ed] out to [be] a bad bargain, she has no fear of leaving him, since her marital relations are not welded by economic dependence." As a result, working-class African American gender roles were more fluid than those of middle-class whites and blacks, and such interdependence created greater levels of parity in those couples.[113] However, less reliance upon husbands resulted in more easily broken commitments and bonds by both men and women, in her estimation.[114]

These views of black marriages are clearly tilted by racial bias, but such research does indicate something unique that was happening for African Americans somewhat hobbled by financial and spatial obstacles. To be sure, black women who sought financially and emotionally supportive marriages sometimes felt betrayed when their expectations went unmet.[115] When Emily Higgens's husband disappeared in 1915 she wrote local police requesting that they scour "pool rooms or houses of ill repute" to find him. Sickness had befallen one of her children and she was "not able to work," but it was her husband's "business to care for us," she beseeched in her message.[116] Without their partners' support or as single parents, women like Higgens might experience depression and anguish that led to health problems and dissolution. In the process of constructing a home for her family, Henrietta Moody left Will Thomas, the father of one of her daughters, because "he was stingy and would not give her any money." The lack of support received from Thomas and the fathers of two other children eventually caused the breakdown of her family and the loss of life through illness, presumably because of poor living conditions. One child died of a bacterial infection as an infant and another of tuberculosis at twelve years old in 1912. Likely struggling to bear the burden of loss and poverty on her own, Moody left her remaining daughter with her mother. She then married a new partner, who she subsequently left for another relationship. Tragically, Moody succumbed to heart troubles only a year later at the age of thirty-seven in 1913, and her daughter Millie Hale experienced similarly scattered and nonsupportive relationships with men as she got older. Although male abandonment did not generally result in the complete disintegration of families, Moody's experience is emblematic of how absentee fathers increased burdens on women who parented alone.[117] Her abnegation of parental duties further strained the resources, budget, and energies of her own mother and ultimately led to the lack of supervision under which her daughter was later molested by a boarder in the house where she lived with her grandmother.[118]

As stated earlier, the predicament of abandonment that women like Moody faced and the consequences her family suffered as a result could sometimes be accompanied by persistent abuse, and some women committed acts of intimate murder in response. Fifty-four-year-old Washington, D.C., native Lucile Sanders killed her husband, Stanley, with a knife in the heat of an argument. Stanley, she told police, had physically abused her, squandered his income on alcohol and gambling, and occasionally took her own earnings without her consent.[119] "My husband stole all my money while [I was] asleep," she explained in court. Wages "I had worked hard for [and] saved" and "left me to pay rent or get food for myself and child." In one fight over cash, Stanley "became enraged [and] drew a knife with intent to cut my throat," she claimed, but she "got hold of the knife," and stabbed him herself.[120] Amelia Shaw more deliberately took the life of her spouse because he mishandled her, drank excessively, and "was a gambler and would not work" leaving her to provide for their family herself. After a short separation Shaw found her husband in bed with another woman, and during an argument she struck him with an axe and killed him.[121]

The responses of Sanders and Shaw serve as stark reminders of the uneven turf black men and women entered when homemaking. Being conducive to sexual violence and abuse, patriarchy itself encouraged some men to

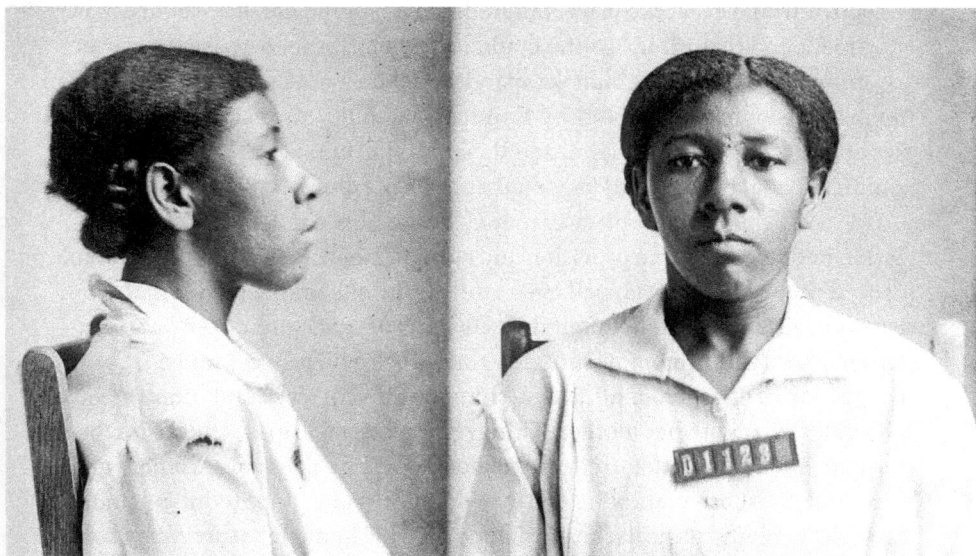

Amelia Shaw (pseud.), an inmate at Auburn prison for women, 1919. Courtesy of New York State Archives and Records Administration, Albany, New York (Inmate #1123, Series B0050).

objectify women as sexual property and, in some instances, retaliatory violence or self-defense might seem like the only options for women fed up with mistreatment. Hence, we can see the affairs of the two women as extremes on a spectrum defined by negotiations common to all relationships at the turn of the century. Just like white women, black women withstood cruelty that ran the gamut from unfair assumptions to infidelity and murder. But they also braved a unique crucible amplified by the hardships endured by their partners, and the often severe physical and emotional cross black men placed upon their shoulders in order to recover their own sense of selfhood.

Likely understanding the adversity women experienced, and hoping to increase their prospects of forging respectable households, black men often pursued women with promises of provision. Caribbean immigrant Julius Redman's attempt to woo Loretta Cunningham in 1911 illuminates black men's awareness about the needs of partners, and likewise makes plain their proclivities toward meeting them, as well as their possible expectation that promises would be enough. Although he married another woman before emigrating to New York in 1890, Redman sought Cunningham's attention through gift-giving, pledges of marriage, and guarantees he would ease her financial stress. Frequent quarrels put the wedding off and Cunningham lost her faith it would ever take place, but Redman reassured her "he would get an apartment and furnish it," so she could leave her mother's house. Once "he got some money . . . we would get married and he would put me in it," Cunningham recounted. Daunted by Redman's inability to make good on his pledge, Cunningham later admitted she only entertained the idea because "I couldn't do any better [and] he wouldn't leave me alone."[122]

Friction around the subject of monetary support elucidates a clear association between resource provision and commitment. At one point, Redman insisted they would be married even after Cunningham rejected him. In order to regain her hand, he offered small sums of money to cover minor expenses, yet Cunningham refused them believing acceptance meant recognition of engagement. Instead, she continued to work and support herself while living with her mother. Things completely fell apart after tense discussions about their deferred union during a Thanksgiving dinner, and Cunningham subsequently moved away without notifying Redman. Undeterred by repeated refusals, he tried to change his financial situation by robbing a safe at his workplace, during which he committed a murder.[123] While Cunningham moved on with her life, Redman faced conviction for the crime and was scheduled for electrocution.[124] However, while awaiting his punishment in Sing Sing prison, he died of a heart attack in 1913.[125]

These stories tug at the strings of one's heart, but they don't define the typical experience of African Americans. In truth, black family life occurred in amphibious form; sometimes submerged in the waters of race-based hardships and other times basking in the sunlight of loving, supportive, and stable relationships. Still, for black men, stereotypes about their lives and intentions further reduced work prospects and demoralized them, and performing the duties of conventional manhood could be impossible. In this predicament, some derived power from their domination of women who worked and supported them in a twist of normative gender roles.[126] They slipped through the crack formed between the realities of their lives and the high bars of popular masculinity standards and their own desires. Being naturally bound to each other romantically, economically, socially, and biologically through childbirth, the interests of black couples converged in ways that significantly defined and influenced their lives and decisions.[127] Yet the heavy burden placed on black women greatly taxed them and sometimes deemphasized the role men played in the life of a family.

For black men in particular, this history answers questions about the connection between conceptions of manhood and crime. Through the prism of intimate relationships, we can see men struggling to reconstruct and reclaim a stake in prominent ideas of masculinity via one traditional pathway: patriarchal control over women. Yet, finding mainstream legitimate modes strained or unavailable, and women unwilling to wait indefinitely or be controlled in marriage, informal markets and crimes like theft and robbery became viable options for seizing power and possibly keeping it. With tensions and conflicts created by poverty and joblessness, things only grew worse when men felt slighted or wronged by women who preferred to live on their own and rejected their advances and support. Black women had the same desires and needs for freedom as their male counterparts, and this discrepancy in expectations every so often combusted into intimate abuse or murder.

"I Shot My Wife, and I Have Good Reason for It"

Like many African American men seeking work, Ham Buckley left his native Bessemer, Alabama, in 1898 and traveled north. Only twelve years old at the time, Buckley shined shoes, cut hair, and waited tables in a series of cities stretching from St. Louis to Buffalo before arriving in New York City in 1900.[128] Still in his teenage years, he entered into a series of short-term service positions and met his eventual wife, Irene, while working as an elevator operator in 1910. Married in 1913 the couple struggled with the terms of their relationship after less than a year. At first, Irene "perform[ed] the duties of a wife regularly" and "behaved herself in a good and orderly manner," Buckley later stated. But the trouble began when she "started staying out late at night," coming home intoxicated, and "she wouldn't connect with me in bed."[129] Buckley made many attempts to change his wife's behavior, but she resisted. "I told her it was not right for her to stay out that late, being a married lady"; but in reply "she said she was twenty-one [and] she knew her business."

Irene's refusal to observe common practices of marriage, as Buckley determined them, led him to speculate about her faithfulness and caused their separation. He theorized she may have changed the parameters of their relationship because he had a stretch of unemployment and she "got tired of me hanging around."[130] Weary of his wife's nightly excursions and suspecting infidelity, Buckley left Irene to live with another woman. However, he subsequently faced resistance when campaigning for their reunion. Confronting her once while she worked at the home of her employer, he promised to "treat her better" since it would be "better for us to go back together and have a nice home, as a married couple should do." Unconvinced by his appeals, Irene withheld her decision indefinitely. "She said she would take her own time," he explained "[and] see a good time before she would consent the matter."[131] Troubled by the unending interruption of the normative standards of wedlock and pained by rumors about her life without him, Buckley once again encountered Irene while she worked and shot her to death in 1915. In the aftermath, he surrendered to police on the sidewalk out front, but not before attempting to take his own life, and failing.[132] Once in police custody he confessed to the murder and expressed a chillingly nihilistic outlook for himself. "I ain't particular about no trial at all," he told investigators, "just go on and kill me."[133]

Ham Buckley's attack on his wife signals a conscious linkage between manhood, household maintenance, and violence that some men wrestled with. As such, the domestic realm became a battleground where they struggled to control space when various other urban fields of activity remained uncontrollable by them. Similar to white working-class men, men like Buckley understood wives, daughters, and romantic partners straddled public and private with some frequency by necessity. Yet, for many men, hegemonic modes of masculinity closely relied upon female domestic attachment and required their strict compliance. Threatened by the prospect of losing such control, they might seek to levy regulations meant to avoid conflict and separations in illegal and merciless ways. Yet, ultimately, the very act of overseeing women's behavior might lead to unavoidable showdowns. In extreme cases like that of the Buckleyes', some men lashed out believing a loss of patriarchal jurisdiction would impact their identification as men.

Citing infidelity and abandonment by his wife Lottie, Clarence Willis described their marriage as "plumb purgatory."[134] However, Lottie claimed she left Clarence for egregious failures as a mate. "He swears he will kill me . . . shoot me or poison me . . . [since] I wouldn't live with him because he mistreated me . . . and didn't half support me."[135] Following a number of extramarital affairs by her husband, Lottie left their home in Virginia for New York, and Clarence followed. After months of stalking his wife, he attempted to kill her by firing multiple gunshots through the window of her sister's apartment.[136] Again we see that waning authority jeopardized nascent concepts of manliness based on household upkeep and submissive spouses. When Ham Buckley killed his wife, and Clarence Willis tried to do the same, they attempted to fulfill what they considered manly directives provoked by their wives' sabotage of their marriages and the derangement it caused them.

Buckley's defense in the murder trial rested on this hysteria induced by Irene's rejection of his interpretation of conjugality.[137] On the day of the shooting he became distraught and suicidal when he learned of a party she organized the night before and the possibility she had become romantic with another man. In his testimony he leveraged common racial perceptions of black men as controlled by passion to prove he experienced temporary insanity. He claimed to have lost control of himself and as a result had a hazy memory of the event. He quit his job, traveled to New Jersey to purchase a revolver, and went to "drown my troubles" with whiskey in multiple saloons.[138] "I just felt as though all my brains had gone," [and] "I didn't have no sense," he said.[139] Buckley first planned to take his own life at Irene's workplace and "fall at my wife's feet . . . to let her know that she did me wrong in life"; yet, in the heat of the moment he shot her multiple times in the back. "We had been separated long enough, and my love to her overpowered me. . . . I could not stand it much longer."[140]

Buckley's defense did not draw the sympathy of the court, and a jury found him guilty of murder and sentenced him to death in 1916.[141] Nevertheless, his account illuminates how criminality and notions of manhood intersected with familial governance. Although it was uncommon for black men to kill their partners, Buckley's case contextualizes how some used verbal and physical threats and actual bloodshed to circumscribe the movements of black women and consolidate relationships around their sense of manhood. Trial transcripts and prison documents allow the reconstruction of numerous violent instances when black men similarly connected matrimonial superintendence and their own sense of identity. Thus, they bridged the movements, aspirations, labors, and freedoms of black women, with an imagined blueprint of manhood while simultaneously inhibiting black women's abilities to imagine and actualize their own places in the urban landscape.

The tragic ending of Ham and Irene Buckley's marriage is a culmination of the Gordian knot of politics that sometimes attended black romance when men lost control over women. Ham's grievous attack on his wife contextualizes the violence some black women performed against men when abused, and it illuminates one dark remote region of marital asymmetry. As somewhat of a counterpoint to Ida Snow's part in the killing of her husband, Elton Snow, Buckley's actions were also meant to remove his spouse as a threat to his interpretation of a life worth living. Experiencing "marital role frustration," the Buckleys both responded to perceived inadequacies in their partner, but Ham Buckley's suicide mission is uniquely telling. As shown, women occasionally assaulted or murdered lovers and husbands because of infidelity, and men in turn might abuse or kill partners for similar offenses. However, beyond desires harbored by both men and women for devotion, support, and intimacy, men pursued domestic and sexual authority and reacted with various levels of outrage to transgressions by women for reasons arising from prevailing notions of early twentieth-century patriarchy. Thus, Buckley committed the ultimate patriarchal crime by taking the life of his estranged wife. In one moment of overwhelming despair, he staked his entire existence on preventing her from living her life outside of his purview, having sexual contact with other men, and from enjoying the city without him.

———

Buckley's actions may also be viewed as a horribly tragic response to the crucible black men faced when aspiring to middle-class standards of family life but missing the mark. Frustrated by external threats to their health and live-lihood, and feeling defeated by the inability to manage internal discord, some men could be especially critical of women who spent their time at parties or in saloons, pool halls, restaurants, and other establishments typically viewed as masculine spaces. They similarly worried individualistic thinking by black mothers and wives would prevent the establishment of sustainable domesti-cally centered lives and households and place women in situations danger-ous to their personal well-being and damage their unions.[142] In the responses of men like Buckley we see attempts to secure stable households, which often meant infringing upon the freedoms and safety of black women and a desire to superimpose their own identity on an imagined form of black womanhood. Just as well, we see criminal, and sometimes violent, measures taken to supplement meager salaries, secure romantic relationships, and make ends meet for the same purposes. Certainly, the stories in this chapter were very rare since most black men did not oppress, abuse, or kill women. How-ever, this study looks at those who did in order to understand how the emas-culation, deprivation, and violence of Jim Crow may have informed their choices. Imbedded in these behaviors is a clear association between mascu-linity and the social and economic construction of the black family. Under the weight of various restrictions placed on pathways to the features of early twentieth-century concepts of masculine identity, black men sometimes attempted to utilize and exploit their relationships with women while con-structing their own destinies.

The unfortunate realities of controlling behavior, abuse, and murder rep-resent remarkable instances where the bond between black men and women ended in violence, death, and imprisonment; yet there were many loving re-lationships and strong families that supported men and women through the most difficult times of their lives. Couples often worked together to find resolutions to marital problems, weather the vestiges of life in the North, and rebuild their lives after poor decisions, injury, or incarceration threatened their livelihoods. Despite separations, disruptions, and disputes, the fates of many couples remained intertwined as they sought to improve their chances of creat-ing stable households and remake themselves as men and women. With men frequently unable to consistently provide for families, durability relied upon the ways in which they depended upon each other as they simply survived or worked to reimagine their lives.[143]

Chapter 5

Been Here Long Enough

Prison, Parole, and the Pursuit of a Better Life in Black Imagination

I'm yours Willie, and you're mine. And when I remember that, ain't nothin' else worth remembering.

—Maya Angelou, skit from *The Richard Pryor Show* (1977)

Circumstantial evidence forced me to take a plea to second degree murder . . . a crime that I [am] not guilty of. At least not of murder.

—Auburn prison, Inmate #38886 (1936)

Recently paroled from a three-year sentence in Sing Sing prison for assault in 1909, New York City native Whitey Burke moved to the Hudson Valley town of Brown Station in an attempt to avoid influences that might lead to a parole violation.[1] However, working at a water treatment facility he found himself in a conflict with a coworker during a card game that resulted in bloodshed. In a police statement Burke admitted to engaging in a struggle for a revolver during which the gun discharged twice. Sustaining injuries himself, he survived the skirmish, but the other man died from a gunshot wound to the groin and Burke received a sentence of twenty years to life at Auburn, New York's correctional facility. After serving only fifteen years he once again received parole in 1924, but his newly gained freedom came with similar caveats as before. As a condition of release Burke would report to Rochester, New York, take a job as a busboy, and live under the direction of his sponsor, Reverend William Doran.[2] In addition, his parole required monthly reports to an officer who would monitor his behavior and progress. With these requirements expiring only upon death Burke understood he would never be free from legal supervision.[3] Still, he expressed optimism about his prospects on the outside in interviews with various prison personnel before his discharge. Hoping to make a career as a candy maker and a cook he affixed a newfound sense of self-discipline to the length of his sentence and a desire for freedom.[4] His current conviction, he explained, resulted from an accident caused by "bad company and drink," and he promised to "work and keep away from evil associations" once free.[5] Questioned by the prison chaplain about his confidence in his rehabilitation Burke plainly responded, "I believe I have been here long enough."[6]

The weariness Burke expressed of the physical, psychological, and emotional displacement of incarceration articulates the deep impression imprisonment made on the spirits and bodies of black men in the early twentieth century. It also illustrates how many men swam against the current of demoralization and sought better lives after release. During confinement, inmates underwent cruel treatment from other prisoners and keepers and withstood inhumane conditions that impacted their corporeal and mental health and strangled their prospects for rehabilitation. Indeed, many men died in prison as long internments or death sentences condemned them for life, but for others shorter sentences and the possibility of parole allowed them to envision life after captivity. No matter the length of their sentence, time away disrupted family connections, ruptured marriages and relationships, and compromised control over one's life. The lack of reformation in prison made release complex. Once paroled, men like Burke pursued economic stability and sought to rejoin their families and start life anew, but they frequently found the very same issues that originally led them to crime magnified by their conviction record. Burke's comments indicate his awareness of a critical aspect of absolution—namely the difficulty of finding pathways to self-reliance and economic freedom without illegality, all while navigating the strictures and surveillance of parole obligations and the limitations of low paid and unstable labor. For Burke these factors combined with unease about his potential to be swept back into illegitimate circumstances by his environment, or the company he kept, and as he left prison he planned to avoid that possible fate. After release he supported himself and kept up the requirements of his parole for some time. However, his efforts to improve his life ended abruptly when he died of unclear causes in the winter of 1929, less than four years after his release.[7]

Burke's experiences shed light on a well-traveled route to imprisonment for many black men and prompt questions about their prospects of remaining free. Unlike more affluent New Yorkers, most African American offenders could not afford adequate legal representation or put together enough money to pay bail, which left them incarcerated at least until trial.[8] Although New York State prisons like the one in Auburn housed men of all ethnicities, black men suffered disproportionately from discriminatory arrests and trials, wrongful accusations, and long prison sentences. Bad living conditions, health hazards, harsh punishments, and violence combined with separation from families, loved ones, and children made prison especially taxing for those men already hobbled by racial discrimination and bias outside of prison. Saddled with prejudicial policing, unsympathetic judges and juries, and poor

Whitey Burke (pseud.), an inmate at Auburn prison, 1909. Courtesy of New York State Archives and Records Administration, Albany, New York (Inmate #32941, Series B0082).

legal representation, men like Burke had little refuge once ensnared in legal processes. They sometimes endured protracted internments for convictions built on insubstantial evidence or uncertain eyewitness accounts, and they suffered parole violations that sent them back to prison for slight infractions. Whether they cooperated with prosecutors or not, time away created crippling setbacks.[9] This study of imprisonment aims to understand the lived experiences of black convicts as well as interrogate the hazards and meanings of deliverance for those who ever saw daylight. For many, prison walls compelled introspection, fostered education, and granted time and space to reimagine one's life in freedom, and many men left with a new perspective about how they wished to live their lives. Although Burke's time free was short, his efforts to remain so and reformulate his life under the tremendous weight of state supervision represent the fortitude with which many other men did the same.

This study additionally brings into view the impact of imprisonment on families and intimate partners. Short or long sentences removed primary breadwinners, fathers, husbands, and sons from households that needed their support, input, and presence. Family composition and survivability hinged upon discharge dates and postincarceration recoveries that were uncertain at best. The imprisonment of women who were just as instrumental to the economic survival of a household as men further complicated the narrative. Black men typically remonstrated women for legal and illegal transgressions they thought undermined patriarchal power and sometimes responded to the roles of reformatory leadership, keepers, and parole personnel as threatening to the formation of their domestic governance. When women entered the carceral state, men aggressively lobbied for their release, visited and wrote regularly, and prepared for their return in ways that required their own personal transformation and expressed complex notions of respectability and manhood. By observing how black men reacted to the incarceration of the women in their lives we can more fully understand their efforts to reform themselves and how they sometimes viewed their own rehabilitation as dependent upon the reformation, or control, of women. Through this phenomenon we can further discern the interdependence, mutuality, and reciprocal exchange that characterized the efforts of both men and women to improve their lives when they experienced the displacement of a jail term and parole. Binding their fates with significant others, men and women endeavored to pull themselves out of poverty, remain on the right side of the law, reconfirm their gendered identities, and find their version of happiness and betterment together.

The conditions Burke faced across the years of multiple imprisonments and his eventual parole resulted from a series of changes to the prison system around the turn of the century. In much of the nineteenth century, New York's penitentiaries primarily adhered to the Auburn model of imprisonment, a system first used in the facility built in 1817 in Auburn, New York. The Auburn system sought to humble and humiliate the prisoner and "produce a mental state of submission" in order to begin the process of reform. Other prisons, such as Sing Sing, took the model to its extreme conclusion with rigid punitive measures and prohibitive regimentation.[10] Because of the "brutal and inhuman treatment" inherent in the system of contracting prison labor at Sing Sing, one article in the inmate-published *New York Star* alleged, some prisoners died or took their own lives.[11] Like most American prisons, New York's penitentiaries rented the labor of convicts to private companies in the last decades of the century. As a result, life and labor rhythms in prisons conformed to the priorities of contractors who designed rules to increase production, control daily activities, and proscribe harsh punishments. Inmate strikes and rebellions of the 1870s, free labor strikes against prison labor, public testimonials about prison life, and progressive reform efforts brought down contract labor. In 1894, New York State ratified the McDonough Amendment to the constitution removing the influence of market forces from penal institutions and enacting reforms to make prisons conducive to prisoner reformation. However, the amendment allowed the "state-use" system of labor, which had internees produce goods that would be used by other state institutions, thereby merely a continuation of forced prison labor.[12] By 1900, a national reform movement sought repeal of the Auburn philosophy, at least in administration if not always in form, and prisons took on more reformatory roles.

In the name of reform, admission to prisons like Auburn, Sing Sing, and Clinton came with a bombardment of tests meant to classify inmates by health, intelligence, body type, and morality, but they were full of racist assumptions. By way of illustration, intake agents evaluated prisoners using the French developed Binet-Simon intelligence test, which was later revised for American standards by Lewis Terman, a Stanford University psychology professor. When applied to African American men and women, the Terman test often gave results that jived with popular opinions of black convicts.[13] Agents regularly determined black men to be mentally impaired, like Derry Peters, who they considered "deficient" and classified as a "moron," and John Gray, who they pegged as "retarded" and "lazy," and both were ascribed mental ages generally below ten years old.[14] Nearly solid low scores for black prisoners collared them for training in "lower grade" trades while inside and impacted their chances of parole once considered.[15] Regardless of whether or not such designations also sometimes fell upon white prisoners, these tests reinforced racial bias and preordained the fates of black inmates.

Ultimately, this study interprets New York's reformatories, prisons, and parole programs as crucibles that mimicked the impact of enslavement on African American men and their families, in some ways.[16] Legal detention literally placed them back into bondage and used their bodies for the state's benefit, while it simultaneously sought to manage their souls for the proper maintenance of the facility. Although jail time uprooted the lives of all incarcerated people and those they cared for, black men entangled in a mesh of scrutiny, restriction, and repercussions on the outside may have seen legal confinement as an eventuality; the likely product of a tentatively designed freedom under Jim Crow. Incarceration existed not only as a possible outcome of the commitment of crimes or criminalized actions but also as a gauntlet that hampered progress for the inmate and interfered with the construction of sustainable lives and households. Black men in prison bore the brunt of the brutality doled out by racially biased prison guards. Captivity stripped them of all they tried to accomplish on the outside and subjected their bodies to labor they could not control, violence they could not prevent, and conditions that mirrored the cruelty and harsh conditions of servitude. Whether guilty of a crime or not, being in the custody of the state plunged them into the belly of a beast that meant to consume them whole, and submerged them in a system that sought to colonize them, mind and body. For those fortunate enough to emerge intact, parole extended that state of sub-jugation into a conditional half freedom. Parolees, like Whitey Burke, often tip-toed through a series of traps set by parole boards and supervisors, un-derstanding that slight infractions might return them to the clutches of a pe-nal institution.

As earlier chapters have shown, many African American men really did commit acts of violence and crime. However, viewing their actions in the con-text of the crucibles of public and commercial space, racial violence, and factors that impeded their progress in legitimate avenues of monetary acqui-sition and the construction of identity allows an appraisal of the impact of the early twentieth-century carceral state on black lives and bodies. Accord-ingly, time in the clink formed one trenchant aspect of the crucible of black criminality. Some incarcerated men leveraged education and vocational skills acquired inside in their determination to remain free. Others found them-selves immersed in a criminogenic environment that exposed them to ag-gression and psychologically subverted their ability to function in the outside world within the boundaries of the law. Among these were men who remained in prison for life never to reunite with families or exercise positive redemp-tive qualities nurtured while away. Others died in prison from untimely ill-ness, brutality, or the slow ritual of capital punishment through execution. And still others failed at attempts to remake themselves, regain what they had lost, and consolidate scattered families and economies when granted parole. Nevertheless, prison can also be viewed as a material site where black men sometimes reimagined their lives in freedom in significant ways.

"A Murder Design on My Life"

Arrest and imprisonment statistics at the turn of the century show sharp in-equalities in the proportions of white and black inmates, and this data shaped contemporary conversations about crime. Joined by many other scholars, Frederick Hoffman, in his 1896 *Race Traits* publication, argued black crime and imprisonment statistics proved blacks had no chance of survival in modern times and that criminality among them would only get worse. But other scholars with an eye toward the evaluation of urban life used those same stats to illuminate inequality not only in the judicial system but in American society.[17] In 1880, there were 77 black prisoners for every 10,000 black New York State residents, a number that jumped by nearly 30 percent to 100 for every 10,000 by 1890. In the same period the ratio of white prisoners to the same proportion of that population only rose 12 percent, from sixteen to eighteen. Aware of these statistics, commentators en-gaged sympathetically in solving the criminal aspect of the "negro problem" by acknowledging crime in black communities and recognizing its root causes.[18] Speaking at the 1909 Hampton Negro Conference, Howard University professor Kelly Miller asserted high crime rates did not indicate "any race trait or defect," but suggested problems that could be ameliorated.[19] Biased viewers might utilize disproportionate conviction figures, but they could not substantiate claims black legal transgressions constituted a "new social plague," since crime was more likely in the lower stratum of all societies.[20] As Miller noted, offenses empirically rose among African Americans as they migrated to urban centers, but he realized the complexity involved in that increase. In some black neighborhoods crime did exceed overall regional rates, and the residents of those communities suffered most from robbery, theft, assault, and other types of violence. Imprisonment numbers did not always accurately reflect actual crime but instead indicated vast problems of discrimination and bias in the judicial system, reflected racial isolation in the public realm, and inequality in the way law enforcers patrolled the streets.[21] "He is handicapped," by a "laborious road his case must travel before it reaches the sentence," wrote Swedish sociologist Thorsten Sellin of African American men, "and this handicap shows in his high rate of conviction."[22]

Once arrested many men went to the city prison in Lower Manhattan commonly referred to as the tombs because of its replicated Egyptian architecture and dank, claustrophobic innards.[23] Entombed in the imposing structure, black defendants met a variety of disadvantages tailored to their intersectionality as prosecutors, juries, and judges convicted and sentenced them with circumstantial evidence. For the recent black migrant, the courts in New York seemed comparatively lenient, reformer Mary White Ovington argued in a 1911 publication, but once before the magistrates "he learns to know that judges differ greatly in their conceptions of justice."[24] Conjecture, duress, and shaky facts often brought about quick convictions of black suspects, and duplicitous plea deals conjured confessions out of innocent and guilty alike. The series of events that led to Floyd Martin's ten-year prison sentence for robbery in 1913 typifies the ordeal awaiting many black men once arrested. In a letter from Auburn prison Martin requested a revision of his sentence from the judge in his case, since his five white accomplices had been acquitted. "It would seem . . . that an unwarranted discrimination was made against me on account of my color," he penned. To make matters worse, he claimed the district attorney told him to plead guilty or "he would see that I got a life sentence." Only two years into his punishment at the time, Martin lamented missing the chance to assert his innocence. "Being without funds or friends to aid me in securing proper counsel I was practically compelled to submit" to the accusations, he concluded.[25] Black Tenderloin resident John Walker learned this lesson when jailed for theft in 1891. Walker did not possess the stolen item when apprehended, but he received a lengthy prison sentence. After more than two years at Sing Sing prison he applied for clemency with an impassioned letter to the governor explaining his innocence. Recalling his arrest, he recounted how his accuser was "under the influence of intoxicating drink" and failed to identify him but told police "it looks like him. It was a colored man anyhow." "Without any means at all," Walker lacked sufficient legal representation and could not appeal his case in court. "Unless you take some action . . . I may be compelled to endure an unjust punishment," he pleaded.[26] Seemingly lost in the metaphorical tombs of New York's detention facilities, both Martin and Walker identified the distinct disadvantage of black men. Race made the streets of New York treacherous for them and it likewise made them uncommon targets in legal proceedings. Martin admitted to the crime of robbery that put him in prison, but his charges of discrimination never received consideration. In contrast, Walker eventually received clemency, but his appeal for release divulges the reality of likely innocent men who never received such regard and underscores the fragility of black freedom.

The city's judicial system also doled out steep fines that added economic setbacks to the list of obstacles incarcerated men had to overcome. The inability to pay cash penalties might confine arrestees to jail long after their sentences ended and affect the budgets of ailing families already clamped under the oppressive weight of the city's expenses.[27] Jailed for assault in 1912, James Pope challenged an eleven-month sentence and a $500 fine in a carefully worded letter to the court that convicted him. Considering some circumstances revealed in his letter, he believed the "punishment was too excess" and that the fine would impact his ability to "become an honest citizen" after release. "All I ask is a chance to start life anew," Pope appealed, "minus the economic strain."[28] Another man, Jasper Gross, wrote a similar message to another judge asking for a revision of his fine. His sentence had changed him for the better, he explained, and he had "decided to live a law abiding citizen the rest of my life." If shown mercy on his fine he promised to "leave New York at once and go to my home and parents in Wilmington, North Carolina, and remain there."[29] Thus, the judicial space of a courtroom reinforced the limitations of public space by merging confinement and legal penalties with police persecution. A probation officer roundly rejected Pope's appeals, affirming the "'nigger' is in the right place and ought to remain there."[30] Gross received a similar judgment and denial from the board of appeals. "[He] is a loafer and does not deserve much consideration," they wrote. "A couple of years in prison might teach him to work."[31] In a city with cultural, structural, and economic imperatives to control black lives and activities, it was clear the consequences of mobility could be unjust incarceration, and once in state control, extortionate fines had the capacity to cinch one's future prospects.

Critical of nineteenth-century prison customs, reformers on the New York State Prison Commission and others like Mary White Ovington and Theodore Roosevelt pursued a "new penology" that would make incarceration more therapeutic and rehabilitative; one that might "normalize" inmates.[32] For women, normalization meant making them more fit for domestic roles in work or housekeeping, and for men the goal was to spark an industrious spirit that could be carried into wage labor once freed. With male convicts making up the largest portion of internments by far, prison reformers emphasized fixing men. Only "human rights, the right to sunshine, to ordinary decencies, [and] to labor" would improve the lives of men on the edge, reformer Florence Maybrick declared at a mass meeting on the subject in 1906.[33] Addressing a church forum as late as 1920, firebrand B. Ogden Chisolm likewise argued current prisons "corrupt rather than improve men," since most jails were built to simply house criminals. True reform would only happen if dignity and greater freedom were part of the process, he concluded.[34] The theory of reformatories maintained that, if inmates would one day be free, incarceration should transform them in preparation for that day.[35] To those ends, the new system allowed organized sports, agricultural activities, and academic and industrial training and discipline with grades and evaluations throughout internment.[36] With the institution of the first indeterminate sentences in 1877, New York instilled its hopes of reforming prisoners in keeping them behind bars until parole officials determined they had transformed. Through work, education, and good behavior, inmates earned credits that eventually made them eligible for release.[37] Prison and parole personnel employed "good time" laws, which reduced sentences for good behavior and implemented indeterminate sentences, parole, and probation strategically, in order to classify convicts in particular grades of offenders, and accurately, if not scientifically, determine when reformation happened.[38] Nevertheless, the void created by the abolition of contract labor left questions about the structure of prison life unanswered, and some of the unhealthy and punitive vestiges of the old system persisted. Upon Whitey Burke's conviction in 1909, prison reformers were in the process of installing modern lighting systems, reshaping labor practices, and improving living conditions, but progress was glacial and administrators and keepers dragged their feet in implementing changes.[39]

In spite of widespread efforts at reform, prisoners suffered health problems caused by the environment. With the ending of the contract system, life expectancy and quality plummeted as prisoners spent far more time confined to cells than previously.[40] Many men arrived with various health issues, but constant enclosure in unclean cells with poor air quality and vermin infestations worsened existing ailments.[41] In his 1926 study of penology, sociologist

John Lewis Gillin criticized the structure of New York's prisons for making health problems inevitable. Likening the living spaces in Auburn prison to "caves," Gillin argued "the central cell block does not permit . . . sunlight," which suffocates prisoners with poor ventilation. To make matters worse, the "floor rests upon the ground, making it damp and cold," and the stone surfaces held moisture encouraging health complications such as rheumatism and tuberculosis. Furthermore, unsanitary conditions and the closeness of prisoners made the transference of disease and illness likely, and deficient health care worsened matters.[42]

In a series of letters to the warden at Clinton Correctional Facility, black inmate Montgomery Redding complained of slow or nonexistent responses to health issues and demanded medical attention. In one note he requested "consent" from the warden "to have the Dentist replace several teeth," because "my teeth became decayed during my long sojourn in prison."[43] In another letter he more explicitly criticized the prison's medical facilities and detailed the lack of care that had deteriorated his health. Redding first mentioned the doctor's failure to follow up after the delay of one medical procedure for a serious reproductive ailment related to blood complications. Promised medicine and a new surgery date he claimed he was discharged from the hospital and left without further medical care. "I suffer also from diabetes. . . . I have had no treatment for that either," he confirmed. Redding then concluded his letter with a rhetorical question meant to trigger the empathy of the warden. "I ask you pointedly if such indifferent treatment is in accordance to law and the spirit of this institution[?]"[44] With very few formalities about health standards and medical treatment, men like Redding often felt vulnerable to the whims of prison officials and physicians but challenged them to uphold humane standards. Left with no other options than to rely upon penitentiary health care, they succumbed to illness at alarming rates.

A damp, dusty, and unsanitary environment and the lack of cleaning protocols especially affected inmates with previous health problems. Upon arrival at Auburn, Whitey Burke suffered from chronic rheumatism, skin eruptions, enlarged tonsils, and deafness in one ear. During his sentence he experienced numerous hospital admissions for influenza and one prolonged visit for tonsillitis.[45] Earl Thatcher bore even more dramatic respiratory difficulties at Auburn. Before his admission, Thatcher had pneumonia, pleurisy, gonorrhea, and swollen thyroid glands. Over the next few years he suffered serious scarring of the lungs, chest pains, and asthmatic breathing irregularities likely due to the lack of ventilation and cleanliness, and inefficient care for previous health issues. He also complained of persistent tuberculosis-like coughing that produced "thick mucoid sputum with occasional lumps . . . discolored with blood." Thatcher seemed to recover after a nearly month-long visit to the prison hospital, but his experience typifies that of many of his fellow inmates.[46] Auburn prison death registers indicate that out of the forty-five black male prisoners that passed away in the 1890s, 66 percent died of complications relating to tuberculosis. The overall number of deaths of black men declined over the next decade by 44 percent, but the rates of tuberculosis cases increased slightly to 68 percent. Those who did not die of lung ailments might succumb to other illnesses aggravated by the environment. In the thirty-year stretch recorded in the register, at least eight black men died because of advanced syphilitic infections and others met their fate from kidney, heart, and brain troubles, and infectious diseases like meningitis, typhoid, and malaria.[47] Confined in cells and at the mercy of prison staff, men received treatment that was inadequate to mitigate the effects of the environment.

Progressive prison reform also failed to rid state institutions of coercive torture and brutal treatment, and some black men complained of being racially targeted, beaten into submission, and generally abused by white guardsmen.[48] Compounding his existing health issues, Montgomery Redding disclosed years of torment and indignities suffered at the hands of one white officer in a psychiatric interview. "That Sergeant . . . has been hounding me since 1926. He beat me up and tells guys to beat me up," he explained. According to Redding the officer expressed his resentment for him because he "cut a white man" in a past fight, and the officer told him "somebody ought to kill you" for that. He had also been attacked by other prisoners egged on by the sergeant, one right "in front of the keepers" and "nothing was done to him but I was put in the cooler," Redding complained. After various incidents and harsh punishments for defending himself, Redding concluded his life was in danger. "That man has beyond a doubt a murder design on my life and I'm left to his hands." The fact that prison psychiatrists classified him as an "emotionally unstable psychopath" with "delusions of persecution" indicates how frivolously prison officials took reports of mistreatment. Whether real or imagined, Redding's accusations against the officer make clear the distress black inmates sustained and the racial tensions that characterized it. With several aspects of his mental and physical health on the line, Redding felt circumscribed by not only the walls of the prison but also the racial biases of the keepers.[49] The space of the prison could then resemble the crucible of public space as white violence might be protected and sanctioned by the very structure of the facility.

Even in the face of severe disciplinary actions and violence, men racked up unfavorable conduct records while trying to ease the misery of imprisonment. In the rebellious behaviors of black male inmates, we can see the merging of their imaginations with the possibilities for self-determination in

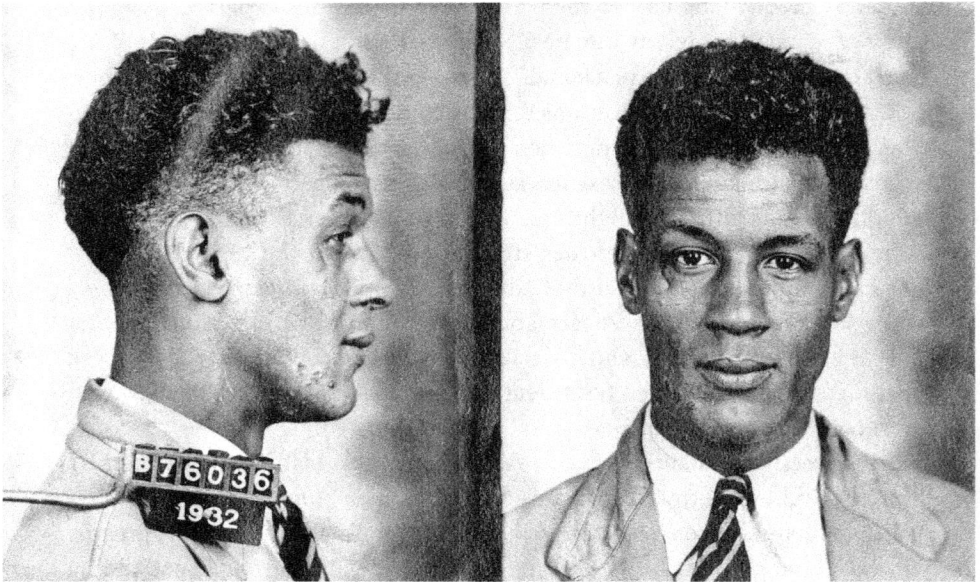

Jesse Sullivan (pseud.), at the time an inmate at Sing Sing prison, 1932. Courtesy of New York State Archives and Records Administration, Albany, New York (Inmate #18208, Series 14610).

ways that copied the tactics they used in the outside world. We also see them struggling to protect their bodies against seemingly insurmountable forces, sometimes in violent ways. Many prisoners who refused to be completely paralyzed by detention seized labor requirements to gain access to freedoms that varied their day-to-day lives and gave them a measure of agency. In less than two years Cornelius Bradley had assignments including removing human waste, working in the clothing shop, and assisting in the invalid quarantine. The principal keeper considered him fairly industrious, but he had multiple violations for fighting and "leaving work ahead of time and insolence," for which he lost time served on his sentence.[50] Jesse Sullivan likewise took the latitude that came with various types of labor as opportunities to enjoy a number of freedoms.[51] In addition to working as a weaver, a barber, and a laborer in a number of shops, Sullivan fixed furniture used by the guards and cleaned the cage of one officer's pet parrot, a task which sent him to the hospital when he was bitten on the hand.[52] All of these positions gave him access to parts of the facility restricted for most inmates. Officers consistently complained of liberties Sullivan took while working including "neglecting his loom," "stalling [and] holding up the job," leaving without permission, and "running around the shop and failing to do his work."[53] Montgomery Redding similarly received discipline for concocting "home-brew," "carrying a knife," multiple stabbings, "hitting another inmate with a hammer," assaulting guards, and refusing to work."[54] These and countless other conduct records show how black men attempted to negotiate the status of their relationships with prison officials. Most infractions were efforts to ease the burden of compulsory chores, deal with disputes with other inmates, or increase mobility. Misbehavior, in some ways, replicated illegal behavior outside of prison. If the crucible of legal and progressive supervision and public racial violence in freedom fostered extralegal responses, the maddening intensification of oversight and immobility in incarceration engendered waywardness and rebellion, as well.[55]

Ultimately, the physical space of prisons like Sing Sing, Auburn, and Clinton placed black men already beset by dilemmas associated with race on the outside into the depths of state control. As felons, lengthy sentences obliged them to make choices about how to maneuver through the hazards and brutalities of government custody. Unlike in the public world, one could not relocate or control one's own spaces of leisure in the carceral state. Prison completely removed them from the possibilities of nurturing patriarchal marriages and households, and it literally supervised and recorded their movements in ways impossible on the outside. The very same aspects of life in freedom that men used their criminal or criminalized behavior to counter hardened into a government-controlled materialization of white supremacy in correctional facilities. Although inadequate to change their plight, resistance symbolized an ongoing struggle that transcended prison walls. Brawls, arguments, theft, and violations of facility rules might allow them to win the battle for a moment, but they would surely lose the war. Trapped between attempting to conform to the regimentation and degradation of their time inside, and a human desire to save one's own spirit and body from complete annihilation, they might form a split personality; one that commandeered advantages by exploiting holes in a literal and figurative wall of restraint, and another that understood acquiescence to be the only chance of salvation and redemption. Hence, behaviors meant to establish, sustain, or defend manhood on the streets of New York City had far less impact in bondage, and the fact of containment had deleterious implications for personal sovereignty and manliness. Men like Bradley, Sullivan, and Redding might experience emotional anguish that was hard to contain when fully realizing their predicament and lash out momentarily. Nevertheless, seeking the approval of parole personnel and release from indeterminate sentences, black inmates frequently humbled themselves, tried to learn work skills for better days, and longed to reunite with families in ways that might bring about personal transformation.

"He Is the Only Support I Has"

The pains of separation from loved ones rivaled the misery of imprisonment itself. Marriages and relationships fell apart, children grew up without fathers, and bonds fractured as family members and lovers strayed emotionally and physically, or sometimes passed away. Married in 1919 in Portsmouth, Virginia, Eugene Crowder and Mabel Jackson bore two children, and Crowder struggled to find employment that did not require him to leave his family. For the first year of their marriage he worked for a contractor in Jacksonville, Florida, but left because of illness in 1920. After a short stint in Virginia he relocated again in 1921, this time joining other members of his family in Haverstraw, New York, a town overlooking the Hudson River less than thirty miles north of Manhattan.[56] Living with his parents in Haverstraw, Crowder labored for a brickyard earning $6 per day as a wheeler, but his stability would not last long. In January 1922 he received a twenty-year sentence to Sing Sing prison for his involvement in a murder with another man Roderick Jenkins.[57] Jenkins had already received a life sentence for his confession to the killing, yet prosecutors believed him to be "under the domination of [Crowder]" when he shot a coworker during a robbery.[58] While serving his sentence, Crowder undoubtedly suffered emotionally when he lost contact with his wife and children in 1927.[59] Discharged in 1936 without knowledge of their whereabouts, Crowder returned to Haverstraw where he once again took a position at a local brickyard and likely struggled to reconnect with his family over the next few years.[60] With their last correspondence mailed from a Brooklyn residence they no longer occupied, he had no means of locating his wife and children but vowed to reconcile with Mabel "if I can find her," he told parole personnel.[61]

One can possibly imagine the yawning void in Crowder's life when finding himself unable to recover his family once returned to society, and how it might have impacted his emotional state and ability to recuperate. Yet, his story is not uncommon.[62] It was not difficult for men to lose connection with loved ones because of the vagaries of prison administration or simply because of the difficulties spouses and children faced without them. In some cases, rules and regulations of the prison prevented the sort of contact inmates and family members desired and relied upon. The gulf between men and their families created by prison walls could leave men distressed about their inability to act. "I have Suffered unspeakable missrey [sic] and am yet Suffering the Same," William Simon wrote a Brooklyn judge in 1913. "My Daughter was to See me today [and said] that her mother could not be left alone" and had recently fainted from illness.[63] Jesse Sullivan lost all contact with his common-law wife through correspondence and visitation restrictions at

Great Meadow's prison. Hoping to reconnect, he requested the right to receive letters and visitors once again. "I desire a chance to correspond with my common-law wife . . . please sir place her name on the visitors [and] corresponding list," he pleaded in a note. Sullivan also issued his request in terms of his right to receive assistance from family members in appealing his criminal case. "It's most important because I am working on my case [and] I have no one els [*sic*] to help me but her."[64] With that request denied, Sullivan later applied for a transfer to another prison, presumably to circumvent the rules of his current institution, but was similarly turned down.[65] The inherent family separation of trips upstate and the difficulty of maintaining bonds from such distances made doing time even harder and involuntarily reformulated some men's expectations for release. Care, support, and housing from loved ones could be pivotal not only for survival in and after prison but also for remaining out of the clutches of the state once free.

The sudden disappearance of men from their families also heavily impacted the women, children, and various other family members who loved them and depended upon their presence and income. Already dire economic situations became significantly worse when the financial contributions of men evaporated, and losing a family member could be particularly jarring for black families often operating under various other strains. Sentenced to more than two years in Sing Sing for transporting stolen property in 1903, Lyndon Freeman contextualized his appeal for clemency in terms of his family's need for his income. Pleading his case, Freeman's various dependents framed their request by revealing the impacts of his incarceration on their well-being and financial security. "I am an old woman and he is the only support I has [*sic*]," Freeman's mother wrote in one letter. "With no money and nothing for my children I can not last long."[66] Lloyd and Mamie Freeman, his young children, also penned multiple notes pressing the governor to release their father so he might fulfill their urgent needs. "Will you please to let my sister see my father before she die [*sic*] . . . [She] is sick and we have nobody to support us," Lloyd wrote. "If you let him free it will never happen again," he later promised.[67] Mamie's letters likewise drew upon the governor's compassion with descriptions of the various difficulties associated with her father's absence. "I have been alful [*sic*] sick . . . will you not spare time to help one little girl [?]," her letter supplicated. "I want to see my poor papa . . . I know he will never be bad anymore."[68] It is unclear whether or not Freeman ever received clemency, but his family's petitions for his discharge likely represent the sentiments of countless other black families. In the process of making their lives in the North, imprisonment changed the course of life for men like Freeman and stalled bids to support their dependents and take care of themselves.

As Freeman's example illustrates, family members generally stood by men when they went to prison by writing letters, visiting, and making efforts to bridge the gap between themselves and their loved one. Such efforts were not only important for the inmate, but also for heartbroken relatives. The exchange of loving missives could be an attempt to make internment less difficult for everyone. Adelaide Bradshaw reassured her son everyone at home anxiously awaited his return from Auburn prison in one letter in 1923. "It won't be long now but we are longing for the time for you to come home," she wrote. She also comforted him about the security of the family business while he was away letting him know they had recently "sold 2 tons of coal" and "cleared [$9] besides paying for the coal." Putting her own money together with that gathered from various family members, Bradshaw enclosed $4 in the letter in hopes he would find some use for it. "Dear son buy yourself some fruit and some smokes," she mothered.[69] In the same way, writing to her forty-five-year-old son during his second time in prison, Edmund Walsh's mother had endearing and encouraging words. Alluding to his possible parole she urged "if you come, come straight and fetch nothing but good in your heart and your head . . . maybe if you come home and do what is right you can get some work." Walsh's extended family collectively wished him well including his "Aunt Alice" who "says she hopes you will be a much better man than when you went away."[70] With returning home always on the mind of the inmate, strong familial bonds played an important role in surviving incarceration and receiving discharge. For those lucky enough to expect parole, family members kept them abreast of important happenings, supplied them with goods and food not available in prison, and gave them hope for their prospects in freedom. Lacking these bonds, and often times with them, some parolees floundered and found themselves on the wrong side of the law once again.

"Working Hard and Doing the Very Best That I Can"

Convicts generally hoped for renewed life after prison but the aggregate of unhealthy conditions, harsh punishments, dislocation while away, and old habits produced mixed results. Instead of preparing inmates for productive lives outside of prison, "the prison system thwarts him," John Gillin argued in his treatise on penology. If prisons and courts expected inmates to "learn by habit to live a proper social life" guided only by "fear and punishment," Gillin supposed incarceration was very unlikely to leave a positive mark. "How can we be surprised if large numbers of these men . . . find it impossible to [live] with the demands of a free society," he wrote. High rates of recidivism and parole violations resulted from the prison's inability to reform inmates and the cruelty that often characterized conditions. Surveys from 1917 indicate 60 percent of New York State's inmates held prior convictions, a number that climbed precipitously for African American men.[71] A sample of black prisoners in Auburn's men's prison between 1922 and 1930 alone reveals more than 91 percent had previous internments, and many had long arrest records that stretched across state lines.[72] As a result, life on parole was not exactly the release parolees hoped for, but instead it represented a liminal state of suspension that postponed redemption indefinitely.

The prevalence of indeterminate sentences in early twentieth-century New York made parole an essential aspect of freedom for most prisoners. Without definite discharge dates convicts regularly left on the discretion of prison officials and parole boards in consideration of good behavior and recommendations by wardens, chaplains, and "reputable" acquaintances. In addition, parole depended upon the willingness of relatives, businessowners, or sponsoring organizations to house, support, and provide work for the parolee while keeping track of their behavior and disclosing transgressions. Reformatories and prisons both used provisional emancipation, not only as an incentive for good behavior while incarcerated but conversely as a tether meant to ensure continued respectable conduct. Eventual discharge from parole relied upon consistent legitimate occupation, various forms of social hygiene, curfews, documentation of earnings and spending habits, and regular reports on the nature of the parolee's daily life.[73] Parole thus officially functioned as a probationary freedom monitored by prison officials but with the distinct purpose of verifying rehabilitation every step of the way.[74]

Parole could be demanding for all men saddled with its list of requirements, but for black men experiencing the hallmarks of Jim Crow, it was a decidedly unsympathetic crucible. It placed the freed convict in invisible chains until the end of their sentence or the approval of their parole officer. The program also represented a global sense of surveillance in the life of the formerly incarcerated since friends, family, or even strangers could imperil a parolee's record with as little as a phone call or letter to the parole board.[75] No matter their race or gender, for all convicts, parole was a conditional commutation that represented confidence in their reformation but also continuously questioned it. The gradual release program allowed inmates to leave prison, often long before serving their maximum sentences. It also created a medial sense of freedom that came with constant scrutiny, monthly progress reports, and work requirements that were difficult to maintain even without a criminal record. Most important, the parole program extended the superintendence of prison officials to the outside world allowing detailed observation of the actions and aspirations of parolees and dangling the constant threat of apprehension and internment. For some men, it proved to be the reprieve they hoped for and they took advantage of support from family members and significant others, jobs offered by parole sponsors and former employers, and skills learned in prison to remake their lives. However, menaced by the possibility of recidivating, a significant portion of parolees floundered after release, struggled to keep employment, and found themselves returned to prison. Whichever category they inhabited, black men sought ways to lessen the impact of surveillance on their lives while on parole, negotiated the nature of their own freedom, and directly confronted the authority of officers, sponsors, and family members. Like their female counterparts, they also experienced racial discrimination and constricted options as felons, and sometimes turned to illicit markets to make ends meet or committed new crimes similar to their original offenses.

To be certain, attempts at rehabilitation began inside of the prison walls.[76] Upon arrival psychiatrists classified new inmates according to observed irregularities in personality makeup and mental fitness in order to begin the process of reforming them for eventual parole.[77] One classification clinic form from Sing Sing prison designated Jesse Sullivan as possessing "borderline intelligence" with limited "general knowledge." Considering him a negligent father of an illegitimate child and "highly emotional and hypersexed," the prison medical officer questioned his fitness for release.[78] After an initial examination, psychiatrists then consulted other experts to corroborate or refute their findings. In addition, educational instructors, industrial supervisors, and chaplains contributed information on academic abilities, work skills, and morality. Parole officers then gathered information on the inmate's previous criminal record, studied his community through interviews and visits, and triaged all biographical, psychological, and physiological information for the purpose of outlining a plan for training, education, and reformatory measures to be taken during internment.[79]

In addition to providing positive evaluations of inmates, personal and professional recommenders and sponsors formed essential aspects of successful parole dockets. However, in trying to help the parolee get on their feet they might become emissaries of the legal system after men received their walking papers. Sponsoring organizations expressed interest in particular prisoners and vowed to help them find work, better themselves, and carry through with their commitments. Graham Glover received acclamatory words recommending his temperament in a letter submitted by Baptist pastor and politician Adam Clayton Powell in 1920. Powell considered the prospective parolee a "straight forward and up-right young man" with a "good reputation" and offered to extend his help if Glover received parole. "Should he be pardoned," Powell wrote, "I will do everything in my power as a minister to assist him in his determination to be a useful citizen."[80] A representative of the Volunteer Prison League expressed "great satisfaction" upon hearing of Glover's possible parole. "My interest in connection with him is largely from the fact that the Wardens, Chaplains and other[s] . . . [have] spoken so well of this man that I feel from their judgement that he is one who will make good."[81] These organizations entered into an agreement with parole officers to surveil parolees and reveal infractions, and men reported directly to them. Once free, a number of edicts governed ex-convicts' movements, social lives, work, and leisure. Through benefactors they found work and housing, but immediately after arrival they were to establish contact with the superintendent of state prisons by mailing the first of many monthly reports, all of which would be signed by their sponsor. Parole prohibited consumption of alcohol and banned spending time in saloons, dance halls, cabarets, and any other "disreputable resorts" that sold liquor. It likewise required avoidance of "evil associations" and that they "respect and cheerfully obey the laws." Considering virtuous employment and industry a preeminent feature of reformation and reliability, parole also obliged men not to change employers or residences unless approved by the board and to remain in the state until the end of the parole period.[82] As a result, recent parolees encountered a mixture of scrutiny and care that might offer opportunities with one hand and foreshadow condemnation with the other.

Family members offered the support they could muster, but penury and tumbledown housing could render their assistance questionable to parole personnel and thrust parolees into substandard circumstances. The poverty many blacks experienced and the poor state of most housing available to them is reflected in the surveys of potential housing for parolees. Some parole investigators communicated concern about the well-being and rehabilitation of the recently released as well as their own biases about the living conditions they believed acceptable to African Americans. Upon visiting the home of John Gray's sister, Emma Wilkins, parole investigators found "rooms poorly furnished" and "very untidily kept" in a "dilapidated two-family frame house." Various residents occupied the eight-room apartment including Wilkins's mother-in-law, her husband, and their four children, an "unemployed musician . . . two married sisters [of Mr. Wilkins] and their respective husbands and three infant children." Commenting on the health of the environment the inspector made assertions about the living expectations of Wilkins's family and their perceived indifference to the surroundings. "The family has evidently never lived in better circumstances . . . they are quite complacent about their present economic condition."[83] Writing about Eugene Crowder's brother's home, investigators similarly disapproved of the location and lodgings. One prerelease report described the home and vicinity as "two rooms of a 6 room frame dwelling located in the towns garbage disposal yard" where "the stench of the garbage heap and nauseating odor of burning rubbish is all pervading." With a monthly rent of only $4 the house was surrounded by "abandoned buildings . . . occupied by unemployed Negroes who crowd . . . into space where only one could be comfortable."[84] Considering the neighborhood a dangerous and unhealthful "squatters colony," the officers recommended Crowder take a position at a brick yard that accommodated employees in dormitories.[85] The economic instabilities of most black communities contributed to the already limited options for parolees. Although family members gave support, their willingness to help did not always guarantee sustainable aid, and men regularly found themselves surviving alone.

Most black parolees left prison with the help of sponsoring organizations and worked to support themselves and sometimes others. Success meant finding work, and as a pivotal aspect of release from prison, employment played a crucial role in continually justifying one's freedom. Standard parole report forms required parolees to verify their source of income, enumerate days employed versus "days idle," and describe all wages and expenditures in detail.[86] Twenty-three days after discharge in August 1923, Cyrus Fischer reported earnings of $75 and listed expenses for rent, food, and clothing that equaled his income. Yet, by his next report in September, Fisher's earnings decreased to $54 and he found himself "looking for employment." Although he found work at a coal company for a two-week stretch in early October, he once again faced joblessness before the end of the month. November brought better news as he acquired a position at a veteran's hospital, yet the bulk of his income went to the support of his father, with whom he lived. Over the next few years Fisher remained intermittently employed making wages that ranged wildly but still allowed him to consistently pay for board and lodging, and occasionally purchase a suit, contribute to his father's needs, or save money.[87] Paroled in 1920 Graham Glover found consistent employment in Auburn, New York, but struggled to keep his job because of the distance between his boarding house and workplace, and he requested permission to change addresses. "I am working hard," Glover wrote to his parole officer, "and doing the very best I can. But under the circumstances here I can hardly get to my work in time in the mornings." With his request ultimately denied Glover managed to continue with the same employer for much of the year, regularly earned more than $100 per month, and saved a large portion of his salary.[88] In one letter to the superintendent of prisons his parole officer reported he had saved nearly $900 in eleven months and his conduct was "all that could be asked of anyone."[89]

Despite clean records early on, both Fischer and Glover stumbled on their parole obligations in the long run. After a period with no infractions, the board suspended formal reports and allowed parolees to check in intermittently to custodian organizations, yet both men faltered once given this liberty. In 1927 Fisher's Salvation Army sponsor noted he "has not been to my office nor have I heard from him for a matter of six weeks now" even after sending "an investigator to look into the matter." Because of his previously "very splendid record" the officer recommended him for a conditional discharge from parole, which the commissioner of corrections denied.[90] Fischer only reappeared in 1929 when a letter sent to his father's home threatened imprisonment.[91] Glover similarly abandoned his parole obligations once his formal reports suspended and absconded to Chicago in 1922 without notifying parole personnel.[92]

Fisher and Glover violated the rules of parole after long stretches of compliance, but others immediately garnered serious violations or resisted the regulation of their daily lives and went back to prison.[93] Following a sentence for a previous parole violation Bert Williams regained his freedom in 1931 but never achieved the stability required by his parole agreement and defied decrees meant to manage his behavior. According to an attending officer's report he was "surly, evasive, a liar and non-cooperative" while free. Acquiring only "odd jobs" and inconsistent employment, Williams's prospects for work worsened after he injured his elbow and advanced complications of syphilis began to take their toll. The officer also conveyed that Williams "boast[ed] of his ability to consume large quantities of liquor without showing any marked effects," which violated his parole, but he refused treatment for alcoholism and housing assistance arguing he was able to "take care of himself." Yet, he subsequently committed petty larceny and returned to prison in 1933.[94]

Some men rejected the entire concept of parole believing it was a violation of their rights after serving their time. When Gregory Pratt left Clinton prison he directly challenged his parole officer, gave false information and addresses, and frittered away $150 saved while in prison. He was "most insolent, refused to answer questions, and remove his hat" during an interview, and "while being searched . . . he tore up numerous slips of paper into small bits in an effort to discard them," officers wrote in their report. Believing the papers indicated the parolee ran numbers in Harlem, parole personnel remanded him to the city jail. Nonetheless, Pratt remained defiant declaring he would not talk if they sent him back to prison for fifty years and threatening to "catch up" with his parole officer if it took him years to do so.[95] The surveillance of probationary release itself sometimes placed parolees in precarious positions, making it difficult for them to remain free even when following the rules. Jesse Sullivan kept up with his parole reports for more than a year when he discovered his girlfriend was already married. Wishing to avoid a parole violation for adultery, Sullivan ended their relationship, but his former love interest falsely accused him of domestic violence out of anger. After convincing the parole board of his innocence, they later discovered his work contract had lapsed, leaving him unemployed, and he was sent back to prison. In most cases, parole complicated the lives of former convicts and kept them precariously poised for recidivation. Even those who avoided the pitfalls of joblessness sometimes succumbed to the temptations associated with freedom and ended up back in prison.[96]

Considering the complex terrain parolees traversed for actual liberation, parole can be seen as a unique type of unfreedom characterized by invisible barriers in physical and psychological space. Leaving prison gates they realized the same literal and figurative landscape that drove them to crime in the first place now had new intrusive legal limitations superimposed upon it in all directions, and friends, neighbors, and sponsors added to the constant baseline of surveillance they had experienced before. Black men sent away for subsistence, pleasure, violent, or patriarchal crimes meant to address impediments tailored to their intersectionality discovered parole only enhanced the features of the color line and made accessing modern pleasures even more problematic. Emblazoned with the mark of criminality, they reentered a world already tilted against them. Some, truthfully determined to remain free, eschewed nightlife, alcohol, and old acquaintances, and adopted attitudes and habits they believed would not only convince parole overseers but sustain them into the future. In the process of resuscitating their social corpus and reclaiming masculine autonomy, many men benchmarked their resumption on a commitment to work and enterprise, respectable associations and housing, and the curative powers of the institution of marriage. As chapter 4 argues, black men in the shadow of looming racial threats often emphasized their control over the domestic realm in hopes of claiming patriarchal power unavailable elsewhere. This impulse was arguably exaggerated for men in the course of shaking off the yoke of bondage and single-minded about upward mobility.

"Become a Woman of Good Character and Live Right"

Nearing his wife's parole date from the upstate Bedford Hills Reformatory in 1919 Adam Pitts's patience ran thin. Married in 1916 Adam and Evelyn Pitts lived together for less than a year when she was arrested for allegedly offering sexual favors for money and sent away.[97] In a series of letters to the parole board at Bedford Hills, Adam questioned Evelyn's guilt and the intentions of the reformatory leadership in keeping her for nearly two years. He furthermore castigated them for taking too many liberties in regulating postal contact with his wife, placing limits on their visitation rights, and intervening in their financial affairs. "You must understand," he wrote to reformatory superintendent Helen Cobb in May 1919, "that [she] is a married [woman] not a child. You [are] not the mother of [Evelyn] . . . you must not take [her] mother['s] place. I tell you Miss Cobb it is [not] slave time with colored people now."[98] In refuting Cobb's legal jurisdiction over his wife, Adam furthermore invoked his status as a military man to compel consideration of his demands. "You must not forget that I am a state soldier, and the government is behind me for right," he explained.[99] "I am going overseas to fight for such as you and your board manager." Leveraging the dignity of his service to enhance his claim to patriarchal authority over Evelyn, Adam characterized her continued imprisonment as an injustice "to a soldier who has [traveled] to France to help bring peace to the world and credit to the country." He also foreshadowed possible action by his commanding officers on his behalf. "I have had citizens locked up for [showing disrespect] to my uniform which mean[s] disrespect to the government."[100]

Distraught by years apart, Adam wrote dozens of similar letters to the reformatory proclaiming Evelyn's innocence, requesting her release, and criticizing keepers and parole personnel for looming watchfully over their marriage. In each letter, he framed his appeals in the context of his manhood, his ability to support his wife financially, and his ultimate patriarchal dominion over their private life. His letters communicated common frustrations black men experienced when intimate partners went to prison and displayed the interdependence and synchronicity many couples yearned for when attempting to rehabilitate themselves after run-ins with the law. Having spent time incarcerated in the past himself, Adam envisioned improving his own life through the prism of a strong and respectable marriage devoid of state interference and parole directives. As a result, he resented the chokehold of superintendence the reformatory placed on Evelyn and continuously contested their power in order to safeguard their marriage from state control.

Adam's assessments of his own character, masculine identity, and competence as a breadwinner featured heavily in his letters to Bedford Hills, elements he thought should influence Cobb and the parole board to send Evelyn home. In many instances he insisted he would be a more suitable corrective agent than the reformatory for his wife's behavior by providing a decent home and all of the securities of domesticity. In one 1919 letter he promised to rent a three-room apartment by the next day, and to prove the worthiness of his prospective dwellings. He indicated it would be in a quiet section of Harlem, with "only one block of colored people." Recently discharged from the military, Adam secured a position as an elevator operator in a high-rise residential tower and reassured Cobb his employment was

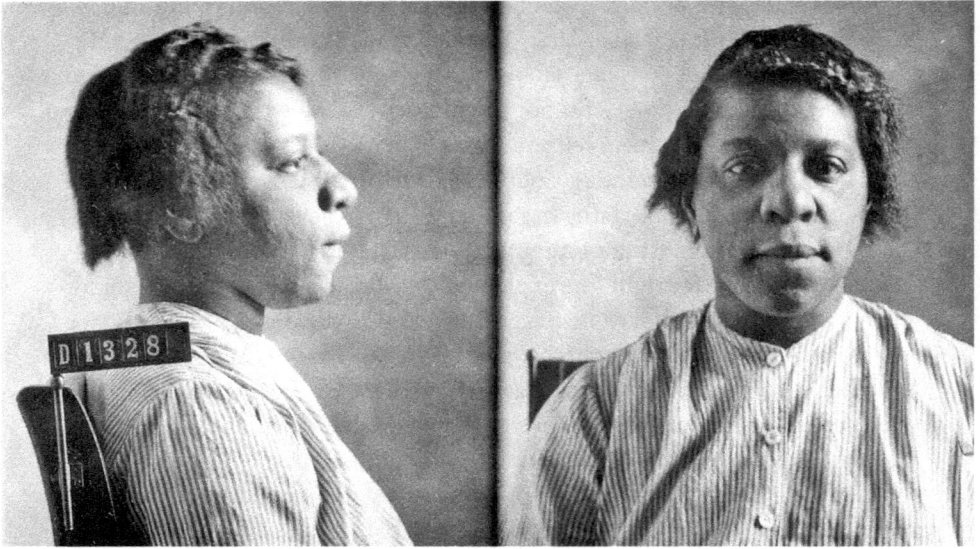

Evelyn Pitts (pseud.), an inmate at Auburn prison for women, 1925. Courtesy of New York State Archives and Records Administration, Albany, New York (Inmate #1328, Series B0050).

stable and paid well enough that he could support Evelyn in their new home. "I make 60 dollars a month [with] tips [which is] very good because we carry rich people in here only," he explained, adding that he "will stick in this job" in order to create "a home . . . which will be clean neat and comfortable." Adam also emphasized how his acquisition of a reliable living space would have implications for Evelyn's ability to turn her life around and remain out of the reformatory. Since 1911, she had been interned in a number of institutions and he hoped to make this committal her last. "The rooms I am getting will give [Evelyn] a chance to make good and will not put her under any strain," he assured. "This house will [be] under my name because I am going to meet all bills . . . like [a] man." The arrangement would also give her the chance to resume her duties as his wife and remake their household which had been split for too long. "Of course . . . my house call[s] for [somebody] to clean and cook and wash," which Evelyn would do having "learned [a] lesson in the wild world of fun and pleasure," Adam conjectured.[101]

Adam's letters reveal amorous eagerness to reconstitute his family with his wife and certainly indicate a true dedication to her as his partner. However, they also say much about how black men intertwined self-image with their capacity to support, protect, and control women. One may interpret his promises of providing respectable and clean living quarters and boasts about his work and earnings as rhetoric meant to win over Cobb's approval, but it is feasible Adam sincerely believed in the transformational qualities of surroundings and propriety. He enthusiastically told the superintendent of how he changed his own life and "came out of the army . . . with a clean mind" having "learned my lesson" through discipline and military service.[102] With his own behavior in check, he worried about Evelyn since "Harlem is the downfall of the colored girls."[103] If he could find housing away from disreputable people, Adam imagined they might eventually have a middle-class life together.

A number of observers of Adam and Evelyn's relationship raised questions about Adam's character, ability to support his wife, and his influences on her. In a 1917 interview with reformatory personnel one of Evelyn's aunts claimed the two "were accustomed to go out late at night and be more or less promiscuous." As a result, she admitted she generally avoided contact with the couple in fear of risking her reputation.[104] In agreeance, Evelyn's mother, Sylvia Cox, gave horrendous reviews of her son-in-law and his effect on her daughter's behavior in a series of letters to Helen Cobb. Cox's writing conveyed apprehension about Adam's alleged illegal activities and the possibility his reunion with his wife would lead to more misconduct. In one of her earliest notes she requested Evelyn be kept in the facility "until she learn some sense" and in order to keep her away from her husband. "I want you to keep my daughter up there," because "I have found out that her [h]usband . . . put her out on the block," Cox wrote implying Adam forced Evelyn into prostitution. Considering her daughter safer locked away she further implored, "don't let her out . . . keep her . . . [and] in that time he might go away or die."[105] Bedford Hills investigators came to similar conclusions about Adam as they conducted a series of examinations and interviews before granting parole.[106] Helen Cobb's 1919 letter to Adam formalized the reformatory's position against his custodial care for Evelyn. "We are under the impression that you have not arranged to provide for a place for [her] which we could consider permanent or satisfactory, also that you are making frequent changes in your work, and . . . there is nothing very definite as yet regarding your income upon which [we] could depend," Cobb wrote.[107]

Cobb's remarks about Adam elucidate a common view of domestic life in the early twentieth century, one that Adam also expressed in his letters. All involved expected him to provide for Evelyn, including himself, but his aspirations for a good salary remained out of reach. His living situation likewise remained unstable, and in many letters he presented yet another neighborhood, flat, or boarding location, and even more plans to find a place where the couple might thrive. Adam continually inhabited a nexus between dreams for the sort of career and home observers would respect and the ever-shifting contours of a public turned against him. He often reported being employed, but his work constantly changed. Undeterred by his own legal and financial troubles Adam remained confident he was capable of supporting his wife and railed against negative comments about his abilities and nature. "I am sorry you do not think I am capable of handling money," he responded to Cobb's letter. "I am a man . . . I have had all kinds of money in life."[108] In another letter he attempted to eliminate all criticisms by reassuring Cobb he would be a good husband and eventually find some sort of stability, if he had not already. "What is more important I am a man who is capable of making a dollar . . . and sometime[s] 20 and sometime[s] more . . . I have more [character] about me than [the investigating parole officer]" who he described as having "unclean" character.[109] By comparing himself favorably to the presumably respectable parole personnel monitoring his relationship with Evelyn, Adam consciously sought to supersede their authority with his own version of propriety and manhood. He likely understood his wife's parole relied entirely upon the discretion of Cobb and the parole board and their perception of the worthiness of their marital bond, and he simultaneously resented the situation while trying to leverage it to his favor. Possibly feeling powerless, Adam obsessively barraged Cobb and other personnel with impassioned letters that framed his wife's freedom as if it was his own bondage, and a matter of life and death. "I will be where [my wife] is or die," he wrote in one indignant letter.[110]

Perhaps because of a combination of Adam's efforts and Evelyn's good behavior, she received her first parole in 1919, and her difficulties remaining free articulate how her own aspirations for self-actualization merged with her love for her husband and her need for his care and support.[111] She became a "fugitive from justice" when the couple fled the state for a short time, and upon returning she once again reentered the reformatory for the violation.[112] Yet both Evelyn and her husband continued to yearn for a stable relationship characterized by the normative hallmarks of middle-class domesticity and collaborated on ways to change their lives for the better. In an exchange of letters preceding a 1920 parole, they lovingly reassured each other about their future together. For women like Evelyn whose lives had been disrupted by imprisonment, dreams of life back home figured prominently in their plans after release. Anticipating her return to freedom Evelyn vowed she would "try I promise I will to keep my parole" since she had "in my mind just [exactly] what I am going to do."[113] Paroled once again in 1920 she worked for a family as a domestic servant in Westchester County north of New York City. In one letter to Adam she requested that he not "disappoint" her when he came to visit because "I will come up in a carriage to the station [and] you can ride in it with me to the house." Wistfully imagining the possibilities for their life after her release from parole, Evelyn fantasized, "Gee I wish we could ride to our own house."[114] This was a strong possibility in her mind, since she had been saving money while away and hoped to "start my little home all over again."[115] However, Evelyn clearly felt her happiness and ability to reconstruct her home life depended upon the actions of her spouse. Complaining of the strenuous nature of her work she expressed assuredness "my husband will start a nice place for me [soon]" in a letter to Cobb.[116] Nevertheless, in another letter only two days later she castigated him for taking so long to work things out. "If my husband would only use his head and get a little home together I would not have all this trouble," she lamented.[117]

Evelyn was not alone in hoping her relationship status might bring about positive change in her own life. Countless letters written by other black women convicts make clear they frequently associated personal improvement with the support of consorts and husbands when released. While on parole from Auburn prison Marilyn Steele framed her eventual freedom from the legal system in terms of marriage and respectability. Claiming to have "been [of] no trouble" since leaving confinement, she requested early release from the requirements of parole. In a letter to her assigned officer Steele confirmed her request was not meant to allow her to "return to a life [of] Crime [and] Prison," but to permit her to marry "a man [of] Clean Princiable [sic] [and] Character." Wishing to start a new life as a respectable married woman, she likewise expressed a desire to keep her disreputable past from affecting her future. "I do not Expect to Ever Be a Woman of the World again an[d] Cause the state further trouble," she wrote. "It is hard for me to Marry as an undesirable."[118]

Arrested for prostitution in 1923 and interned at Bedford Hills Reformatory, Wilma Heywood also believed wedlock would change her life for the better. Paroled in the same year, Heywood agreed to the requirement of requesting permission if she planned to marry, but she violated that agreement when she married Samuel Butler months after her release.[119] Once discovered, she apologized to parole personnel in a letter claiming she did it because "it would keep me from going out anywhere that I shouldn't go." "Maybe I would keep my parole more better" by remaining "safe at home" with a "very nice and accommodating husband," she reasoned. Heywood hinged her ability to remain "obedient to the state" and to God on her husband's support and rectitude. Having known him for three years she was certain he was "a man of Quality," and "as he is willing to live a straight and honest life I will endeavor to keep my parole."[120]

These sentiments linking romantic relationships with the chances of one's improvement make two things clear about black women's aspirations when tying the knot. As argued earlier, women frequently struggled to reconcile traditional values and notions of respectability in relationships with their own desires and emerging thought about female independence. With that considered, they also sometimes sought the material and recreational options city living engendered through the prism of romantic relationships and conjugality. For some women, the prospect of a durable relationship and a respectable household seemed like a surefire way to achieve financial and personal stability and consumer power. Yet, women like Steele, Heywood, and Pitts might find that the strictures of marriage trifled with their imagined lifestyles, which presented a troublesome paradox. Just as men regularly found a sense of identity in patterns of consumption and profligacy, so did some women seek the ability to control their buying power and live their version of a good life without the asymmetrical compromises of traditional marriage.

Adam Pitts was also not alone in believing his patriarchal presence to be essential to his wife's chances in life. Like women, men could be pulled between objectives to author pictorial narratives of normative home lives while surviving the crucibles in their paths and fulfilling their own appetites for diversion. Many settled on a version of marriage that might allow them to do both. Jerome Bowman's letters to his wife Camille in 1924 demonstrate this best. Lamenting Camille's arrest for prostitution, Jerome blamed himself. "I lived with her," he told one official, "but if I had married her right this trouble would never have happened." However, in his mind, that ship had not yet sailed.[121] Although currently interned in the city jail himself, he promised to get her out and marry her immediately "so that we could be happie [sic] again."[122] "[I] am with you all the way, just depend on me Honey," he reassured her in a letter.[123] Bowman's message, like those of Adam Pitts, convey how much of the weight of women's reformation men placed on themselves. Although often self-serving and rife with unevenness, their concepts of patriarchy required their full physical, psychological, and spiritual support of women, at least in theory.

Some men, angry about the behavior of paramours, or rejection of their advances, attempted to sabotage women's parole. In 1925, Joseph Perkins penned a letter to the state superintendent of prisons telling of parole violations he claimed Jacqueline Ray was getting away with. According to Perkins, Ray was "hang[ing] out with her gang which is of absolutely no [good] to the world," spending "late hours [in] Cabarets Drunk," and "work[ing] when she feels like it." Perkins also intimated the parolee was involved with prostitution since she could be found "on the Streets all hours of the night with all kinds and any kind of men," which he considered "absolutely fierce."[124] After checking in on Perkins's story parole officers determined Ray was living up to her parole agreements but had refused Perkins's advances, and they realized he wrote his letter only out of spite.[125] Whether the officers' suspicions were true or not, Perkins's actions contextualize the sometimes provisional terms of men's devotion to imprisoned women. Writing to his wife before her parole, Will Linton expressed belief in their common fates. "I hope you will turn out a good woman as I am trying hard to do the same," he wrote, adding that it would be good if she learned a lesson "as I have learn [already]. If we can agree together we will go back together and let the pass [sic] be forgotten." Linton ended his letter by vowing his conditional support as long as his wife did her part. "[D]ear my arms are always open to you if you will treat [me] good."[126]

Even more devotedly, Adam Pitts remained by Evelyn's side across multiple parole detainments and consistently tried to make both of their lives better. Preceding her release in 1919 he informed his wife of new developments and encouraged her about her ability to live a quiet life with him when she returned to New York City. "I have a good position now dear heart," he wrote, "I have made up my mind to give you a chance to make good while on parole." Promising to pay all bills as long as Evelyn agreed to the restrictions of domesticity, Adam cautioned her against outside employment. "Understand me good," he warned, "if you go to work I am not hav[ing] anything to do with it. . . . So long as you wanted to work out it stands only up to you to make good." He concluded his letter by reassuring her he would provide for her and create the durable private life they both wanted, with her compliance. "Good things comes [sic] to men" who use their brains he wrote. "I will do that because it is my duty as a man and of my character."[127]

Once allowed to relocate to her husband's home in 1921, Evelyn reported on her progress to parole personnel at least once a month. A series of communications indicate the level of guardianship the institution imposed upon her freedom and likewise illustrate the couple's resolution to determine their own fate.[128] When the Bedford Hills superintendent inquired about her husband's support, Evelyn expressed contentment with her new home and optimism about her marriage.[129] "My husband and I are getting along lovely indeed," she wrote adding, "[Adam] has money enough to take care of me."[130] In later letters both Evelyn and Adam voiced a level of harmony and reciprocation they could not achieve during her incarceration. Evelyn in particular regained a sense of place in her household and vowed to remain faithful to the duties and responsibilities of married life. On New Year's Day of 1921 she "made a promise never to get in any place far from home again [because] [t]here is no place like home sweet home." She spoke this vow while praying with her husband "thank[ing] God that we were living."[131] Evelyn also told of plans to purchase a house with money from her own work washing clothes at home and her husband's earnings from prizefighting and his nascent notary enterprise.[132] With their lives seemingly repaired and on track they fantasized about summering in the country in the belief that time together and stable finances would allow them to "enjoy the very best of health that life can afford," Evelyn penned.[133]

Counter to their optimism, the Pitts's legal troubles continued into the latter part of the decade, and their household never stabilized. Not long after Evelyn's high-spirited 1921 letter she was arrested once for grand larceny and a month later caught in the act of burglary by a homeowner.[134] Adam's last recorded letters conveyed exhaustion with Evelyn's inability to remain out of jail and detailed the impact of her misgivings on his own rehabilitation. They make clear he hoped to improve his own circumstances through acquiring property in a respectable neighborhood and starting his own enterprise, which he believed would provide a more sustainable and consistent income. However, while in the process of remaking his own life, Adam alleged Evelyn was influenced by a group of gamblers, pimps, and robbers who taught her a number of illicit trades and abandoned her each time she went to jail. Angry about his wife's disloyalty, lawless behavior, and lapses in their marriage, and hurt by accusations about his own misgivings from the parole board and Evelyn's family, Adam finally wrote "I have Washed my hand I give up. Let these [men] do it."[135] If Evelyn returned to him for good he promised to then "give her a chance as my wife to redeem herself, and be a woman and live within the law."[136] Prison documents make clear Adam's wishes for a consolidated and respectable home would never be granted. Evelyn served time for burglary in 1921, then multiple times again for unlawful entry and grand larceny in 1923 and 1924. In 1925 prosecutors accused her of burglarizing houses while pretending to look for domestic work in Poughkeepsie, New York, and she received a sentence of up to five years in prison.[137] Upon release she faced arrest once more in 1930 for a similar charge, and during her intake she reported her husband had passed away not long before.[138]

The saga of the Pittses' marriage and fragmentation is hard to read because it conjures the grievances of hundreds of thousands of black men and women blown in the winds of racial inequality in spaces, places, and ideological schemas constructed to limit their capacity to visualize their lives for themselves. Most assuredly, Adam and Evelyn made their paths by walking them, and they often suffered the consequences of their own choices. Yet they made those choices in a broader context of racially specific dangers, housing segregation, financial deprivation, and possibly a feeling of powerlessness in the face of white supervision and authority. As hard as he evidently tried, Adam confronted a city unwilling to admit him to "respectable" housing and restricting him to work that fell short of his expectations and those of his wife and others. Both of them dreaming of a bucolic and quiet existence, the Pitts likely had difficulty avoiding the temptation of illicit trades surging around them, and lacking the resources to insulate themselves from the legal system, it intruded on their lives for the length of their marriage. However, their story also indicates how black couples drove deep roots into the terra firma of matrimony in an attempt to withstand the cyclones raging around them. Despite their frequent disintegration, affectionate and complementary romantic bonds eminently figured in a black imaginary dimension that men and women entered when determined to improve their lives. For men in particular, the literal and figurative architecture of the private domain became a proxy for the jurisdiction they lacked elsewhere, and they sometimes swiveled on the axis of the women in their lives, for better or worse.

––––––––––

Adam Pitts's attempts to recover his marriage and his failure to do so also tells a story that exemplifies the experiences of countless other black men as they navigated the legal system in the North. In the middle of a process of reformation in the early twentieth century, New York's prison and parole systems had a stake in rehabilitating prisoners, releasing them, and preventing high rates of recidivism. However, like policing, public racial attacks, and surveillance by progressive and civic organizations, imprisonment had broad existential effects on the lives of black men and their families. In addition to the unrecoverable impacts of internment on inmates themselves, short and long prison sentences had implications for spouses, children, extended families, and communities. Men and women like Adam and Evelyn Pitts faced legal challenges for innumerable reasons, yet typically endured similar physical, psychological, financial, and emotional difficulties that impacted their time in prison and their chances for recuperation once released. Already struggling to survive, support families, and navigate the labyrinthine racial politics of New York City in freedom, imprisonment seemed like a structural manifestation of all the restrictions, surveillance, and violations materialized in three dimensions, and supported by the state in explicit terms.

Black men and women sent to prison often possessed a common awareness about the uneven nature of law enforcement and had relatively resistant attitudes about the treatment they experienced. In prison they worked, learned, and fought to survive, all while harboring fantasies of better days after release. Adam's letters reveal an awareness of the vagaries of internment and a radically resistant perspective that exemplifies the endurance many black men showed when interfacing with the carceral state. For some, living in New York proved to be too much, and they believed returning to the South might ease their burdens. Paroled back to his family in Beech, Virginia, after multiple imprisonments and parole violations, Cornelius Bradley's freedom depended upon him staying put and not giving in to the "itch" to return to the North. But Bradley did not believe it would be a problem, plainly telling the parole board "I have had enough of New York."[139]

Sadly, for many like the Pittses, better days never arrived. Planting the very seeds of their identity in the rich soil of relationships, they held tight through prison walls. They rethought past behaviors, sought stable employment, and interlaced their lives with their significant others before and after their return. Many recognized the benefits of maintaining a respectable countenance when interacting with prison personnel and parole boards, when seeking work, and when convincing sponsors, family members, and parole officers of their rehabilitation. However, some still pushed against the authority of others in shaping their own existence. In some cases, intimate partners were the only refuge on the complex terrain of being jailed and released, and couples frequently navigated it together. Insecurity sometimes defined these unions, but black men and women continued to depend upon one another in hopes of weathering various storms intact and ultimately finding happiness together.

Epilogue

Real Niggaz Don't Die: Revolution and Continuity

Will there ever be peace, or are we all just,
Headed for doom, still consumed by the beast,
And I know, there will never be peace,
That's why I keep my pistol when I walk the streets.

—Tupac Shakur, *Never B Peace* (2002)

The pages of this book are filled with narratives of momentary triumph, but different forms of ultimate defeat often followed for men who decided to take radical measures to meet their needs and desires. Their stories may seem unfamiliar, veiled by time and context, isolated in the distant past, and disconnected from the present by decades of change and progress. Yet, for many of us, these men are recognizable as our uncles, brothers, fathers, friends, and ourselves. They did not exist in some foreign land in a culture discrete from our own, and they were not inhabitants of another dimension. All of the men and women in this history, including the reformers, politicians, and police officers, white and black, are us—or more accurately, we are them. We carry their genes and names, inhabit the same spaces, face or maintain the same systems, and make decisions to fulfill similarly entrenched compulsions, obligations, and appetites. Our society did not spontaneously combust into being as each of us became aware of it, but it is firmly rooted in the past, a mere evolution of the complex structures and cultures that have come before. We are not enlightened beings perched atop the wreckage of the past, but live inside of history itself, imbedded in the same unending moment that saw the enslavement and emancipation of Africans, a moment interrupted only by forgetfulness and the requirement of daily sleep. Just as early twentieth-century blacks contended with the vestiges of racist frameworks devised in the centuries before, we in the twenty-first century are still haunted by the ghosts of slavery, Jim Crow, and an ever-evolving racial caste system that will not biodegrade on its own.

The election of Barack Obama as American president in 2008 certainly indicated a sort of breakthrough, a towering place of rest on a long voyage to a distant mountaintop. However, liberation is not one location to be reached but a sprawling landscape, and progress in one place can say little about the improvement needed in another. African Americans largely live in marginalized communities, segregated into districts severely impacted by deindustrialization, white flight, red lining, and urban disinvestment that began in earnest in the post–World War II period. Lacking economic cores, these neighborhoods are still more likely to host underground markets—many of which serve the desires of the broader city, not only the black communities they are grounded in. Black men are still profoundly affected by legacies of job discrimination, spatial marginalization, unjust surveillance, police brutality, and systems that set them up for imprisonment more than any other demographic. These men today still confront the same labeling as their early twentieth-century counterparts, markers of criminality defined by color, class, and the perceptions of others. And, some still may understand illegality to be their most potent form of resistance to a legal and economic system specifically turned against them.

Much of this study invokes a very important aspect of black development in the years following slavery's end—geography. Space, the ability to relocate, and the forging of landscapes where blacks might truly experience freedom became even more important as they realized the half-hearted nature of emancipation. Many Americans at the time sought renewal by migrating, but for African Americans, movement was existential. Southern plains, flood valleys, and plantations were drenched in the blood of their ancestors, recent and distant, and by leaving the region, they registered social and political discontent, pursued imagined new lives, and simply wished to avoid the same brutal fate. Cities like New York offered what rural spaces did not—rapture, anonymity, and overt and clandestine economies in some ways more concerned with profit than racial custom. But blacks soon realized the limitations of their lives in the North. In this moment we see the crystallization of modes of engagement and self-expression on both sides of the lines of racial scrimmage. Whites responded to the country's demographic and racial changes hoping to preserve and expand their racial privilege; and blacks, determined to maintain and strengthen their personhood, used whatever resources they had in an ever-evolving, asymmetrical war.

The violence of segregation formed as whites relegated blacks to the most unhealthy and deleterious housing, often through outright attacks and policing that amounted to terrorism. They also moved away from neighborhoods that blacks occupied, beginning the century-long flight that continues today, although slightly abated. That exodus has steadily bloated and distended metropolitan regions like Detroit, Chicago, and New York far beyond necessary geographical perimeters, simultaneously abandoned and exploited the urban core, and rearranged it and destroyed it with impunity. The violence of segregation continues. Not only are neighborhood boundaries maintained by militaristic policing in the twenty-first century, but containment itself is destructive, particularly on topographies serviced with polluted amenities; marked by inequality in housing, education, and resources; and rife with gun violence. Like in the early twentieth century, claiming urban space has remained important to African American communities in ongoing campaigns for resources, revenue, and respect. One need only listen to New York hip-hop artists like Nas, Jay-Z, and 50 Cent to hear black men attaching their personas to very specific parts of the city such as Jamaica, Brooklyn's Marcy Projects, Queens Bridge, and Harlem. It is clear, one's literal and figurative location in America's racial political labyrinth is crucial, as it can often mean the difference between thriving and failing, freedom and unfreedom, and life and death.

Black criminality can only be understood in the context of this maze, a social and physical construction embedded in American culture and shaped by the towering double presence of racism and capitalism. With the conclusion of the original sin of enslavement, free market enterprise set the stage for unending rivalry; but racism doused that stage in gasoline and lit it on fire. In Robert K. Merton's 1938 publication *Social Structure and Anomie*, he attempted to explain the country's relatively high crime rate as the result of normlessness, a cultural state created by a high emphasis placed on monetary success and a low emphasis on the means of acquiring it. The American dream exists in fiction and reality in the gap between these two. As a culture we revere those lucky, ruthless, persistent, or corrupt enough to achieve it, whether they are inheritors of wealth, captains of industry, shady politicians, or gangsters.[1] Those deprived of such dreams, the working class and poor, the marginalized and forgotten, are "on the one hand . . . asked to orient their conduct toward . . . accumulating wealth and on the other, they are largely denied effective opportunities to do so institutionally," in Merton's words. The "strain" caused by such limitations produces deviant behavior and rebellious activities. Crime is thus partially produced by the predominant values of capitalism and competition, and by a caste system that denies normative, legitimate access to prevailing cultural markers of success for certain citizens, effectively rendering the American dream into fantasy.[2] As such, we can understand contraband enterprises, theft and robbery, and the performance of black toughness as power for the powerless, exploits pregnant with radical content and meaning for the economically deserted.

Uncontrollable Blackness contextualizes this radicalism as resistance to systems of power fashioned in the Jim Crow era and fossilized at the turn of the twenty-first century as mass incarceration.[3] Relatively progressive pre–World War II outlooks on criminality, imprisonment, and reform became more punitive and retaliatory after the war, particularly as politicians like

Lyndon Johnson vowed to stop the "disorder" attending the urban crisis of the 1950s and 1960s. Just as Jim Crow policies in cities like New York responded to demographic changes and challenges to racial order blacks posed at the time, the "tough-on-crime" policies enacted at midcentury responded to the pressures from the civil rights movement and fear of urban insurrections. Civil disorder like that experienced in places like Harlem, Rochester, and Philadelphia in 1964 coincided with hardening assumptions about black delinquency and shaped federal policy.[4] Founded in 1968, Johnson's Law Enforcement Assistance Administration involved the federal government in local policing and imprisonment more than ever before by disbursing funds that broadened local and state carceral programs. Subsequent leaders such as Richard Nixon and Ronald Reagan ramped up the punitive nature of policing even further by segueing the War on Crime into the War on Drugs, a campaign that largely targeted African American communities.[5] From 1976 to 1996 the rate at which blacks were arrested climbed by 400 percent, and men composed the vast majority of those busts.[6]

The growth of the incarceration of poor and minority Americans reflects a broad change in dominant views of criminality in the mid-twentieth century. Adhering to more conservative criminological theories in the 1960s and 1970s, the country largely abandoned rehabilitation for capital punishment. Indeterminate sentences, drug rehabilitation programs, and early parole were swapped for "three-strikes" laws, mandatory minimum penalties, and "truth in sentencing" statutes that precluded parole.[7] Influential scholars like James Q. Wilson, in his 1975 book *Thinking About Crime*, rejected structural inequality as a determinant of criminal behavior, proposed ending social welfare programs, and supported inflicting greater punishments on criminals in order to stop crime.[8] With George L. Kelling in 1982 he published the essay "Broken Windows," which saw poverty and disrepair simply as the backdrop for the activities of wicked people, not as evidence of inequality, deprivation, and economic isolation that could be criminogenic for some. Arguing one smashed window on a block signaled no one cared and invited more destruction, broken windows theory recommended meticulous police patrols that would treat all infractions against the social order as precursors to greater evils.[9] Officers would repress disturbances, rein in rowdy teenagers, and round up drunks and petty offenders in an effort to maintain public peace, which would theoretically prevent a neighborhood's slide into more serious disorganization and crime. Like other conservative criminological theories, Wilson and Kelling's work influenced policing in many American cities, including New York City where Mayor Rudolph Giuliani fully embraced it during his tenure in the 1990s and implemented programs like "stop and frisk," which gave police permission to search and arrest people with impunity.[10] With black men being stopped, arrested, and imprisoned at rates that far surpassed their proportion of the population across the twentieth century and into the next, *Uncontrollable Blackness* represents a long overdue analysis of the historical causal factors for this imbalance. Viewing this subject through a historical lens facilitates our understanding of the admixture of racial and structural continuities, and resistance and revolution that forms the logic of black crime or behaviors criminalized by others.

Measures of fascination and fantasy have always been involved in the criminalization of black bodies by white Americans. Black illicit districts like those in early twentieth-century New York have morphed, expanded, and relocated over the decades, but they have remained spaces where outsiders might come to find substances and pleasures unavailable elsewhere. But, as cities have changed, crumbling black communities have become the source of another often intangible and psychic thrill for nonresidents. As disremembered nether-regions of an opulent capitalist society, for some those spaces and their cultural production represent authenticity and realness, a primal state of humanness unfiltered by the extravagant absurdity of modern American excess.

We can track the origins of such a perspective through this study. At the turn of the twentieth century, "modernity" was located in the city. Middle-class white Americans flocked to modern spaces seeking to participate in the avant-garde and stylish, new-fashioned technologies, and the bliss of unfamiliar freedoms. However, there was a strain in American culture that sought to escape the fatigue of overindulgence, crime, and pollution in cities by embracing simpler, more natural aspects of life, rebuking cities to some degree. For interested whites, black bodies writhing to jazz and blues music, black and tans, coon songs, and minstrel shows conjured cathartic daydreams of primitive contact, worlds away from the suffocating, over-regulated culture of work, time, and responsibilities. Whites restive about the anxieties of modern life sought such carelessness by listening to hopped up ragtime jingles that invoked comical black plantation watermelon thieves and gun-wielding "coons"; songs that reaffirmed white superiority but also allowed those listeners to explore the wilderness on the flip side of the color line. They journeyed into black sections of American cities on urban safaris for whisky, cocaine, and interracial sex, as well as to imbibe the untroubled, devil-may-care spirit they expected to find there. It was the same thrill that made an overnight sensation out of Ota Benga, the Congolese Mbuti man brought to New York by a missionary in 1906 and placed on display at the Bronx Zoo.[11] During his engagement keepers kept Benga in a cage where visitors observed him as he played with chimps, counted money, carved arrows, and "swings himself" on the branches, one observer wrote.[12] Some clergy members and

African Americans condemned the exhibit but white visitors rushed in to see him and a letter arrived from a woman asking to purchase him. "If he is in good condition write me his age and the care he ought to have," she requested, eager to negotiate a price.[13] The surreal magnetism of black life to a mesmerized white middle class ripened into a full-blown craze in white writer Carl Van Vechten's vulgarly titled 1926 novel, *Nigger Heaven*. Van Vechten acted as a tour guide of black Harlem in the book and further provoked white slumming parties.[14] Paul Laurence Dunbar wrote of this phenomenon as early as 1903 in the play, *In Dahomey*. "When dey hear dem ragtime tunes, [w]hite fo'ks try to pass fo' coons."[15]

Such antimodern interest in the primitive and unworldly partially fed movement away from urban centers, which began most sincerely in the post–World War II period. With the help of federal government programs like the Home Owners Loan Corporation and the G.I. Bill, white Americans fled the vagaries of urban life for the relatively natural setting of the suburbs in droves, a move that helped move along an urban crisis. Because of this exodus from cities and a deluge of consumer products and ideas that accompanied it, by the 1960s and 1970s the suburbs became the new location of over-modernization, culturally considered a place of living death, flooded with conveniences and frozen by tedium that minimized the human spirit and eclipsed individual autonomy. Novels and films like *Revolutionary Road* (1961) and *The Stepford Wives* (1975) brought these attitudes to life for those experiencing them. At that same time and in the decades that followed, cities emerged as antimodern spaces, regions with old-timey amenities, hulking Victorian homes, and streetscapes considered the antithesis of suburban dullness. In the late twentieth and early twenty-first centuries, former suburbanites have thronged to erstwhile glorious industrial urban centers rebirthed from rust, and they have remodeled ailing communities to fit their version of urbanity, often interrupting the lives of residents already residing there in a process of gentrification. And, just like past black cultural expression, "gangsta" hip-hop music has fulfilled an antimodern impulse for suburban residents searching for the authenticity of black life. *I'm America's nightmare, young black and just don't give a fuck, I just wanna get high and live it up.*[16] The music of rappers like NWA, Wu-Tang Clan, Jay-Z, Notorious B.I.G., Mobb Deep, and Onyx became conduits into the spirit of urban realness for some white Americans tired of suburban unreality.

However, for African American men in the 1990s and beyond, hip-hop, "gangsta" or not, often serves as a salve on ailing parts of the soul. Like blues songs that came before, hip-hop expresses the bottomless discontent of black men still seeking the respect, inclusion, and potentiality an American ethos promises but denies them. They may see lyrics as revolutionary incantations that instill power in their masculine identities, romanticize the pains of racial isolation, and convey the profound strength it takes to have hopes and dreams in a world tilted against them. *I grew up on the crime side, the New York Times side, staying alive was no jive.*[17] Many of the men presented in lyrics, real or imagined, are modern-day Stagolees and Railroad Bills, resolved to not be swallowed by racial circumstance; literal badmen christened in the blood of street battles and shining in the darkness of subterranean economies. Some have superhero qualities, the ability to morph or conjure magical effects, and to survive against impossible odds. *Shell hit my jaw, I ain't wait for doc to get it out, Hit my wisdom tooth, *hock too* spit it out; I don't smile a lot, cause ain't nothing pretty, Got a purple heart for war and I ain't never left the city.*[18] Like black folkloric heroes they might openly challenge authority by threatening to shoot law enforcers or gain credibility for having done so, like Tupac Shakur who was arrested and released after shooting two off-duty police officers in 1993. Like the fabled Railroad Bill, Tupac seemed immortal after being shot multiple times himself. In his own words, *busters shot me five times, real niggaz don't die.*[19] Killed in another shooting in 1996, fans still deny his death and report sightings even decades later, elevating his outlaw status to mythological hero. Whether physically alive or not, Tupac lives on because he represents the complex duality African American men have experienced for the length of the nation's history. They have both understood the insurgent nature of rule-breaking and unlawful acts when deep in the humid bowels of human captivity, and harbored the desire to be successful men in a society of laws and order. Able to express the violent, sexist, and materialistic trappings of "thug life" alongside political testimonials about racist structures and black womanhood, Tupac remains a towering figure because he embodies the enduring dilemmas of black masculinity. *When it's time to die, be a man and pick the way you leave, Fuck peace and the police, my ambitions as a ridah.*[20]

Uncontrollable Blackness addresses both how American society has historically constrained black men and how extra-legal activities became effective responses to a legal system that double-crossed those men. Conservative criminology asserts that crime stems from individual immorality and will only stop when the punishment is greater than the rewards. In contrast, critical criminology theorists understand that "crime" is often defined by those in power to ensure continued control, and is largely generated by social, structural, and economic inequality. With such a deep look at illegality, we can grasp how closely aligned crime and protest often are. How protest takes place is often technically criminal or criminalized by others, while crime frequently happens because of the same issues that make people protest. As a result, a nuanced understanding of the black freedom struggle must include black men who have been driven or seduced onto the other side of the law, very often for reasons that are outside of their control. It is true that people are ultimately accountable for their own choices, but those choices are always made within a societal context that is pivotal when discussing crime. There is a monster in America's past and present; one that swallows black men whole on the streets, in popular culture, in police custody, and in prisons. This book confronts that beast with an uncomfortable truth: the maze-like crucible of American racism and violence has produced black criminality.

The men and women in this book did not see the future, but if they could, they may not have fully detected the differences in the realm of race in the twenty-first century. They might have marveled at technologies unimaginable in their time but recognized the long shadow of inequality and racial disparity looming across the decades, still dimming pathways to economic and social justice. So many aspects of the *crucible of black criminality* are still present at the time of this writing. Racial violence and police brutality still underscore spatial and economic markers of imparity, continue to delimit black men's mobility, and constrict their command of the public world. *I can't breathe!*[21] Underground markets are still enticing for men largely affected by the reverberations of inherited and present-day injustices, groping for sovereignty in a society that only truthfully recognizes selfhood through the prism of economic and physical power. *I'ma start selling drugs around my way. . . . Shit, they gon' get it from somebody, I rather it be me.*[22] Ancestral, physical, and psychological wounds still impact community and family formation, and black women still face their own crucibles, made that much more severe because of the hardships black men confront. Local and national legal malpractices have persevered and worsened making imprisonment even more of a crucible than before. And black masculinity is still politically and socially examined for defective parts, feared and fantasized about in popular culture, and subjected to measures meant to contain or neutralize it.

As such, the men in this book have so much to teach us, not only because their own lives illuminate societal strains that have shaped future realities, but also because many of us are them, simply retrofitted with modern ways to communicate, and that much more history behind us. In a sense, these men have never died but have lived on in a continuum through their sons and grandsons still facing the same crucible. Their stories should function as histories that uncover the humanity inspiriting anarchical behavior, for better or worse. As black men continue to confront the future, the term *uncontrollable blackness* contextualizes that confrontation as an ancient struggle for personhood, no matter what form it takes. It invokes a powerful spirit of resistance that knows no limits; an insurgency that makes breaking the law a tool that might allow one to rise above the restrictions placed on their lives by others, at all costs. Criminality can be a force that saps the vitality from a community, harms property and individuals, and takes lives, a subject not to be romanticized. Yet it can also be viewed as an enlivening resort for the lionhearted, those for whom everyday needs and wants compete with a moral or legal compass when vastly deprived, or for whom the glacial pace of racial progress is too slow. Although the men in this book could not see where things were heading, they might have predicted another century of strife and black struggle, a prognosis that may have instilled their actions with a melancholy quality. But there is also hope in their defiance, a belief in their ability to wrestle power from the jaws of defeat, in an effort to remain free in the face of condemnation, self-governing, and uncontrollable.

Notes

Partial List of Archival Abbreviations

ARD Auburn Register of Deaths, Records of the Department of Corrections, New York State Archives, Albany, New York

AU Auburn Correctional Facility, Records of the Department of Correctional Services, New York State Archives, Albany, New York

AUP Auburn Division of Parole, Records of the Department of Corrections, New York State Archives, Albany, New York

AUWP Auburn Women's Prison, Records of the Department of Correctional Services, New York State Archives, Albany, New York

BH Bedford Hills Correctional Facility, Inmate Case Files, Records of the Department of Correctional Services, New York State Archives, Albany, New York

CCF Clinton Correctional Facility, Inmate Case Files, Records of the Department of Correctional Services, New York State Archives, Albany, New York

COF Committee of Fourteen Paper Collection, Rare Books and Manuscripts Division, New York Public Library, New York City, New York

DACCF District Attorney Closed Case Files, New York Municipal Archives, Records and Information, New York, New York

DCFL Dowridge-Challenor Family Letters, Schomburg Center for Research in Black Culture, New York City, New York

ECP Executive Clemency and Pardon Case Files, Records of the Department of Correctional Services, New York State Archives, Albany, New York

NYPR New York Municipal Archives, Probation Records

SSP Sing Sing Prison Admission Registers, 1865–1939, New York State Archives, Albany, New York

TTC Trial Transcript Collection, Crime in New York 1850–1950, Special Collections, Lloyd Sealy Library, City University of New York, John Jay College of Criminal Justice/CUNY, New York City

Introduction

1. New York State Census 13th Assembly District, Borough of Manhattan, 1900; Inmate Case File #44016, Preliminary Investigation, January 4, 1929, box 8, AU.

2. Inmate Case File #44016, Preliminary Investigation, January 4, 1929, box 8, AU.

3. Inmate Case File #44016, Sing Sing Prison Hospital, Personal History, September 3, 1929, box 8, AU. Census records show that Katherine Whitehead was listed as

unemployed and doing "housework" in the 1905 enumeration. New York State Census, 13th Assembly District, Borough of Manhattan, 1905.

4. Inmate Case File #44016, Receiving Blotter, Bureau of Identification, Auburn State Prison, July 14, 1930, box 8, AU. In this burglary he climbed into the kitchen window of a flat by the fire escape and stole four gold watches, two gold chains, a gold lavalier, one lady's gold chain, and a pearl necklace, altogether valued at $63. Complaint Record #115710, Affidavit—Burglary, June 13, 1917, box 1350, folder 359.

5. Inmate Case File #44016, Preliminary Investigation, January 4, 1929, box 8, AU; and Inmate Case File #81658, Sing Sing Receiving Blotter, February 1, 1929, box 44, vol. 8, SSP.

6. Inmate Case File #44016, Preliminary Investigation, January 4, 1929, box 8, AU.

7. Urban theorists, such as Susan S. Fainstein and Scott Campbell, recognize "race, class, ethnicity, gender, citizenship status, and disability all interact as part of the process of creating social advantage and disadvantage." Fainstein and Campbell, *Readings in Urban Theory*, 111.

8. Gilfoyle, *City of Eros*, 203–10.

9. The murder of the "mulatto woman" took place in the Criterion Club at 331 West Thirty-Seventh Street, only eight blocks south of Dell Whitehead's home. "Mulatto Woman Murdered," *New York Times*, November 12, 1906.

10. Wallace, *Greater Gotham*, 81; "War in 'Hell's Kitchen'" *New York Times*, August 4, 1898.

11. Parts of Hell's Kitchen were affected by the Tenderloin riots in 1900. See "West Side Race Riot: Mob Attacks Negroes for Policeman's Death," *New-York Tribune*, August 6, 1900; "Negro Finds Hard Fighters in New York," *Atlanta Constitution*, August 17, 1900; and "War on the Blacks," *Los Angeles Times*, August 17, 1900.

12. Inmate Case File #44016, Preliminary Investigation, January 4, 1929, box 8, AU.

13. New York City has long been a place in the black imagination that represents freedom. During the American Revolution black bondsmen flocked to the city hoping to take advantage of an offer of freedom if they fought with the British, and the "city became an island of freedom in a sea of slavery" (Berlin and Harris, *Slavery in New York*, 14). Long before other states, New York began the process of gradual emancipation in 1799 that continued until 1850, and the city became a bastion of abolitionist sentiment leading up to the Civil War. Berlin and Harris, *Slavery in New York*, 13–24. For more on African Americans in New York City during the period of the Great Migration, and Harlem Renaissance, see Lewis, *When Harlem Was in Vogue*; Anderson, *This Was Harlem*; Douglas, *Terrible Honesty*; Frazier, "Negro Harlem." For other books on the Great Migration, see Drake and Cayton, *Black Metropolis*; Grossman, *Land of Hope*; Wilkerson, *The Warmth of Other Suns*; Lemann, *The Promised Land*. For more on New York City history, see Ellis, *The Epic of New York City*; Lankevich, *A Brief History of New York City*; Homberger, *The Historical Atlas of New York City*; Jackson and Dunbar, *Empire City*.

14. Brooklynites did not celebrate the annexation but Manhattanites "rejoiced" with a parade in front of City Hall. Weil, *A History of New York*, 165–67.

15. Wallace, *Greater Gotham*, 5.

16. For more on "other-directedness," see Riesman, *The Lonely Crowd*. German theorist Ferdinand Tönnies had a similar theory as Riesman's. He argued modern soci-

ety had experienced a change from *community* to *society*, a development where traditional communal relations dispersed in the wind of urban life. According to Tönnies,
the "relationship" between people in a society "and the social bond that stems from it,
may be conceived either as having real organic life, and that is the essence of *Community [Gemeinschaft]*; or else as a purely mechanical construction, existing in the mind,
and that is what we think of as Society *[Gesellschaft]*." Tönnies, *Community and
Civil Society*, 17. This dramatic urban change led to increased tension and even nervous disorders. As historian Arthur Schlesinger put it, "hordes of people habituated to
a rural environment had suddenly to adapt themselves to the frantic pace of urban
communities. This circumstance is attributed to the startling growth of nervousness
or neurasthenia, designated by one contemporary as 'the national disease of America.'" Schlesinger, "The City in American History," 60.

17. Croly, "New York as the American Metropolis."

18. As Sven Beckert writes in his work on late nineteenth-century capitalists in Gotham, "nowhere did economic, social, and political power coalesce more than in New
York City." Beckert, *The Monied Metropolis*, 4.

19. Sacks, *Before Harlem*, 14–17.

20. "Sketches of Gay New York: No. 10. In the Tenderloin," *National Police Gazette*,
May 20, 1899.

21. Osofsky, *Harlem*, 3.

22. Sacks, *Before Harlem*, 18–19; Wallace, *Greater Gotham*, 808–9.

23. Osofsky cites a 1907 survey in which only 18 out of 240 black respondents had
been born in New York; Osofsky, *Harlem*, 17–20; Mary White Ovington, in *Half a
Man*, shows that the majority of blacks in the areas she studied were "largely newcomers" from the "South and the West Indies." Ovington, *Half a Man*, 48.

24. This work follows a number of works on New York City's black community.
For example, see Osofsky, *Harlem*; Hodges, *Root and Branch*; Wilder, *A Covenant
with Color*; Harris, *In the Shadow of Slavery*; Lepore, *New York Burning*; White,
Stories of Freedom in Black New York; Alexander, *African or American?*; Dabel, *A Respectable Woman*; Hicks, *Talk with You Like a Woman*; Peterson, *Black Gotham*.

25. Lombroso's work is quoted in Cullen and Agnew, *Criminological Theory*, 26–27.
Also see Lombroso and Lombroso-Ferrero, *Criminal Man*; Gibson, *Born to Crime*;
and Horn, *The Criminal Body*. Interestingly, Cesare Lombroso partially blamed the
high number of homicides in the United States on the history of white colonial and
slaveholding violence. "Those who invaded the territory of the Indian and who based
their rights upon conquest, thought no more of killing a red-man than a hunter would
of killing a monkey. . . . The same can be said of the former slave holders, who were so
used to disposing of the lives of their slaves that no more importance was attached to
the life of a negro than to that of a domestic animal in Europe. The barbarous condition still continues in those States which have been but recently admitted to the
Union, and is rampant in those where gold is sought." Lombroso, "Why Homicide Has
Increased in the United States, II," 3–4.

26. Hicks, *Talk with You Like a Woman*, 128–29.

27. Sing Sing Prison Admissions Registers, box 9, vol. 25, 1865–1939.

28. Case #26267, New York State Reformatory Department of Research, October 3, 1916, box 2, ECF.

29. Quotes taken from Elmira Reformatory Biographical Registers and Receiving Blotters, box 8; and Inmate Case File #38795, Occupational Sheet, undated, box 1, AU.

30. "Dr. Parkhurst on Race Problem," *New York Times*, May 11, 1903.

31. Inmate Case File #44016, Preliminary Investigation, January 4, 1929, box 8, AU. White blood could also be considered an improvement, as many whites believed "mulattoes" had superior intellects. For example, when discerning the difference between what he considered to be advanced blacks and the "bad" and "ignorant" ones, William Fielding Ogburn wrote: "those who have much white blood in their veins are different from the black ones." Ogburn, "The Richmond Negro in New York City," 2.

32. In the words of anti-black sociologist Edward Byron Reuter in his 1918 book, *The Mulatto in the United States*, those of mixed ancestry like Whitehead were "peculiar people," trapped between black inferiority and the transcendency of white blood. Reuter, *The Mulatto in the United States*, 338–39.

33. Bruce, *The Plantation Negro as a Freeman*, 146, 242.

34. Straton, "Will Education Solve the Race Problem?" 788. Booker T. Washington replied to Straton only a month later arguing education would solve the race problem but recognized the "sincere and kindly spirit in which Professor Straton's article is written." Washington conceded that "much that he emphasizes as to present conditions is true" but refocused the debate on "education which begins in the home and includes training in industry and in habits of thrift, as well as mental, moral and religious discipline, and the broader education which comes from contact with the public sentiment of the community in which one lives." He also believed that if Southern whites were educated "race prejudice will be tempered and they will assist in lifting up the black man." Washington, "Education Will Solve the Race Problem: A Reply," 221.

35. McGerr, *A Fierce Discontent*, 182–83.

36. Litwack, "Jim Crow Blues," 7.

37. The best account of race relations in New York during the Civil War and the draft riots is in Bernstein, *The New York City Draft Riots*.

38. Osofsky, *Harlem*, 35–36; McBride, "Fourteenth Amendment Idealism," 207–33; and Wallace and Burrows, *Gotham*, 1034.

39. Other New York–based civil rights laws followed in the new century, including one in 1909 and the Levy Law in 1913, which broadened the laws. Fronc, "The Horns of the Dilemma," 8; "The Last Bill is Signed," *New York Times*, June 16, 1895; "The New York Equal Rights Law," *The Sun*, August 25, 1895.

40. Sacks, *Before Harlem*, 42; "The Last Bill is Signed," *New York Times*, June 16, 1895.

41. Wallace, *Greater Gotham*, 825. Newspaper articles from the *New York Times* often instigated stereotypical images of blacks as criminal similar to those found in vaudeville shows and popular music. For instance, one 1898 *Times* article told of a "burly negro" named "Steve" Small charged with "stealing watermelons and mayhem." The article reads out like a comical play, calling the defendant a "lazy, good-for-nothing fellow who lounges about . . . along with other negroes, watching for opportunities to get hold of watermelons" by the docks. When workers on steamships carrying produce from the South miscalculated a throw and dropped a watermelon, the paper claimed, "there is a rush of darkies who hang around like vultures over a battlefield." In this case, Small, impatient for a dropped melon, stole one and fought his

captors, wounding one badly. "The Luscious Watermelon," *New York Times*, July 12, 1898; Sacks, "Re-Creating Black New York at Century's End," 334; and Woodward, *The Strange Career of Jim Crow*, 74. The surge of support and sympathy in the North for white Southern racist rhetoric at the turn of the century represented a consolidation of white Americans in both regions around a common goal of propping up white supremacy. Lears, *Rebirth of a Nation*, 92–93.

42. Kendi, *Stamped from the Beginning*, 278–79.

43. Woodrow Wilson's promises to the black community are exemplified by an optimistic letter he penned to black bishop Alexander Walters in 1912 during his presidential campaign. Wilson attempted to "assure my Colored fellow citizens of my earnest wish to see justice done them in every matter, and not mere grudging, but justice executed with liberality and cordial good feeling." Letter from Woodrow Wilson to Bishop Alexander Walters, October 16, 1912, box C 1, folder Administrative File, LOC.

44. Wolgemuth, "Woodrow Wilson and Federal Segregation," 158–73.

45. Barbeau and Henri, *The Unknown Soldiers*, 178; and Roth, *American Homicide*, 438.

46. Shaped by population increases, penury, gangs, and sporadic economic downturns, crime was up in New York City at the beginning of the twentieth century. The rate of homicide jumped precipitously in the 1890s and thieves and robbers stalked the streets, affecting all New Yorkers. Timothy Gilfoyle cites only one officer per 400 of New York City's residents between 1855 and 1900. With so few police on the beat, officers had little control over groups of youths and gangs that took over sections of the city and were sometimes afraid to wrangle with them. Gilfoyle, *A Pickpocket's Tale*, xiii, 186. In 1904 prominent judge Rufus B. Cowing noted "highway robberies" like those "depicted in the stories of Western life" plagued the city's byways. Cowing was noticing a period of morphing criminal complexity as offenders became evermore connected to an underground industry, and social scientists, police, and reformers defined a "class of criminals" ranging across all spaces. "Highwaymen More Active," *New York Times*, January 23, 1904. It is worth noting some prominent New Yorkers disagreed with Judge Cowing, although likely for political reasons. For example, police commissioner at the time, Theodore Roosevelt, made a statement on the same day indicating his agreement with the judge that criminals need to be punished more severely but also saying "the facts by no means warrant the alarmist tone of Judge Cowing's charge. "City's Streets Not Safe," *New York Times*, January 7, 1896.

47. Harris, *In the Shadow of Slavery*, 247–48.

48. Wiebe, *The Search for Order*, 168.

49. Many scholars have charted the history of political protest, racial destiny, and civic sources of redress that blacks have employed in a fight for civil rights, fair housing, and protection from racial violence, yet few have foregrounded the ways in which illegality, self-defense, and retaliatory violence figured into black responses including Lane, *Roots of Violence in Black Philadelphia*; and King, *Whose Harlem Is This Anyway?*

50. For African Americans in the decades following slavery, relocation was radical and involved the grand opening of an entire universe of possibilities. As one freed woman told her former owners when they offered to pay her for her services, "I must go. . . . If I stay here I'll never know I'm free." Quoted in White, *Ar'n't I a Woman?*, 169.

51. As historian Lawrence Friedman put it, "the soul was now exposed . . . to the whole bursting, blooming, noisy world." Friedman, *Crime and Punishment in American History*, 193–94.

52. Fainstein and Campbell, eds., *Readings in Urban Theory*, 10. Like Elsa Barkley Brown and Gregg Kimball's 1995 work on black Richmond, this work interrogates the black deployment of concrete and ideological urban nodes and the meaning of the "invisible landscapes" constructed from real and imagined factors that black people navigated. Brown and Kimball, "Mapping the Terrain of Black Richmond."

53. Racist constructions of the black mentality often pegged blacks as too simple to be diabolical criminals. "The Negro is possessed of a hot, violent temper but this does not lead to crime unless it finds immediate opportunity of venting its self," sociologist John Clyde wrote in 1890. "The Negro lacks fortitude and ingenuity that are necessary in the make up of the high class criminal." As such, their crimes related to petty, hedonistic impulses like fights, gambling, theft, and rape, but "never with a Colored woman," Clyde chimed, implying they favored white women. Clyde, "The Negro in New York City," 20.

54. Muhammad, *The Condemnation of Blackness*, 15–35.

55. Muhammad, *The Condemnation of Blackness*, 8.

56. Hoffman's *Race Traits and Tendencies of the American Negro* became a standard and helped solidify the idea that blacks migrating north were "spreading vice, crime, and disease in their wake." Muhammad, *The Condemnation of Blackness*, 5–7, 56.

57. Muhammad, *The Condemnation of Blackness*, 35–36. Following Frederick Hoffman's eugenic work on black crime, Father Thomas F. Price bluntly argued it resulted from exaggerated sensuality and dishonesty, a weakness of willpower, and a lack of stigma against criminals among blacks. Men like Father Price saw Anglo-Saxon contact with "inferior races" as a repetitive story of declension. Lesser peoples died off not because of "persecution that came from without, [but] lack of moral stamina within," despite attempts by whites to save them. Black crime represented the inability of people with African ancestry to cope with civilization and would therefore be their undoing. Price, "Race War and Negro Demoralization," 97, 96, 103. Anna Julia Cooper saw inspiration in the advancement of individual blacks since emancipation because, in her words, it proved "there is nothing irretrievably wrong in the shape of the black man's skull." Cooper, *A Voice from the South*, 26.

58. Grant, *The Passing of the Great Race*, 77. The only way to save the white race, in Grant's opinion, was to allow black evolutionary shortcomings to remove them as a threat. "The stoppage of famines and wars and the abolition of the slave trade [in Africa] while dictated by the noblest impulses of humanity, are suicidal to the white man. Upon the removal of these natural checks Negroes multiply so rapidly that there will not be standing room on the continent for white men, unless, perchance, the lethal sleeping sickness, which attacks the natives far more frequently than the whites, should run its course unchecked" (80).

59. Conrad, *Heart of Darkness*; and Burroughs, *Tarzan of the Apes*.

60. Kendi, *Stamped from the Beginning*, 269.

61. Kendi, *Stamped from the Beginning*, 281. Less than fifty miles from Manhattan, biologist Charles Davenport opened the Eugenics Record Office in Cold Spring Har-

bor, New York, in 1910, with the mission of promoting the preservation of superior white stock and the disappearance of others considered lesser (Kendi, 301).

62. Black Northern elites often used the same "respectability" rhetoric as their white counterparts, especially when dealing with migrants, yet they were still more likely to cite environment and race discrimination when addressing crime. Muhammad, *The Condemnation of Blackness*, 10–11.

63. Miller, "Review of *Race Traits*."

64. Du Bois, "Review of *Race Traits*," 22.

65. Kellor, "The Criminal Negro: A Sociological Study," 61–65.

66. Other notable publications that espoused the same focus on environment over race include one by black educator J. H. N. Waring, who saw black crime spreading like "the white plague of tuberculosis" but still understood that "criminality among the colored people may be properly charged to a lack of proper education, the alley home, and the whiskey shop, to ill-advised arrests, chiefly of children, to reformatories that do not reform, and the 'Topsy class.'" Waring, "Some Causes of Criminality Among Colored People," 45; Miller, *Race Adjustment*; and Ovington, *Half a Man*.

67. Kendi, *Stamped from the Beginning*, 282–83.

68. Du Bois, *The Philadelphia Negro*, 166.

69. In *Righteous Propagation*, Michelle Mitchell looks at both middle-class and working-class ideas about race, gender, and racial destiny. Mitchell, *Righteous Propagation*; Peterson, *Black Gotham*; Gaines, *Uplifting the Race*.

70. Many scholars have engaged black masculinity. For examples, see Mutua, *Progressive Black Masculinities*. In his work, Craig Steven Wilder connected the African roots of antebellum voluntary associations with the construction of black manhood and political development. Wilder, *In the Company of Black Men*. Many authors have approached the subject of black masculinity by analyzing literature such as Hoch, *White Hero Black Beast*; Ikard, *Breaking the Silence*; Leiter, *In the Shadow of the Black Beast*. For more general studies on masculinity, see Seidler, *Rediscovering Masculinity*.

71. Recent studies have emphasized the importance of black romantic relationships in black civil rights and self-determination. Chief among them is Hunter, *Bound in Wedlock*; see also Jones, *Labor of Love, Labor of Sorrow*; Hudson, *To Have and to Hold*; and White, *Ar'n't I a Woman?*

72. Ascribed statuses such as gender, race, and social class are assigned at birth and achieved statuses are those acquired through life if one is able to be socially and economically mobile. Those with low ascribed statuses experience stigma, marginalization, and vulnerabilities custom-fit to their intersectionality. The act of migration, in many ways, was meant to enact a process of refocusing on achieved statuses and denying ascribed statuses. Linton, *The Study of Man*, 113–16.

73. Historians of masculinity, such as Anthony Rotundo and Michael Kimmel, chart the factors that altered white men's conceptions of self at the turn of the century and describe how those men constructed manhood in response to marginalized others and the changing structure of culture and economy. Both acknowledge, to varying degrees, the multiplicity of manhood but don't engage so thoroughly with how black men struggled with the same urges for sovereignty and control over their own lives. The work of a number of scholars has redressed this neglect in the past few

decades and informs the background on black masculinity for this volume. See Wallace, *Constructing the Black Masculine*; Buckner and Caster, *Fathers, Preachers, Rebels, Men*; Madhubuti, *Black Men*; Wallace, *Black Macho and the Myth of the Superwoman*. Riché Richardson interrogates black and white cultural production that portrays black men as emasculated in an effort to establish the rural South as a site of black masculinity studies, in addition to the urban environment. Richardson, *Black Masculinity and the U.S. South*. Anthony J. Lemelle Jr. argues social and political forces reduced prevailing racist perceptions of black manhood into polar opposites, effeminate and ineffectual versus hypersexualized and unbounded, in order to justify subjugation after slavery. The uneven juxtaposition of white and black masculinity, performed on opposite sides of a gulf in the dynamic of American power, leads to tremendous inequity, Lemelle concluded. Lemelle, *Black Masculinity and Sexual Politics*. As Kobena Mercer and Isaac Julien have argued, "black male gender identities have been culturally constructed through complex dialectics of power," since identity itself is adjudicated through "a variety of material, economic, social and political structures." Mercer and Julien, "True Confessions," 196. Martin Summers's work on the interplay of middle-class Victorian masculinity and Jazz Age black conceptions that reveled more openly in sexuality and "revolved around consumption and the body" blueprints a bifurcation between "new negroes" and an older generation. Summers, *Manliness and its Discontents*, 8–9, 288.

74. Baldwin, *Chicago's New Negroes*; also see Gates Jr. and Jarrett, *The New Negro*; Pochmara, *The Making of the New Negro*; King, *Whose Harlem Is This, Anyway?*; and Harold, *New Negro Politics in the Jim Crow South*.

75. Du Bois, *The Souls of Black Folks*, 33, 37.

76. Pochmara, *The Making of the New Negro*, 39–40.

77. "The South Blamed for Negro Exodus," *New York Times*, July 2, 1917; Dumenil, *The Modern Temper*, 284–85.

78. Quoted in Osofsky, *Harlem*, 22.

79. A number of historians recognize that white men at the turn of the century were "born anxious and insecure, uncoupled from the more stable anchors of landownership or workplace autonomy." As such, they were experiencing a "crisis" of masculinity. Kimmel, *Manhood in America*, 4–5, 7. For more on American masculinity, see Rotundo, *American Manhood*. Gail Bederman more completely engages with race by looking at the subject of white antimodernist thought at the turn of the century and arguing that emasculating "other" men bolstered the project of constructing novel versions of civilized masculinity for white men. Bederman, *Manliness and Civilization*.

80. Guterl, *The Color of Race in America*, 6. For more on the subject of the transformation of whiteness, see Roediger, *The Wages of Whiteness*; and Roediger, *Working Toward Whiteness*. Eugenicist T. Lothrop Stoddard, in his work condemning the inmigration of people of color and the growth of the black population, coined the term *bi-racialism*, which aided in the bifurcation of Americans into categories of "white" and "black." Stoddard, *Re-Forging America*.

81. Sociologist Robert Staples makes this argument in *Black Masculinity*, 2–7.

82. Anthony, *Searching for the New Black Man*, 4.

83. Historian Cheryl Hicks used the women's case files from the New York State Archives extensively in the past, including in her book, *Talk with You Like a Woman*.

84. Gross, "Exploring Crime and Violence," 57.

85. The popular idea of a "culture of poverty" comes primarily from Daniel Patrick Moynihan's 1965 report to President Lyndon B. Johnson, "The Negro Family: The Case for National Action," in which he argued African American communities were hindered by a "tangle of pathologies" resulting from matriarchal households, absent emasculated fathers, and cultural inadequacies acquired under slavery. Much of the following sociological work on black crime endeavored to refocus attention on the impact of urban conditions and economic isolation. Kendi, *Stamped from the Beginning*, 391. For sociological scholarship contemporary to the Moynihan report and after that refuted claims of black pathologies, see Myrdal, *An American Dilemma*; Osofsky, *Harlem*; Liebow, *Tally's Corner*; Clark and Myrdal, *Dark Ghetto*; and Wilson, *The Truly Disadvantaged*.

86. Majors and Billson, *Cool Pose*; Liebow, *Tally's Corner*; Anderson, *Code of the Street*. Drawing from these and other works I've also considered the arguments of sociological researchers who have made arguments about the connection between crime and masculinity. Considering sixty interviews of black teenagers, *Cool Pose* authors Richard Majors and Janet Mancini Billson conclude that some employed a "cool pose," that helped them to project a masculine identity and navigate the unique hazards and structural limitations that black men face. The psychological castration of race forced them to realize normative behaviors failed to reap the expected rewards for them. Billson and Mancini argued that "striving for masculinity" presented a predicament unique to black men under these circumstances. "Being male and black has meant being psychologically castrated—rendered impotent in the economic, political, and social arenas that whites have historically dominated. Black men learned a long time ago that the classic American virtues of thrift, perseverance, and hard work did not give them the same tangible rewards that accrued for whites" (1–2). Building off of this scholarship I'm writing about men who responded to externally constructed ideas of black manhood while caught between old and new versions of manliness designed by black men. The men in my study are working class and thus faced imperatives and restrictions that were less prominent for the black bourgeoisie. However, many of them had middle-class aspirations and accordingly existed somewhere along the spectrum between new and old concepts of black manhood.

87. Bell, *Race, Racism, and American Law*; Alexander, *The New Jim Crow*.

88. Hine and Jenkins, *A Question of Manhood*; also see scholars such as Eric Arnesen, Craig Steven Wilder, Michele Mitchell, and Allison Dorsey who have engaged black masculinity through the lens of politics, labor, military combat, fraternal organizations, sports, and respectability. Arnesen, *Brotherhoods of Color*; Wilder, *In the Company of Black Men*; Mitchell, *Righteous Propagation*; Dorsey, *To Build Our Lives Together*.

89. Summers, *Manliness and Its Discontents*; Hornsby-Gutting, *Black Manhood and Community Building in North Carolina*; Black, *Dismantling Black Manhood*. Historian Martin Summers argues that black conceptions of manhood in the early twentieth century ran the gamut from middle-class Victorian versions of restraint to Jazz Age interpretations that eschewed the primacy of the marketplace and patriarchy in constructing manhood, reveled more openly in sexuality, and "revolved around consumption and the body." Ultimately, Summers's blueprints a bifurcation between

"new negroes" coming of age during and after World War I, and an older generation "attentive to the fact that black middle-class youth were rapidly jettisoning the Victorian framework of values that had structured their parent's gender and class identities," 8–9, 288.

90. See Mumford, *Interzones*; Schatzberg and Kelly, *African American Organized Crime*; Hunter, *To 'Joy My Freedom*; see also Wolcott, *Remaking Respectability*; Campbell, *Crime and Punishment in African American History*; LeFlouria, *Chained in Silence*. Also Khalil Gibran Muhammad's seminal study of the implementation of social scientific theories on race, crime, and heredity to shape reform and public policy laid a formidable historiographical foundation for continued analysis of black crime. Muhammad, *The Condemnation of Blackness*.

91. Muhammad, *The Condemnation of Blackness*.

92. Gross, *Colored Amazons*; Hicks, *Talk with You Like a Woman*.

93. Blair, *"I've Got to Make My Livin'"*; Haley, *No Mercy Here*; and Harris, *Sex Workers*.

94. Roger Lane used W. E. B. Du Bois's *Philadelphia Negro* study and various other municipal records to argue that as whites became more integrated and stabilized by the burgeoning industrial economy, African Americans became more detached and destabilized, which caused the growth of a criminal subculture. However, in his analysis he found the justice system not to blame and that blacks benefitted from illegal underground markets. Lane, *Roots of Violence in Black Philadelphia*.

95. For more on the subject of the moral construction of criminality, see Friedman, *Crime and Punishment in American History*, 125–26.

96. Roth, *American Homicide*, 3–24.

97. Roth, *American Homicide*, 399.

98. Theories such as labeling theory, differential association, control theory, and anomie and strain theory explain the impact of society on the individual and how crime is produced. My work is not adhering to any one of these theories but is considering them collectively in my analysis of criminogenic factors, the gaze of others on black behaviors, and the responses of black men to various environmental stimuli. On labeling theory, see Tannenbaum, *Crime and the Community*. For differential association, see Shaw and McKay, *Juvenile Delinquency and Urban Areas*; Sutherland and Cressey, *Principles of Criminology*; Sutherland and Cressey, "A Theory of Differential Association"; Cullen and Agnew, *Criminological Theory*, 95. Travis Hirschi was not the first control theorist, but his work is exemplary in Hirschi, *Causes of Delinquency*. Robert K. Merton's criminological work on anomie and strain theories are best represented in Merton "Social Structure and Anomie," 672–82.

99. Cullen and Agnew, *Criminological Theory*, 294–303. For more on critical criminological theory, see Bonger, *Criminality and Economic Conditions*; Quinney, *Class, State, and Crime*; and Currie, *Confronting Crime*.

100. Bonger, "Criminality and Economic Conditions," in *Criminological Theory*, Francis T. Cullen and Robert Agnew, 307.

101. These wounds began with invasion on the African continent and in the Middle Passage. For more on the devastating traumas of slavery, see Genovese, *Roll, Jordan, Roll*; Brown, *The Reaper's Garden*; Smallwood, *Saltwater Slavery*; Mustakeem, *Slavery at Sea*; Berry, *The Price for Their Pound of Flesh*; and Fuentes, *Dispossessed Lives*.

102. Some authors have acknowledged that structural issues produced many of the problems facing African Americans in the twentieth century but sometimes reacted moralistically to single-parent households, "illegitimate" children, and matriarchy as "problems" associated with the "pathologies" caused by a history of enslavement. See Frazier, *The Negro Family in the United States*.

103. Recent scholarship has shown how integral slavery was to the unbridled capitalism that followed it, as well as how important the separation of families and other cruelties were to maintaining the system. See Baptist, *The Half Has Never Been Told*.

104. In New York City specifically, blacks lacked the political pull to make changes through policy. Constituting less than 3 percent of the population until 1910, and lacking money to influence city machine politics, they were also excluded from many local party club units. By 1920 the situation was not much better when they made up only 4.8 percent of the population. Blacks typically voted Republican, against the white majority of Democrats, and their votes rarely impacted the outcomes of races. As a result, they never partook of the political patronage jobs that others benefitted from, including the Irish who dominated police rosters. Lewinson, *Black Politics in New York City*, 34–35.

105. Some historians have looked at manhood as a perpetual state, uncompromised by culture, time, place, and individual, while others have considered it composed of changeable cultural aspects, a list that morphs over time. Neither of these interpretations allow for the diversity of "manhoods" that might exist at one time side by side across race, class, and power dynamics. Historian Gail Bederman called "gender" a "historical, ideological process" where individuals are "positioned and position themselves as men or women." Bederman, *Manliness and Civilization*, 6–7; also see Rotundo, *American Manhood*, 1.

106. Rotundo, *American Manhood*, 3–6.

107. Rotundo, *American Manhood*, 227.

108. Beynon, *Masculinities and Culture*, 16.

109. Lindsey, *Gender Roles*, 285–86.

110. Before the feminist movement of the second half of the twentieth century, criminology was primarily male-centered. In the 1960s and 1970s more women became involved in the study of criminology and more complex questions about the gendered differences of crime began to be asked seriously. I attempt to understand crimes committed by black men by analyzing the role of patriarchy in their actions. Theorists such as Meda Chesney-Lind have offered explanations for crimes committed by women that are rooted in the idealization of inequality in heterosexual relationships and attempts by women to escape sexual and physical abuse. See Hicks, *Talk with You Like a Woman*; Gross, *Colored Amazons*; Chesney-Lind and Shelden, *Girls, Delinquency, and Juvenile Justice*; and Chesney-Lind, *The Female Offender*. In addition, Rita James Simon argues women's crime stems from grievances with the unfulfillment and servility of traditional male and female relationships in Simon, *Women and Crime*.

111. John Beynon argues that hegemonic norms of masculinity reduce the statuses of all others. Beynon, *Masculinities and Culture*, 16; and Lindsey, *Gender Roles*, 286.

112. Bederman, *Manliness and Civilization*, 47.

113. Scholars such as Judith Kegan Gardiner have made it clear how hegemonic masculinity "gives men a sense of superiority and of entitlement to advantages over

women, and it valorizes in men characteristics such as aggression that harm women as well as other men." Gardiner, "Theorizing Age with Gender," 90.

114. See Bonger, *Criminality and Economic Conditions*; Greenberg, *Crime and Capitalism*; Gordon, "Capitalism, Class, and Crime in America," 163–86.

115. Sugrue, *The Origins of the Urban Crisis*, 5.

116. Sociologists have argued that black economic isolation led to urban crisis and increased crime rates in the post–World War II period. See Wilson, *The Truly Disadvantaged*. Race impacted the tenor of disparity for blacks while whites were engaged in the process of "becoming white," as scholars like David Roediger have noted. Roediger, *The Wages of Whiteness*.

117. Rotundo, *American Manhood*, 3–4.

118. Beckert, *The Monied Metropolis*, 237–38.

119. Dumenil, *The Modern Temper*, 7.

120. Dormon, "Shaping the Popular Image of Post-Reconstruction American Blacks."

121. Sacks, *Before Harlem*, 48–50; and "The Dominant 'Coon Song,'" *Los Angeles Times*, November 28, 1897.

122. Sacks, *Before Harlem*, 51.

123. Sacks, *Before Harlem*, 51.

124. Reed and Ward, *Leave Your Razors at the Door.*

125. Sacks, *Before Harlem*, 51.

126. Sacks, *Before Harlem*, 54.

127. Levine, *Black Culture and Black Consciousness*, 239–41.

128. Levine, *Black Culture and Black Consciousness*, 411; Gussow, "Shoot Myself a Cop," 9–12.

129. Gussow, *Seems Like Murder Here*, 162–63, 168–69; Eberhart, "Stack Lee."

130. McKee and Chisenhall, *Beale Black and Blue*, 28.

131. Gussow, *Seems Like Murder Here*, 3.

132. Gussow, *Seems Like Murder Here*, 170.

133. Wright, *Black Boy*, 64–65.

134. Michael J. Carter and Celene Fuller outline symbolic interactionism in "Symbols, Meaning, and Action," 931–61. For other prominent sociologists on the subject, also see Mead, *Mind, Self, and Society*; Kuhn, "Major Trends in Symbolic Interaction Theory," 61–84; Blumer, *Symbolic Interaction*; and Stryker, *Symbolic Interactionism.*

135. Fanon, *The Wretched of the Earth*, 15–16; and Patchay, "Transgressing Boundaries," 149.

136. Sociologist Jack Katz, in his 1988 publication, argued scholars should give more attention to "those aspects of criminality that make its various forms sensible, even sensually compelling, ways of being." Katz, *Seductions of Crime*, 3, 9–10.

137. Baldwin, *The Fire Next Time*, 98; also quoted in Kimmel, *Manhood in America*, 196.

Chapter 1

1. Jeremiah Dunn's biography bears out in his trial for murder in 1901. Trial Transcript #257, March 18, 1901, reel 47, 414–16, TTC.

2. Trial Transcript #257, 452–53, TTC.

3. Trial Transcript #257, 418–19, TTC.

4. "Negro Shoots Messenger," *New York Times*, August 26, 1900.

5. "Police Find 'Lamplighter,'" *New York Times*, August 30, 1900; "Pistol-shooting Negro Caught," *The Sun*, August 30, 1900.

6. "More Attacks on Negroes," *New-York Tribune*, August 27, 1900.

7. "More Attacks on Negroes," *New-York Tribune*, August 27, 1900.

8. Ottley, *New World A-Coming*, 26–27; and Hicks, *Talk with You Like a Woman*, 55.

9. "More Attacks on Negroes," *New-York Tribune*, August 27, 1900.

10. Trial Transcript #257, 78–79, TTC.

11. Trial Transcript #257, 412, TTC.

12. Sacks, *Before Harlem*, 80. "There was excitement every night," police captain Cornelius Willemse remembered from his rookie year in San Juan Hill in 1899. "Brawls were common and serious fights were regular events." Willemse, *Behind the Green Lights*, 29.

13. Sacks, *Before Harlem*, 80; Kisseloff, *You Must Remember This*, 190.

14. Campbell, "You Needn't Be Afraid Here," 259. In his work, historian Shannon King has argued that the emphasis many scholars have placed on riots has, to some extent, rendered everyday racial violence invisible. On the contrary, life in the North for African Americans included small- and large-scale racial attacks as well as instances of police brutality that were not anomalous, but were frequent and institutional in nature. King, "Ready to Shoot and Do Shoot," 757, and in King, *Whose Harlem Is This, Anyway?*

15. Fainstein and Campbell, *Readings in Urban Theory*, 111.

16. Osofsky, *Harlem*, 43.

17. In an interview for the *Times*, black pastor R. F. Hurley argued this mixture afflicted blacks most since foreign-born and "illiterate white people, with whom in our poverty we are thrown in competition for our livelihoods . . . perpetuate this prejudice against us." "Prejudices of Landlords," *New York Times*, April 14, 1889.

18. Quoted in Sacks, *Before Harlem*, 124.

19. Myrdal, *An American Dilemma*, 527.

20. Hicks, *Talk with You Like a Woman*, 26–27; and Haynes, "Conditions among Negroes in the Cities," 108. Also see Henri, *Black Migration*; Grossman, *Land of Hope*; Trotter, *The Great Migration in Historical Perspective*; Griffin, *"Who Set You Flowin'?"*; Hahn, *A Nation Under Our Feet*.

21. Paul, "A Group of Virginia Negroes in New York City," 35. Black commentators often invoked religious imagery of exodus and arrival and considered the North a "promised land" of deliverance from the neoslavery of the South. Jones, *Labor of Love, Labor of Sorrow*, 131.

22. Corbould, "Streets, Sounds and Identity in Interwar Harlem," 870–71.

23. Kiser, *Sea Island to City*, 133. Writers like Kingsley Moses echoed the idea that life would be better in the North. Moses, "The Negro Comes North," 181–90.

24. Kiser, *Sea Island to City*, 137.

25. Johnson, *Along This Way*, 152.

26. Johnson, *The Autobiography of an Ex-Coloured Man*, 93.

27. It is interesting to note only six men and women indicated they moved North because of employment they had already acquired, particularly considering the efforts

of job recruiters to entice migrants to relocate. Wright, "The Migration of Negroes to the North," 566.

28. Ogburn, "The Richmond Negro in New York City," 33.

29. Very well explained in Wallace, *Greater Gotham*, 432–38.

30. The Amenia Conference, 1925, W. E. B. Du Bois Papers, 1868–1963, Special Collections, University of Massachusetts Amherst Libraries, 3–4.

31. The Amenia Conference, 1925, W. E. B. Du Bois Papers, 1868–1963, Special Collections, University of Massachusetts Amherst Libraries, 3–4.

32. Notes on Amenia Conference, 1916, W. E. B. Du Bois Papers, 1868–1963, Special Collections, University of Massachusetts Amherst Libraries, 3.

33. The Amenia Conference, 1925, W. E. B. Du Bois Papers, 1868–1963, Special Collections, University of Massachusetts Amherst Libraries, 13.

34. "Spingarn Home Burns," *New York Times*, December 16, 1917.

35. The Amenia Conference, 1925, W. E. B. Du Bois Papers, 1868–1963, Special Collections, University of Massachusetts Amherst Libraries, 17–18.

36. The Amenia Conference, 1925, W. E. B. Du Bois Papers, 1868–1963, Special Collections, University of Massachusetts Amherst Libraries, 18. [Mention: This observation is not to disparage the contributions of the Amenia conference-goers.]

37. An explicit barrier of race and class disconnected the proletarian and poor blacks most concerned with issues of subsistence and racial violence, and the white and black elites that comprised the NAACP. Wallace, *Greater Gotham*, 845.

38. The Amenia Conference, 1925, W. E. B. Du Bois Papers, 1868–1963, Special Collections, University of Massachusetts Amherst Libraries, 12.

39. Trial Transcript #478, January 16, 1905, reel 82, 7, 382, TTC.

40. Trial Transcript #478, 28–31, TTC.

41. Trial Transcript #478, 90, TTC.

42. Trial Transcript #478, 152, TTC.

43. Trial Transcript #478, 92, TTC.

44. Trial Transcript #478, 116–124, TTC.

45. Trial Transcript #478, 382, TTC.

46. Trial Transcript #478, 581–86, TTC.

47. Trial Transcript #478, 587, TTC. Some white observers blamed migration itself for the unfavorable change in demographics and represented migrants as interlopers in a relatively calm racial environment. Prominent defense attorney Lewis Stuyvesant Chanler summed these sentiments up during the trial of a black New York native accused of killing a migrant from South Carolina. In making an argument of self-defense he told the jury "there are good and bad negroes. . . . There are the men who come up from the south . . . who are thronging our city, and making its streets dangerous to us [and] there are the negroes of that class, who render New York unsafe to whites and blacks, and who live in herds together, ready to assist each other in every crime." These "herds," he argued, grew in size and would continue unless something halted their multiplication. "They are coming, day by day, from the south, and I hope that something will be done soon to remedy that evil." In contrast, he described the defendant as a "boy, coming of honest people, of good old colored stock, that we used to make our servants . . . and our work was done well and faithfully." Although Chanler's rhetoric about the virtues of black New Yorkers served oratorical purposes in the

trial it indicates a level of enmity that whites felt about surging populations of migrants. As the number of blacks skyrocketed in the city white tenants and landholders resented the new spatial competition and sometimes romanticized native-born blacks in order to emphasize the nuisance of new arrivals. "In other words," Chanler concluded, the defendant "has a right to live in New York, for he was born and reared here . . . and [the right] to resist the attack of a mob of furious southern negroes." Trial Transcript #478, February 9, 1904, reel 71, 116–18, TTC.

48. On the subject of black leisure and public space, see Harris, *Sex Workers*, 31. Representing the viewpoint of the people of Sixty-Second Street, Assistant District Attorney Charles Nott asserted their rights to occupy public space for work and leisure and challenged unofficial edicts about popular decorum. "The night in question was a warm, sultry night, and in accordance with the habits of these colored people, and their sociability . . . the block was not deserted," Nott explained. "If what they are doing does not disturb that neighborhood, and no complaint is made, they have the right to be there," he remonstrated. With this statement, Nott confronted long-established customs of police brutality enacted by the New York Police Department on poor and working-class citizens. Trial Transcript #478, 6, 596, TTC.

49. Jury finds Frederick Miller guilty of manslaughter in Trial Transcript #478, 675, TTC. A number of factors stacked against Miller in his case. Less than a month before his trial he assaulted a journalist without provocation. He also had "half a dozen [victims] . . . ready to prefer charges of assault against him." The assault on the journalist helped prosecutors bring the case of murder against him. Miller originally convinced magistrates he shot Joseph Poole in self-defense, but an assistant district attorney reopened the case and discovered police had colluded to make him look like the aggressor. "Murder Charge, Too," *New-York Tribune*, December 29, 1904. District Attorney Charles Cooper Nott also brought the inconsistency of Miller's story about the attack to the surface during his closing statement. "Was he stamped on, kicked, slugged? Not a scratch on him? And yet he says he had this frightful struggle down the street, and this enormous man, Poole, taller and heavier than himself, fell down on him, and he was pinioned under Poole, and here was this crowd around him crying 'Kill the son of a bitch,' but they did not touch him, though they could have punched him and kicked him and not a scratch on him." Trial Transcript #478, 453, 426; "To Arrest Patrolman," *New-York Tribune/Herald Tribune*, December 22, 1904; "Clubbed By Policeman," *New-York Tribune/Herald Tribune*, December 21, 1904; "Murder Charged, Too," *New-York Tribune*, December 29, 1904. Although the allegations of Miller slashing his own coat were not entered into the trial as evidence, the assistant district attorney's investigation concluded the slashes could not have been dealt by a razor in a fight because there was no evidence of slashing on Miller's shirt or skin beneath his coat; Trial Transcript #478, 660, 675, TTC.

50. For more on police brutality in New York City, see Johnson, *Street Justice*. Miller's attorney blamed public opinion on his conviction saying "the recent efforts of the district attorney's office to purify the police have prejudiced the public mind against the force to a great degree, and I believe this feeling affected the jury." "Victim of Public Opinion," *The Evening Post*, February 3, 1905.

51. McFarland, *Inside Greenwich Village*, 11; Scheiner, *Negro Mecca*, 15–16.

52. Cuyler, "A Peep Into Cut-Throat Alley," *The Independent*, February 7, 1861, 6.

53. Bernstein, *The New York City Draft Riots*, 3.

54. Gilfoyle, *A Pickpocket's Tale*, 184–88.

55. "Defense of the Negro," *New York Times*, September 2, 1900. For more on early black life in New York City, see McManus, *A History of Negro Slavery in New York*; White, *Somewhat More Independent*; Berlin and Harris, *Slavery in New York*; Harris, *In the Shadow of Slavery*.

56. Osofsky, *Harlem*, 17–18, 128.

57. Locke, *Harlem*, 630. For more on the diversity of African descended residents of neighborhoods like Harlem, see Watkins-Owens, *Blood Relations*.

58. Wallace, *Greater Gotham*, 807–10.

59. By 1910, the black populations of Manhattan and Brooklyn inflated by 60 percent and 62 percent respectively rivaling numbers in Washington, D.C, which had the largest black community in the country at the time. Osofsky, "Race Riot, 1900," 1. Seth M. Scheiner explains that New York City's black population growth at the turn of the century can be explained partly by natural increase counting a population of 38,504 New York–born blacks in the state in 1870. That year 74 percent of the black population had been born in the state. From 1870 to 1880 the black population jumped 56 percent and, less impressively, it jumped 17.6 percent in the 1880s. The 1890s witnessed yet another spectacular increase of 79 percent. While migration was inconsistent, it remained significant until 1900. This indicates not only a large increase of migrant blacks in New York City but also a significant influx that precedes the historical parameters of the "Great Migration" by more than a decade. Statistics on black migration into New York City in the nineteenth and early twentieth centuries can be found in Scheiner, *Negro Mecca*, 7–8, 10.

60. Osofsky, *Harlem*, 14–15.

61. Osofsky, *Harlem*, 12–13. San Juan Hill's boundaries also defined in Ovington, *Black and White Sat Down Together*, 26. In William Fielding Ogburn's master's thesis for Columbia University he claimed the San Juan Hill neighborhood got its name "because of its slope and the fighting that used to occur there between the negroes and the Irish or Italians." Ogburn, "The Richmond Negro in New York City," 52.

62. A "baby belt" of black entertainment and housing existed on South Fifth Avenue crisscrossed by Bleeker, Sullivan, and Thompson Streets. Brown, *Brownstone Fronts and Saratoga Trunks*, 361; Clyde, *The Negro in New York City*, 3a; and Osofsky, *Harlem*, 12–13.

63. Wallace, *Greater Gotham*, 584, 591–92, 595. In his 1909 exposé of the Tomb's jail John J. Munro wrote about the Hell's Kitchen Gang headquartered on Thirty-Ninth Street and Eleventh Avenue, and how they "usually fought negroes with guns, while the negroes in turn fought with razors. The negroes and whites are far from being friendly in this neighborhood, and many battles have taken place in recent years." Munro, *The New York Tombs Inside and Out!*, 187–88.

64. Osofsky, Harlem, 11–13, 71; Connolly, *Blacks in Brooklyn*, 115. A tremendous increase in black migration corresponded with a notable decrease in the movement of Southern white residents. Between the Civil War and 1900 100,000 fewer whites migrated from the South to other parts of the country than did blacks. Sacks, *Before Harlem*, 9. In Queens blacks often settled in South Jamaica and Flushing in areas formerly inhabited by the descendants of slaves. Wallace, *Greater Gotham*, 812–14.

65. White et al., *Playing the Numbers*, 14. In 1898, sociologist John P. Clyde identified a constellation of blacks in Harlem living here and there from "river to river." Clyde, "The Negro in New York City," 3a–4a. in his study on Harlem, E. Franklin Frazier noted how the black population of the neighborhood increased over time from 1910 to 1934 by 631 percent, advancing from 27,827 to 203,482. Frazier, "Negro Harlem," 75.

66. Connolly, *Blacks in Brooklyn from 1900–1960*, 81–82; Wallace, *Greater Gotham*, 812–14; and Pritchett, *Brownsville, Brooklyn*, 40.

67. "Where New York's Population Is Growing Most Rapidly," *New York Times*, September 4, 1910.

68. Lewinson, *Black Politics in New York City*, 48–49.

69. McKay, *Harlem*, 18.

70. Johnson's chapter on the racialization of police brutality from 1900–1911 makes clear how police violence increasingly targeted African Americans and Jewish immigrants. Johnson, *Street Justice*, 19, 56–86.

71. Political machines, or clubs, represented a connection between national politics and voters through local party bosses, and they often doled out resources and jobs in exchange for loyalty. In New York City at the turn of the century, the Democratic Party operated through Tammany Hall and controled much of city politics, including the police. Boehm and Corey, *America's Urban History*, 170.

72. Friedman, *Crime and Punishment*, 149–50, 154; and Callow, "The Crusade Against the Tweed Ring," 191.

73. Robertson et al., "Disorderly Houses," 445–52.

74. McGerr, *A Fierce Discontent*, 190–91.

75. Most New York City census records from the turn of the century show black and white inhabited buildings on the same blocks and avenues, but rarely do the races live in the same buildings. As an example, from the 1900 census, in one stretch of buildings in the Tenderloin African Americans inhabited a stretch from 11–17 Thirtieth Street, interrupted only by one white residence at number 14. German immigrants rented the buildings from 18–19, followed by a number of other buildings tenanted by African Americans. This is the dominant trend found in the census documents for this section of the city. New York State Census, 11th Assembly District, Borough of Manhattan, 1900.

76. As an accomplice of eugenics, the pseudoscience of euthenics promised to improve human morality through better environments and households, since abjection and disorderliness doomed children to immoral lives, regardless of heredity. Mitchell, *Righteous Propagation*, 141–42, 147. According to Annie Dewey, the wife of famed librarian Melvil Dewey, the "betterment of living conditions, through conscious endeavor, for the purpose of securing more efficient human beings, is what is meant by euthenics, and the home is its most important factor, relating education and science to life." Dewey, "Standards of Living in the Home," 9, 491.

77. "High Negro Mortality," *New York Amsterdam News*, August 31, 1927.

78. Observant of the conditions blacks lived in and the "pressure" they felt from "the less moral elements of both races," sociologist George Edmund Haynes wrote "the marvel is not that the criminal records outrun other elements of our urban population [among blacks], but that impartial observers both North and South testify to the large law-abiding Negro citizenship, and to the thousands of pure individuals, Christian homes and communities." Haynes, "Conditions Among Negroes in the Cities," 115.

79. Moore, "A Study of a Group of West Indian Negroes in New York City," 23.

80. "Tenement Commission Makes Its Report," *New York Times*, February 26, 1901.

81. In framing the Tenement House Law, the inaugural leaders of the Tenement House Commission, Robert W. De Forest and Lawrence Veiller, implemented many of the ideas from Ernest Flagg's 1894 *Scribner's Magazine* article which called for larger buildings and lots that would allow for sunny internal courtyards, larger rooms, bathrooms, fire safety policies, new windows on older constructions, and other measures meant to make life better for low-income renters. Flagg, "The New York Tenement-House Evil and Its Cure"; and Wallace, *Greater Gotham*, 254–56. Part of the problem for blacks looking for housing stemmed from a shortage of housing for whites. A report by the New York Bureau of Social Hygiene noted in 1922 that "during the past few years owing to lack of building it has been impossible for the whites to get houses elsewhere, and the colored have been hemmed in with no possibility of expansion." As a result, "Negro families have a much narrower limit of choice than white people . . . [and] the situation [in Harlem] is probably more acute than in other sections of Manhattan." Bureau of Social Hygiene, *Housing Conditions of Employed Women in the Borough of Manhattan*, 57.

82. Scheiner, *Negro Mecca*, 38.

83. For example, the Ugly Club, the Sons of Virginia, and the Manhattan Club all catered to professionals, educators, and wealthy blacks explicitly. Scheiner, *Negro Mecca*, 94.

84. Little more than a decade into the overwhelming black occupation of Harlem, one writer for *Outlook* observed houses "in good repair" and determined that "windows, entrances, halls, sidewalks, and streets are clean, and the houses comfortable and respectable inside to a degree not often found in a workingman's locality." Dyckoff, "A Negro City in New York." However, others regularly considered housing in Harlem to be unclean, overcrowded, and neglected by landlords and tenants. See "Sees Negro Housing Crisis," *New York Times*, January 13, 1928; "Harlem Conditions Called Deplorable," *New York Times*, September 6, 1927.

85. Press accounts of Southern communities divided along lines of race and disease generated public apprehension about closeness with the swelling populations of black newcomers in New York City. Believing blacks to be more proficient carriers of disease, white Southerners responded violently to contact with blacks they believed to be diseased. In 1897 smallpox ravaged communities in and surrounding Birmingham, Alabama, and primarily affected African Americans, scores of whom were removed to a "pesthouse" on nearby Red Mountain. Frightened of the possible contagion from the quarantine, a group of whites "almost splintered the house with bullets" causing the inmates to flee in panic. See "Smallpox in Alabama," *New York Times*, July 28, 1897. In another case, New Orleans residents experienced "alarm and anxiety" over a quarantine packed with 197 smallpox cases, of which 192 were black men and women. "The only danger of a possible spread," declared the *New-Orleans Picayune*, "is from negroes coming to the city from the country." In order to minimize their contact with the white population, civic leaders had "the negro quarters . . . vigilantly patrolled, and suspicious cases . . . promptly looked after." Story reprinted in "The Smallpox in New-Orleans," *New York Times*, March 20, 1896.

86. *New York Times* writers reporting on the epidemic sweep of smallpox across the South made certain to mention that many of the counties plagued by the disease were "populated chiefly by negroes." States like Alabama, Georgia, and Louisiana experienced increased rates of the disease, and violent conflicts between white communities and black neighborhoods were considered the source of diseases like smallpox and tuberculosis. "At North Brother Island," *New York Times*, June 16, 1901. It is interesting to note that in reporting on the mystery of black vulnerability to smallpox and tuberculosis, another *Times* article reported on the Hampton Institute's recommendations for "race improvement" and mentioned the suggestions of black leaders on how to handle disease. The institute, the paper reported, "emphasized that negro mortality must be looked after" and believed themselves that blacks were dying more frequently from disease than whites. However, they rejected the notion that it was due to a weaker racial constitution and instead pointed to the conditions of their communities. In pushing for improved conditions in black homes and public spaces, Dr. J. W. Prather highlighted the "duties of mothers" and schools in eradicating disease by aiding in the enforcement of vaccinations. "Negro Problems from the Negro Standpoint," *New York Times*, July 19, 1903, 11.

87. Story taken from "Fighting the Smallpox," *New York Times*, December 1, 1900; and "Smallpox on West Side," *New York Times*, November 30, 1900. In another case one *Times* columnist described black domestic servant Mary Loftus as a roaming menace in 1899 delivering disease to her white employers. Making matters worse, the New York Health Department believed Loftus contracted the disease from her brother who distributed handbills in a busy shopping district. "Brooklyn Smallpox Scare," *New York Times*, November 11, 1899, 4.

88. "War on Disease Germs," *New York Times*, July 12, 1900.

89. The *New York Indicator* quoted in Wallace, *Greater Gotham*, 852.

90. "Dislike Negroes in Harlem," *New York Times*, July 7, 1912. Responding to unfavorable investigative reports by the crime-fighting Committee of Fourteen, business-owner John O'Connor claimed it was due to the unfortunate transformation of his neighborhood "so that my customers are almost entirely colored people." Harlem experienced great demographic change later than the Tenderloin, and John O'Connor's letter to the Committee of Fourteen indicates that even as late as 1917 large white populations still lived in the area of 683 Lenox Avenue on 144th Street. It is interesting to note that his establishment changed from a primarily white drinking spot to one that was mostly black, and he remained in business to serve the new clientele. When investigated by the committee and pressured to eliminate prostitution from the rear room, he promised to "avoid the repetition of this offense" by no longer allowing women to "be served with liquor to be consumed on the premises, [and] the service of liquor to women" would be "restricted to pint and bottle trade." Letter from John O'Connor, September 26, 1918, box 17, folder Lenox Avenue-Lexington Avenue, COF.

91. Osofsky, *Harlem*, 105.

92. "Invasion of Negroes Cuts Harlem Values," *New York Times*, December 1, 1911.

93. "Invasion of Negroes Cuts Harlem Values," *New York Times*, December 1, 1911; Scheiner, *Negro Mecca*, 30–31.

94. African American real estate entrepreneurs eventually entered the market in Harlem in ways that flipped the script of racial exclusion. Entering the market at the

perfect time and taking advantage of a glut of housing in upper Manhattan, black real estate investors like Philip A. Payton and Reverend Hutchens C. Bishop bought newer constructions and rented to blacks. Facing opposition from white real estate companies that actively campaigned to remove black tenants, Payton and Bishop both bought buildings and evicted white tenants in retaliation. In 1905 Payton acquired three tenements on West 135th Street where blacks had been evicted a year earlier, and expelled white renters only days before Christmas. Declaring the start of a "Real Estate Race War" in Harlem, the *New York Times* reported on "white folks, hat in hand," filing into Payton's office begging to be "left in undisturbed possession of their little flats over the holidays." Wallace, *Greater Gotham*, 850–52; "Real Estate Race War is Started in Harlem," *New York Times*, December 17, 1905.

95. In an interview in 1889 one real estate agent admitted "the rents are made higher to the colored people than to the white because the demand for habitations for colored people is larger than the supply." "Prejudices of Landlords," *New York Times*, April 14, 1889.

96. The writer of the *New York Times* article on the racial practices of landlords described the interviewee as "a colored women, a widow of excellent reputation" in order to confirm her "respectability." "Prejudices of Landlords," *New York Times*, April 14, 1889.

97. Osofsky, *Harlem*, 136.

98. Process of speculation explained in "Rent Strike for Harlem Proposed," *Chicago Defender*, April 6, 1918; Scheiner, *Negro Mecca*, 30.

99. Osofsky, *Harlem*, 140–41; Harris, *Sex Workers*, 26. Blacks very often were not allowed to inhabit a building until it was too run down for white tenants. Clyde, *The Negro in New York City*, 3a. In one representative situation, buildings "absolutely filled with white people" in Harlem yielded up to $19 per month for the owner until adjacent construction made them undesirable. When the owner opened the property to black tenants the buildings then drew rents up to $24 per month. "The unreasonable percentage of family income paid for rent makes a housekeeper accept dangerous risk," one *Times* article posited. "Planning to Solve Negro Housing Problem," *New York Times*, December 19, 1915.

100. Inmate Case File #2493, Laboratory of Social Hygiene, Home Conditions, July 21, 1917, box 1, folder 31, BH.

101. Comments about housing in McKay, *Harlem*, 18, 28. Columbia graduate student William Fielding Ogburn noted the discrepancy between expectations and the high cost of living in New York City that jarred many black migrants. "Many come to save money . . . they do not however take sufficiently into consideration the fact that expenses . . . are increased also in like proportion." Lacking the consumer power and financial stability they sought, black migrants often languished in rapidly forming and increasingly dilapidated and constricted communities in the Tenderloin, northern Manhattan, and central Brooklyn. "From individual instances observed," he concluded, "I learned that it is very difficult to save; and I did not meet any who had accomplished their purpose" in migration. Ogburn, "The Richmond Negro in New York City," 47–54.

102. Hicks, *Talk with You Like a Woman*, 43.

103. New York State Census, 17th Assembly District, Borough of Manhattan, 1905.

104. A study by the National League on Urban Conditions Among Negroes found similar numbers indicating the large percentage of lodgers in Harlem and cited 32 percent of the population as boarders. Statistics quoted in Scheiner, *Negro Mecca*, 28.

105. At 336 people per acre, black communities far outstripped Manhattan's average of 223 per acre. Osofsky, *Harlem*, 140–41. Compared to white districts, primarily black areas were 50 percent denser with up to 336 residents per acre, and lodgers made up a significant portion of those numbers. Statistics quoted in King, *Whose Harlem Is This, Anyway?*, 11.

106. Bureau of Social Hygiene, *Housing Conditions*, 58.

107. McKay, *Harlem*, 28. A study of Harlem concluded "brownstone dwellings" failed to meet the spatial needs of incoming black residents and led to "a widespread lodger evil with its inevitable attacks on privacy, morality and the integrity of family life." Report, A Summary of Vice Conditions in Harlem, 1929, box 12, folder James Pedersen, Committee of Fourteen Papers Collection, New York Public Library.

108. Sacks, *Before Harlem*, 78–79.

109. Inmate Case File #41462, Partial Report, January 17, 1933, box, 15, AUP.

110. Inmate Case File #41462, Parole Interview Form, February 17, 1933, box 15, AUP.

111. The offense of sexual assault took place when her family lived in Washington, D.C., before relocating to New York City. Inmate Case File #2480, Statement of Girl, June 23, 1917, box 1, folder 18, BH.

112. Inmate Case File #2493, Letter from Bedford Hills to State Charities Aid Association, April 17, 1920, box 1, folder 31, BH.

113. Wood, "The Costs of Bad Housing," 145; Sacks, *Before Harlem*, 73. The conditions African Americans faced after migration became the subject of a lot of debate about the efficacy of relocating North. As historian and journalist Ray Stannard Baker observed in 1908, blacks encountered oppressive conditions upon arrival, some of which were worse than in the South. "In the first place the poorer sort . . . in New York" lived in "the deadly tenement," he wrote, and overcrowding turned it into "a hotbed of disease" where the air is "unendurably warm and impure." In contrast, "in the South the great mass of Negroes have lived with their doors open, fireplaces have kept their homes ventilated, [and] they could leave the matter of sanitation to fresh air and sunshine." Baker, *Following the Color Line*, 112–17. Paul Laurence Dunbar agreed, arguing blacks were better off in the South. "They have given up the fields for the gutters . . . [and] bartered the sweet-smelling earth of their freshly turned furrows for the stenches of metropolitan alleys," Dunbar surmised. "They have a right to strength and to health, but they have neither." Although Dunbar meant much of his writing to discourage black migration, his biased reporting on the well-being of black New Yorkers held truth. Dunbar, "The Negroes of the Tenderloin."

114. Clyde, *The Negro in New York City*, 2b–4b.

115. Refuting claims about the inherent susceptibility of African Americans to disease in 1929, the chairman of the Harlem chapter of the New York Tuberculosis and Health Association, Dr. Henry O. Harding, connected the discrepancy of white and black deaths with "the economic condition of the average Negro family." With powerful and unwelcoming workers' unions "it is difficult for an uneducated Negro to

earn more than $23 weekly," he argued, "and this sum is today insufficient to maintain a family in decent surroundings and with proper food." As a result of "high rents and high food prices" children languished and became "non-resistant to tuberculosis," he concluded. "'White Plague' Threatens Negroes in United States," *Philadelphia Tribune*, July 4, 1929, 9. As more evidence that the situation continued to get worse in the late 1920s, statistician of the Metropolitan Life Insurance Company, Dr. Louis L. Dublin, enumerated Harlem's death rate as 17 deaths per 1,000 residents in 1929 and specifically cited pneumonia, which killed blacks at three times the rate of whites. Likewise, blacks succumbed to tuberculosis at a rate 300 percent higher than their white counterparts by that time. "Harlem's High Death Rate Studied," *New York Amsterdam News*, October 30, 1929.

116. Clyde, *The Negro in New York City*, 13b. Mary White Ovington described miserably crowded, dirty, and unventilated tenements as "human hives, honeycombed with little rooms thick with human beings." In such conditions disease prevailed, and deficient health care doomed many blacks with curable ailments. Ovington quoted in Sacks, *Before Harlem*, 76–77. Although dissatisfied with their options, most blacks occupying dilapidated housing aspired to make their living quarters bearable through decorations and cleaning. After surveying "thousands of Negro dwellings" Mary White Ovington argued black tenants kept their houses even cleaner than their white working-class counterparts. "Pictures decorate the walls, the sideboard contains many pretty dishes, and the table is set three times a day." As a result of this effort "the tenement dwelling becomes a home, and the boys and girls pass a happy childhood in it." Undoubtedly idealized and overgeneralized, Ovington's account still indicates how some African Americans endeavored to cope with decaying housing and unhealthful surroundings. Ovington, *Half a Man*, 64.

117. A 1915 statement by the New York Department of Health indicated a black mortality rate of 26.31. Referenced in Sacks, *Before Harlem*, 78; "White Plague Deaths on Increase in Harlem," *New York Amsterdam News*, October 14, 1925. At one peak between 1923 and 1927 Harlem's death rate exceeded that of the larger city by 42 percent, and for infants the rate towered by 72 percent. Osofsky, *Harlem*, 141.

118. Inmate Case File #2493, Statement of Girl, July 12, 1917, box 1, folder 31, BH; Cheryl Hicks, *Talk with You Like a Woman*, 44.

119. Inmate Case File #2486, Laboratory of Social Hygiene, Information Concerning the Patient, undated, box 1, folder 24, BH (J. Johnson).

120. Sacks, *Before Harlem*, 77. In another notable effort to solve the problem of tuberculosis, Booker T. Washington and the National Negro Business League established National Negro Health Week in 1915, meant to instruct blacks on how to rectify "bad houses" with basic sanitation and an understanding of the true pathogenic causes of the disease. The *Afro-American* indicated that most blacks believed "consumption was inherited," but through the prism of National Negro Health Week and their publication, the aim was to make clear that it formed from germs and bad air. The solution would be "abundant fresh air." "If you want to live and to keep from having consumption live with your windows open!" "How to Keep Good Health," *Afro-American*, March 27, 1915; and "Plans for the Conservation of Negroes' Health," *New Journal and Guide*, November 18, 1916.

121. Anderson, *This Was Harlem*, 13–15.

122. Wallace, *Greater Gotham*, 828. Black elites simultaneously criticized the actions and lifestyles of a black working class, and worked against racial bias and violence by forming organizations to deal with increasing racial animosity and poverty, and increase access to education, jobs, and resources. While help of this kind often came with judgment, many black progressives had positive intentions that empirically benefitted the broader black community. Peterson, *Black Gotham*, 345–84; and Haynes, "Conditions Among Negroes in the Cities," 111.

123. Hughes, *The Big Sea*, 238–40.

124. McKay, *Harlem*, 23.

125. Berlin and Harris, *Slavery in New York*, 21.

126. Berlin and Harris, *Slavery in New York*, 829. An 1895 *Times* article recognized some wealthy black Brooklynites owned and occupied "brownstone dwellings in fashionable neighborhoods, employ[ed] white servants, and [rode] in their own carriages," but most in Manhattan lived in depressed black districts. The article went on to catalog a number of wealthy black men and women and their businesses, including retired tea and spice dealer Theophilus I. Fisher, Dr. Susan McKinney who lived in a "fashionable quarter" of Brooklyn, and carpet cleaner Peter Freeman who employed a number of white men. "We are not to be judged by the street loungers and drunkards of our race," proclaimed one black middle-class woman. "It would be just as sensible to judge the white race by its criminal classes." "Wealthy Negro Citizens," *New York Times*, July 14, 1895. Some blacks, like William Hannibal Thomas, openly condemned black criminals as the source of race hatred and condoned society's right to "protect itself in every possible way," even if that meant disenfranchisement, heavy policing, and the acceptance of white tutelage by blacks. In his 1901 book, *The American Negro*, he cast them as "open and avowed enemies of mankind," that may be held in check only by "fear of bodily harm." Thomas, *The American Negro*, 208.

127. Dunbar, *The Sport of the Gods*.

128. Dunbar also blamed ignorance and an unhealthy environment for what he saw as poor behavior among blacks in the Tenderloin. "In these seemingly careless, guffawing crowds lies a terrible menace to our institutions," he wrote. "Everything in their environment tends to the blotting of the moral sense, everything to the engendering of crime." Dunbar, "The Negroes of the Tenderloin."

129. "Dragging the Race Down," *New York Age*, June 9, 1910. Another writer linked the presence of sex workers with the vulnerability of "respectable" citizens in black sections of the city. "Street-walking women and the animals that live upon their dirty money and boldly loaf in the path of good people, must go," the author declared. "Clean 'Em Out," *New York Age*, April 6, 1911.

130. "Labor of Colored Men," *New York Times*, December 31, 1911.

131. In the *Times* news article Reverend Bishop defended the housing "agents and landlords" implying that they are "not altogether responsible for the condition of things." Some of the agents he spoke with insisted that black tenants took better care of the apartments that they rented. Instead, the landlords maintained that fear of renting to African American tenants stemmed from "the objection of white people to living in the same building or in the same neighborhood with colored people." Although this is not uniformly true of all landlords and agents, this further indicates that black Manhattanites around the turn of the century were facing great opposition from

white residents and were forced to find housing where they could, whether it was adequate or not. This also indicates the great role that popular perception of black migrants as uniformly unruly and undesirable neighbors clashed with reality and played a large part in determining the city's residential demographic configuration. "The Northern Color Line," *New York Times*, April 28, 1889, 9; "Prejudices of Landlords," *New York Times*, April 14, 1889, 10.

132. W. E. B. Du Bois, "The Black North," *New York Times*, November 17, 1901. As a settlement house pamphlet stated in 1910, "there was scarcely a house where a decent family could live with the assurance that the worst element would not sooner or later find lodgings across the hall." White Rose Mission Settlement Pamphlet, undated, folder 1, White Rose Mission and Industrial Association collection, Schomburg Center for Research in Black Culture, NYPL.

133. Trial Transcript #39, 19, TTC.

134. Trial Transcript #39, 29, TTC

135. "Killed His Man with a Brick," *New York Times*, November 16, 1893.

136. Trial Transcript #39, 35, TTC. William McKenzie, one of the men shooting craps with Harper, testified that Dunham attacked Harper first and minimized his response, 123–26.

137. Trial Transcript #39, 202–3, TTC.

138. "It is the colored people who are hedged in by prejudice to particular localities . . . in the meanest tenement districts," one *New York Times* writer noticed before the turn of the century. "Their environment is not what they would make it—it is what is made for them, and it is made as depraved . . . as the prejudice and selfishness of man can make it." "Prejudices of Landlords," *New York Times*, April 14, 1889.

139. Hicks, *Talk with You Like a Woman*, 42.

140. Sacks, *Before Harlem*, 172; Inmate Case File #44009, Preliminary Investigation Form, June 5, 1929, box 8, AUP. Many other men had similarly unstable housing records. Before arriving in New York City men like Jackson Burns at times lived in several other cities and that transience continued after arrival. "My first residence was 32 West 135th Street," Burns recounted. "The next one was . . . 1 West 135th Street; and the next one was 107 West 132nd Street." After subsequently living in two other addresses in Harlem, he moved to Chicago and Jersey City before joining the navy and resettling in New York once again. Trial Transcript #2784, March 22, 1920, reel 339, 124–26, TTC.

141. Scheiner, *Negro Mecca*, 37. As one example of the Utopia Neighborhood Club's work, the organization implemented an annual fashion show that was meant to raise money for neighborhood improvements. In 1923 the fashion show netted more than $2,100, which was then used to "help establish in Harlem a Child Welfare Center, from which can be directed a general Community program of activities for children and young people." "Utopia Neighborhood Club Thanks Friends," *New York Amsterdam News*, May 16, 1923.

142. Inmate Case File #44076, Preliminary Investigation, April 22, 1929, box 8, AUP.

143. Inmate Case File #44076, Receiving Blotter, Bureau of Identification, May, 20, 1929, box 8, AUP.

144. Inmate Case File #44076, Preliminary Investigation, April 22, 1929, box 8, AUP.

145. Inmate Case File #44076, Preliminary Investigation, April 22, 1929, box 8, AUP.

146. Sacks, "To Be a Man and Not a Lackey," 53.

147. Osofsky, *Harlem*, 3–4; and Muhammad, *Condemnation of Blackness*, 106. In 1910 there were eighty-five black men to every hundred women, and only slightly more at ninety by 1920. Researcher Ruth Reed surmised this imbalance hurt the marriage prospects of working-class black women more than the middle-class since "women of this class are under ordinary circumstances less sought after in marriage and more often sought for unsanctioned sex relations than are women of other classes." I would have liked to see her reword this to acknowledge the responsibility of men who are either less inclined to be married or are unable to meet the financial requirements of fatherhood and marriage. Reed, *Negro Illegitimacy in New York City*, 83.

148. Researcher John P. Clyde also found multitudes of black men unable to get work at all, a state he considered a "great breeder of sloth and inefficiency" and forced them to depend on women and children for support. Clyde, *The Negro in New York City*, 2c.

149. Wallace, *Greater Gotham*, 816, 819. It was sometimes possible for black working-class men to earn the living they hoped for, albeit within boundaries. A 1907 article in the *Colored American Magazine* celebrated the occasional entrance of black mechanics into the construction industry "despite the general belief to the contrary." *Colored American Magazine* quoted in Scheiner, *Negro Mecca*, 55. At times, working as a porter was a lucrative position. A survey of a black church in the Tenderloin showed the largest portion of the men employed as "red caps" at the Grand Central Depot. In addition to their regular salaries they received as much as $3 a day in tips. Hopper, "A Northern Negro Group," 23. By 1912, more than 34,000 factories drove New York City's economy employing 700,000 workers in an array of small industries producing garments, sheet iron, food, leather, furniture, and various other luxury and essential items. Sixty-eight percent of this production happened on Manhattan island, the bulk of which sat close to working-class communities on the West Side, like the massive manufacturing complex of the National Biscuit Company, or Nabisco, between Tenth and Ninth Avenues on Fifteenth Street. With such proximity, African Americans were still often barred from this type of work. Wallace, *Greater Gotham*, 305, 315–16.

150. Sacks, "To Be a Man and Not a Lackey," 47; and Sacks, *Before Harlem*, 109, 123. With skilled and industrial largely off limits, black men were compressed into a field they were steadily losing. Scheiner, *Negro Mecca*, 48–61.

151. Statistics quoted in Sacks, *Before Harlem*, 109. Even black craftsmen plying trades such as blacksmiths, carpenters, and mechanics often gave up searching for work in their fields and resigned themselves to whatever they could find. Bloch, "The New York City Negro," 34–35.

152. Sacks, *Before Harlem*, 108–9, 114. One apartment superintendent told an interviewer, "We can't keep a decent white fellow when we get one," since building tenants frequently helped them find other work and they left. "This wouldn't happen . . . to one of my colored men [so] we can keep our decent colored boys." Plus, these men determined they made up to $15 less each month than their white counterparts. Washington, *A Study of Negro Employees*, 17, 21. The study also found that in some cases wages were raised in order to bring in white workers and then lowered again when those workers left and blacks reentered the field. Two large department stores displaced black elevator men and switchboard operators with whites and raised the salary from

$30 per month to $40. Yet, after losing the white workers "colored men were re-employed" and the wage was once again lowered to $30. Sacks, *Before Harlem*, 21.

153. Quoted in Baker, *Following the Color Line*, 133. One hiring agency sought two "elevator boys"—one "colored" and one white, but promised to pay the white worker $25 more per week for fewer hours of work. New York Commission on Congestion of Population, *Report of the New York City Commission on Congestion of Population*, 265. Employers also might dispute claims of job discrimination by arguing blacks had, in fact, not risen to the challenge of wage labor since they lacked ambition and the ability to work hard at tedious or difficult tasks. Commenting on the reduction of black laborers in certain fields one writer argued, "if they rendered service considered as efficient as that by whites, they would have been retained." "Labor of Colored Men," *New York Times*, December 31, 1911. In his investigation of the industrial work prospects of African Americans in New York, school principal William L. Bulkley told a story of how he inquired at an electric company about whether or not they would hire a fictitious "colored boy who could answer the qualifications stated. The next mail brought the expected reply that no colored boy, however promising, was wanted. I heaved a sigh and went on." Bulkley, "The Industrial Condition of the Negro in New York City," 130.

154. Hughes, *The Big Sea*, 85–86.

155. Only 12 percent of the black men in the survey had skilled positions including work as undertakers, tailors, clerks, and painters. Survey of vocations held by men in Manhattan's fifth district conducted by author from the Twelfth Federal Census of the United States, Manhattan's Fifth District, Election Districts 10 & 11, 1900.

156. Sacks, *Before Harlem*, 108–12, 124. Some African American men were able to participate in skilled trade industries outside of unions in black communities and created their own organizations such as the Negro Printer's Union in 1907 and the Colored Chauffers' Association in 1912. Wallace, *Greater Gotham*, 816; and Hopper, "A Northern Negro Group," 23. George Edmund Haynes argued this was partly due to black migrants being unprepared for Northern industrial labor, but primarily to "a whimsical dislike of any workman who is not white and especially one who is black!" Haynes, "Conditions Among Negroes in the Cities," 111–12. In 1900 only 5 percent of black men and women had mechanical and manufacturing jobs in the state. Statistics taken from Bulkley, "The Industrial Condition of the Negro in New York City," 129. Mary White Ovington elaborated on the consignment of harsh labor to black men. "The only place in the world of labor that the colored man can win as a segregated race in New York," she wrote in 1906, "is the place that no one else wants. He may sweep down the subway steps, run the elevators in cheap apartment houses, act as porter in stores, where the work is heavy and the pay small," she wrote. Ovington, "The Negro in the Trades Unions in New York," 92, 95.

157. Being concerned about his students and realizing the unfairness of racial discrimination, principal William L. Bulkley lamented the student's response. "I shall remember that scene till my dying day. All the monster evils of prejudice passed before me in procession like the hideous creatures of an Inferno, and I thought of the millions of hopes that have been blighted . . . all because the iron heel of this base, hell-born caste is upon the neck of every boy, of every girl who chanced to be born black." Bulkley, "The Industrial Condition of the Negro in New York City," 131.

158. Letter from Frederick Challenor to Aletha Dowridge, March 14, 1913, box 1, DCFL.

159. The report noted that "at the present time practically all of the superintendents are white, mostly Swedes and Germans, some English, and a very few Irish," many of whom earned "from $75.00 to $125.00 per month and a free apartment." Washington, *A Study of Negro Employees*, 10–12. The report also noted differences between "American Negroes" and West Indians. Fifty-eight percent of the employees surveyed came from the Caribbean, primarily because, the report claimed, superintendents preferred them as workers. "It is their practice of a sort of co-operation that does not exist among American Negro employees." That cooperation was paramount since managers had an incentive to fire workers for slight infractions. "Certain employment agencies paid these superintendents a commission for every man hired through that agency. The latter received this commission back in exorbitant fees they charged men." As a result, there was a crooked symbiosis between agencies and employers who both had incentives and motivations for making keeping a high turnover. Washington, *A Study of Negro Employees*, 13–15.

160. Washington, *A Study of Negro Employees*, 24.

161. Washington, *A Study of Negro Employees*, 19–21; information on a "living wage" in More, *Wage-Earners' Budgets*, 269–70.

162. Washington, *A Study of Negro Employees*, 22–23.

163. McKay, *Jean Toomer*, 28; and Whalan, *The Letters of Jean Toomer*, 13.

164. Du Bois told stories of how he coped with such labor that included the theft of food. "The waiters stole their food and they stole the best. We gulped and hesitated. Then we stole, too . . . and we all fattened, for the dainties were marvelous. You slipped a bit here and hid it there; you cut off extra portions and gave false orders; you dashed off into darkness and hid in corners and ate and ate! It was nasty business." Between theft and the black waiter who he caught "crouching, grinning, assuming a broad dialect when he usually spoke good English," and "playing the clown," he recoiled from the "dishonesty and deception of it all." Du Bois, *Darkwater*, 110–13.

165. Kiser, *Sea Island to City*, 252. To find work, some men resorted to trickery. Desperate in 1917, Barbadian immigrant William Grimes had a friend falsify the signature of the Republic Steamship Company president on a recommendation letter in order to secure work on one of their vessels but was caught and charged with forgery. Grimes told an elaborate story of securing the stationary of the Republic Steamship Company from a stenographer from the company's office, having a third party type it for him, and then asking his friend, a custodian from the shipmaster's club, to sign the company president's signature on it for him. Once caught, Grimes tore the letter apart, but it was kept as evidence in his case and reassembled. It reads: "The bearer . . . has served as master of the S/Y Condor, from September 15th 1916 until December 23rd 1916, on a cruise to the Indies. I take pleasure in stating that Captain [Grimes] has always proven himself to be . . . trustworthy in the performance of his duties, and I cheerfully recommend him as an able master." Complaint Record #114903, April 16, 1917, box 1338, folder 288, DACCF.

166. Inmate Case File #44076, Preliminary Investigation, May 6, 1929, box 8, AUP.

167. Men might steal from employers, like porter George Lambert who allegedly stole a typewriter from his workplace and pawned it for $30 in 1920. Complaint

Record #128234, Affidavit—Larceny, November 22, 1920, box 1480, folder 1483, DACCF. Other essential expenses, like medical costs, could likewise motivate theft. Arrested in 1928, Queens resident Cornelius Wright admitted to police he stole a barrel of block tin and lead from a local shop and sold it to a "junk man" for $30, in order to continue expensive treatments for gonorrhea." Inmate #43822, Indictment Sheet No. 10295, undated, box 7, AU.

168. Inmate Case File #44000, Preliminary Investigations, December 30, 1929, box 8, AU.

169. Information about inmates' arrests in Inmate #44000, Receiving Blotter, January 8, 1930, box 8, AU; 1929 offense and quotes from Lawrence and from intake agent found in Inmate Case File #44000, Preliminary Investigations, December 30, 1929, box 8, AU.

170. Inmate Case File #43996, Preliminary Investigations, September 10, 1929, box 8, AU.

171. Complaint Record #117615, Affidavit-Burglary, October 14, 1917, box 1372, folder 523, DACCF; and Complaint Record #118003, Form from Court of General Sessions of the Peace, filed October 14, 1917, box 1372, folder 523, DACCF.

172. Lane, "Ambushed in the City," 692. It is unclear where the Clearing House game originated although it is possibly an import from the Caribbean. On the shrouded origins, see White et al., *Playing the Numbers*, 58–62.

173. Schatzberg and Kelly, *African American Organized Crime*, 74–75.

174. Shane White et al., give a full explanation of how the Clearing House games were run and how the numbers were determined in White et al., *Playing the Numbers*, 12–14, 21; also see Harris, *Sex Workers*, 55, 97; and Kiser, *Sea Island to City*, 47.

175. White et al., *Playing the Numbers*, 18.

176. White et al., *Playing the Numbers*, 144.

177. White et al., *Playing the Numbers*, 150–59. There is also a very good biography of Holstein's life in Turnbull, *Casper A. Holstein*.

178. Claire M. Halley, "'Fickle Lady Luck,' A Story of A 'Number' Player," *New York Amsterdam News*, February 23, 1927; also used in White et al., *Playing the Numbers*, 147–48.

179. White et al., *Playing the Numbers*, 136.

180. Complaint Record #126245, Affidavit—Larceny, July 29, 1919, box 1460, folder 1272, DACCF.

181. Inmate Case File #39003, Classification Clinic, February 27, 1934, box 1, AU.

182. Complaint Record #133603, Statement of Witness, March 18, 1921, box 1541, folder 2089, DACCF.

183. Indictment #158900, Preliminary Investigation, March 6, 1925, box 2, folder 231, NYPR.

184. Complaint Record #120290, Testimony of Officer Edwin F. England, September 30, 1918, box 1404, folder 789, DACCF.

185. Bloch, "The New York City Negro."

186. Inmate Case File #39003, Classification Clinic Psychiatric Report, February 27, 1934, box 1, AUP.

187. Inmate Case File #43988, Auburn Prison Department of Correction Admission Form, June 21, 1930, box 8, AU.

188. Job discrimination did not entirely deprive black men of the ability to map out their lives in the North, and when able, they took advantage of work and business ventures. From the end of the Civil War until 1900 various groups such as the Brooklyn-established American Freedman's Friend Society and Manhattan's Colored Mission placed African Americans in positions. Other organizations like the Young Men's Industrial League helped black men find jobs and promoted business and industrial education. More organizations meant to help black migrants successfully transition into New York City's economy appeared around the turn of the century. With an uptick in migration, groups like the League for the Protection of Colored Women and the Committee for Improving the Industrial Conditions of Negroes continued this endeavor with noticeable results. In 1909 the committee reported they had placed over 1,000 blacks into positions in the city and simultaneously made headway in a number of new industries. Both organizations merged with the Committee on Urban Conditions in 1911 to form the National League on Urban Conditions (Urban League), which focused on addressing migrants' employment concerns by offering training for various trades and assistance in finding jobs. Additionally, the Urban League acted as a broker between job-seeking blacks and white employers, ran campaigns to promote the value of their labor, and helped organize for better pay and common rights once hired. Sacks, *Before Harlem*, 26, 125–26; Scheiner, *Negro Mecca*, 58. Wishing to avoid the vagaries of wage labor, others took advantage of entrepreneurial opportunities and established saloons, pool halls, restaurants, cigar and candy stores, when they were able. In a 1901 article for the *New York Times* W. E. B. Du Bois explained the variations in black employment experiences in the North and underlined the unobserved reality of black business holdings. According to Du Bois more than 5 percent of black New Yorkers held over $1.5 million in real estate and small businesses such as catering, drug stores, undertaking, and hotel and restaurant establishments at the time. One exceptional business leader built a business cleaning houses worth over $20,000 and employing a staff of twelve. While this was not the experience of most black New Yorkers and may have been unattainable for most working-class blacks, some circumvented the labor market by saving money and establishing businesses. Du Bois, "The Black North," SM10.

189. Lears, *No Place of Grace*, 218.

190. Mary Rock's letter quoted in Sacks, *Before Harlem*, 137.

191. Charles Morris, "Race Question in New York," *New York Times*, June 15, 1904, 6.

192. "Many Persons Wounded, But One Fatally Hurt," *Brooklyn Daily Eagle*, August 16, 1900. Harris later claimed Officer Thorpe assaulted him before he took his life. "Negro Who Killed Policeman," *The Sun*, October 26, 1900. Tenderloin riot outlined well in Shapiro, *White Violence and Black Response*, 93–96; Johnson, *Street Justice*, 57–69; also see Hicks, *Talk with You Like a Woman*, 53–55; and Osofsky, "Race Riot, 1900," 16–24. The rioting began after an interracial fight at a gathering site near the slain officer's home. Osofsky, *Harlem*, 47.

193. "Police in Control in Riotous District," *New York Times*, August 17, 1900. African Americans implicated officers in all large-scale racial conflicts in the early decades of the twentieth century, and New York race papers covered large- and small-scale attacks against black citizens. Sacks, *Before Harlem*, 81–82. It is interesting to note that in some instances, white onlookers stepped in on behalf of African American victims

of the riot. When two officers attacked Stephen Small on a streetcar "a white man in-terfered, and the police desisted." Later a mob of whites boarded the car and attacked him but "the car had quite a number of women in it, who began to scream, and some of them told me to get under the seat, which I did," he testified. "I reached the neigh-borhood of the Hudson Street House of Relief, where the white gentleman who had interfered in the first instance took me, and where I had my head bandaged." Small slept in the cellar of the House of Relief that night to avoid further danger, but was as-saulted by an officer on his way home in the morning. "I was stopped by an officer who wanted to know where I was going, and what weapon I had on me. I told him I had nothing on me. He said, 'You look as if you had been in the scrap. They ought to have killed you; get out of here.' As he said this he struck me across the back with his club, and I yet am unable to lay flat on my back without suffering extreme pain. Citizens' Protective League, *Story of the Riot*, 7.

194. Osofsky, *Harlem*, 49; and Citizens' Protective League, *Story of the Riot*, 2. Sev-eral women who lived across a courtyard from the Thirty-Seventh Street police sta-tion house told of the sounds and voices they heard coming from the building on the night of August 15, 1900. One woman, Alice Lee, claimed she heard "people scream-ing and groaning, and shouts of people pleading not to be clubbed anymore. I saw one man lying on the station house floor, apparently almost helpless." Another caught the sounds of "persons in agony, and cries of 'Why are you hitting me? I haven't done anything!'" Trial Transcript #478, 48–49.

195. A group of women living near the precinct heard agonizing cries and shouts coming from the building, and through the windows they witnessed "one man lying on the station house floor, apparently almost helpless," and others gravely injured. Citizens' Protective League, *Story of the Riot*, 48–49.

196. The house Chester Smith fell in front of belonged to a white lady identified only as "Mrs. Davenport." She took Smith into her house and protected him from the mob telling them "if they would not leave she would kill them." Mrs. Davenport de-clined to submit an affidavit, but told George P. Hammond, the notary collecting the affidavits for Frank Moss that she "sheltered two or three Negroes during the night" and that several police officers who attempted to get into her house, at the time that she rescued the said Smith, acted and spoke in an insulting manner, one of them say-ing, "What kind of a woman are you, to be harboring niggers?" Citizens' Protective League, *Story of the Riot*, 14–15. Many sustained serious injuries, like John Wolf who was hit so hard with a billy club his jawbone was crushed and "it caused my chin to fall down. . . . My jaw is still loose, and will not hold in position without the bandages that almost cover my face and head." Another man, Nicholas Sherman, claimed a "blow on the small of my back made my left limb almost paralyzed." Citizens' Protective League, *Story of the Riot*, 66–67, 78.

197. Citizens' Protective League, *Story of the Riot*, 50–51; Johnson, *Street Justice*, 63.

198. Letter reprinted in opening of pamphlet. Citizens' Protective League, *Story of the Riot*.

199. Although the efforts of the CPL only garnered few punitive results for police officers, they alerted progressive organizations to the plight of black communities and placed police brutality on the agenda. Marilyn Johnson notes that such riots in-cluding police violence did not happen again after the 1905 riot in San Juan Hill until

after World War I, and at that point police were far less overt in their attacks. Johnson, *Street Justice*, 85–86.

200. Reeling from the 1900 riots in the Tenderloin one Brooklyn resident implored blacks to "get a permit to carry a revolver," adding "to be caught unprepared once is no disgrace, but don't be caught again." "Negroes Demand Justice," *New-York Tribune*, September 13, 1900. A survey of the area conducted the day following the initial clash discovered black residents bought more than 145 revolvers and large amounts of ammunition. Johnson, *Street Justice*, 49–50. Arthur Harris was eventually convicted for Robert Thorpe's murder and sentenced to life in prison. "Thorpe's Slayer Sentenced," *Evening Post*, November 2, 1900.

201. The "third degree" was not only used on black suspects, but it figured prominently in the fear that African Americans felt about being in police custody. The black press makes this clear. "The Third Degree," *New York Amsterdam News*, August 18, 1926; Friedman, *Crime and Punishment*, 152–53; and Richardson, *The New York Police*, 193–94.

202. Johnson, *Street Justice*, 122; quote taken from "The Third Degree," *New York Amsterdam News*, August 18, 1926.

203. "Policemen Beat Up Near-Riot Witness in Station House," *New York Amsterdam News*, August 22, 1928. To make matters worse, arrestees frequently reported blatant assaults. Appearing in court on suspicion of public intoxication, Tenderloin resident John Rowls complained of being beaten on the street and in the station house in full view of others without any recourse to stop it. The arresting officer denied the charge, but witnesses watched him assault Rowls again as he removed him from the courtroom. Such trumped up charges and outright maltreatment from police altered the psychology of public space for African Americans, often making them feel alienated and unsafe where others moved about freely. "Kicked and Beaten by a Policeman," *New York Times*, October 15, 1894.

204. Many newspaper articles recount instances where arrests of black men and women were interrupted by gathering crowds that assaulted police with fists and projectiles when they felt the detainment was unjust. For example, "Ninety Police Out to Quell Negro Riot," *New York Times*, July 31, 1909; "Negro Loiterers Arrested," *New York Times*, August 8, 1911; "Policeman Felled in a Bronx Riot," *New York Times*, November 6, 1911; "Negroes in Riot to Rescue Prisoner," *New York Times*, September 3, 1912.

205. "Police in a Fight With 1,000 Negroes," *New York Times*, July 5, 1907.

206. Black interviewees in San Juan Hill expressed antipathy toward police to researcher William Fielding Ogburn in 1909, citing how they overlooked solvable issues. Ogburn, "The Richmond Negro in New York City," 51.

207. Samuel Battle faced discrimination after taking the police officer's exam in 1910 and scoring well but being passed over. He eventually elicited the help of "a friend of mine," Fred R. Moore, the editor of the *New York Age*, who used his connections as a friend of the current mayor to get him assigned in Manhattan. Battle, "Reminiscences of Samuel J. Battle," 16–19. That discrimination only continued after his appointment. His fellow officers reportedly ignored him. "Silence for Negro Policeman," *The Sun*, August 16, 1911.

208. Blascoer, *Colored School Children in New York*, 23.

209. Blascoer, *Colored School Children in New York*, 24.

210. "One Negro Killed, One Wounded," *Evening Post*, December 30, 1904; "Murder, Fire and Fight in Negro Athlete's Wake," *New York Times*, December 31, 1904.

211. Quoted in Kiser, *Sea Island to City*, 50. In extensive interviews of black migrants in San Juan Hill William Fielding Ogburn noted frequent "expressions of contempt for the . . . police," which he considered justified. "I was told that the police did not make raids on the 'dens' but only came down when there was a robbery, stabbing, or a fight; they are brought down by results but do not remove the cause," he wrote. As a result of the neglectful quality of policing "street scenes of a very disorderly and depraved nature are permitted," Ogburn concluded. Ogburn, "The Richmond Negro in New York City," 51.

212. Sacks, *Before Harlem*, 80–81.

213. Battle, "Reminiscences of Samuel J. Battle," 35–36.

214. Story taken from Gilfoyle, *City of Eros*, 203. The area, formerly home to New York's elite, had been abandoned by those residents as it became increasingly racially and ethnically diverse and catered to brothels, bars, and illicit commercial spaces. Once abandoned, well-built and beautiful brownstones were very often either divided into rental flats, made into lodging houses, or rented out as brothels, since properties furnishing prostitution often paid the highest rents. Thus, the more buildings abandoned by bourgeois and middle-class New Yorkers, the more prostitution flourished in the area. Gilfoyle, *City of Eros*, 204. Because of graft, anyone patrolling the Tenderloin "could live on tenderloin steaks the rest of his life," another officer claimed. Quoted in Osofsky, *Harlem*, 14.

215. Many sources from the time argued that police commissioners and political organizations like Tammany Hall were in on the corruption scheme. As an example, in an article labeling New York as cursed by pool rooms or gambling dens, the *Times* argued "with the necessary 'pull' nothing seems to be illegal either in New-York City or in the State of New-Jersey." "A Pool Room Cursed City," *New York Times*, March 22, 1891.

216. Trial Transcript #2191, April 17, 1916, reel 276, 7, TTC.

217. Inmate Case File #44000, Preliminary Investigation Form, December 30, 1929, box 8, AUP.

218. Trial Transcript #2751, November 18, 1919, reel 47, 142–43, TTC. Philadelphia migrant Kathleen Evans suffered this sort of treatment by police repeatedly. Police once jailed her on a charge of grand larceny as she sat outside her home, a charge that she claimed was a case of mistaken identity. She had also been fined twice for public intoxication, once for $5, and another time for $2. Information about the life of Kathleen Evans in Trial Transcript #1356, April 19, 1911, reel 175, 178–79, TTC.

219. Willemse, Behind the Green Lights, 84–86.

220. The Magistrate Court Documents from Manhattan's fifth district show a great imbalance in the number of men and women arrested in 1901. Out of 541 arrested 349 were men, making up nearly 68 percent of those detained. Magistrate's Court Documents, 1800–1930: Manhattan's Fifth District, rolls 29, 30, 31, 32, NYCMA. Frankie Y. Bailey and Alice P. Green explain the complexities of class involved in the usage of public space for leisure in black communities recognizing that not all African Americans spent time on street corners. "The arrest of a lounging black man would not necessarily have been viewed as an injustice by everyone in the black community," they

write, arguing that "the migration of more blacks into urban centers marked the point at which black neighborhoods began to decline." Yet migrants were not entirely at fault for the change in the communities they settled in. Ghettos, they argue, "were created by whites who placed boundaries on black settlement and enforced those boundaries with petitions, restrictive covenants, and sometimes violence." Bailey and Green, *Law Never Here*, 78.

221. "Negroes Fight Police," *New-York Tribune*, August 5, 1911. For more on policing in New York City, see Richardson, *The New York Police*; and Johnson, *Street Justice*.

222. Homosexual acts and conduct was not written into code as illegal until a 1923 state statute that considered "lewd" behavior unlawful and made male on male sexual experiences criminal. Chauncey, *Gay New York*, 172.

223. Story and quotes related in Van Notten, *Wallace Thurman's Harlem Renaissance*, 95–96.

224. Heap, *Slumming*, 85–86; and Chauncey, *Gay New York*, 255–56. In 1928 W. E. B. Du Bois ousted one editor of his *Crisis* periodical for such a misgiving. Chauncey, *Gay New York*, 264. Adam Clayton Powell's 1929 rant against same-sex contact makes this denunciation clear. Powell accused a coterie of minsters with sexual perversion, the kind that "causes men to leave their wives for other men." As such, these trysts threatened the reproduction and collective destiny of the race, he claimed. Many dismissed Powell's rigid representations of correctness. He expected a "vote of thanks" from his fellow ministers but received silence and felt shunned by his community. "One very familiar friend said as he passed me with a scrutinizing look . . . 'I thought you had some sense,'" he recalled. Story related in Powell's autobiography. Powell, *Against the Tide*, 215–17.

225. Heap, *Slumming*, 254.

226. Barbeau and Henri, *The Unknown Soldiers*, 184–85.

227. The *Age* changed ownership in 1907 when Booker T. Washington purchased the paper and Fred R. Moore bought T. Thomas Fortune's shares. With new leadership came new politics, and the *Age* no longer took the same radical stance against racial violence as it did before. King, "Ready to Shoot and Do Shoot," 760. As a close friend of Booker T. Washington and the editor of the conservative *New York Age*, Timothy Thomas Fortune's advocacy of self-defense against public racial violence is ironic. Fortune often defended Washington's views when attacked by more militant African Americans for being too accommodating because he understood the value in Washington's viewpoints about thrift, industry, and economic black nationalism, and because he understood "how powerful were the racist currents Washington was trying to navigate." However, he was militant himself and joined black leaders and writers who saw self-defense as the only recourse. Fortune quoted in Wallace, *Greater Gotham*, 837.

228. Wallace, *Greater Gotham*, 838–40.

229. Rudwick, *W. E. B. Du Bois in the Role of Crisis Editor*, 214.

230. Marcus, "Hubert Harrison," 18; and Makalani, "Internationalizing the Third International," 155.

231. Garvey speech paraphrased in "Hundreds Hear Marcus Garvey," *New Journal and Guide*, November 10, 1923. Garvey launched his United Negro Improvement Association (UNIA) in Harlem in 1916 with the philosophy of black nationalism; a platform

that recognized a worldwide pan-African community responsible for its own fate and esprit de corps. Kendi, *Stamped from the Beginning*, 309.

232. Kendi, *Stamped from the Beginning*, 309. African American folklore and blues music often celebrated black combatants historian Lawrence Levine called "heroes who were not to be contained by the limits of the actual." These songs provided a sense of cultural legitimacy to a burgeoning belief that violence would be necessary to deal with pervasive racial attacks. Levine, *Black Culture and Black Consciousness*, 400.

233. Josie Miles's "Mad Mama Blues" quoted in Gussow, "Shoot Myself a Cop," 36.

234. Locke, *Harlem*, 631.

235. King, "Ready to Shoot and Do Shoot," 758.

236. Shapiro, *White Violence and Black Response*, 145. Observing the reactions of black men to the violence of the Red Summer, one black woman subscriber rejoiced writing, "I thank God" that "at last our men had stood like men [and] struck back." Haywood, *Let Us Make Men*, 55; and Kendi, *Stamped from the Beginning*, 314.

237. Hartt, "The New Negro," 59.

238. Sacks, *Before Harlem*, 88–89.

239. Washington, "Recreational Facilities for the Negro," 278.

Chapter 2

1. "Policeman Dead, Two Dying," *New-York Tribune*, May 3, 1903; "Three Policeman Shot by Negro Ex-Convict," *New York Times*, May 3, 1903; and "Police Parade Past Cheering Thousands," *New York Times*, May 3, 1903; also in "Fatal Saloon Fight," *Hartford Courant*, May 4, 1903; "Negro Kills Policeman," *Washington Post*, May 3, 1903; "Shot Tormentors," *Boston Daily Globe*, May 3, 1903; "Three Policemen Are Shot," *Chicago Daily Tribune*, May 3, 1903.

2. A number of prominent progressive voices railed against saloons early in the century. After counting 111 Protestant churches and other places of worship versus 4,065 saloons below Fourteenth street in 1890, Jacob Riis condemned drinking dens as portentous of the ruin of the working class. "I am afraid . . . that the congregations (of the saloons) are larger by a good deal; certainly the attendance steadier and the contributions more liberal the week round, Sunday included," he concluded. "The saloon is the one bright and cheery and humanly decent spot to be found" in a crowded tenement district and was irresistible to slum dwellers. Although it represented temporary relief from the sickness, filth, and squalor of the unventilated tenement flat he argued it also depleted the resources of the poor and put them in proximity with other forms of vice. "Upon the direst poverty of their crowds it grows fat and prosperous, levying upon it a tax heavier than all the rest of its grievous burdens combined." Riis, *How the Other Half Lives*, 165. For sociology professor John Marshall Barker, liquor was not the problem, but the dark space of the saloon itself that he believed prepared the imbiber for criminality, unhinged reasoning, and put him into dangerous proximity with "the gamblers, the thieves, the prostitutes, and the vicious class." Barker, *The Saloon Problem and Social Reform*, 57.

3. McGerr, *A Fierce Discontent*, 274–75. As has been shown, outbursts of such bloodshed happened frequently on streets and in leisure spaces, and press coverage carica-

tured the specter of interracial combat in popular imagination. An 1899 *Times* article reported on a group of men who attacked a black boxer and his friends and drove them from a white saloon; *New York Times*, October 22, 1899; and during the summer of 1905 sporadic fighting sparked in the San Juan Hill district leaving scores wounded; "Riot in New York," *Washington Post*, July 15, 1905. The fact that much of this violence took place or began in saloons is worth noting. As race relations chilled at the turn of the century, public spaces of leisure became hotly contested and African Americans squeezed into increasingly isolated spaces. Before black-owned saloons became more frequent, African American alcohol consumption often took place in private spaces. "One great reason for this is that in many saloons the negro is served only with the understanding that the consumption be at home," wrote one Columbia University master's student in 1911. In combination with a popular progressive fear of white and black proximity in sexualized spaces of amusement, white de facto intolerance of black association and frequent violent outbreaks forced black men to reconsider their patronage of mixed race and white saloons, bars, and dives and to create their own racially exclusive spaces of leisure. Robert Zachariah Johnstone's master's thesis was one of a grouping of theses that emerged in the 1900s examining the lives of African Americans who had recently migrated North from Virginia. In his section on saloons he discusses black exclusion from white leisure spaces explaining that blacks were expected to take their alcohol to go. However, he justifies this exclusion by stating that "this works a certain good in that [black men] may be saved from being intoxicated on the street. It saves the women this experience too. But it cannot be said to lessen the loathsome effect on the children at home." Johnstone, "The Negro in New York—His Social Attainments and Prospects," 46.

4. A number of black community leaders in New York City protested the attention the COF gave to African American saloons in the early twentieth century believing it reflected bias against black saloon owners. COF leader Frederick Whitin replied to these accusations that race prejudice had nothing to do with COF decisions to investigate or not investigate any establishments and that, in fact, there was not enough attention paid to black saloons because of a "lack of colored police and excise agents available for detective work." See Memo written by Frederick Whitin, August 14, 1911, box 13, folder 31, COF; and Sims, "Blacks, Italians, and the Progressive Interest," 91.

5. As an example, the 1895 Malby Act provided "full and equal" access to all "accommodation or amusement" regardless of race. Quote taken from "Equality by Legislation," *New York Times*, June 30, 1895; "The New York Equal Rights Law," *The Sun*, August 25, 1895; and Wallace, *Greater Gotham*, 814.

6. Powers, *Faces along the Bar*, 55–56. Separation in leisure also stemmed partially from the inclination of black men to spend time among other black men. Powers, *Faces along the Bar*, 63–64.

7. "Police Kill Negro in Race Riot; 7 Hurt," *New York Times*, May 27, 1917.

8. "Policeman Dead, Two Dying," *New-York Tribune*, May 3, 1903.

9. "Policeman Dead, Two Dying," *New-York Tribune*, May 3, 1903; "Three Policemen Shot by Negro Ex-Convict," *New York Times*, May 3, 1903.

10. A deeper record of Singleton's history found in "Two Policeman Dead," *The Sun*, May 4, 1903.

11. Sing Sing Prison Inmate Admission Registers, 1877; Sing Sing Prison Register, box 7, series B0143; and Auburn Prison Register, 1886; "Two of the Policemen Dead," *The Sun*, May 4, 1903.

12. The term *hidden transcripts* is used in Scott, *Domination and the Arts of Resistance*; also referenced in Robin D. G. Kelley, "We Are Not What We Seem," 77–78.

13. A number of historians have made similar arguments about consumption and its role in inculcating claims to citizenship. For example, Davarian Baldwin's work on the black community of Chicago asserts that participation in various types of trade was important in a generational shift toward self-actualization for African Americans. "Black working-class migrants attempted to use the mass consumer marketplace to challenge the dehumanizing effects of capitalism and etch out a world of leisure that could cater to their own labor demands," Baldwin wrote; Baldwin, *Chicago's New Negroes*. Martin Summers also argued that black men in particular had social, economic, and political imperatives to connect themselves with a consumerist version of manhood. Like most men, they at least somewhat adhered to dominant normative modes of American masculinity that were in flux at the time alongside broader economic and cultural developments. "Achieving manhood became less dependent upon imbibing the producer values of industry, thrift, sobriety, self-control, and character" that pervaded the Victorian era, Summer's argues, "rather, individuals constructed a masculine sense of self that was tied to the consumer goods they owned, the leisure practices they engaged in, and their physical and sexual virility"; Summers, *Manliness and Its Discontents*. Also see Green, *Selling the Race*; Caddoo, *Envisioning Freedom*; Greer, *Represented*; and Parker, *Department Stores and the Black Freedom Movement*.

14. In addition to the way that saloons functioned as sites for political engagement in terms of voting and gathering information, black men often engaged in conversations and arguments about politically controversial subjects. In one example, a quarrel between two men over some subject regarding the high cost of living resulted in the shooting death of Isaac Lee in 1910. "Quickest Murder Trial," *New York Times*, December 22, 1910.

15. Newspapers indicate illegal prizefights often took place in the backs of saloons. For example, "Killed in a Prizefight," *New York Times*, February 28, 1908.

16. Robin D. G. Kelley's superlative work on the importance of leisure and informal lifestyles to working-class African Americans is pivotal in that it inserts "spaces of pleasure" into discourse about the politics of black institutional and organizational life. See Kelley, *Race Rebels*, 47–49.

17. Powers, "The 'Poor Man's Friend,'"1. Popular historical arguments have depicted early twentieth-century urban vice among lower-class individuals as conscious or unconscious subaltern social resistance to the culturally dominant upper and middle class. See, for example, Gilfoyle, *City of Eros*; Chauncey, *Gay New York*; and Mumford, *Interzones*. The saloon has been depicted as an institution that provided a space of leisure for this form of resistance and served as a middle man between New York City's economic and political structure and working-class European immigrants. For African American men the saloon similarly served as a place of subaltern social resistance but it fell short as a middle man between blacks and the civic power structure. For this reason, it more often served as a refuge for black participation in underground economies.

18. Argument made for similar function in the lives of white ethnic immigrants in Rothbart, "The Ethnic Saloon."

19. In her book, historian Madelon Powers deals with the subject of black men and saloons to some extent but focuses on white ethnics primarily. Powers, *Faces along the Bar*; for other books about American saloons and alcohol prohibition, see Duis, *The Saloon and the Public City*; Okrent, *Last Call*; McGirr, *The War on Alcohol*.

20. A Summary of Vice Conditions in Harlem, 1928, box 12, folder "James Pedersen," COF; reported digested in the black New York newspaper in "They Won't Keep Away," *New York Amsterdam News*, October 23, 1929.

21. Heap, *Slumming*, 2–3.

22. In his work, Jack Katz argues the "badass" states with their actions "not only am I not here for you, I come from a place that is inherently intractable by your world." As such, they make themselves into an "alien" that others might find unnerving. Katz, *Seductions of Crime*, 80–81, 87.

23. "Two of the Policemen Dead," *The Sun*, May 4, 1903.

24. "Policeman's Slayer Free," *New York Times*, August 18, 1903; "Negro Not Held for Murder," *Washington Post*, August 18, 1903; "Killed Two Cops, But Is Free," *The Sun*, August 18, 1903.

25. Willemse, *Behind the Green Lights*, 112.

26. "Negro Rearrested," *New York Times*, August 25, 1903; and "'King of Coons' Is Little Jeff," *Evening World*, August 24, 1903; "[Singleton] in Trouble Again," *Evening Post*, August 24, 1903.

27. Powers, *Faces along the Bar*, 27; Moore, "The Social Value of the Saloon," 4–8.

28. Willemse, *Behind the Green Lights*, 13–14.

29. Robertson et al., "Disorderly Houses," 445.

30. Kiser, *Sea Island to City*, 44–45.

31. Sacks, *Before Harlem*, 187.

32. Gilfoyle, *A Pickpocket's Tale*, 111.

33. Gilfoyle, *A Pickpocket's Tale*, 111; and Czitrom, "The Politics of Performance," 525–26.

34. Wallace, *Greater Gotham*, 394–427.

35. McGerr, *A Fierce Discontent*, 274–75.

36. Eric Avila engages the racialized construction of the "new mass culture" very well in Avila, *Popular Culture in the Age of White Flight*, 3; and Gilfoyle, "White Cities, Linguistic Turns, and Disneylands," 178–79.

37. King, *Whose Harlem Is This, Anyway?* 122; Powers, "The 'Poor Man's Friend,'" 1–5.

38. King, *Whose Harlem Is This, Anyway?* 132; Lerner, *Dry Manhattan*, 201.

39. Heap, *Slumming*, 1–2.

40. Harris, *Sex Workers, Psychics, and Numbers Runners*, 2–3.

41. Peiss, *Cheap Amusements*, 20.

42. Michael Kimmel engages this subject in his work on the cultural breakdown of the "self-made man." Kimmel, *Manhood in America*, 88–89. Further, historian Martin Summers argues "manhood became less defined by production (or engagement in the marketplace), character, respectability, and the producer values of industry, thrift, regularity, and temperance. Rather, middle-class Americans increasingly unlinked manhood from the market, at least from the orientation of the producer, and

began to define it in terms of consumption." However, it is clear this was not only a phenomenon of the monied middle class but also a shift that pervaded many aspects of the social world concerning labor, gender, sexual relationships, spaces of leisure, and paradigms of consumption across classes, as Summers acknowledges. Summers, *Manliness and Its Discontents*, 8.

43. Jones, *Recreation and Amusement among Negroes in Washington, D.C.*, 131.

44. "In the Negro Cabarets," *New York Times*, September 5, 1922.

45. Powers, *Faces along the Bar*, 12.

46. Heap, *Slumming*, 1–2.

47. Powers, *Faces along the Bar*, 64.

48. Johnson, *Along This Way*, 176.

49. Wallace, *Greater Gotham*, 452–53.

50. Powers, *Faces along the Bar*, 66–70.

51. Lewinson, *Black Politics in New York City*, 38; "Negro Republican Clubs," *The Sun*, March 25, 1904.

52. Wallace, *Greater Gotham*, 820.

53. Pegram, *Battling Demon Rum*, 88–89.

54. Wallace, *Greater Gotham*, 634–35. On the beginnings of the Anti-Saloon League, Pegram, "The Dry Machine."

55. Barker, *The Saloon Problem and Social Reform*, 41–42.

56. Barker, *The Saloon Problem and Social Reform*, 21.

57. The Committee of Fifty did not see anything wrong with drinking in general, but that in its abuse it posed a problem to health and society. They proposed an innovative alternative of removing private profitmaking from the sale of liquor and sending all profits to the state, which would then be redistributed to communities "for the purpose of public betterment." Billings, *The Liquor Problem*, 17–19, 125.

58. Many white progressives expressed panic about this sort of contact, including Police Commissioner McAdoo. In his memoir he described allegations of racial bias from a "delegation of colored saloon-keepers" who "asserted with great emphasis their legal right to entertain white as well as colored women." Questioning the legality of forcing segregation in private businesses, they protested the practice of singling out racially mixed black-owned barrooms as targets for arrests, raids, and sanctions. McAdoo remained steadfast in his conviction to police these places because of their danger "for a certain class of white women" and at the same time defended himself against accusations of racism. "They accused me of being prejudiced against the colored race . . . which is quite untrue, I being a much better friend of the honest, decent, respectable colored people . . . than the owners of these brothels." Nevertheless, he later expressed strong disapproval of white and black intimate contact and equated it with prostitution. "The mixed-race resort, besides running counter to violent racial prejudices and traditions, is an unmitigated and disgusting evil, and the technical arguments as to the legal rights of a licensed resort should not prevent the police in placing it under constant surveillance and in enforcing the law with the greatest vigor," he concluded. McAdoo, *Guarding a Great City*, 95–96, 100.

59. The Committee of Fourteen was initiated by members of the New York Anti-Saloon League and first endeavored to stop vice by closing saloons that violated liquor laws. While investigating saloons, the organization refocused on interracial vice

and sex in spaces of leisure. See Fronc, *New York Undercover*; also see Sacks, *Before Harlem*, 64; and Wallace, *Greater Gotham*, 109, 419. Another organization, the Committee of Fifteen, founded in 1900, published an influential report on the "Social Evil" of prostitution in 1902 just before it discontinued. Committee of Fifteen, *Social Evil*; and Wallace, *Greater Gotham*, 604. Andrea Friedman gave great attention to the mindsets of such progressive organizations. Friedman, *Prurient Interests*.

60. The COF formed primarily in response to saloons that bypassed state legislation regulating liquor sales. The 1896 Raines Law restricted Sunday sales of spirits to restaurants or hotels, thereby criminalizing consumption in saloons on the one day most workers had for leisure. In response proprietors converted storage areas into sleeping quarters and served inedible meals consisting mostly of unsavory "Raines Law sandwiches" in an effort to circumvent the law. The COF first set out to end these fraudulent business configurations by partnering with brewers to choke the alcohol supply of noncompliant saloonkeepers. Fronc, *New York Undercover*, 6, 66–68.

61. Report on Marshall's Hotel, March 17 1910, box 28, folder 1910–1912, COF.

62. Report on Saloons, 1913, box 28, folder "1913-June–July," COF. Yet another sleuth made a direct connection between the risky environment of black and tans and the forecasts for the "very bad looking white girls" found within. These women "seemed to be all in, broken down," he claimed. "All the paint and make up they had on their face could not disguise the kind of life they had been living." Report by W. M. Franklin, box 28, folder 1913 June–July, COF.

63. Anonymous Letter to Police Commission Arthur Woods, undated, box 2, folder Citizen's Complaints, COF. In another letter dated 1909 a Tenderloin resident asked the COF to "pay attention" to a basement saloon "only patronized by disorderly Negroes [and] White Women." Above the rathskeller was a brothel "run by a Negress very openly" and frequented by young white men. "It is really a disgrace to the Young People of the Neighborhood," the resident plied. Letter to Frederick Whitin from "A Resident," September 14, 1909, box 22, folder "Complaints," COF.

64. Letter to the Committee of Fourteen from John H. Fife of the Gilsey House, January 1910, box 22, folder "Complaints," COF. Built during the early Gilded Age, the Gilsey House was well known for famous guests such as Mark Twain, as well as its architecture, food, and accommodations for the rich. Stuart Sprague, "Lure of the City," 81. With more personal concerns, worried parents, husbands, and wives begged reformers to shut down or improve saloons, dance halls, and theaters, and pay attention to worsening conditions on city streets. Distressed by his daughter's patronage of the Great Eastern saloon a father appealed to the COF to investigate it. "I am white but this is a nigger place [and] I can't stop her so I wish you would see that [the proprietor] would run a decent place," he entreated. "I have been in the back room and it is awful." Letter from "A Father" to Committee of Fourteen, undated, box 22, folder "Citizens' Complaints," COF. Another man told of an errant sister who preferred to spend her free time in the Benson Café with "negro women." Claiming authorities ignored his requests to arrest the prostitutes and pimps in the establishment, he considered the COF his last chance to save her. Letter to the Committee of Fourteen, box 22, folder "Citizen's Complaints," COF.

65. Fronc, *New York Undercover*, 6; and Report on the Police Department and the Committee of Fourteen, box 82, folder 3, COF.

66. Sacks, *Before Harlem*, 43–45; and Strausbaugh, *Black Like You*, 134–49. According to writer Tony Fletcher, Harlem nightlife along 133rd Street from Lenox to Seventh Avenue catered "mostly to white 'Negrophiliacs' who journeyed uptown in cavalcades, some with good intentions to share 'genuine' Negro experience, others out on what they openly admitted were 'slumming parties.'" Fletcher, *All Hopped Up and Ready to Go*. Intellectuals like Columbia University historian William Dunning fostered delusions of Utopian plantation contentment and characterized the Civil War and Reconstruction as the demise of an amiable paternalistic system. Dunning, *Reconstruction*, 212.

67. Graham, *New York Nights*, 17–19.

68. T. J. Jackson Lears engages the subject of antimodernism best in his book, *No Place of Grace*, 4–5; and Lears, *Rebirth of a Nation*.

69. Heap, *Slumming*, 154–55, 189.

70. McAdoo, *Guarding a Great City*, 93–95.

71. The *Brooklyn Citizen* quoted in Hicks, *Talk with You Like a Woman*, 62.

72. Statement from District Attorney's Office, November 3, 1891, box 43, folder 12, ECF.

73. The letter confirming Stokes eventual release is Letter from Warden to Governor Roswell P. Flower, September 18, 1894, box 43, folder 12, ECF.

74. Multiple letters in Wendell Stoke's clemency file vouched for his good character and condemned not only Monte James but integrated bars and their clientele. One exemplary letter states: "The provocation was a very aggravated one on the part of his assailant, that of assault with intent to rob Mr. [Stokes] and he was forced, from what I learn from the most reputable and truthful gentlemen, to kill the negro, and under the circumstances I cheerfully unite in a petition . . . for Executive Clemency, believing from all I hear that it was a case of justifiable homicide." Letter from John W. Lawson to T. J. Campbell, Esquire, June 23, 1891, box 43, folder 12, ECF.

75. In the process of establishing these spaces men participated in a "discourse of the street," which included aspects of style, consumption, and cultural representation. Writing about this discourse, Elsa Barkley Brown and Gregg D. Kimball emphasized the usage of city space and the built environment to fulfill the social, economic, and cultural priorities of urban residents. In their work, they interrogated the meaning black Richmonders "gave to the spaces they shared and the rhetoric and ideologies of urban space they developed." For all urban dwellers, they argued, "the City—its spaces, its forbidden and inviting areas, its pleasures and dangers, even its boundaries—existed in people's minds as much as on street maps." Finding themselves marginalized out of other public spaces some African American men may have found a sense of exclusivity in the alleys, backstreets, rathskellers, and uninviting conditions of black quarters. Brown and Kimball, "Mapping the Terrain of Black Richmond." Elsa Barkley Brown and Gregg D. Kimball are part of a group of urban historians whose work became popular in the 1980s and 1990s when they began to reevaluate urban subcultures. Recent urban historical writers have reinserted the influence, adaptability, and agency of historically ignored groups such as migrants, sex workers, and the working class. Much of this work has centered on the construction of social identities and the persistence of subcultural norms in the face of a dominant culture in an urban environment. They have given priority to the usage of space, the built environment, and

identity created through cultural consumption, domestic configuration, and leisure. For more on urban space, see Kusmer, "African Americans in the City Since World War II," 458–504; Joe William Trotter, *Black Milwaukee*; Earl Lewis, *In Their Own Interests*; Stansell, *City of Women*; Celik, Favro, and Ingersoll, eds., *Streets*, 4; and especially Gilfoyle, "White Cities, Linguistic Turns, and Disneylands," 175–204.

76. Investigations and other documentation make it clear women, involved in sex work or not, had a definite presence in saloons. Powers, *Faces along the Bar*, 32–33.

77. Complaint Record #127541, Report from Great Meadow Prison on inmate #10643, June 6, 1934, box 1473, folder 1414, DACCF.

78. "Negro Kills Policeman," *New York Times*, November 11, 1919; during the murder trial of Jackson Burns, he makes very clear that he envisioned his attack on his wife as justified because of the insanity caused by her disobedience and abandonment. Trial Transcript #2784, March 22, 1920, roll 339, 3–4, 233–39, TTC.

79. Trial Transcript #2784, 243, 360, TTC.

80. Burns and his attorney offered a plea of guilty to reduce his sentence at the outset of the trial, but the district attorney refused the offer with a terse statement. "People are critical of the police at times. But nobody disputes their bravery, and when an officer is killed this office will make every effort to have the extreme penalty meted to the assassin." "Becker Case Recalled," *New York Times*, March 23, 1920; "Life Term for Policeman's Slayer," June 24, 1920; and Complaint Record #127541, Report from Great Meadow Prison on inmate #10643, June 6, 1934, box 1473, folder 1414, DACCF.

81. Ella's responses to Jackson's pleas are taken from Jackson's recollection during his testimony in the murder trial. Trial Transcript #2784, roll 339, 233–43, TTC.

82. Bederman, *Manliness and Civilization*, 16–17; and Peiss, *Cheap Amusements*, 20.

83. Rotundo, *American Manhood*, 279–83.

84. Heap, *Slumming*, 233, 254; *Interzones* is a term used in Mumford, *Interzones*, 35.

85. Wallace, *Greater Gotham*, 786; Heap, *Slumming*, 254–56; and Chauncey, *Gay New York*, 246. A survey of materials from the Committee of Fourteen, done by historian Kevin Mumford, showed that most of the clubs where same-sex behavior was reported were "colored," or exclusively or primarily black. Mumford, *Interzones*, 35, 80–82; for more see Hartman, *Wayward Lives, Beautiful Experiments*.

86. Wallace, *Greater Gotham*, 784; and Chauncey, *Gay New York*, 65–66.

87. Chauncey, *Gay New York*, 99–100, 126; and Wallace, *Greater Gotham*, 785.

88. Chauncey, *Gay New York*, 244–57. Many of the publications of the Harlem Renaissance examined and celebrated same-sex relationships, including Nella Larsen's *Quicksand* (1928) and Wallace Thurman's *Infants of the Spring* (1932). Vogel, *The Scene of Harlem Cabaret*, 18–19.

89. "Masquerade Ball Draws 5,000," *New York Amsterdam News*, February 20, 1929.

90. Letters from Police Inspector John Daly, September 23, 1916, box 17, folder Seventh Avenue, COF.

91. Special Grand Jury Report Arranged by Streets, 1910, box 28, folder 1910 Grand Jury (John D. Rockefeller) Arranged by Streets, COF; Sims, "Blacks, Italians, and the Progressive Interest," 88; in his address to the National Negro Business League Convention in 1903, Fred R. Moore praised New York City's black community for supporting "a large number of so-called saloons." Moore, "Negro Business Enterprises in New York," 69; the information of the previous note contradicts that of statistics from

the National Negro Business League on black businesses in New York City quoted in Haynes, *The Negro at Work in New York City*, 99. Haynes's records indicate that out of 309 black establishments in the city, only five could be classified as "saloons and cafes." Those businesses most represented on the list were barbershops at fifty, groceries at thirty-six, and restaurants at twenty-six. *The Negro at Work in New York City*, 99.

92. *New York Times*, July 1, 1895.

93. Letter to S. Liebmann's Sons Brewing Co., box 17, folder West 109th St.–137th St., COF.

94. Hazzard-Gordon, *Jookin'*, 97–111; and Powers, *Faces along the Bar*, 27.

95. Hughes, *The Big Sea: An Autobiography*, 224–25.

96. Hughes, *The Big Sea: An Autobiography*, 228–29.

97. Report of Investigator W. M. Franklin, December 5, 1914, box 28, folder "1913 Aug–Sept," COF. A black Brooklyn saloon allowed white customers but forbade them from certain areas. Agent W. S. Rainsford observed what he could about an upstairs section that was seemingly secured by a "well dressed lot of coons." Rainsford watched "a lot of white girls coming down [with] some niggers" and assumed they were involved in the sex trade. "These girls are not maidens." Night Inspection by W. S. Rainsford at 176 Myrtle Avenue, June 20, 1912, box 29, folder blank, COF. In another case, also in Brooklyn, a white investigator inquiring about the company of a group of black women received rejection because they only solicited black men. Investigation of Karl's Hotel, August 17, 1916, box 30, folder blank, COF.

98. Report of Investigator W. M. Franklin, December 5, 1914, box 28, folder 1913 August–September, COF.

99. Report on Chadwick's Novelty Café, November 21, 1915, box 30, folder 9, COF.

100. "Report for Saturday Evening, August 9," box 28, folder 1913 August–September, COF.

101. "Barron Wilkins Murdered," *Chicago Defender*, May 31, 1924.

102. Juli Jones Jr., journalist for the *Indianapolis Freeman*, quoted in "Old-Timer Recalls History of Barron," *Chicago Defender*, May 31, 1924.

103. "Barron D. Wilkins Slain in Harlem," *New York Times*, May 25, 1924.

104. Ellington, *Music Is My Mistress*, 64.

105. "Stay for Negro Resort," *New York Times*, July 17, 1910.

106. "Bits of New York Life," *Atlanta Constitution*, August 20, 1924.

107. "Sportsman's Murder Stirs East," *Pittsburgh Courier*, May 31, 1924.

108. "Barron Wilkins Murdered," *Chicago Defender*, May 31, 1924; and "In and around New York," *Chicago Defender*, January 10, 1925.

109. Report on Harlem Saloons, September 22, 1912, folder 1913 June–July, COF.

110. Report on Baron Wilkins' Café, March 16 1910, box 28, folder 1910–1912, COF.

111. Report on Barron Exclusive Club, undated, folder 1913 August–September, COF.

112. "Four Gambling Raids," *New York Times*, December 21, 1910.

113. "Raids on Negroes Trap Slummers," *New-York Tribune*, October 11, 1915.

114. "Baron Wilkins in Trouble," *Chicago Defender*, January 20, 1917. Barron Wilkins faced arrest less than a month after his January 1917 arrest when one of his waiters served drinks to undercover detectives afterhours, and police discovered dancing in his saloon without a dancehall license. Case Record #114529, Affidavit of Violation of Liquor Tax Law, February 22, 1917, box 1334, folder 259, DACCF; and "De-

tectives Who Raided Barron Wilkins' Cabaret, Pinch 23," *Chicago Defender*, March 11, 1922.

115. "Cabarets," *Variety* 47, no. 6 (July 6, 1917): 13.

116. Editorialized in "Sportsman's Murder Stirs East," *Pittsburgh Courier*, May 31, 1924.

117. Other men like John Parker showed similar aspirations as Wilkins. After holding many different jobs for ten years, Parker hoped to escape meaningless drudgery by starting his own business. Dissatisfied with his position as a chauffeur and handyman for a wealthy family, he asked his employer Sofia Moretti for a loan to begin the new enterprise. In his request he told Moretti he was "tired of being a chauffeur" and wished to open a restaurant for which he would need $300. "You must give it to me," Parker demanded. When Moretti refused Parker threatened to kill her. Although he never received the money, Parker was later convicted of attempted robbery and given a ten-year prison sentence. Nevertheless, his crime represents the frustration some black men felt with marginal, inauspicious job prospects and severely limited financial potential, and his aspirations of leaving wage labor were very common. Since arriving in the city from North Carolina a decade earlier, Parker never progressed past underpaid domestic service and aimed to reap the full rewards of his labor, even if it meant risking imprisonment and doing harm to another person. Story from Trial Transcript #623, January 23, 1907, reel 100, 14, 16–17, 59, TTC.

118. Wallace, *Greater Gotham*, 606–7.

119. Wallace, *Greater Gotham*, 596.

120. Zacks, *Island of Vice*, 8–9.

121. "Fear Sweeney Will Confess," *New York Times*, February 20, 1913. There is a great explanation of how graft worked at the turn of the century in Key, "Police Graft."

122. Annual Report of the Committee of Fourteen, 1916–1917, 4. Conducting an investigation himself, Hooke had also reported a fight in a saloon to an officer who turned his back and said "let the 'niggers' fight it out." Letter from Walter G. Hooke to Police Inspector Thomas T. Ryan, December 22, 1916, box 12, folder "Police Inspectors," COF.

123. "Fear Sweeney Will Confess," *New York Times*, February 20, 1913; "To Tell New Graft Story," *Evening Post*, February, 20, 1913.

124. Johnson, "The Making of Harlem," 635.

125. Wallace, *Greater Gotham*, 455. Marshall's was an important center for a black middle class. Marshall's hotel, planted in adjacent brownstones on Fifty-Third Street, contained handsome suites on upper floors, a cellar for performances, and a fancy dining room on the first floor, one of few such restaurants that allowed blacks. Famed black musicians began to use it as a hangout and networking space and in 1910, composer Jim Europe opened the Clef Club across the street, a hiring bureau for bandleaders and instrumentalists that helped them gain ground in the live music sector in Manhattan. Wallace, *Greater Gotham*, 455, 471.

126. Wallace, *Greater Gotham*, 455.

127. It was a sight that made him and his brother rent space in the Marshall's back room so they might begin their musical work in such an atmosphere. It also opened many doors for black performers that were previously closed to them. Johnson, *Along This Way*, 175–77.

128. Clubs, Hotels, Saloons, etc. cont'd, box 31, folder untitled, COF.

129. It is clear from Fred R. Moore's letter that he had a friendly relationship with the COF leadership and wished to diffuse the situation in a way that pleased both parties. However, Moore expressed the sentiments of many African Americans who worried about the impact progressive reformers had on men like Marshall who were widely considered heroes engaged in enterprises of "race progress." Letter from Fred R. Moore to Committee, box 21, folder 1911–1914, COF.

130. W. E. B. Du Bois's letter to the Committee of Fourteen quoted in Sacks, *Before Harlem*, 65.

131. Letter from Frederick H. Whitin to Ebling Brewing Co., February 16, 1918, box 17, folder "West 41st–81st St.," COF.

132. Letter to Inspector John F. Dwyer, box 17, folder 41st–81st St., COF.

133. Letter from Investigator H. O. Harding to Walter G. Hooke, March 30, 1911, box 22, folder complaints, COF.

134. Investigation Report, September 14, 1912, box 28, folder Aug–Sept, COF.

135. Letter from Committee of Fourteen Secretary Thomas H. Reed to Police Commissioner Theodore A. Bingham, October 17, 1908, box 13, folder 1904–09, COF.

136. Letter to Walter G. Hooke from Leroy Wilkins, February 5, 1915, box 19, folder Protest List Correspondence 1915–1916, COF.

137. Letter from William Banks to Walter G. Hooke, December 18, 1910, box 17, folder West 4, COF.

138. Complaint Record #112738, Transcript of the Court of General Sessions of the Peace, September 21, 1916, box 1313, folder 119, DACCF.

139. Complaint Record #112738, Affidavit of Violation of Liquor Tax Law, Selling on Sunday—Rear Room, September 21, 1916, box 1313, folder 119, DACCF.

140. Letter to the Committee of Fourteen from Barron Wilkins, September 26, 1912, box 17, folder Seventh Avenue, COF. 0658.

141. Letter to Walter G. Hooke from Leroy Wilkins, February 5, 1915, box 19, folder Protest List Correspondence 1915–16, COF.

142. *New York Amsterdam News* article clipping, undated, box 82, folder Attacks on Committee, COF.

143. Letter to Walter G. Hooke from Leroy Wilkins, February 5, 1915, box 19, folder Protest List Correspondence 1915–1916, COF.

144. "Saloonkeepers Organize," *New York Age*, June 8, 1911; and "To Raise the Moral Tone of Local Saloons," *New York Age*, December 14, 1911. *Age* writers agreed that wrestling control of black businesses from whites was essential to the moral and economic life of Harlem and other black communities, since whites did not care about the welfare of black women entangled in saloon life nor did they have a stake in black entrepreneurialism. King, *Whose Harlem Is This, Anyway?* 121; Fronc, *New York Undercover,* 114; also see Scheiner, *Negro Mecca*, 120.

145. Various Committee of Fourteen reports show racial integration in member institutions into the 1920s.

146. Letter to the Committee of Fourteen from William Banks, September 23, 1913, box 17, folder "Bronx," COF.

147. Letter to the Committee also included a promise not to allow single women "unaccompanied by escorts" into the rear of the saloon after 7 P.M. and that no women would be admitted to the business after 12:30 or served alcohol after 1 A.M. Dancing

and the singing of vulgar songs would also not be allowed, and performers would be kept from mingling with customers. He reiterated these promises four years later when in a 1918 letter to the committee he apologized for not keeping his promises. "I promise that this year I will conduct the place strictly as one for men only unless released in some way from this promise by the Committee or its representative." Letter to the Committee of Fourteen, box 17, folder West 4th–40th Sts., COF.

148. Letter to the Committee of Fourteen from Barron Wilkins, January 10, 1918, box 17, folder Seventh Avenue, COF.

149. Letter to Committee of Fourteen from Leroy Wilkins, September 28, 1916, box 17, folder Eldridge Street—Fifth Avenue, COF.

150. Committee of Fourteen, *Annual Report, 1915–1916* (New York, 1916), 58.

151. Committee of Fourteen, *Annual Report, 1914* (New York, 1915), 10–12, 15.

152. Committee of Fourteen, *Annual Report, 1915–1916* (New York, 1916), 58.

153. "Charleston Tells Story of Wilkins Slaying," *Chicago Defender*, October 25, 1924.

154. "Barron Wilkins Left $125,000 Estate to His Wife, Sister, and Brother," *Afro-American*, June 6, 1924.

155. "Barron Wilkins Shot Dead in Front of Harlem Cabaret," *Philadelphia Tribune*, May 31, 1924; numbers on funeral from "Barron Wilkins Funeral," *Chicago Defender*, June 7, 1924.

156. "Barron Wilkins Left $125,000 Estate to His Wife, Sister, and Brother," *Afro-American*, June 6, 1924; "Barron Wilkins Leaves a Fortune," *Philadelphia Tribune*, June 14, 1924; "Barron Wilkins Leaves $125,000.00 Estate," *Pittsburgh Courier*, June 7, 1924.

157. Weather report for the night of W. S. Rainsford's investigations taken from "The Weather," *New York Times*, June 20, 1920.

158. Night Inspection by W. S. Rainsford at 205/4 Myrtle Avenue, June 20, 1912, box 29, folder blank, COF.

159. Night Inspection by W. S. Rainsford at 173 Myrtle Avenue, June 20, 1912, box 29, folder blank, COF.

160. Night Inspection by W. S. Rainsford at 164 Myrtle Avenue, June 20, 1912, box 29, folder blank, COF.

161. Jacob Riis described the black "Minettas" neighborhood in Greenwich Village (made up of Minetta Place, Minetta Lane, and Minetta Street) as inhospitable to respectable whites and criticized interracial communion in "black and tan" saloons as the "commingling of the utterly depraved of both sexes." "There can be no greater abomination," he penned. In "The Color Line in New York," Riis's chapter on African Americans in New York City, he describes blacks as very dichotomous characters. On one hand, he sees "Little Africa" as a place shaped by black optimism in the face of oppression. "Poverty, abuse, and injustice alike the negro accepts with imperturbable cheerfulness," he writes. Blacks, he argues, are clean and blithesome, and always "putting the best foot foremost" by "disguising his poverty." On the other hand, he argues that a black inclination toward crime and violence makes the "black 'tough' . . . as handy with the razor in a fight as his peaceably inclined brother is with it in pursuit of his honest trade." Riis never reconciles these two distinct black characters. Describing mixed saloons as the "worst and desperately bad" of venues, he condemned "black and tans" as places of "common debauch." Primarily troubled by racial violence Riis

criticized "foul cellar dive[s]" that gathered together "all the lawbreakers and all the human wrecks within reach," into one place. "When a fight breaks out during the dance a dozen razors are handy in as many boot-legs, and there is always a job for the surgeon and the ambulance" afterward, Riis surmised. Riis, *How the Other Half Lives*, 119.

162. Crane's descriptions of Minetta Lane seem far more narrowly constructed than many of his descriptions of other parts of New York City. At the time of his writing in 1896 he seems to imply that the Minettas were no longer as affected by crime as they used to be. In his interviews with current residents he notes that they spoke of the earlier part of the decade as "the old gorgeous days" of violence and crime and that Italian immigrants were quickly encroaching on formerly black housing in Little Africa. Hagemann and Stallman, *New York City Sketches*, 178–79, 179–84.

163. Moss and Parkhurst, *The American Metropolis,* 286–87. Observing the reputation of the area, police, clergy, and citizens proposed removing the "offending streets" as "city sore spots" in 1912 and replacing the area with an extension of Sixth Avenue or a plaza, although it never happened. "May Wipe Out Minettas," *New York Times*, April 7, 1912. Another proposal to make the area into a playground was made in 1914. "To Save Washington Sq." *New York Times*, March 1, 1914; and "Minetta Square Playground," *New York Times*, April 26, 1914.

164. "With Hot Fat and Dishes," *New York Times*, January 2, 1896.

165. "Minetta Street, Tough, Crooked and Dilapidated, to Be Wiped out under Civic Betterment Plan," *The Sun*, December 10, 1916.

166. Willemse, *Behind the Green Lights*, 112.

167. Mainstream newspaper reporters joined the chorus of condemnation of black crime and often overdramatized conflicts that happened in integrated venues. In one typical article in 1896, the *New York Times* described a "miniature race war" in a Greenwich Village restaurant. Commenting on the mélange of racial groups in the area of the eatery the writer implied that integration provoked violent encounters. "The peculiar civilization that exists in the vicinity . . . is strongly impregnated with a feeling of animosity between its various elements." Sketching a scene of hysteria and chaos, the article blamed black residents. Donning colorful sobriquets such as "Black America," and "Pete the Pig," a group of black men reportedly "created havoc" in a restaurant during a New Year's Day celebration. Frenzied because of some insult or slight, a crowd of more than five hundred called "their champions" to "exterminate the white trash that was giving them battle with hot fat, pitchers, catsup bottles, and such dishes as could be handily converted into weapons of defense." After the melee, "the negroes who caused the trouble were escorted through Minetta Lane in triumph by their friends," the *Times* reported. This scene, and others like it, consciously mapped out divisions between white and black spaces by impressing upon readers the volatility of interracial proximity. Story found in "With Hot Fat and Dishes," *New York Times*, January 2, 1896.

168. Testimony in Trial Transcript #39, November 10, 1893, reel 10, 62, TTC.

169. Trial Transcripts #1356, April 19, 1911, reel 175, 356, 369, 376, TTC.

170. "Clean 'Em Out," *New York Age*, April 6, 1911.

171. In his work on nineteenth-century gangs and crime in New York City, historian Timothy Gilfoyle makes the argument that more than money, white gang members sought "respect, honor, and adulation from other neighborhood youths for performing

deeds others feared. . . . For gangsters violence was an accepted element of their social order, the defining element of their self-worth and honor." Gilfoyle, *A Pickpocket's Tale*, 189–90.

172. Exaggerated accounts of instances of interracial violence in New York City's spaces of leisure caused much alarm for observers. In one case, the *New York Times* reported the murder of a white man in an interracial saloon when a black man shot him dead for an unknown reason. "Negro Defends His Race," *New York Times*, August 28, 1899, and "Shot Down in a Saloon," *New York Times*, June 27, 1899. In another instance, a group of black men eluding police during a riot fled into a saloon and opened fire with revolvers when they were pursued. "Race Rioters at It Again," *New York Times*, July 18, 1905; *New York Times*, August 28, 1899.

173. One witness corroborated Caldwell's story adding that Maxwell "always had one or two girls on the block for him." Trial Transcript #3176, April 5, 1906, reel 379, 150, TTC.

174. Trial Transcript #3176, August 24, 1903, reel 379, TTC.

175. Trial Transcript #3176, 47, 117–18, 120–21, 150–85, TTC.

176. Branch quoted on 196 and 198. Trial Transcript #3176, roll 379, 107, 212, TTC.

177. "Negro Killed in Street, Men Dodging the Shots," *New York Times*, February 11, 1906.

178. Trial Transcripts #3176, 155, TTC.

179. Trial Transcript Case #3176, 259, TTC.

180. Trial Transcripts Case #3176, 175–84, TTC.

181. Branch made it clear in his testimony he purposely did not involve the police. Trial Transcripts #3176, 212, TTC.

182. New York State Census, 3rd Assembly District, Borough of Manhattan, 1905; and New York State Census, 9th Ward of the City, Borough of Manhattan, 1910.

Chapter 3

1. Trial Transcript #575, roll 93, March 21, 1921, 33, TTC.

2. Trial Transcript #575, 37, TTC; some details of the trial in "Negro's Prison Slaves Tell Court Their Story," *New York Times*, March 22, 1906.

3. "White Slave's Story," *New-York Tribune*, March 22, 1906.

4. "Negro's Prison Slaves Tell Court Their Story," *New York Times*, March 22, 1906. "The houses in question were not only barred and bolted like prisons, but negro guards on the outside were on watch continually to prevent any of the inmates escaping." "Trial Begun," *Evening Post*, March 20, 1906.

5. For scholarship on "white slavery," see Lubove, "The Progressives and the Prostitute," 308–30; De Young, "Help! I'm Being Held Captive!" 96–99; D'Emilio and Freedman, *Intimate Matters*; Grittner, *White Slavery*; Keire, "The Vice Trust," 5–41; and Donovan, *White Slave Crusades*. A number of newspapers claimed there was a "syndicate of resorts, patronized by colored men, where white women are forcibly detained." "Jerome Finds Strange Crime in Tenderloin," *St. Louis Post-Dispatch*, March 10, 1906; "Women Held for Years in Slavery," *San Francisco Chronicle*, March 10, 1906. Sharp evidently ran a few houses of prostitution with very little interference from police for several years but his luck changed in 1905 when Hattie Ross,

a former brothel proprietor turned missionary worker, pressured police to raid his house. Ross, the *Tribune* noted, knew "the Tenderloin better than any other person, as she has lived there for years" and at one point "was the proprietor of several disorderly resorts." She "got religion" after a stint in jail and decided to work providing aid to women in the sex trade. En route past one of Sharp's houses, she encountered an injured woman claiming to be a sex slave and subsequently aided the district attorney with information that led to his arrest. "Roosevelt Restored [Sharps's] Citizenship," *New York Times*, March 14, 1906, 6. "Net Tightens," *New-York Tribune*, March 14, 1906.

6. Quote of Sharp's charge found in "$9,000 Bail," *New York Times*, March 17, 1906. One *Times* reporter attempted to convey the dread and anger he perceived in the courtroom by depicting spectators on the edges of their seats. "The jurors took it all in. They followed closely the testimony given by the women, but every now and then one of the men in the box would turn quickly to watch the defendant for a moment before giving his attention once more to the gruesome story unraveled by the questions." This sort of report indicted and convicted Sharp before the trial was complete and helped create the public perception that he was guilty. "Negro's Prison Slaves Tell Court Their Story," *New York Times*, March 22, 1906.

7. Wallace, *Greater Gotham*, 607–9. Joanne Meyerowitz thoroughly tackles the subject of women living on their own in cities in Meyerowitz, *Women Adrift*.

8. See Connelly, *The Response to Prostitution in the Progressive Era*; Rosen, *The Lost Sisterhood*; McDermott and Blackstone, "White Slavery Plays of the 1910s," 141–56; and Doezema, "Loose Women or Lost Women?," 23–50.

9. See Felton, *The Romantic Story of Georgia's Women*. As Crystal Feimster argues, during Reconstruction "southern Democrats had made clear their intentions of excluding black men from politics, 'protecting' white women from the perceived 'dangers' of black citizenship, and maintaining sexual and political power over both black and white women." Feimster, *Southern Horrors*, 62–63.

10. May, *Great Expectations*, 94. Alan Hunt wrote about the creation of "heterosocial space" in amusement venues during the time. Hunt, "Regulating Heterosocial Space," 1–34.

11. Clement, *Love for Sale*, 1–12; and Peiss, *Cheap Amusements*. Progressives' intent on reversing the trend of this courting culture saw it as a bridge between the lives of good girls and prostitutes. Activists like Belle Lindner Israels, the director of the Committee on Amusements and Vacation Resources of Working-Class Girls, published a prominent article in 1909 that described social clubs as traps for unwary women. Those simply seeking wholesome fun in the glitzy dance palaces of Coney Island, as an example, would inadvertently find "unnatural forms of excitement" and lecherous men, and come to realize too late that their trip to the beach "costs more than carfare." Israels, *The Way of the Girl*, 486–97.

12. *Atlanta Constitution*, March 11, 1906. "The trial gives promise of revealing a system of revolting slavery of white women in negro resorts." "Trial Begun," *Evening Post*, March 20, 1906.

13. Books from authors like Charles Loring Brace and Harriet Beecher Stowe had been published long before Stephen Crane's work making it clear these ideas of prostitution had begun to take root long before the turn of the century. Brace, *The Dangerous Classes of New York*; and Stowe, *We and Our Neighbors*.

14. Gilfoyle, *City of Eros*, 275. "Traffic in Souls" showed how "attractive emigrant girls are spotted and netted, how girls from country towns are lured at railway stations, how some of the captives struggle for liberty after being forcibly detained in traffic houses," according to *Variety* magazine. "Traffic in Souls," *Variety* 32, no. 13 (November 28, 1913). However, a writer for the *Chicago Daily Tribune* considered it an "exaggerated view of red light life" without one shock and "no special mission other than furnishing good entertainment." Together they make clear how prevailing this view of prostitution had become by 1913. "'Traffic in Souls' Has Thrills; but Nary Shock," *Chicago Daily Tribune*, April 16, 1914.

15. Mumford, *Interzones*, 14–18.

16. Donovan, *White Slave Crusades*, 5–6; Lears, *Rebirth of a Nation*, 106.

17. Price, "Race War and Negro Demoralization," 93–95, 99. In 1892, Memphis activist and newswoman Ida B. Wells published the *Southern Horrors* leaflet in which she surveyed more than 728 lynchings and showed that in only one-third of the cases had black men been formerly charged with rape. Thus, the generic argument that ravenous black men were to blame for the prevalence of lynching, was bogus, she protested. Wells, *Southern Horrors and Other Writings*, 61.

18. Quoted in Kendi, *Stamped from the Beginning*, 296.

19. Donovan, *White Slave Crusades*, 1; and Campbell, *Crime and Punishment in African American History*, 146.

20. As historian Brian Donovan has noted, white slavery as a "genre" was deployed in many ways by advocates, not simply for the purpose of locking up black or immigrant men. Some progressive reformers worked to change women's lives by opening rescue homes and advocating for the end of vice districts or pointing the finger at corrupt police. White slavery also became the linchpin of conversations about women's suffrage, the virtues of domesticity, the problems of urban life, and the issues of consumerism. Donovan, *White Slave Crusades*, 2.

21. The idea of the "new woman" "imbued women's activity in the public domain with a new sense of female self," in the words of historian Kathy Peiss. Peiss, *Cheap Amusements*, 6–7.

22. Wallace, *Greater Gotham*, 758–59.

23. The use of the line "burst into a flaming jubilee before it hit the ground" is a tribute to Mable King's character, Mable Thomas, in the 1970s television show *What's Happening*. She used the phrase when referring to the charms of her children's absent father in the episode entitled, "When Daddy Comes Marching Home."

24. Donovan, *White Slave Crusades*, 6; and Lears, *No Place of Grace*, 4–6. On primitivism, Lears writes "many advisors exhorted Americans to cultivate relaxation and repose, to learn from 'Oriental people, the inhabitants of the tropics, and the colored peoples generally.' Americans had had enough moral and intellectual strenuosity; they need to husband their psychic resources." Lears, *No Place of Grace*, 52.

25. Pinar, *The Gender of Racial Politics and Violence in America*, 322; and Kimmel, *Manhood in America*, 61–68. A number of scholars have argued there was a "crisis" of masculinity beginning in the 1890s and continuing into the new century including Kimmel, in *Manhood in America*, and Derrick, *Monumental Anxieties*. Others have questioned the meaning of the "crisis" of white masculinity including in Carnes and Griffen, *Meanings for Manhood*. Gail Bederman argues that white masculinity was

simply in flux but never lost its power and "was hardly in crisis." Bederman, *Manliness and Civilization*, 15.

26. Derrick, *Monumental Anxieties*, 157.

27. Lears, *No Place of Grace*, 107–8.

28. Roosevelt, "The American Woman as a Mother," 3–4.

29. When Dixon's *Clansman* theatrical production played in New York in 1906, school principal William L. Bulkley wrote a letter to the *Times* drawing great contrasts between that spectacle and a nearby African American–serving industrial school. "Within this building hundreds of the maligned race are at the same moment quietly but earnestly working at their books or in trades. . . . What a refutation to all pessimism would it be if the audience in the theatre would take a recess for a few moments and go through our classrooms!" Bulkley, "The Industrial Condition of the Negro in New York City," 134. D. W. Griffith's 1915 film, *The Birth of a Nation*, gave currency to the belief that black men were criminal and covetous of white power by depicting Reconstruction-era freedmen as rapists and pillagers. After forty-five weeks of showings at Forty-Second Street Liberty Theatre nearly one million New York City residents had watched the film, soaking in theatrics that defended the open lynchings of black men. "Written on the Screen" *New York Times*, January 2, 1916.

30. Grant, *The Passing of the Great Race*, 18.

31. For more on interracial sex in American history, see Horowitz and Peiss, *Love across the Color Line*; Mumford, *Interzones*; Hodes, *White Women, Black Men*; and Hodes, *Sex, Love, Race: Crossing Boundaries in North American History*.

32. Lacking photos, Sing Sing prisoner registers give great detail about the features of inmates, including the size and shape of body parts, the location of scars, and the general appearance. Sing Sing Prison, Inmate Admission Registers, 1842–1852, 1865–1971 (bulk 1865–1971). New York (State). Dept. of Correctional Services, Series B0143. New York State Archives, Albany, New York.

33. Cynthia Blair makes this point explicitly in Blair, *"I've Got to Make My Livin,'"* 19; Cheryl Hicks, *Talk with You Like a Woman*; and Harris, *Sex Workers*.

34. "Jerome Arrest Stirs Tenderloin," *Evening World*, March 9, 1906.

35. "Where King Vice Reigns," *Evening World*, December 27, 1889.

36. "City News Items," *New York Herald*," September 25, 1879.

37. "Memories Revived by a Legacy," *New York Daily Tribune*, September 8, 1879.

38. "Helplessly Adrift," *National Police Gazette*, September 20, 1879, 7.

39. "The Virginia House Raided," *Brooklyn Daily Eagle*, April 9, 1884.

40. The *Tribune* reported that "under the influence of liquor," the two argued when Mayo declined an invitation to drink and Sharp threw water into his face. "As they rolled together on the floor, [a] knife was plunged into Mayo's neck, the point penetrating his lung." "A Probably Fatal Fight between Negroes," *New-York Tribune*, November 6, 1889, 10.

41. Sing Sing Prison Inmate Admission Registers, box 9, vol 25; quote from Recorder Smyth in Sharp's trial for assault found in "Where King Vice Reigns," *Evening World*, December 27, 1889.

42. New York State Census, 15th Election District, Borough of Manhattan, 1900 and 1905.

43. Executive Restorations of Citizenship Rights, Sing Sing State Prison, October 30, 1899, SSP; quote on Jennie Allen from "Where King Vice Reigns," *Evening World*, December 27, 1889; Sharp's address found in records of the 1900 Census. It is unclear exactly when Sharp and Allen married, but they appear as a married couple in the twelfth census living at 14 Cornelia Street, the same house where Sharp is eventually accused of trapping Helen Watts and Caroline Kelly, among others. New York State Census, 54th Enumeration District, Borough of Manhattan, 1900.

44. Wallace, *Greater Gotham*, 606; Peters, "Suppression of the 'Raines Law Hotels,'" 86–88. Ivan Light's work differentiates African American vice districts and prostitution rings from those in the Chinese vice industry in New York City. While the black vice industry consisted mostly of streetwalking prostitutes and individual pimps who controlled them and protected them, syndicates of brothels and gangs who settled disputes in gang warfare controlled the Chinese vice industry. This simply indicated a difference in the level of organization between the two groups. African American prostitution, although sometimes organized into large brothels with up to one hundred prostitutes, was mostly a lower-scale affair that consisted of individual pimps with one to fifteen prostitutes in hotels, brothels, apartments, and businesses like candy shops and saloons. Light, "The Ethnic Vice Industry," 471.

45. Gilfoyle, *City of Eros*, 209; Fronc, *New York Undercover*, 40.

46. Report, "National League for the Protection of Colored Women, Night Investigation of April 30, 1910," folder 1910–1912, COF.

47. Report, "Special Grand Jury Report Arranged by Streets, 1910," box 28, folder 1910 Grand Jury (John D. Rockefeller) Arranged by Streets, COF.

48. Wallace, *Greater Gotham*, 608.

49. Wallace, *Greater Gotham*, 608–9. Reflection on how progressive campaigns changed sex work also in Trial Transcript #3317, January 10, 1910, reel 420, 622, TTC.

50. Gilfoyle, *City of Eros*, 284–86.

51. Gilfoyle, *City of Eros*, 287.

52. Mumford, *Interzones*, 99–101.

53. As historian Marcy Sacks put it, "the popular perception of black women as willing participants in the sex industry emerged at precisely the same time in which victims of the 'white slave trade' became the targets of sympathy and protection." Sacks, *Before Harlem*, 60.

54. On the subject of black women's vulnerability to sexual assault, Darlene Clark Hine argues that the prevalence of the threat and reality of rape for black women "influenced the development of a culture of dissemblance among Black women that created the appearance of openness and disclosure but actually shielded the truth of their inner lives and selves from their oppressors." Black women faced the constant terror of this threat, and black men encountered the constant inability to legally secure them. Hine, "Rape and the Inner Lives of Black Women," 912; also Sacks, *Before Harlem*, 11.

55. Report, "Special Grand Jury Report Arranged by Streets, 1910," box 22, folder 1910, COF.

56. McAdoo, *Guarding a Great City*, 98–99.

57. "A Ghastly Bundle This," *New York Times*, April 1, 1895. The victim, Mary Martin, had arrived in New York City four years before from a town near Fredericksburg,

Virginia, to live with her husband, Thomas S. Martin, but left him a year before her murder to live with William Caesar, who eventually confessed to her murder. "Caesar is the Murderer," *New York Times*, April 4, 1895. The *Times* described Martin in a way that betrays a casual indifference to her death: "She used to wear a wig, penciled her eyebrows, dressed neatly, and wore high-heeled shoes. She was well-formed, but not good-looking. "Caesar Loses His Nerve," *New York Times*, April 5, 1895. William Caesar was sentenced to death for murder on June 25 and executed a month later. "William Caesar Sentenced to Death," *Washington Post*, June 25, 1895.

58. Mumford, *Interzones*, 5–6.

59. White, *Ar'n't I a Woman?* 67–68, 176–77.

60. White, *Ar'n't I a Woman?* 177.

61. Blee, *Women of the Klan*, 12–13.

62. In his book Wyn Craig Wade argued white men had placed white women on a pedestal during slavery, one that made them sexually inaccessible, and they found an outlet in raping black women. When slavery ended, they realized it was possible black men would seek sex with white women in retaliation, and they simultaneously lost the sexual dominance they enjoyed over black women. Wade, *The Fiery Cross*.

63. Blee, *Women of the Klan*, 14.

64. Blee, *Women of the Klan*, 14.

65. Bederman, *Manliness and Civilization*, 46–47.

66. Bederman, *Manliness and Civilization*, 49.

67. The KKK's ideas most evidently continued in the new century in the popularity of D. W. Griffith's 1915 film, *The Birth of a Nation*, but other cultural production at the time illustrated how saving white women from interracial sex, rape, and enslavement would require the bravery of white men. Narratives like H. B. Gibbud's *The Story of Nellie Conroy* made this clear. In the account, Gibbud finds Conroy on the streets tattered, dirty, and "bruised and swollen" from abuse, and he rescues her from a "huge negro" who beat her for yielding meager profits from sex work. H. B. Gibbud's story retold in Sacks, *Before Harlem*, 64.

68. Wallace, *Greater Gotham*, 469.

69. Hobson, *Uneasy Virtue*, 16. Cornelius Willemse encapsulated the sentiments of white men in New York when commenting on interracial relations in his autobiography. Remembering the "strange combination" of a "German shoemaker married to a colored woman" Willemse commented that he liked the couple. "The woman helped her husband with his work and they were contented and quiet and it was nobody's business why they had married." In contrast, the captain disliked relationships between white women and black men because the women "were of questionable reputation, and that was a horse of a different color." While many agreed with Willemse about sexual relationships between white men and black women, interactions between white women and black men were frequently seen as illicit and in need of regulation. Where the law did not provide for such intervention, white men often worked to create sufficient boundaries. Willemse, *A Cop Remembers*, 142–43.

70. Bederman, *Manliness and Civilization*, 47.

71. Mumford, *Interzones*, 13–14.

72. The term *white slavery* was originally used to highlight exploitative labor arrangements in the industrial North by juxtaposing the laboring experiences of white

workers to that of black bondspeople in the Southern states. Muhammad, *The Condemnation of Blackness*, 133.

73. Willemse, *A Cop Remembers*, 36–37.

74. Turner, "The City of Chicago," 576. Writing about the perils of leisure spaces where races and genders mixed, Bureau of Social Hygiene writer George Kneeland depicted young white women as guiltless casualties of the relentless growth of paid adultery. He admitted that some women frequented cafes, bars, movie theaters, and dancehalls because they had "loose morals" but argued, "many are innocent working girls [seeking] legitimate recreation." In the pursuit of good times, these women often came into contact with men and women who lured them into the lifestyle. The "agents of commercialized vice," in Kneeland's description, often well-groomed and attractive, seduced women into submission. These "agents" operated sex clubs, worked in brothels, and steered customers to hotels, saloons, and parlor rooms, and Kneeland worried most about interracial spaces that fed this industry. Kneeland, *Commercialized Prostitution in New York City*, 72.

75. Miner, *Slavery of Prostitution*, xi.

76. Miner, *Slavery of Prostitution*, 38, 84.

77. For more on racialized ideas about cocaine, crime, and miscegenation in the early twentieth century, see Musto, *The American Disease*; Spillane, *Cocaine*, 90–122; Cohen, "Jim Crow's Drug War"; Provine, *Unequal Under Law*, 63–90; Courtwright, "The First American Cocaine Epidemic"; and Courtwright, "The Hidden Epidemic."

78. Miner, *Slavery of Prostitution*, 2.

79. Miner, *Slavery of Prostitution*, 2, 84.

80. McAdoo called out the black community to help reduce interracial resorts arguing that they were most detrimental to respectable blacks. "The true friends of the negro among the whites, and the real leaders like Booker T. Washington, cannot, in my judgment, impress too strongly the necessity of the colored people themselves repudiating these men and women and aiding the law officers in bringing them to justice." McAdoo, *Guarding a Great City*, 94–97.

81. Roe, *The Great War on White Slavery*, 19. The White Slave Traffic Act of 1910, originally meant to attack commercialized sex traffic, continually widened in scope over the years after its implementation. "The Supreme Court of the United States has not as yet finally decided how wide that scope shall be, but the tendency of the lower Federal courts has been to extend rather than limit its operation," wrote Arthur Spingarn in his manual for social workers dealing with sexual immorality. As such, the law was flexibly designed and deployed selectively. Spingarn, *Laws Relating to Sex Morality in New York City*, 45.

82. Unlike the Committee of Fourteen, Johnson saw the Marshall, and the Maceo which was nearby, as alternatives to the sorts of resorts often investigated by progressive reformers. Johnson, *Black Manhattan*, 118–19; Letter from Fred Moore to Walter G. Hooke, October 9, 1912, box 21, folder 1911–1914, COF.

83. The Committee of Fourteen Special Grand Jury Report not only concerned large and popular saloons like Marshall's but also mentioned tenements believed to be involved in the sex trade. It cataloged a number of places a few blocks away from Marshall's Hotel on the same street including the residence of a "negro cadet" named Ford Davinne who had only one girl, and Bill George who lived on West Fifty-Eighth Street.

Another brothel at the Gosford Apartments, apparently run by a Ms. M. Edwards, had two women it described as "bed makers" and was reportedly supplied with women from "Mrs. Dix." Special Grand Jury Report Arranged by Streets, 1910, box 28, folder 1910, COF. Another report acknowledged the status Marshall's held for catering to elite white and black crowds and putting on a "good grade of theatrical performances" but cast doubt on the significance of the clientele and entertainment to the place's overall reputation. "Supposed to be a high class restaurant for colored people," the inspector scoffed, but instead "it is patronized largely by white women and colored men . . . [and] open nearly all night." Left without notable evidence of the saloon's indelicacy, the COF stamped the Marshall with a general seal of disapproval. "Most questionable orgies and revels are held there nightly," the report concluded with a recommendation that it be treated as any other black and tan. Another investigation in the spring of 1910 yielded more actionable evidence in the case against the Marshall and exhibits the connection investigators made between interracial contact and prostitution. "The place was fairly well filled with both white and colored people" when the agent arrived at 2:30 in the morning, and he noted a number of white women sitting with "their colored men friends." After consuming champagne, the group began to sing loudly and the women rose to dance. "They raised their skirts so high, their person could be seen," he complained, "the motions they went through were outrageous." He concluded his account of the scene by flatly stating that the dancing women "are both prostitutes. This hotel is a meeting place for white women and their colored lovers." "Report on Marshall's Hotel, box 28, folder 1910–1912, COF. Although the Marshall was criticized for its interracial inclination, its popularity was unquestionable. Even the investigator in the "Popular Resorts" report for the Committee of Fourteen wrote it was "perhaps the most popular place in town." However, the involvement of the owner in concealing any wrongdoing helped to keep its doors open according to the report. The Marshall was "very hard to get, because of its popularity and the discreet manner in which it is run." Report on Popular Resorts, box 28, folder 1910–1912, COF.

84. "Clean 'Em Out," *New York Age*, April 6, 1911.

85. Donovan, *White Slave Crusades*, 90.

86. Turner, "The Daughters of the Poor," 45. The Rockefeller Grand Jury inquiry came about as a result of an effort to determine whether "white slavery" claims were in fact real and not overly exaggerated. Some reformers and journalists openly questioned its veracity. As an ex-police commissioner in 1909 William McAdoo denounced Turner's article as "slander" against Jewish immigrants claiming "there is no more vice on the east side in proportion to the population than in any other part of the city." "City Slandered—McAdoo," *New York Times*, October 28, 1909. Many other publications questioned the movement against white slavery. This debate led to a need to fully unpack the city's sex work problems in the trial.

87. Wallace, *Greater Gotham*, 610.

88. Wallace, *Greater Gotham*, 610.

89. The *Evening Post* labeled her a "black-and-tan procurer . . . holding and selling white girls for the use of both colored and white men," and prosecutors portrayed her as a veteran of the sex trade who regularly entertained men "by dancing with her skirt up over her knees." *Evening Post*, April 30, 1910. The ensuing trial defined the contours of the color line, demarcating racial spaces by contrasting Moss with two white

women she allegedly kidnapped and intended to sell and a harrowing story of under-cover investigators who seemingly entrapped her. Trial Transcript #1169, roll 153, January, 22, 1906, TTC.

90. The *New-York Tribune* noted, "neither of [the two women] cried yesterday, but each boldly acknowledged her 'profession' and told of the negotiations preceding their agreement to go to Seattle." "Found Guilty of Selling Two Women," *New-York Tribune*, May 20, 1910; Trial Transcript #1169, 291, TTC; "Prison For [Belinda Moss]," *New-York Tribune*, May 27, 1910; *New York Times*, May 27, 1910.

91. "Found Guilty of Selling Two Women," *New-York Tribune*, May 20, 1910; Trial Transcript #1169, 291; "Prison For [Belinda Moss]," *New-York Tribune*, May 27, 1910; *New York Times*, May 27, 1910; there is a full description of Belinda Moss's case in Donovan, *White Slave Crusades*, 93–109.

92. Fosdick, *John D. Rockefeller, Jr.*, 137.

93. Donovan, *White Slave Crusades*, 92.

94. Trial Transcript #3317, 10, TTC.

95. Trial Transcript #3317, 4, TTC.

96. "Cleanest Large City, White Slave Report," *New-York Tribune*, June 29, 1910.

97. Rockefeller quoted in Wallace, *Greater Gotham*, 611; and Donovan, *White Slave Crusades*, 108–9.

98. "Cleanest Large City, White Slave Report," *New-York Tribune*, June 29, 1910.

99. Donovan, *White Slave Crusades*, 1.

100. Donovan, *White Slave Crusades*, 2–3.

101. See Leab, "Women and the Mann Act," 55–65; Connelly, *The Response to Prostitution in the Progressive Era*; Bristow, *Prostitution and Prejudice*; Rosen, *The Lost Sisterhood*; Boyer, *Urban Masses and Moral Order in America*; and Clement, *Love for Sale*.

102. "White Man Assaults Booker Washington," *New York Times*, March 20, 1911; "Ulrich, Who Thrashed Washington, Is Freed," *New-York Tribune*, November 7, 1911. Questions arose about whether or not Albert Ulrich was indeed married to the woman involved in the case. She is first reported as "Lola Ulrich" but later revealed to possibly be his "landlady" in "Can You See the Point," *Chicago Defender*, November 11, 1911; and "Booker T. in Row," *Washington Post*, March 20, 1911.

103. "Angry Husband Wields a Club on Washington," *Atlanta Constitution*, March 20, 1911; "Ulrich, Who Thrashed Washington, Is Freed," *New-York Tribune*, November 7, 1911.

104. "Booker T. in Row," *Washington Post*, March 20, 1911.

105. "White Man Assaults Booker Washington," *New York Times*, March 20, 1911; and "The Assault on Booker T. Washington," *Outlook* 97, no. 13 (April 1, 1911): 707.

106. "Angry Husband Wields a Club on Washington," *Atlanta Constitution*, March 20, 1911; "Dr. Washington's Assailant Dismissed," *Afro-American*, November 11, 1911. A thorough recounting of this incident can be found in Gatewood, "Booker T. Washington and the Ulrich Affair."

107. Financier George Peabody and steel magnate Andrew Carnegie both offered "any assistance that [he] might wish to command," and the chairman of Washington's Tuskegee Institute pledged his support and the aid of the school's board of directors. "Aid Is Offered," *Atlanta Constitution*, March 21, 1911.

108. "Press Commentt [*sic*] on Assault upon Dr. Washington," *Afro-American*, April 1, 1911.

109. *Charleston Messenger* quoted in "Press Commentt [*sic*] on Assault upon Dr. Washington," *Afro-American*, April 1, 1911.

110. "Race Stands By Booker T.," *Washington Post*, March 27, 1911; "B. T. Washington Beaten on New York Streets Like Dog," *Chicago Defender*, March 25, 1911.

111. In President Taft's letter he pledged his support to Washington writing "I want you to know that your friends are standing by you in every trial and that I am proud to subscribe myself as one." "President Taft's Letter to Dr. Booker T. Washington Expressing Confidence in Him," *Afro-American*, April 8, 1911.

112. Adam Clayton Powell quoted in "Race Stands By Booker T." *Washington Post*, March 27, 1911.

113. *Rochester Sentinel* quoted in "Press Comment [*sic*] on Assault upon Dr. Washington," *Afro-American*, April 1, 1911.

114. Franklin and Moss, *From Slavery to Freedom*, 246–47.

115. Booker T. Washington's speech at the Cotton States Exposition quoted in "A Negro Honored Who Honored Himself and His Race," *Zion's Herald*, September 25, 1895.

116. Kendi, *Stamped from the Beginning*, 277–78.

117. "Press Commentt [*sic*] on Assault upon Dr. Washington," *Afro-American*, April 1, 1911.

118. Quoted in "Press Comment [*sic*] on Assault upon Dr. Washington," *Afro-American*, April 1, 1911.

119. "Press Commentt [*sic*] on Assault upon Dr. Washington," *Afro-American*, April 1, 1911.

120. "Fund to Aid Ulrich," *Chicago Daily Tribune*, March 25, 1911.

121. "Dr. Washington Forgiving," *New-York Tribune*, March 27, 1911; "Booker T. Admits Ulrich is Right," *Chicago Daily Tribune*, March 27, 1911; "Ulrich, Who Thrashed Washington, Is Freed," *New-York Tribune*, November 7 1911; "Did the Manly Thing," Says Negro Educator of Assailant," *Los Angeles Times*, March 28, 1911.

122. "Negro Educator Prosecutes Man Who Beat Him," *St. Louis Post-Dispatch*, November 6, 1911, 1.

123. Bederman, *Manliness and Civilization*, 4–5; "Ulrich, Who Thrashed Washington, Is Freed," *New-York Tribune*, November 7 1911. In other news reports of police violence against black men police officers often used the same tactic to explain injuries taken by black suspects. In one *Tribune* article a white police officer arrived at his station house with a black prisoner who had suffered a number of scalp wounds. When the officer was asked how "his prisoner had been so severely wounded he replied, "he fell down on his way to the station and struck his head on the sidewalk." "More Attacks on Negroes," *New-York Tribune*, August 27, 1900.

124. Gatewood, "Booker T. Washington and the Ulrich Affair," 41.

125. Gilmore, *Bad Nigger!* 88. For more on the meaning of prizefighting for black men and manhood, see Moore, *I Fight for a Living*.

126. Baldwin, *Chicago's New Negroes*, 3.

127. Quote taken from "Eight Killed in Fight Riots," *New York Times*, July 5, 1910. Reporting on the death of a black police officer and the burning of a black tenement

from "Racial Clashes Follow Victory of Jack Johnson," *Atlanta Constitution*, July 5, 1910. Various stories of the aftermath of the Jack Johnson and Jim Jefferies fight in New York City can be found in "Negro Slain By Fellows," *New York Times*, July 6, 1910; "Crowd is Saddened When Johnson Wins," *New York Times*, July 5, 1910; "Fight News Starts Many Race Riots," *The Hartford Courant*, July 5, 1910; "Eleven Killed in Many Race Riots," *Chicago Daily Tribune*, July 5, 1910.

128. "Negro Slain By Fellows," *New York Times*, July 6, 1910; "Eight Killed in Fight Riots," *New York Times*, July 5, 1910, 1; *New York Herald*, July 5, 1910, quoted in Bederman, *Manliness and Civilization*, 3; "Negro Slain By Fellows," *New York Times*, July 6, 1910.

129. Bederman, *Manliness and Civilization*, 3.

130. Farr, *Black Champion*, 72; Roberts, *Papa Jack*, 117; and Gilmore, *Bad Nigger!* 16.

131. Bederman, *Manliness and Civilization*, 8.

132. Bederman, *Manliness and Civilization*, 9–10.

133. Information on Johnson's trip taken from Farr, *Black Champion*, 72; Roberts, *Papa Jack*, 117; Gilmore, *Bad Nigger!*, 16; and Bederman, *Manliness and Civilization*, 3. With Johnson's arrival by train in New York City's Grand Central Station a week after the fight, black New Yorkers celebrated him as a symbol of triumphant black masculinity. Caught in the convulsions of celebration, many blacks praised the fighter for his demonstration of manliness and paraded his attributes with a sense of ownership. "Mobbed by a crowd of negroes . . . till he begged for respite," Johnson disembarked to fans "parading, shouting, shooting off fireworks, and carrying on in hilarious fashion," according to one of his aids. Bederman, *Manliness and Civilization*, 3. In appreciation for the pugilist's visit and his business, saloonkeeper Baron Wilkins and a coterie of black businessmen raised funds to purchase a $25,000 championship belt "of solid gold, studded with two hundred diamonds" for Johnson. "Johnson's Arrival a Negro Gala Day," *New York Times*, July 12 1910; "Stay for a Negro Resort," *New York Times*, July 17, 1910.

134. "Europe Good to Jack Johnson," *The Sun*, December 23, 1911.

135. "'Jack' Johnson Arrested," *New York Times*, July 20, 1910. After his arrest for reckless driving Johnson claimed he had been informed "that the bicycle police all over the city had made the declaration that they were 'out to get him.'" "'Jack' Johnson Arrested," *New York Times*, July 20, 1910.

136. "'Jack' Johnson Arrested," *New York Times*, November 26, 1910; Mumford, *Interzones*, 7–8. Johnson was also arrested nearly a year after the Jeffries fight in San Francisco for speeding. "Champion 'Jack' Doesn't Like Jail," *Afro-American Ledger*, April 8, 1911.

137. "Johnson's Arrival a Negro Gala Day," *New York Times*, July 12, 1910.

138. "Jack Johnson Sees Jefferies Defeated," *New York Times*, July 14, 1910.

139. *Beaumont Journal* quoted in Gilmore, *Bad Nigger!*, 96–97; and Conference of the Governors of the States of the Union. *Proceedings of the Fifth Meeting of the Governors of the States of the Union Held at Richmond, Virginia*, December 3–7, 1912, 52, 199–200.

140. One white New York clergyman appealed to state leaders to show "morality" by "not allowing the motion picture of this deplorable and savage exhibition to be displayed." Quoted in Farr, *Black Champion*, 133; and "Fight-Picture Ban is Now Widespread," *New York Times*, July 7, 1910.

141. Gilmore, "Jack Johnson and White Women," 24. Jack Johnson, in an autobiographical work, later admitted to having relationships with multiple black women in his youth. However, one of these women, Clara Kerr, ran away with a friend of his, taking with her "all my clothes, all other personal property of mine which was of any value." After this occurrence Johnson tracked Kerr down in Tucson, Arizona, and reconciled with her only to have her disappear once again in the same fashion. "The next woman who came into my life was Hattie McLay," Johnson wrote. The anguish that "Kerr had caused me, led me to forswear colored women and to determine that my lot henceforth would be cast only with white women." Jack Johnson, *Jack Johnson in the Ring-and Out*. Also see Kendi, *Stamped from the Beginning*, 298–99; Bederman, *Manliness and Civilization*, 3–4, and Mumford, *Interzones*, 11–12. Johnson's explanation for his preference of white women only served to distress his black supporters. In a conversation with the black actress Ethel Waters he admitted he "could love a colored woman, but they never give me anything." Black leaders and commentators saw this perspective as a dereliction of his duties as a black icon, and an irresponsible way to squander the progress his defeat of Jefferies represented. Roberts, *Papa Jack*, 74–75.

142. Kendi, *Stamped from the Beginning*, 298.

143. "Jack Johnson, Dangerously Ill, Victim of White Fever," *Philadelphia Tribune*, October 26, 1912; and Gilmore, *Bad Nigger!*, 100.

144. Reporter quoted in Mumford, *Interzones*, 9.

145. "Dr. Washington Raps Jack Johnson," *Baltimore Afro-American Ledger*, October 26, 1912; "Condemns J. Johnson's Acts," *Chicago Daily Tribune*, October 21, 1912.

146. Johnson's remarks in response to Washington found in *Chicago Daily Tribune*, October 24, 1912.

147. "Long Island Home for Dr. Washington," *New York Times*, April 2, 1911.

148. Roberts, *Papa Jack*, 119–22, 140–41; "Jack Johnson Marries Lucille Cameron," *Cornell Daily Sun*, December 4, 1912. Johnson's marriage to Cameron created a controversy when her mother accused him of abduction and certified her daughter as deranged commenting, "I would rather see [her] spend the rest of her life in an insane asylum than see her the plaything of a nigger." Cameron's mother quoted in Mumford, *Interzones*, 9.

149. Mumford, *Interzones*, 11–12; Muhammad, *Condemnation of Blackness*, 133; and Campbell, *Crime and Punishment in African American History*, 146.

150. Mumford, *Interzones*, 11.

151. "Jack Johnson is Crucified for his Race," *Chicago Defender*, July 5, 1913.

152. In less than subtle language, white Southern commentators condemned Northern men as less masculine and incapable of keeping black men in a subordinate position. The *Houston Post* delineated the difference between North and South by explaining that growing up in Texas, Johnson "understood that he was a negro." Johnson's confusion about his place had to do with loose racial boundaries in the North, the *Post* concluded, calling him "much better than those with whom he associates away from Texas." Further implying the consequences for Johnson's actions would be markedly different if they took place in the South, the *Fort Worth Citizen-Star* declared, "we bet we know one person that isn't singing 'I Wish I was in Dixie.'" This rhetoric contended that sexual relationships between black men and white women would ultimately lead to national racial conflict. According to Representative Seaborn A.

Roddenberry of Georgia "this slavery of white women to black beasts will bring the nation to a conflict as fatal and as bloody as ever reddened the soil." All Texas newspapers quoted in Gilmore, *Bad Nigger!* 96–97, 108.

153. "Disorderly Negro Gets Subway Lesson," *New York Times*, July 20, 1910.

154. Mumford, *Interzones*, 48

155. Sacks, *Before Harlem*, 62.

156. Inmate Case File #3486, Recommendation for Parole Form, undated, box 5, folder 17, BH, also used in Hicks, *Talk with You Like a Woman*, 27.

157. Inmate Case File #3247, Abstract of Personal History, undated, box 3, folder 24, BH.

158. Mumford, *Interzones*, 94; and Hicks, *Talk With You Like a Woman*, 11–26. In addition, undercover investigations into domestic employment agencies by social reformer Frances Kellor in 1902 determined that black women migrants were regularly threatened into positions in "questionable places" and tricked into sex work. Kellor, *Out of Work*, 83; and Wallace, *Greater Gotham*, 532.

159. Inmate Case File #2507, Report from Laboratory of Social Hygiene, September 15, 1917, box 2, folder 10, BH; Hicks, *Talk with You Like a Woman*, 11–26.

160. Inmate Case File #2507, Empire Friendly Shelter Report, undated, box 2, folder 10, BH.

161. Inmate Case File #2507, Verified History Form, August 12, 1917, box 2, folder 10, BH.

162. Celia Greensmith's Bedford Hills Reformatory file indicates she was molested in her mother's home by more than one man. Forced to live in a one-room Brooklyn flat and sleep in the same bed with her mother and stepfather as a child, Greensmith accused her stepfather of molestation in 1915. Upon her complaint she was removed from the household and sent to the New York Training School for Girls in 1915, but her troubles continued. After six months there she went to another facility as a "mental case" and remained for three years. Once reunited with her only parent, Greensmith was once again molested in her mother's rooming house, this time in Atlantic City. After leaving her mother, she entered into a series of relationships, including a marriage in 1921 that ended when she discovered her husband was already married, and an affair marred by a miscarriage in 1923. Inmate Case File #3486, Recommendation for Parole Form, undated, box 5, folder 7, BH; and Inmate Case File #3486, Probation Officer's Report, General Information, undated, box 5, folder 7, BH; materials from this file also used in Hicks, *Talk with You Like a Woman*, 27.

163. Like Sharp, Bennett had also spent time in prison for assault with a deadly weapon after a dispute in 1888. "Murder May Be the Charge against Negro," *New York Times*, March 11, 1906, 12.

164. "Band of Slave Dealers," *New York Times*, March 10, 1906.

165. "Murder May Be Charge against Negro," *New York Times*, March 11, 1906.

166. "Negro Denkeeper Held," *New-York Tribune*, March 13, 1906, 11.

167. "[Sharp] is Reindicted," *New York Times*, March 16, 1906.

168. Trial Transcript #575, 5–8, 32–34, 37–41, 45–47, TTC. One *Times* reporter attempted to convey the dread and anger he perceived in the courtroom by depicting spectators on the edges of their seats. "The jurors took it all in. They followed closely the testimony given by the women, but every now and then one of the men in the box

would turn quickly to watch the defendant for a moment before giving his attention once more to the gruesome story unraveled by the questions." This sort of report indicted and convicted Sharp before the trial was complete and helped create the public perception that he was guilty. "Negro's Prison Slaves Tell Court Their Story," *New York Times*, March 22, 1906.

169. Trial Transcript #575, 32–34, 37–41, 45, 47, TTC; some details of the trial in "Negro's Prison Slaves Tell Court Their Story," *New York Times*, March 22, 1906.

170. "Negro's Prison Slaves Tell Court Their Story," *New York Times*, March 22, 1906.

171. Stephen Crane's *Maggie* was originally published in 1893 and, like other novels, included a tale of a white woman who departs from accepted decorum and either dies or takes her own life. Crane, *Maggie*; see also books such as Chopin, *The Awakening*; and Wharton, *The House of Mirth*.

172. Trial Transcript #575, 79–84, TTC.

173. Helen Watts's testimony is frustrating to read and somewhat baffling as she often contradicts herself and explains her behavior in ways that makes one wish the defense attorney would have pressed her further. Trial Transcript #575, 49, 66–67, 70, 73–74, TTC.

174. Trial Transcript #575, 161–63, TTC; second quote from "Divekeeper Guilty of Abduction," *New York Times*, March 23, 1906.

175. By the time of the Sharp trial Helen Watts's trial for "disorderly conduct" had still not been resolved. Although she was the main witness in the white slavery case against Sharp, she had still not been absolved of the crimes she was accused of committing in his house. Trial Transcript #575, 158–59, TTC. Making the case for prosecution Assistant District Attorney Francis Garvan asked the jury to withhold judgment of their character until their testimony was complete. "You must not judge them as you would judge the women of your acquaintance," he implored. "Try to put your mind within theirs and understand their state of mind." Defending Watts's admitted lifestyle before encountering Sharp, Garvan conceded "this is not a good woman. She has admitted it on the stand." Nevertheless, he sought to defend her transgressions by focusing on the mental incapacitation caused by alcohol. A nearly unbroken state of obligatory intoxication influenced the state of mind that allowed Watts to endure such defilement, he argued. "During the entire time they were in the house . . . they were kept soaked with liquor," he charged, and even appeared to be in a "besotted condition" at the time of their rescue. Trial Transcript #575, 83, 125–26, 130–36, TTC.

176. Trial Transcript #575, 202, TTC.

177. Trial Transcript #575, 179, TTC.

178. Trial Transcript #575, 164–68, TTC.

179. Trial Transcript #575, 164–69.

180. Trial Transcript #575, 164–69.

181. Trial Transcript #575, 165–66, 167–68, 170–72, 175.

182. Trial Transcript #575, 188.

183. Trial Transcript #575, 210–12, 252; defense attorney's statement about Helen Watts summed up in a *New-York Tribune* article declaring Sharp's guilt. "[Sharp] Found Guilty," *New-York Tribune*, March 23, 1906; "[Sharp] Gets 20 Years," *New-York Tribune*, Mach 28, 1906.

184. Judge Cowing also admonished Sallie Bennett who was also convicted of abduction as a first offense and received a ten-year sentence. "I believe you have been a party to the death of many women who have been lured by you into the places you kept," Cowing said to Bennett after sentencing. "[Sharp] Found Guilty," *New-York Tribune*, March 23, 1906; "[Sharp] Gets 20 Years," *New-York Tribune*, March 28, 1906. After his time in prison, Sharp reappears in the 1920 census living with his wife Jennie, his daughter Mamie, his son-in-law John, and his granddaughter Jeannette. New York State Census, 221st Assembly District, Borough of Manhattan, 1920.

185. "Negro Pastor Attacks Tenderloin 'Clubs,'" *New York Times*, March 26, 1906.

186. "Murder May Be Charge Against Negro," *New York Times*, March 11, 1906, 12; "Net Tightens," *New-York Tribune*, March 14, 1906, 10; "Roosevelt Restored Citizenship," *New York Times*, March 14, 1906; "[Sharp] is Reindicted," *New York Times*, March 16, 1906, 16.

187. Ross, the *Tribune* noted, knew "the Tenderloin better than any other person, as she has lived there for years" and at one point "was the proprietor of several disorderly resorts," herself. She "got religion" after a stint in jail and decided to work providing aid to women in the sex trade. "Net Tightens," *New-York Tribune*, March 14, 1906; "Roosevelt Restored Citizenship," *New York Times*, March 14, 1906, 6. "Net Tightens," *New-York Tribune*, March 14, 1906.

188. Trial Transcript #575, March 21, 1921, 134, TTC.

189. New York City Police Department, *Annual Report*.

190. Kneeland, *Commercialized Prostitution in New York City*, 100–106. Arrested on charges of robbery in 1913, white New England migrant Grace Le Gendre insisted that a focus on white slavery was too narrow and blamed loneliness, alcohol, and a "kink" in her "moral sense" for her downfall. "I blame myself . . . and this spell which New York casts over all pleasure-seeking girls," she regretted. "Grace Le Gendre Says New York Women are Hitting up the Booze," *The Day Book*, December 5, 1913.

Chapter 4

1. Trial Transcript #3174, January 19, 1905, 588, TTC.

2. Trial Transcript #3174, 589, 592, TTC.

3. Walter Reed's brutal murder of Elton Snow clarifies the conviction of some black men to protect themselves and the women they cared for, even if it meant facing long-term imprisonment or death and taking the life of someone else. The fact that Reed left Snow's half-dismembered body on display near the front steps hints at the often-public nature of homicide and violence, and invites questions about the benefits he believed this presentation afforded him. Trial Transcript #3174, January 19, 1905, 594, 634–71, TTC.

4. Trial Transcript #448, July 19, 1904, 366–69, 385, 402–10, 441, 474, TTC.

5. Ida Snow was originally tried in 1904 but the jury could not decide the case. She was tried once again in 1905 and this time unanimously convicted of manslaughter.

6. Harris, *Sex Workers*, 45.

7. Mitchell, *Righteous Propagation*, 147–53.

8. Lears, *No Place of Grace*, 220–21; and Lindsey, *Gender Roles*, 287.

9. Men's job prospects remained poor into the 1930s and black women, even those who were married, worked more frequently than their white counterparts. Jones, *Labor of Love, Labor of Sorrow*, 139–40.

10. In *Righteous Propagation*, Michele Mitchell masterfully connects progressive precepts of racial destiny to various aspects of black home economics, sexuality, and respectability. Mitchell, *Righteous Propagation*, 141–42. Also see Higginbotham, *Righteous Discontent*; Gaines, *Uplifting the Race*; and White, *Too Heavy a Load*.

11. Mitchell, *Righteous Propagation*, 433.

12. Certainly, many scholars have shown that black working-class women did not always seek the same sort of respectability as middle-class whites and blacks, and often their male suitors attempted to impose it upon them, and instead they set about "remaking respectability," as historian Victoria Wolcott put it. But in the process of customizing their versions of propriety, they collided with men who had their own understanding of the life best lived. Wolcott, *Remaking Respectability*.

13. Dumenil, *Modern Temper*, 98.

14. Jones, *Labor of Love, Labor of Sorrow*, 139–42. This is substantiated by statistics. Fewer than 3 percent of all black working women in the country held manufacturing positions in 1900, which pales in comparison to American-born white women—38 percent of whom found industrial employment. Cited in Jones, *Labor of Love, Labor of Sorrow*, 143. In a 1940 article Carl Offord described black women's domestic work as slavery. Offord, "Slave Markets in the Bronx."

15. Jones, *Labor of Love, Labor of Sorrow*, 153.

16. Trial Transcript #3174, January 19, 1905, 601–2, TTC.

17. See Chesney-Lind, *The Female Offender*.

18. Hicks, *Talk with You Like a Woman*, 32.

19. Inmate Case File #1513, Auburn Prison Intake Sheet, June 2, 1929, box 2, folder 9, AUWP.

20. The Hampton Conference goers also generally gave "hearty endorsement" to industrial education, agricultural work, and living in the South. "Good proof of the value of the work Hampton (University) is doing for the country is shown in the reports made by her graduates of a few years ago, now engaged in business of various kinds. These young men and women are farmers, merchants, school teachers, workers in many fields, all doing good service in their communities and taking a cheerful view of the future of their people. It was evident from what was told of the various sections of the country that while Negroes have some privileges and advantages in the North and West, by far the best chances for the majority are to be found in the South, where land is chap, their labor sought for, and climatic conditions are favorable." Langhorne, "The Hampton Conference," 157.

21. "Race Gleanings," *Afro-American*, August 27, 1898; and "The Hampton Conference," *Afro-American*, July 30, 1898.

22. Victoria Earle Matthews's remarks in Annual Report, Hampton Negro Conference, c. 1, v. 2, 1898, 62–69.

23. "Colored Man's Chances," *New York Times*, July 25, 1898.

24. Annual Report, Hampton Negro Conference, c. 1, v. 2, 1898, 11.

25. Annual Report, Hampton Negro Conference, c. 1, v. 2, 1898, 11.

26. African Americans were not alone in linking human behavioral patterns with the national or racial destiny. Middle-class whites also saw manly behavior, success, and self-control, tempered by a strong moral female presence, as essential to the future of the nation. The influence of women in the home would therefore impact the actions of men in public in ways that would contribute to building a stable community and republic. May, *Great Expectations*, 17–18.

27. L. H. Harris, "Negro Womanhood," *The Independent* 51, June 22, 1899, 1688; and "The Moral Status of the Negro," *New York Evangelist*, 71, February 22, 1900, 6.

28. Mitchell, *Righteous Propagation*, 8.

29. Mitchell, *Righteous Propagation*, 12.

30. Cooper, *A Voice from the South*, 24–25.

31. Kramer, "Uplifting Our 'Downtrodden Sisterhood,'" 243.

32. Partial History of White Rose Mission and Industrial Association, undated, White Rose Mission and Industrial Association Collection, Schomburg Center for Research in Black Culture, NYPL.

33. Victoria Earle Matthews, "The Awakening of the Afro-American Woman" (Address delivered at the annual convention of the Society of Christian Endeavor, San Francisco," July 11, 1897, Beinecke Rare Book and Manuscript Library).

34. White Rose Mission Settlement, undated, White Rose Mission and Industrial Association collection, Schomburg Center for Research in Black Culture, NYPL. More on the White Rose Mission in Kramer, "Uplifting Our 'Downtrodden Sisterhood,'" 243.

35. Mitchell, *Righteous Propagation*, 152.

36. White, *Ar'n't I a Woman?*, 142–43; Frazier, "The Changing Status of the Negro Family," 387.

37. Dabel, *A Respectable Woman*, 43–44.

38. Hunter, *Bound in Wedlock*, 16.

39. Hunter, *Bound in Wedlock*, 7.

40. Other journals included *Freedom's Journal*, which ran only between 1827 and 1829; the *Ram's Horn*; and Frederick Douglass's *North Star*. Although these advocates were fighting for abolition as well as civil rights, their rhetoric about the family survived into the post-emancipation period. Dabel, *A Respectable Woman*, 4–5.

41. Hicks, *Talk with You Like a Woman*, 57.

42. Barbara Welter argues "True Womanhood" involved a commitment to "piety, purity, submissiveness and domesticity. Put them all together and they spelled mother, daughter, sister, wife—woman. Without them, no matter whether there was fame, achievement or wealth, all was ashes." White women had the option of conforming into the "cult of True Womanhood," but black women could not achieve such a status no matter their efforts. Barbara Welter, "The Cult of True Womanhood," 152.

43. Hicks, *Talk with You Like a Woman*, 57–58.

44. Du Bois, *Writings*, 184–86. Du Bois's thoughts on the burden of black men and protecting women from sexual violence in Du Bois, *The Souls of Black Folk*, 12, 27. Deborah Gray White clarifies how men "who tried to protect their spouses were themselves abused. . . . Only the uncommon bondman mustered suicidal courage and took revenge on the white man who had whipped or raped his wife. More common . . . was

the man who slipped away and feigned ignorance of the attacks on his wife." As a result, she argued, some men refused to create marital bonds with women in order to avoid such shame. White, *Ar'n't I a Woman?*, 146.

45. Du Bois also solemnized the glory of black women in his *Darkwater* volume in 1920, honoring "the women of my race" for their beauty, perseverance, and unmatched instincts for motherhood. Du Bois, *Darkwater*, 166, 185–86.

46. In his study of Philadelphia, Du Bois identified the features of urban life as the catalyst for women's dissipation, which was exacerbated by an imbalance in the male and female populations. Hence, a large number of single women fell into the traps of "illicit sexual intercourse and restricted influence of family life." The combination of the freedoms of urban living, low standards of sexual propriety, and financial instability that discouraged marriage inevitably led to "prostitution and illegitimacy," Du Bois argued. Du Bois, *Writings*, 826; Du Bois, *The Souls of Black Folk*, 171; and Gutman, *The Black Family in Slavery and Freedom*, 450.

47. Victoria Earle Matthews in a letter to the editor, "The Negroes of New York," *The Sun*, September 14, 1897.

48. Francis Kellor quoted in Carby, "Policing the Black Woman's Body in an Urban Context," 739–41.

49. Although Tayleur's attitudes about slavery departed sharply with those of writers like Du Bois and Matthews, she shared their skepticism about the chances of black families in urban settings. "There is something almost sardonically humorous in the thought of this woman, with the brain of a child and the passions of a woman . . . playing with the die of fate," she concluded. Tayleur, "The Negro Woman," 266–71.

50. Tayleur, "The Negro Woman," 270.

51. Wolcott, *Remaking Respectability*, 13–14.

52. Wolcott, *Remaking Respectability*, 17–18.

53. For black progressives, "respectability" was complex, not simply derivative of the ideas they may have gleaned from their white contemporaries. As an example, historian Victorian Wolcott makes clear how the National Training School straddled the line between countering stereotypes of black women and rethinking the avenues women could take to respectability. Through such programs black women remade respectability so it fit their needs more precisely. Wolcott, "Bible, Bath, and Broom," 90–91.

54. Inmate Case File #3494, Admission Record, August 7, 1923, box 5, folder 20, BH.

55. Inmate Case File #3489, History Blank, July 24, 1923, box 5, folder 19, BH.

56. Inmate Case File #2819, Medical History, October 1, 1919, box 3, folder 21, BH.

57. In one extreme case, women performed abortions on themselves to end unwanted pregnancies. Martha Azier performed such procedure in 1916 with the use of a catheter after five months of pregnancy. When an officer arrived at her flat he noticed "a dead female child," and Azier admitted to inducing the miscarriage herself. Complaint Record #112889, Affidavit—Plain, November, 1916, DACCF.

58. Reed, *Negro Illegitimacy in New York City*, 77–78. Placing a child in a boarding home was not an uncommon strategy. Some parents, when struggling to support children, saw it as an option that eliminated the threats of poverty from their child's life and eased financial burdens on the rest of the family. San Gupta, "Black and 'Dangerous,'" 105.

59. Reed, *Negro Illegitimacy in New York City*, 54–55.

60. For more on the changing conceptions of women's lives, see Rothman, *Woman's Proper Place*; Mintz and Kellogg, *Domestic Revolutions*.

61. Dumenil, *Modern Temper*, 142.

62. Dumenil, *Modern Temper*, 112.

63. Dumenil, *Modern Temper*, 130.

64. Dumenil, *Modern Temper*, 130–32.

65. Dumenil, *Modern Temper*, 98–99.

66. Engels, *The Origins of the Family, Private Property and the State*, 89–90.

67. Lindsey, *Gender Roles*, 9.

68. Guy-Sheftall, *Daughters of Sorrow*, 24.

69. Sacks, *Before Harlem*, 115–18.

70. For instance, these sentiments can be found in Inmate Case File #3486, Admission Record, July 18, 1923, box 5, folder 17, BH; and in Inmate Case File #3365, History Blank, February 2, 1923, box 4, folder 19, BH.

71. Sacks, *Before Harlem*, 60–61.

72. This material also used in Cheryl Hicks, *Talk with You Like a Woman*, 34–37; Inmate Case File #2490, Laboratory of Social Hygiene, Information Concerning Patient, July 9, 1917, box 1, folder 28, BH.

73. Inmate Case File #2490, Laboratory of Social Hygiene, Information Concerning Patient, July 9, 1917, box 1, folder 28, BH.

74. Inmate Case File #2490, Verified History, July 9, 1917, box 1, folder 28, BH.

75. Various letters, interviews, and statements in Ruby Wilcox's inmate case file give information on her lifestyle choices, aspirations, personality, and background. Inmate Case File #2505, box 2, folder 7, BH.

76. Inmate Case File #2505, Statement of Girl, August 10, 1917, box 2, folder 7, BH.

77. Inmate Case File #2490, Statement of Girl, July 9, 1917, box 1, folder 28, BH.

78. Harris, *Sex Workers*, 42–43. For more on the subject of black women and leisure, see Gross, *Colored Amazons*; Hicks, *Talk with You Like a Woman*; Blair, *I've Got to Make My Livin'*; and Wolcott, *Remaking Respectability*.

79. Hicks, *Talk with You Like a Woman*, 142.

80. Cheryl Hicks's work on marriage and familial support is pivotal in understanding the aspirations of black women in New York City. Hicks, *Talk with You Like a Woman*, 141–43; Information on Victoria Winters taken from interview with agent from Laboratory of Social Hygiene during investigation of an inmate of Bedford Hills Reformatory. Inmate case file #2486, Laboratory of Social Hygiene Interview, box 1, folder 24, BH.

81. Historian Eleanor Alexander writes about "marital role frustration" in Alexander, *Lyrics of Sunshine and Shadow*, 147–48.

82. Inmate case file #2505, Statement of Girl, August 10, 1917, box 2, folder 7, BH.

83. Raising children alone can also be identified as a part of black women's crucible, a factor that can sometimes be criminogenic and a holdover from enslavement. In Deborah Gray White's research on the lives of slave women she notes, "the responsibilities of childbearing and child care seriously circumscribed the female slave's life." She makes this point most saliently by looking at the statistics of runaways. Most male and female absconders were in the child bearing age range, which White argues

accounts for the low numbers of women among their ranks. "A woman of this age was either pregnant, nursing an infant, or had at least one small child to care for. While all the men between sixteen and thirty-five could count on was hard work and severe punishment if they angered the master or overseer, it was during these years that many slave women got their best care." Also, "women tended to be more concerned with the welfare of their children, and this limited their mobility." This does not indicate that men cared less for their children, but that the nature of plantation life gave men more mobility as women took on child-care responsibilities. White, *Ar'n't I a Woman?*, 69–71.

84. Inmate #2493, Verified History, July 12, 1917, BH.

85. Quote on relationships with Hunt and Sykes taken from Hale's statement forms filled out by principal keeper at Bedford Hills Reformatory. There are also interviews with Gerald Sykes, Hale's grandmother, and many other interested parties in Hale's file from Bedford Hills Reformatory. Inmate Case File #2493, Verified History, July 12, 1917, BH.

86. In a series of letters written by Taylor to her parole officer she tells of how her life is going on parole and makes requests for assistance and advice. Inmate Case File #2493, BH.

87. May, *Great Expectations*, 17.

88. Eliot, "Containing the Transactions of the American Association," 139.

89. William Pinar lays out the scholarly controversy around the subject of a "crisis of masculinity" very well. Pinar, "The 'Crisis' of White Masculinity."

90. Kimmel, *Manhood in America*, 62–63; Eliot, "Containing the Transactions of the American Association," 139; and Wallace, *Greater Gotham*, 756.

91. Victoria Earle Matthews in a letter to the editor, "The Negroes of New York," *The Sun*, September 14, 1897.

92. *New York Tribune* quoted in Sacks, "To Be a Man and Not a Lackey," 53.

93. Letter from Inmate to Governor Roswell P. Flower, February 1, 1893, box 47, folder 13, ECP.

94. Prosecutors claimed Jones left his victim staggering in the street "with blood oozing from his face . . . all swelled, [and] his hat in pieces" before he died at home. Investigators trailed Jones after identifying him as the man who pawned the stolen watch at a shop in Manhattan. The arrestee gave multiple conflicting explanations for how he acquired Roxbury's watch including claiming he found it while on a work trip in Connecticut. In the end, prosecutors used a positive identification from a witness and the testimony of Jones's domestic partner, Liddy Wells, to convict him of first-degree murder. Details of Roxbury's robbery found in Trial Transcript #379, reel 68. Media interpretations of the robbery and events in courtroom in newspapers articles include "Negro Arrested in Roxbury Murder Case," *New York Times*, July 18, 1903; "Miss Tomasch Repulsed by Roxbury's Widow," *New York Times*, August 26, 1903; and "[Jones] Trial Halted by Recorder Goff," *New York Times*, August 28, 1903.

95. Trial Transcript #379, 598; In Jones's testimony he describes hours of wandering around Manhattan and standing on various corners with no clear objective or activity. At the end of the day he explains waiting around near the river before making his way home. "I stood there, watching the people going down to the Recreation pier, at 50th Street, and, when the crowd come up from the dock, I went home." Assuming

Jones was concerned about his money trouble, one must question whether or not spending time in various parts of the city may have afforded him contact with formal and informal markets. Wells's testimony on 406–19. Details on Jones's relationship with Wells on 476 and 558.

96. For information on African Americans and job insecurity in New York City, see Sacks, *Before Harlem*, 107–13.

97. Greenberg quoted in Cullen and Agnew, *Criminological Theory*, 298.

98. In Gutman's work he argues against scholars like E. W. Burgess who described African American communities as having persistently "unorganized and disorganized" families. He presents evidence that a husband or father was present in slightly more than four in five (83 percent) of San Juan Hill and Tenderloin households and subfamilies. Gutman's analysis of the 1905 census on black families and household composition show striking limitations on the job prospects of African American men. He makes it clear that six in seven adult black men in New York City worked in labor positions or various types of service work. The same statistics apply to men living in nuclear families. Age did not significantly impact the positions that men held. Eighty-four percent of men older than forty-five, whether they were fathers or not, worked in the same sorts of positions. Gutman, *The Black Family in Slavery and Freedom*, 433, 452–56.

99. If women brought men to court and proved their paternity, men might be forced to pay around $4.50 per week if they won the case. Reed, *Negro Illegitimacy in New York City*, 83.

100. Ruth Reed, a doctoral student at Columbia University, was given access to the social service department of the Sloane Hospital for Women, and the hospital records and case files of other social agencies. Reed, *Negro Illegitimacy in New York City*, 65–66.

101. Survey conducted by the author looking at women who reported motherhood, Bedford Hills Collection boxes 1–2; and Auburn Prison for Women collection boxes 1–2.

102. Inmate Case File #1337, Letter from District Attorney Albert Fach to Warden E. S. Jennings, June 2, 1927, box 2, folder 6, APW; and Inmate Case File #1337, Statement of the Prison Physician Relative to the Application for Parole, September 23, 1927, box 2, folder 6, APW.

103. Reed, *Negro Illegitimacy in New York City*, 87.

104. One-hundred and fifty-three were single, and only seventeen had lost their wives through death or divorce. Reed, *Negro Illegitimacy in New York City*, 83.

105. Cheryl Hicks's analysis of black women and families in Hicks, *Talk with You Like a Woman*, 141.

106. Dabel, *A Respectable Woman*, 42.

107. Sacks, *Before Harlem*, 120.

108. Ovington, *Half a Man*, 138–41.

109. Case Record #458, Documentation on inmate, undated, BPD.

110. Ogburn, "The Richmond Negro in New York City," 63.

111. Clyde, "The Negro in New York City: His Social Attainments and Prospects," 29.

112. Ovington, *Half a Man*, 149.

113. Dabel, *A Respectable Woman*, 41.

114. Ovington, *Half a Man*, 138–41; and Ovington, *Black and White Sat Down Together*, 26–27. Columbia University graduate student William Fielding Ogburn did ethnographic work in the San Juan Hill neighborhood around the same time as Ovington and reached similar, although far more biased, conclusions about his black study subjects. He made a similar observation about the endurance of relationships under these conditions. "There was a great amount of non-legal marriages . . . easily made and easily broken" he wrote. "The women," he continued "[were] economically independent," and the ease of finding "nurses who for a small sum take care of children while the parents work" created "conditions favorable to the laxity of conjugal relationships." Although both Ovington and Ogburn viewed these communities with their own biases, their ethnographic perspectives are important because they indicate much about the outside appearance of black relationships. While they were far more complex than either of these analysts perceived, economic conditions and the necessities of survival certainly affected their vitality, as both Ovington and Ogburn argued. Ogburn, "The Richmond Negro in New York City," 63.

115. Cheryl Hicks addresses the many ways intimate relationships and marriages fell apart because of the gap between women's expectations and the expectations or inadequacies of their husbands. Hicks, *Talk with You Like a Woman*, 141–49.

116. Emily Higgens quoted in Sacks, *Before Harlem*, 141.

117. Hicks, *Talk with You Like a Woman*, 141–42.

118. Inmate Case File #2493, Statement of Girl, July 2, 1917, box 1, folder 31, BH.

119. In statements written to the Board of Parole recommending Sanders's release from her sentence for murder, her employer considered her a "much abused woman," often arriving at work "with discolored eyes caused by her husband brutally beating her." Inmate Case File #1145, Recommendation Letter for Inmate's Parole, undated, box 1, AUPW.

120. Lucile Sanders's account in Inmate Case File #1145, Prisoner's Preliminary Statement, October 25, 1919, AUPW. One eyewitness account indicates once Sanders had the knife she followed her husband as he walked into their building and stabbed him in the neck before fleeing. Complaint Record #126592, Recommendation, October 10, 1919, box 1464, folder 1319, DACCF.

121. Inmate Case File #1123, Prisoner's Preliminary Statement, January 16, 1919, box 1, folder 13, AUPW; information also from Complaint Record #121793, Report of the Court of General Sessions of the Peace, box 1422, folder 929, DACCF.

122. Trial Transcript #1476, December 15, 1911, reel 192, 360, TTC.

123. Trial Transcript #1476, TTC; "Murdered Dealer's Jewels Not Found," *New York Times*, December 8, 1911.

124. Quotes from Cunningham's testimony in Julius Redman's murder, Trial Transcript #1476, 100–106.

125. "Murderer Dies of Fear," *New York Times*, January 24, 1913.

126. Marcy Sacks argues this point in Sacks, *Before Harlem*, 165–66.

127. Sacks, *Before Harlem*. After serving her time in prison, Ida Snow reappears in the census records in 1930 as a resident of 205 W. 134th Street in Harlem living in a home valued at $20,000 with her sisters and four male lodgers. See New York State Census, Enumeration District No. 31, Borough of Manhattan, 1930.

128. Questioned in the trial about the year of his arrival in New York City, Buckley is unable to recall. However, in a police statement read earlier in the proceedings he indicates he arrived fifteen years prior to the interview, which took place in 1915. From this information I have determined he likely migrated from Buffalo to New York City in 1900. Trial Transcript #2146, January 14, 1916, 278–79, TTC.

129. Trial Transcript #2146, 171–72, 284. Some of Buckley's statements to the police read during trial beginning on page 235.

130. Trial Transcript #2146, 240.

131. Trial Transcript #2146, 290.

132. Trial Transcript #2146, 247.

133. Trial Transcript #2146, 242.

134. Trial Transcript #2842, reel 346, June 15, 1920, TTC.

135. Trial Transcript #2842, reel 346, TTC, 6.

136. Trial Transcript #2842, reel 346, TTC, 10–11.

137. Defense attorney Frank Aranow argued his delirium occurred because of his wife's broken matrimonial commitments and his inability to manage his own emotions. Appealing to prevailing attitudes about the conduct of women, Aranow asked the jury to identify with Buckley's plight. He had primarily chosen married men as jurors, he explained, "because I wanted them to understand the things that an ordinary and single man does not." In the process of proving his point Aranow implored the jury to consider how they would respond if "you came home . . . after a hard day's work . . . to find your wife had been out, with influences of drink upon her." Depicting Buckley as a poor migrant lacking education and "the power of inhibition," he hinted racial underdevelopments were a factor in the shooting. "You have had two thousand years of . . . education, while this man has had about sixty," Aranow asserted. "He is somewhat of the animal." In closing for the defense, he furthermore drew attention to the discrimination Buckley likely faced because of his race. "Here is a poor devil, colored, prejudiced against, without the advantages that other men have, animal instinct greatly in him . . . [he] loses the balance of his head and asks you to deal with him justly." Trial Transcript #2146, 247, 284, TTC.

138. Trial Transcript #2146, 351, TTC.

139. Trial Transcript #2146, 235, 247, 282, 284, 287, TTC.

140. Trial Transcript #2146, 172, 176, 191, TTC.

141. Inmate Case File #66897, Receiving Blotter, January 28, 1916, box 25, volume 60, SSP.

142. Harris, *Sex Workers, Psychics, and Numbers Runners*, 43.

143. White, *Ar'n't I a Woman?*, 184–85.

Chapter 5

1. Inmate Case File #32941, Prisoner's Preliminary Statement, January 30, 1924, box 1, AUP.

2. Inmate Case File #32941, Statement of Crime, box 1, AUP.

3. Inmate Case File #32941, Notice of Prisoner Paroled, February 25, 1924, box 1, AUP.

4. Inmate Case File #32941, Statement of the Prison Physician Relative to the Application for Parole, January 25, 1924, box 1, AUP.

5. Inmate Case File #32941, Statement of the Prison Chaplain Relative to the Application for Parole, February 15, 1924, box 1, AUP.

6. Inmate Case File #32941, Statement of the Prison Chaplain Relative to the Application for Parole, February 15, 1924, box 1, AUP. Paroled in 1932, also to Rochester, New York, another parolee was just as enthusiastic about his future outlook as Burke, telling interviewers it did not matter whether or not he was given a job before the prison doors opened for him. "I will find something out there, shine shoes. Be my own boss anyway." Inmate Case File #41682, Parole Hearing Interview, June, 14, 1932, box 16, AUP.

7. Inmate Case File #32941, Letter from Roy B. Hill to Dr. Raymon F. C. Kieb regarding Parolee, April 10, 1930, box 1, AUP.

8. John Lewis Gillin did not directly mention the likely impossibility of African Americans hiring lawyers but made clear that most poor defendants, black and white, failed to secure representation in court. Information about arrest and imprisonment in Gillin, *Criminology and Penology*, 247.

9. Sacks, *Before Harlem*, 103.

10. Colvin, *Penitentiaries, Reformatories, and Chain Gangs*, 91; Roberts, "The Historic Roots of American Prison Reform"; Muth and Gehring, "The Correctional Education/Prison Reform Link."

11. Quote from *New York Star* in McLennan, *The Crisis of Imprisonment*, 166.

12. Jackson, "Prison Labor," 234–35.

13. Kendi, *Stamped from the Beginning*, 311; and Woodbury, "General Intelligence and Wages," 698.

14. Inmate Case File #43225, Admission Record, December 29, 1928, box 4, folder 137, AU; and Inmate Case File #42686, Psychologist's Report, January 20, 1934, box 4, AU.

15. Inmate Case File #38798, Admission Record, January 23, 1922, box 1, folder 64, AU.

16. For others who have done work on New York's carceral state, see Wicker, *A Time To Die*; and Thompson, *Blood in the Water*.

17. The impact of Hoffman's work and conversations about the subject in the early twentieth century in Muhammad, *The Condemnation of Blackness*, 35–87.

18. Contradicting arguments about the inherent criminality of African Americans, economist Walter Willcox admitted black prisoners in New York "contributed over five times as many as the whites to the prison population." This meant that "under present conditions in the country the African race . . . is much more likely to fall into crime than a member of the white race." However, Willcox wrote, "a negro is convicted, on average, upon less evidence than is required to convict a member of the dominant race . . . if guilty, he is less likely to escape prison by paying a fine [and] if both are imprisoned, the negro is likely to receive a longer sentence for a like offense." Willcox, "Negro Criminality," 78.

19. Quote from Kelly Miller summarized in "Negro Morals," *Outlook*, July 31, 1909, 770.

20. Miller, "The Negro's Part in the Negro Problem," 289.

21. "Race Question in New York," *New York Times*, June 15, 1904; statistics on imprisonment taken from Willcox, "Negro Criminality."

22. Sellin, "The Negro Criminal: A Statistical Note," 56.

23. Trumble, *New York Tombs*, 5; Sutton, *New York Tombs*; also see Munro, *New York Tombs, Inside and Out!*.

24. Ovington, *Half a Man*, 201–2.

25. Case #431, Letter to Judge Norman Dike, March 1, 1913, box 1, BDPR. In his letter to Judge Norman Dike, Floyd Martin recognized that "my previous record is very much against me and doubtless I owe the severity of my sentence to that fact, but never the less it seems to me that a somewhat lighter term would have satisfied the requirements of justice in my case." Martin had been arrested in Savannah, Georgia, in 1898 for vagrancy under an alias, for fighting and shooting craps in Philadelphia in 1904, and multiple times in New York City for robbery and grand larceny. Case #431, Prisoner's Criminal Record, undated, box 1, BDPR. In a 1917 case, Wayne Oscar Anderson told a district attorney he only plead guilty to the charge of theft because "I got no lawyer, no money to get no lawyer," and he believed entering a plea of guilty was his only chance of avoiding prison or receiving leniency. Complaint Record #118193, Statement of Defendant made to D.A.D.A Edelson, December 21, 1917, box 1379, folder 584, DACCF.

26. Letter to Governor Roswell P. Flower, February 1, 1893, box 47, ECP.

27. Sacks, *Before Harlem*, 103–5.

28. Case Record #653, Letter to General Sessions Judge Campbell, May, 6, 1913, BPD.

29. Case Record #458, Letter to Judge Lewis Fawcett, May 18, 1913, BPD.

30. Case Record #653, Appeal Response Letter, undated, BPD.

31. Case Record #458, Appeal Response Letter, undated, BPD.

32. McLennan, *The Crisis of Imprisonment*, 195.

33. "Mrs. Maybrick Condemns the Sing Sing Prison," *New York Times*, December 21, 1906.

34. "Says Prisons Corrupt Men," *New York Times*, June 21, 1920.

35. Previously dominant ideas about imprisonment as punishment faded and "in its place had been written the right of the convict to his freedom, within certain limitations, as soon as he could be reformed." McKelvey, *American Prisons*, 263–64.

36. McKelvey, *American Prisons*, 242.

37. Friedman, *Crime and Punishment in American History*, 159–61.

38. Friedman, *Crime and Punishment in American History*, 159–62; and Charles L. Chute, "Probation and Suspended Sentence." Parole was also an arrangement that served the purposes of the prison system by allowing wardens to incentivize prisoners and by reducing the cost of imprisonment periodically. Campbell, "African Americans and Parole in Depression-Era New York," 1067.

39. McLennan, *The Crisis of Imprisonment*, 87, 191, 195, 197. There is an extensive body of work on progressive prison reform in the North: Friedman, *Crime and Punishment in American History*, 159–62; Sullivan, *The Prison Reform Movement*; McKelvey, *American Prisons*; Freedman, *Their Sister's Keepers*; Keve, *Prisons and the American Conscience*; and Rothman, *Conscience and Convenience*.

40. In 1898 one editorialist with intimate knowledge of Sing Sing wondered about the difficulty of maintaining sanity under such limitations. "The most lonesome and wearisome hours of day or night are those spent in the cells, where it would seem as if

a prisoner would knock his head against the stone walls to put an end to his existence." "Within Prison Walls," *New York Evangelist*, December 15, 1898.

41. Inmates expressed disapproval of the combination of conditions with continual confinement in the *Star of Hope* and found support from the members of the New York Prison Association who argued state prisons posed threats to the convict as well as the public. McLennan, *The Crisis of Imprisonment*, 285–86.

42. Gillin, *Criminology and Penology*, 530–31, 557. Acting as an emissary of Governor William Sulzer in 1913 George Blake wrote on continued poor conditions and the refusal of treatment for sick prisoners at Auburn. In addition to unhealthful surroundings, Blake condemned the current doctor as "brutal in his treatment of the sick [and] neglectful of their needs," charging "every nook and cranny of the prison reeks with tales of [the] cruelty of this man." "Finds Gross Cruelty in Auburn Prison," *New York Times*, April 28, 1913.

43. Inmate Case File #17802, Correspondence with Warden Lewis E. Lawes, July 31, 1937, box 2, CCF.

44. From Redding's letter it sounds that he was likely suffering from sickle cell anemia. He claimed the prison doctor delayed his surgery and told him, "Your blood is not in the proper shape. I am going to give you medicine for your blood. I will be back here in perhaps two weeks or a month to operate upon you." Inmate #17802, Correspondence with Warden Lewis E. Lawes, box, 2, October 19, 1937, CCF.

45. Inmate Case File # 32941, Statement of the Prison Physician Relative to the Application for Parole, January 25, 1924, box 1, AUP.

46. Inmate Case File #43474, Hospital Admission Form, January 17, 1935, box 5, folder 126, AU.

47. Sent to Auburn for life on a charge of murder, Horace Greaves gave in to a blood infection caused by an old injury in 1889. Distressed by a similar illness, Sidney Bolton remained "under constant treatment" for four months "until death came and relieved his sufferings." Across the time span recorded in the register 65 percent of all black men to die in Auburn prison experienced some sort of respiratory illness, whether tuberculosis or pneumonia. Auburn Register of Deaths, box 1, ARD.

48. In terms of punishment, some investigators, such as George Blake, found inmates placed in "perfectly dark" unventilated cells and deprived of "sleep and rest as well as . . . food, drink, air, and light." "Finds Gross Cruelty in Auburn Prison," *New York Times*, April 28, 1913. Surveying Sing Sing one journalist put himself in the shoes of the inmates punished in the "dark cell." After learning of "a negro of giant strength" who suffered four days in "this horror of great darkness," the journalist asked to be closed inside of one of the cells himself. "For the first time I knew what was meant by . . . 'darkness that might be felt'" he wrote. "It was as if I had been buried alive. Nothing ever 'took the starch' out of me so quickly and in less than a minute I banged away for deliverance." "Within Prison Walls," *New York Evangelist*, December 15, 1898.

49. Inmate Case File #17802, Prison Classification Clinic, Psychiatric Report, undated, box 2, CCF.

50. Inmate Case File #39494, Principle Keeper's Report, May, 15, 1939, box 7, AUP.

51. Inmate Case File #18208, Indeterminate Sentence Record Card, December 20, 1929, box 2, CCF.

52. Inmate Case File #18208, Great Meadow Prison Hospital, May 9, 1936, box 2, CCF.

53. Inmate Case File #18208, Indeterminate Sentence Record Card, December 20, 1929, box 2, CCF.

54. Montgomery Redding's inmate number changed to #74590 when he was returned to Sing Sing prison for a parole violation in 1937. I have continued to use his previous number since documents from that internment are found in the Clinton Prison folder. Inmate Case File #17802, Correspondence Between Warden and Principal Keeper, April 30, 1937, box 2, CCF.

55. A number of documents indicate Redding aggressively attacked guards and inmates. Inmate Case File #17802, Disciplinary Note to Warden from Ivan Carpenter, undated, box 2, CCF; Inmate Case File #17892, Report for Bad Conduct, February 24, 1938; and Letter to Principle Keeper J. J. Sheehy from Warden, April 30, 1937.

56. Inmate Case File #38886, Executive Department Division of Parole Form, January 15, 1935, box 1, folder 71, AU.

57. Inmate Case File #38886, Executive Department Division of Parole Form, box 6, AUP.

58. Inmate Case File #38886, Classification Clinic Report, December 14, 1933, box 6, AUP.

59. Inmate Case File #38886, Auburn Prison Division of Psychiatry Form Interview, December 4, 1930, AU.

60. It is unclear from Crowder's record whether or not he found his wife and children after his release or if he was able to keep up with the requirements of parole. Inmate Case File #38886, Executive Department Division of Parole Form, December 18, 1934, box 1, AU.

61. Inmate Case File #38886, Executive Department Indeterminate Sentence Form, box 6, AUP.

62. Many men leaving prison suffered similar losses. Serving time for manslaughter in 1915, Sonny Wilks remained in connection with his spouse and child, but an unforeseen tragedy disintegrated their family when his wife unexpectedly passed away and the child went to live with one of Wilks's aunts in Long Island. Paroled in 1935, Wilks intended to "live with [the] Aunt and support the child," however, his monthly parole reports indicate he had trouble attaining stable employment over the next several years and resorted to living on his own in Manhattan. Inmate Case File #34772, Parole Reports, box 2, AUP.

63. Case Record #1716, Letter to Judge Thompson from Inmate, July 22, 1913, BPD.

64. Inmate Case File #18208, Note to the Chief Clerk, undated, box 2, CCF.

65. Inmate Case File #18208, Letter from Department of Corrections to Inmate, July 15, 1935, box 2, CCF.

66. Letter from Inmate's Mother and Son to Governor Benjamin Odell, July 3, 1904, box 67, folder 28, ECP.

67. Letter from Inmate's Son to Governor Benjamin Odell, March 20, 1904, box 67, folder 28, ECP.

68. Letter from Inmate's Daughter to Governor Benjamin Odell, November 16, 1904, box 67, folder 28, ECP.

69. Inmate Case File #37394, Letter from Mother of Inmate, May 12, 1923, box 4, AUP; Bradshaw's son, John Bradshaw, had been arrested for robbery in 1919.

Complaint Record #127178, Affidavit—Robbery, October 11, 1919, box 1469, folder 1369, DACCF.

70. Inmate Case File #37164, Letter from Mother of Inmate, undated, box 3, AUP.

71. Gillin, *Criminology and Penology*, 535–36.

72. The author formulated these statistics by surveying prison case files of forty-eight black men in Auburn between 1922 and 1930 and determined forty-four had previous convictions, and many were returned to prison for parole violations. Auburn Prison Case Files, boxes 1–8.

73. Information on how parole functions found in Gillin, 679, 713, and in Hicks, *Talk With You Like a Woman*, 238–39.

74. Gillin, *Criminology and Penology*, 679.

75. Hicks, *Talk with You Like a Woman*, 238–39.

76. Exemplifying official thinking on rehabilitation in prison, a 1920 report by the Prison Survey Committee of New York recommended the board of parole "base its discussions for granting or refusing parole upon definite and supporting data" that would ensure prisoner improvement before release. The committee saw it as crucial that parole hearings consider a variety of materials and factors including a record of the original offense, the history of the prisoner's behavior, certificates vouching for mental and physical ability, educational records, and statements from receiving care-takers and institutions indicating employment possibilities once paroled. These mea-sures were meant to prevent the parole board from advancing those "unfit to reenter society." *Prison Survey Committee Report*, State of New York, Albany, 1920, 254.

77. Gillin, *Criminology and Penology*, 692–93.

78. Sing Sing Prison Classification information appears copied in Inmate #18208, Clinton Prison Classification Clinic, March, 13, 1935, box 2, CCF.

79. In Gillin's description of the intake and parole processes, he is specifically refer-ring to the state of New Jersey; however, prison documents from New York indicate that the processes are identical in both states. In addition, a 1920 report from the Prison Survey Committee of New York recommended the reformation of New York's parole program in the model of New Jersey's. Gillin, *Criminology and Penology*, 692–93.

80. Inmate Case File #32913, Recommendation Letter from Adam Clayton Powell to Warden Jennings, January 19, 1920, box 1, AUP.

81. Inmate Case File #32913, Letter from the Volunteer Prison League to the Parole Board, January 26, 1920, box 2, AU.

82. Inmate Case File #35321, Parole Application, August 10, 1920, box 5, AU.

83. Inmate Case File #42686, Executive Department Form, June 26, 1934, box 4, folder 28, AUP.

84. Inmate Case File #38886, Executive Department Division of Parole Form, De-cember 18, 1934, box 1, AUP.

85. Inmate Case File #38886, Partial Pre-Parole Report, August 11, 1936, box 1, AUP.

86. Inmate Case File #38399, Parole Reports, 1923–1925, box 5, AUP.

87. Inmate Case File #38399, Parole Reports, 1923–1925, box 5, AUP.

88. Inmate Case File #32913, Parole Reports, 1920, box 2, AUP.

89. Inmate Case File #32913, Letter from Parole Officer to Superintendent of Pris-ons, January 26, 1922, box 2, AUP.

90. Inmate Case File #38399, Correspondence between the Salvation Army and Department of Correction, November 30, 1927—December 5, 1927, box 5, AUP.

91. Inmate Case File #38399, Letter from Department of Corrections to Inmate, October 23, 1929, box 5, AUP.

92. Inmate Case File #32913, Letter from Parole Officer to Superintendent of Prisons, January 26, 1922, box 1, AUP.

93. Frank L. Heacox did a comprehensive study of parole violators returned to Auburn prison in September 1915 that gives many reasons for violation, but it does not indicate race for all cases. Heacox, "Parole Violators."

94. Inmate Case File #40652, Auburn Prison Division of Psychiatry Report, June 28, 1933, box 2, AU. Inmate Case File #40652, State of New York Executive Department Division of Parole, Report of Violation of Parole, box 2, AUP.

95. Inmate Case #18675, Report of Violation of Parole, May, 10, 1934, box 5, CCF.

96. Inmate Case File #18208, Clinton Prison Classification Clinic Psychiatric Report, June 2, 1933, box 2, CCF; Hicks, *Talk with You Like a Woman*, 238–39.

97. Inmate Case File #2504, Verified History Form, folder 5, BH and Inmate Case File #1328, box 2, folder 2, AU; Hicks, *Talk with You Like a Woman*, 152–54.

98. Inmate Case File #2504, Letter May 4, 1919, folder 5, BH.

99. Inmate Case File #2504, Letter May 12, 1919, folder 5, BH.

100. Inmate Case File #2504, Undated Letter to Helen Cobb, folder 5, BH; Inmate Case File #2504, Undated Letter to Board of Managers, folder 5, BH.

101. Inmate Case File #2504, Letter to Superintendent Helen Cobb, July 28, 1919, box 2, folder 6, BH.

102. Inmate Case File #2504, Letter to Superintendent Helen Cobb, March 26, 1919, box 2, folder 6, BH.

103. Letter to Superintendent Helen Cobb, undated, box 2, folder 6, BH.

104. Inmate Case File #2504, Verified History Interview August 8, 1917, box 2, folder 5, BH.

105. Inmate Case File #2504, Letter to Helen Cobb, October 13, 1917, box 2, folder 5, BH. In another letter Cox referred to Adam Pitts as a "dirty young man" who "won't work and [h]as not worked for God knows [h]ow long." She doubted he had the ability or the will to support his wife because "he is drawing his money spending and drinking it up." Cox also worried about the possible repercussions of Adam Pitts learning of the contents of her letters. "Don't say I [w]rote when he comes because he will just get drunk and cuss me out. . . . I am [a]fraid I have to lock him up because I am not going to take his insults any longer . . . he is an awfull [*sic*] young man." Inmate Case File #2504, Letter to Helen Cobb, June 9, 1920, box 2, folder 5, BH.

106. Investigators even questioned Adam's intentions in requesting his wife's release. "Judging from what we have seen of him," wrote one parole officer to the superintendent, "I would say that he is not fit to be made responsible for [Evelyn], and that he doesn't care a great deal about her any way." Inmate Case File #2504, Undated Letter from Parole Officer to Helen Cobb, box 2, folder 5, BH.

107. Inmate Case File #2504, Letter from Helen Cobb to Husband, May 1, 1919, box 2, folder 5, BH.

108. Inmate Case File #2504, Letter to Helen Cobb from Husband of Inmate, undated, folder 5, BH. Job insecurity likely made it so Adam Pitts had trouble establishing

a household with a solid foundation, and the alluring profitability of underground markets presumably drew him in. He also had his own legal troubles. Some of his messages imply he had been incarcerated in previous years, and in one letter to Evelyn he admits being "locked up for fighting" in a saloon while she was at Bedford. Inmate Case File #2504, Undated Letter to Helen Cobb from Husband, folder 5, BH.

109. Inmate Case File #2504, Undated Letter to Helen Cobb from Husband, box 2, folder 5, BH.

110. Letter to Helen Cobb from Husband of Inmate, May 4, 1919, box 2, folder 6, BH.

111. More on women and parole in Hicks, *Talk with You Like a Woman*, 238–52.

112. Inmate Case File #2504, Letter from DPH: W to E. H. Decker at the Bureau of War Risk Insurance, October 16, 1919, folder 5, BH.

113. Inmate Case File #2504, Letter from Inmate to Husband, June 1, 1919, box 2, folder 5, BH.

114. Inmate Case File #2504, Letter to Parolee's Husband, July 10, 1919, box 2, folder 5, BH. When paroled from Bedford Hills Reformatory women very often worked as domestic servant for families outside of the city. The idea was to place them in a reputable white home where they might be taught how to live a quiet domestic existence, earn some money, and possibly become an example for other women at Bedford Hills. Hicks, *Talk with You Like a Woman*, 240.

115. Inmate Case File #2504, Letter to Helen Cobb, May 16, 1919, box 2, folder 5, BH.

116. Evelyn was discouraged by the difficulty of the work she had at a boarding house in Jefferson Valley, New York, and attempted to explain what she thought might be an impending parole violation. "So Miss if you hear of me back there it won't be because I have broken my parole. Only to change my place," she explained. Inmate Case File #2504, Letter to Helen Cobb, July 5, 1919, box 2, folder 5, BH.

117. Inmate Case File #2504, Letter to Helen Cobb, July 7, 1919, box 2, folder 5, BH.

118. Inmate Case File #1312, Letter to Parole Officer, box 2, folder 2, AUP.

119. Inmate #3377, Recommendation for Parole, undated, box 4, folder 31, BH; and Hicks, *Talk with You Like a Woman*, 244.

120. Inmate Case File #3377, Letter from Parolee to Amos T. Baker, January 9, 1924, box 4, folder 31, BH. Florence Parkerson made similar requests as Wilma Heywood but did not violate the rules of parole. Instead she and her fiancé wrote letters to the institution requesting the right to get married. In one letter, Parkerson wrote, "I am trying to live a better life," which she believed marriage would help. She then asked for understanding of the fact that "you don't know what girls like me are driven to do. I [did not] do them just for the fun . . . life has not been so kind to me." Inmate Case File #3458, Letter from Parolee to Parole Board, December 4, 1927, box 5, folder 2, BH.

121. Jerome Bowman's statements about Camille cited in a letter from Catholic Charities of the Archdiocese of New York to Bedford Hills. Inmate Case File #3723, Letter from Supervisor of Parole Delinquency to Dr. Amos T. Baker at Bedford Hills, September 29, 1924, box 7, folder 6, BH.

122. Inmate Case File #3723, Letter to Superintendent Amos T. Baker, November 28, 1924, box 7, folder 6, BH.

123. Inmate Case File #3723, Letter Inmate, November 28, 1924, box 7, folder 6, BH.

124. Inmate Case File #1141, Letter to Prison Superintendent James L. Long, February 10, 1925, box 1, folder 15, AWP.

125. Inmate Case File #1141, Letter from Prison Superintendent James L. Long to A. L. Bohn, February 20, 1925, box 1, folder 15, AWP.

126. Linton also urged his wife to consider how her past actions affected their relationship and to use that knowledge to improve her behavior like he would. "I know we all make mistakes and now I am asking you if you are going to be a wife to me . . . for you let your friends ruin our lives and now God has punished us . . . are you going to behave [?]" Inmate Case File #2778, Letter from Inmate's Husband to Inmate, August, 11, 1920, box 2, folder 33, BH.

127. Inmate Case File #2504, Letter, June 25, 1919, BH.

128. A letter dated November 16, 1920, from the Bedford Hills superintendent, presumably Helen Cobb, indicates that Evelyn was paroled to her husband at Grand Central Station on November 17. The note informing Adam of her impending release includes a request for "assurance that both [of you] will do all in your power to keep the remaining months of her commitment here." Inmate Case File #2504, Letter from Bedford Hills Reformatory, November 16, 1920, BH.

129. Bedford Hills superintendent's request for information on her marriage and living circumstances found in Inmate Case File #2504, Letter from Bedford Hills Superintendent Ann Hedges Talbot, November 26, 1920, BH.

130. Inmate Case File #2504, Letter to Bedford Hills Superintendent Ann Hedges Talbot, December 5, 1920, BH.

131. Inmate Case File #2504, Letter to Bedford Hills Superintendent Ann Hedges Talbot, January 4, 1921, BH, 5357.

132. Inmate Case File #2504, Letter to Bedford Hills Superintendent Ann Hedges Talbot, March 29, 1921, BH, 5623.

133. Inmate Case File #2504, Letter to Superintendent Talbot, March 17, 1921, BH.

134. Complaint Record #139002, Affidavit—Burglary, September, 15, 1921, box 1574, folder 2449, DACCF; and Complaint Record #139002, Prisoner's Criminal Record, undated, box 1574, folder 2449, DACCF.

135. Adam alleged Evelyn's "gang of niggers" thwarted his attempts to achieve financial stability by opening his own enterprises. "This crew has Broke up Fruit stand Employment office [Cigar] store notary Public office," he explained, claiming "[Evelyn] stole for the [syndicate] and Broke up my office." Another time police arrested Evelyn for stealing and "pawning stolen diamonds under my name," he wrote, and "the gang . . . got her out on bail." Inmate Case File #2504, Undated Letter to Board of Managers at Bedford Hills Reformatory, folder 5, BH.

136. Inmate Case File #2504, Letter to the Parole Board, undated, box 2, folder 2, BH.

137. Inmate Case File #1328, Letter from District Attorney of Dutchess County Allen S. Reynolds, July 23, 1926, AUP.

138. Inmate Case File #2504, Letter from Bedford Hills Superintendent to Commissioner on Jails, February 14, 1934, BH.

139. Inmate Case File #39494, Parole Interview, April 15, 1936, box 7, AUP.

Epilogue

1. Cullen and Agnew, *Criminological Theory*, 162; and Merton, *Social Structure and Anomie*. Many other theorists have engaged with the anomie theory after Merton

drawing from his interpretation and adding to it, including Bernard, "Testing Structural Strain Theories"; Cullen, *Rethinking Crime and Deviance*; Messner, "Merton's 'Social Structure and Anomie'"; Rosenfeld, "Robert Merton's Contribution to the Sociology of Deviance."

2. Merton, "Social Structure and Anomie," 679.

3. A number of scholars have previously engaged the subject of mass incarceration and racial caste, including Alexander, *The New Jim Crow*; Forman, *Locking Up Our Own*; and Hinton, *From the War on Poverty to the War on Crime*.

4. See Suddler, *Presumed Criminal*.

5. Hinton, *From the War on Poverty to the War on Crime*, 1–4, 11.

6. Provine, *Unequal Under Law*, 17.

7. Cullen and Agnew, *Criminological Theory*, 452–53.

8. Wilson, *Thinking About Crime*.

9. Wilson and Kelling, "Broken Windows Theory."

10. Cullen and Grawert, "Fact Sheet."

11. Wallace, *Greater Gotham*, 356.

12. The description of Ota Benga's time in the cage as described in one letter to the *New York Times* editor meant to defend the Bronx Zoo against criticism for placing the visitor in a compromised position. "Ota Benga Having a Fine Time," *New York Times*, September 13, 1906.

13. "Wants to Buy the Pigmy," *New York Times*, October 2, 1906. Ota Benga left the exhibit and continued to work in the park, albeit as an oddity. Eventually, he lived in Lynchburg, Virginia, and presumably out of homesickness he took his own life in 1916. "Ota Benga, Pygmy, Tired of America," *New York Times*, July 16, 1916.

14. Van Vechten, *Nigger Heaven*.

15. Cook, Shipp, and Dunbar, *In Dahomey*, 104.

16. "All We Got Iz Us (Evil Streets)," compact disc, track 3 on Onyx, *All We Got Iz Us*, JMJ Records, 1995.

17. "C.R.E.A.M.," compact disc, track 8 on Wu-Tang Clan, *Enter the Wu-Tang (36 Chambers)*, Loud Records, 1993.

18. "U Not Like Me," compact disc, track 18 on 50 Cent, *Get Rich or Die Tryin'*, Shady/Aftermath/Interscope Records, 2003.

19. "No More Pain," compact disc, track 7 on Tupac, *All Eyez on Me*, Death Row Records, 1996.

20. "Ambitionz Az a Ridah," compact disc, track 1 on Tupac, *All Eyez on Me*, Death Row Records, 1996.

21. When New York City Police placed Eric Garner in a chokehold in 2014, video footage shows, he gasped for air and shouted "I can't breathe" several times to no effect. Due to his treatment he died in a hospital approximately one hour later.

22. "Last Dayz," compact disc, track 2 on Onyx, *All We Got Iz Us*, JMJ Records, 1995.

Bibliography

Manuscript Collections

Columbia University, Rare Book and Manuscript Library, New York, New York
  Reminiscences of Samuel J. Battle: Oral History, 1960
  Society for the Prevention of Crime Records, 1878–1973
District Attorney Indictment Papers, Closed Case Files, New York County, Court of
    General Sessions
  Brooklyn Probation Records
  Manhattan Probation Records
  Magistrates' Court Documents
John Jay College, Lloyd Sealy Library
  Criminal Trial Transcripts of New York County Collection, 1883–1927
Library of Congress, Manuscripts Division, Washington, DC
  National Association for the Advancement of Colored People Collection
New York City Municipal Archives, Records and Information Services, New York,
    New York
New York Public Library Rare Books and Manuscripts Division, Stephen A.
    Schwarzman Building, New York, New York
  Committee of Fourteen Collection
New York State Archives, State Education Department, Albany, New York
  Auburn Correctional Facility Records
    Inmate Case Files (Classification Clinic), 1914–1950
    Auburn Prison Inmates, Division of Parole Files, 1918–1955
    Register of Deaths, 1888–1937
    Auburn Prison Female Inmate Case Files, 1920–1930
  Bedford Hills Correctional Facility Records
    Inmate Case Files, 1915–1930
  Clinton Correctional Facility Records
    Inmate Case Files, 1930–1956
  Executive Clemency Collection
  Sing Sing Correctional Facility
    Inmate Admission Registers, 1865–1971
    Admission Registers for Prisoners to Be Executed, 1891–1946
Schomburg Center for Research in Black Culture, Manuscripts, Archives, and Rare
    Books Division, New York Public Library, New York, New York
  Dowridge-Challenor Family Letters, 1904–1917
  White Rose Mission and Industrial Association Collection
University of Massachusetts, Special Collections and University Archives
  W. E. B. Du Bois Papers, 1803–1999

Newspapers and Periodicals

Afro-American	*New Journal and Guide*
Afro-American Ledger	*New York Age*
Atlanta Constitution	*New York Amsterdam News*
Boston Daily Globe	*New York Daily Tribune*
Brooklyn Daily Eagle	*New York Evangelist*
Chicago Daily Tribune	*New York Herald*
Chicago Defender	*New York Sun*
Columbus Dispatch	*New York Times*
Congregationalist	*New-York Tribune*
Cornell Daily Sun	*OAH Magazine of History*
Day Book	*Outlook*
Evening Post	*Philadelphia Tribune*
Evening World	*Pittsburgh Courier*
Forum	*San Francisco Chronicle*
Hartford Courant	*St. Louis Post-Dispatch*
Independent	*Survey*
Ladies' Home Journal	*Survey Graphic*
Los Angeles Times	*Variety*
McClure's	*Washington Post*
National Police Gazette	*Zion's Herald*
New-Orleans Picayune	

Published Primary Sources

Annual Report. *Hampton Negro Conference.* Hampton: Hampton Institute Press, 1898.

Barker, John Marshall. *The Saloon Problem and Social Reform.* Boston: Everett Press, 1905.

Billings, John S. *The Liquor Problem: A Summary of Investigations Conducted by the Committee of Fifty, 1893–1903.* Boston: Houghton, Mifflin, 1905.

Blascoer, Frances. *Colored School Children in New York.* New York: Public Education Association of the City of New York, 1915.

Bonger, Willem Adriaan. *Criminality and Economic Conditions.* Boston: Little, Brown, 1916.

———."Criminality and Economic Conditions." In *Criminological Theory*, edited by Francis T. Cullen and Robert Agnew, 304–11. New York: Oxford University Press, 2006.

Brace, Charles Loring. *The Dangerous Classes of New York.* New York: Wynkoop & Hallenbeck, 1872.

Bruce, Phillip A. *The Plantation Negro as a Freeman: Observations on His Character, Condition and Prospects in Virginia.* New York: G. P. Putnam's Sons, 1889.

Bulkley, William L. "The Industrial Condition of the Negro in New York City." *Annals of the American Academy of Political and Social Science* 27 (May 1906): 134.

Bureau of Social Hygiene. *Housing Conditions of Employed Women in the Borough of Manhattan.* New York: Bureau of Social Hygiene, 1922.

Burroughs, Edgar Rice. *Tarzan of the Apes.* New York: Oxford University Press, 2010.

Chopin, Kate. *The Awakening.* Chicago: H.S. Stone, 1899.

Chute, Charles L. "Probation and Suspended Sentence." *Journal of the American Institute of Criminal Law and Criminology* 12 (February 1922): 558–65.

Citizens' Protective League. *Story of the Riot.* New York: Arno Press, 1969.

Clyde, John. "The Negro in New York City: His Social Attainments and Prospects." Master's thesis, Columbia University, 1898.

Committee of Fourteen. *The Social Evil in New York City: A Study of Law Enforcement by the Research Committee of the Committee of Fourteen.* New York: A. H. Kellogg, 1910.

Conrad, Joseph. *Heart of Darkness.* New York: W. W. Norton, 1988.

Cooper, Anna Julia. *A Voice from the South.* New York: Oxford University Press, 1988.

Cox, Earnest Sevier. *The South's Part in Mongrelizing the Nation.* Richmond, VA: White America Society, 1926.

Crane, Stephen. *Maggie: A Girl of the Streets.* New York: W. W. Norton, 1979.

Croly, Herbert. "New York as the American Metropolis." *Architectural Record* 13 (1903): 193–206.

Cuyler, L. "A Peep Into Cut-Throat Alley." *Independent* 13 (1861): 6.

Deane, Sidney. "The 'Tenderloin' District." *Christian Union* 45 (June 1892).

Dewey, Annie. "Standards of Living in the Home." *Outlook* 101 (June 1912).

Drachsler, Julius. "Intermarriage in New York City." Master's thesis: Columbia University, 1921.

Drake, St. Clair, and Horace R. Cayton. *Black Metropolis: A Study of Negro Life in a Northern City.* New York: Harcourt, Brace, 1945.

Du Bois, W. E. B. "The Black North: A Social Study New York City." *New York Times,* November 17, 1901.

———. *Darkwater: Voices from Within the Veil.* New York: Harcourt, Brace, & Howe, 1920.

———. *The Philadelphia Negro: A Social Study.* New York: Oxford University Press, 2007.

———. "Review of *Race Traits and Tendencies of the American Negro,* by Frederick L. Hoffman, F.S.S." *Annals of the American Academy of Political and Social Science* 9 (January 1897): 127–33.

———. *The Souls of Black Folk.* New York: Bantam Books, 1989.

———. *Writings.* New York: Literary Classics, 2007.

Dunbar, Paul Laurence. "The Negroes of the Tenderloin." *Columbus Dispatch,* December 19, 1898.

———. *The Sport of the Gods.* New York: Dodd, Mead & Co., 1902.

Dunning, William Archibald. *Reconstruction: Political and Economic, 1865–1877.* New York: Harper & Bros., 1907.

Dyckoff, E. F. "A Negro City in New York." *Outlook,* December 23, 1914.

Eliot, Samuel. "Containing the Transactions of the American Association." *Journal of Social Science* 4 (1871): 139–50.

Ellington, Duke. *Music Is My Mistress.* New York: Doubleday, 1973.

Engels, Friedrich. *The Origins of the Family, Private Property and the State.* Chicago: C. H. Kerr, 1902.

Felton, Rebecca Latimer. *The Romantic Story of Georgia's Women*. Atlanta: Atlanta Georgian and Sunday American, 1930.

Gillin, John Lewis. *Criminology and Penology*. New York: The Century Co., 1926.

Graham, Stephen. *New York Nights*. London: Ernest Benn Limited, 1928.

Grant, Madison. *The Passing of the Great Race; or, The Racial Basis of European History*. New York: C. Scribner, 1916.

Hagemann, Edward R., and Robert Wooster Stallman. *The New York City Sketches of Stephen Crane, and Related Pieces*. New York: New York University Press, 1966.

Halley, Claire M. "'Fickle Lady Luck,' A Story of a 'Number' Player." *New York Amsterdam News*, February 23, 1927.

Harris, L. H. "Negro Womanhood." *Independent* 51 (June 1899): 1688.

Hartt, Rollin Lynde. "The New Negro." *Independent* 105 (January 1921): 59.

Haynes, George Edmund. "Conditions among Negroes in the Cities." *Annals of the American Academy of Political and Social Science* 49 (September 1913): 105–19.

———. *The Negro at Work in New York City*. New York: Arno Press, 1968.

Heacox, Frank L. "Parole Violators: A Study of One Year's Parole Violators Returned to Auburn Prison." *Journal of the American Institute of Criminal Law and Criminology* 8 (July 1917): 233–58.

Hopper, Ernest Jasper. "A Northern Negro Group." Master's thesis, Columbia University, 1912.

Hughes, Langston. *The Big Sea: An Autobiography*. New York: Thunder's Mouth Press, 1986.

Jackson, Henry Theodore. "Prison Labor." *Journal of the American Institute of Criminal Law and Criminology* 18 (August 1927): 218–68.

Johnson, Jack. *Jack Johnson in the Ring and Out*. Chicago: National Sports Publishing, 1927.

Johnson, James Weldon. *Along This Way: The Autobiography of James Weldon Johnson*. New York: Viking Press, 1943.

———. *The Autobiography of an Ex-Coloured Man*. New York: Alfred A. Knopf, 1927.

———. *Black Manhattan*. New York: Alfred A. Knopf, 1930.

———. "The Making of Harlem." *Survey Graphic* 6 (March 1925): 635.

Johnstone, Robert Zachariah. "The Negro in New York—His Social Attainments and Prospects." Master's thesis, Columbia University, 1911.

Jones, William H. *Recreation and Amusement among Negroes in Washington, D.C.: A Sociological Analysis of the Negro in an Urban Environment*. Washington, DC: Howard University Press, 1927.

Kellor, Frances. "The Criminal Negro: A Sociological Study." *Arena* 25 (January 1901): 61–65.

———. *Out of Work: A Study of Unemployment Agencies: Their Treatment of the Unemployed, and Their Influence Upon Homes and Business*. New York: G. P. Putnam's Sons, 1904.

Key, V. O. "Police Graft." *American Journal of Sociology* 40 (March 1935): 624–36.

Kneeland, George. *Commercialized Prostitution in New York City*. New York: Century Publishing, 1913.

Lane, Winthrop. "Ambushed in the City: The Grim Side of Harlem." *The Survey* (March 1925): 692–94.

Langhorn, Orra. "The Hampton Conference." *Congregationalist* 83 (1898): 157.

Larsen, Nella. *Quicksand.* New York: Alfred A. Knopf, 1928.

Lerner, Michael A. *Dry Manhattan: Prohibition in New York City.* Cambridge, MA: Harvard University Press, 2008.

Locke, Alain. *Harlem, Mecca of the Negro.* Baltimore, MD: Black Classic Press, 1980.

Lombroso, Cesare. "Why Homicide Has Increased in the United States. II. Barbarism and Civilization." *North American Review* 166 (January 1898): 1–11.

Lombroso, Cesare, and Gugliemo Ferrero. *Criminal Woman, the Prostitute, and the Normal Woman.* Durham, NC: Duke University Press, 2004.

Lombroso-Ferrero, Gina, and Cesear Lombroso. *Criminal Man: According to the Classification of Cesare Lombroso.* New York: Putnam, 1911.

Matthews, Victoria Earle. "The Awakening of the Afro-American Woman." An Address Delivered at the Annual Convention of the Society of Christian Endeavor, San Francisco, July 11, 1897.

McAdoo, William. *Guarding a Great City.* New York: Harper & Bros., 1906.

McKay, Claude. *Harlem: Negro Metropolis.* New York: E. P. Dutton, 1940.

Merton, Robert K. "Social Structure and Anomie." *American Sociological Review* 3 (October 1938): 672–82.

Miller, Kelly. *Race Adjustment: Essays on the Negro in America.* New York: Neale Publishing, 1908.

———. The Negro's Part in the Negro Problem. *Forum* 36 (October 1904): 289–305.

———. "Review of *Race Traits and Tendencies of the American Negro*, by Frederick L. Hoffman." *American Negro Academy Occasional Papers* 1. Washington, DC: The Academy, 1897.

Miner, Maude E. *Slavery of Prostitution: A Plea for Emancipation.* New York: Macmillan, 1916.

Moore, E. C. "The Social Value of the Saloon." *American Journal of Sociology* 4 (July 1897): 1–12.

Moore, Fred R. "Negro Business Enterprises in New York." Report of the Fourth Annual Convention of the National Negro Business League, Nashville, Tennessee, August 19–21, 1903. Wilberforce, OH: Charles Alexander, 1903.

Moore, Garrie W. "A Study of a Group of West Indian Negroes in New York City." Master's thesis, Columbia University, 1913.

More, Louise Boulard. *Wage-Earners' Budgets: A Study of Standards and Cost of Living in New York City.* New York: Henry Holt, 1907.

Morris, Charles. "Race Question in New York." *New York Times,* June 15, 1904, 6.

Moses, Kingsley. "The Negro Comes North." *Forum* (August 1917): 181–90.

Moss, Frank, and C. H. Parkhurst. *The American Metropolis: From Knickerbocker Days to the Present Time: New York City Life in All Its Various Phases: An Historiograph of New York.* New York: P. F. Collier, 1897.

Munro, Josiah J. *The New York Tombs, Inside and Out!: Scenes and Reminiscences Coming Down to the Present—A Story Stranger Than Fiction, With an Historic Account of America's Most Famous Prison.* Brooklyn, NY: The Author, 1909.

New York City Police Department. *Annual Report of the Police Department of the City of New York.* New York: New York Printing, 1920.

New York Commission on Congestion of Population. *Report of the New York City Commission on Congestion of Population*. New York: Lecouver Press, 1911.

Offord, Carl. "Slave Markets in the Bronx." *The Nation* (June 1940): 780.

Ogburn, William Fielding. "The Richmond Negro in New York City: His Social Mind as Seen in His Pleasures." Master's thesis, Columbia University, 1909.

Ovington, Mary White. *Black and White Sat Down Together: The Reminiscences of an NAACP Founder*. New York: Feminist Press at the City University of New York, 1996.

———. *Half a Man: The Status of the Negro in New York*. New York: Longmans, Green, 1911.

———. "The Negro in the Trades Unions in New York." *The Annals of the American Academy of Political and Social Science* 27 (May 1906): 89–96.

Paul, Seymour. "A Group of Virginia Negroes in New York City." Master's thesis, Columbia University, 1912.

Peters, John P. "Suppression of the 'Raines Law' Hotels." *Annals of the American Academy of Political and Social Sciences* 32 (November 1908): 86–96.

Popenoe, Paul, and Roswell H. Johnson. *Applied Eugenics*. New York: Macmillan, 1935.

Powell, Adam Clayton. *Against the Tide: An Autobiography*. New York: R. R. Smith, 1938.

Price, Thomas F. "Race War and Negro Demoralization." *American Catholic Quarterly Review* 25 (January 1900): 89–105.

Reed, David, and Chas B. Ward. *Leave Your Razors at the Door*. New York: Chas. B. Ward Publishing, 1900.

Reed, Ruth. *Negro Illegitimacy in New York City*. New York: Columbia University Press, 1926.

Reuter, Edward Byron. *The Mulatto in the United States; Including a Study of the Role of Mixed-Blood Races Throughout the World*. Boston: R. G. Badger, 1918.

Riis, Jacob. *How the Other Half Lives: Studies among the Tenements of New York*. New York: Charles Scribner's Sons, 1890.

Roe, Clifford G. *The Great War on White Slavery; or Fighting for the Protection of Our Girls*. S.I: C. G. Roe and B. S. Steadwell, 1911.

Roosevelt, Theodore. "The American Woman as a Mother." *Ladies' Home Journal* 22 (July 1905): 3–4.

Sellin, Thorsten. "The Negro Criminal: A Statistical Note." *Annals of the American Academy of Political and Social Science* 140 (November 1928): 52–64.

Spingarn, Arthur. *Laws Relating to Sex Morality in New York City*. New York: Century, 1915.

Stoddard, T. Lothrop. *Re-Forging America: The Story of Our Nationhood*. New York: Scribner's, 1927.

Stowe, Harriet Beecher. *We and Our Neighbors, or, The Records of an Unfashionable Street*. New York: Fords, Howard, & Hulbert, 1875.

Straton, John Roach. "Will Education Solve the Race Problem?" *North American Review* 170 (June 1900): 785–801.

Sutton, Charles. *The New York Tombs: Its Secrets and Its Mysteries: Being a History of Noted Criminals with Narratives of Their Crimes*. New York: United States Pub. Co., 1874.

Tayleur, Eleanor. "The Negro Woman—Social and Moral Decadence." *Outlook*, January 30, 1904.

Thomas, William Hannibal. *The American Negro: What He Was, What He Is, and What He May Become; a Critical and Practical Discussion.* New York: Macmillan, 1901.

Tönnies, Ferdinand. *Community and Civil Society.* New York: Cambridge University Press, 2001.

Towns, Charles B. "Help for the Hard Drinker: What Can Be Done to Save the Man Worth While." *The Century* (March 1912).

Trumble, Alfred. *The New York Tombs: Its History and Its Mysteries: Life and Death in New York's Famous Prison.* New York: R. K. Fox, 1881.

Turner, George Kibbe. "The City of Chicago: A Study of the Great Immoralities." *McClure's Magazine,* April 1907.

———. "The Daughters of the Poor." *McClure's Magazine* 34, November 1909.

Van Vechten, Carl. *Nigger Heaven.* New York: Knopf, 1926.

Waring, J. H. N. "Some Causes of Criminality Among Colored People." *Charities* 15 (October 7, 1905): 45–49.

Washington, Booker T. "Education Will Solve the Race Problem: A Reply." *North American Review* 171 (August 1900): 221–32.

———. "Negro Crime and Strong Drink." *Journal of the American Institute of Criminal Law and Criminology* 3 (September 1912): 384–92.

Washington, Forrester B. "Recreational Facilities for the Negro." *Annals of the American Academy of Political and Social Science* 140 (November 1928): 272–82.

———. *A Study of Negro Employees of Apartment Houses in New York City.* New York: National Urban League for Social Service Among Negroes, 1916.

Wells, Ida B. *Southern Horrors and Other Writings: The Anti-Lynching Campaign of Ida B. Wells, 1892–1900.* Boston: Bedford Books, 1997.

Wharton, Edith. *The House of Mirth.* New York: Charles Scriber's Sons, 1905.

Willcox, Walter F. "Negro Criminality." *Journal of Social Science, Containing the Proceedings of the American Association* 37 (December 1899): 78–98.

Willemse, Cornelius W. *Behind the Green Lights.* New York: Alfred A. Knopf, 1931.

———. *A Cop Remembers.* New York: E. P. Dutton, 1933.

Wood, Edith Elmer. "The Costs of Bad Housing." *Annals of the American Academy of Political and Social Science* 190 (March 1937): 145–50.

Woodbury, Robert M. "General Intelligence and Wages." *Quarterly Journal of Economics* 31 (August 1917): 690–704.

Wright, Richard. *Black Boy: A Record of Childhood and Youth.* New York: Harper & Brothers, 1945.

Wright, R. R. "The Migration of Negroes to the North." *Annals of the American Academy of Political and Social Science* 27 (May 1906): 97–116.

Secondary Sources

Alexander, Eleanor. *Lyrics of Sunshine and Shadow: The Tragic Courtship and Marriage of Paul Laurence Dunbar and Alice Ruth Moore.* New York: New York University Press, 2001.

Alexander, Leslie. *African or American?: Black Identity in New York City, 1784–1861.* Chicago: University of Illinois Press, 2008.

Alexander, Michelle. *The New Jim Crow: Mass Incarceration in the Age of Colorblindness*. New York: New Press, 2010.

Anderson, Elijah. *Code of the Street: Decency, Violence, and the Moral Life of the Inner City*. New York: W. W. Norton, 2000.

Anderson, Jervis. *This Was Harlem: A Cultural Portrait, 1900–1950*. New York: Farrar, Straus and Giroux, 1982.

Anthony, Ronda C. Henry. *Searching for the New Black Man: Black Masculinity and Women's Bodies*. Jackson: University of Mississippi Press, 2013.

Arnesen, Eric. *Brotherhoods of Color: Black Railroad Workers and the Struggle for Equality*. Cambridge, MA: Harvard University Press, 2001.

Avila, Eric. *Popular Culture in the Age of White Flight: Fear and Fantasy in Suburban Los Angeles*. Berkeley: University of California Press, 2004.

Bailey, Frankie Y., and Alice P. Green. *Law Never Here: A Social History of African American Responses to Issues of Crime and Justice*. Westport, CT: Praeger, 1999.

Baker, Ray Stannard. *Following the Color Line: American Negro Citizenship in the Progressive Era*. New York: Harper & Row, 1964.

Baldwin, Davarian. *Chicago's New Negroes: Modernity, the Great Migration, and Black Urban Life*. Chapel Hill: University of North Carolina Press, 2007.

Baldwin, James. *The Fire Next Time*. New York: Dial Press, 1963.

Baptist, Edward E. *The Half Has Never Been Told: Slavery and the Making of American Capitalism*. New York: Basic Books, 2014.

Barbeau, Arthur E., and Florette Henri. *The Unknown Soldiers: Black American Troops in World War I*. Philadelphia, PA: Temple University Press, 1974.

Bay, Mia. *The White Image in the Black Mind: African-American Ideas about White People, 1830–1925*. New York: Oxford University Press, 2000.

Beckert, Sven. *The Monied Metropolis: New York City and the Consolidation of the American Bourgeoisie, 1850–1896*. Cambridge: Cambridge University Press, 2001.

Bederman, Gail. *Manliness and Civilization: A Cultural History of Gender and Race in the United States, 1880–1917*. Chicago: University of Chicago Press, 1995.

Bell, Derrick. *Race, Racism, and American Law*. Boston: Little, Brown, 1973.

Berlin, Ira, and Leslie M. Harris. *Slavery in New York*. New York: New Press, 2005.

Bernard, Thomas J. "Testing Structural Strain Theories." *Journal of Research in Crime and Delinquency* 24 (November 1987): 262–80.

Bernstein, Iver. *The New York City Draft Riots: Their Significance for American Society and Politics in the Age of the Civil War*. New York: Oxford University Press, 1990.

Berry, Daina Raimey. *The Price for Their Pound of Flesh: The Value of the Enslaved, from Womb to Grave, in the Building of a Nation*. Boston: Beacon Press, 2017.

Beynon, John. *Masculinities and Culture*. Philadelphia, PA: Open University Press, 2002.

Black, Daniel P. *Dismantling Black Manhood: An Historical and Literary Analysis of the Legacy of Slavery*. New York: Routledge, 1997.

Blair, Cynthia M. *"I've Got to Make My Livin'": Black Women's Sex Work in Turn-of-the-Century Chicago*. Chicago: University of Chicago Press, 2010.

Blee, Kathleen M. *Women of the Klan: Racism and Gender in the 1920s*. Berkeley: University of California Press, 2009.

Bloch, H. D. "The New York City Negro and Occupational Eviction, 1860–1910." *International Review of Social History* 5 (1960): 26–38.

Blumer, Herbert. *Symbolic Interaction: Perspective and Method*. Berkeley: University of California Press, 1969.

Boehm, Lisa Krissof, and Steven H. Corey. *America's Urban History*. New York: Routlege, Taylor & Francis, 2015.

Boyer, Paul. *Urban Masses and Moral Order in America, 1820–1920*. Cambridge, MA: Harvard University Press, 1992.

Bristow, Edward W. *Prostitution and Prejudice: Jewish Fight Against White Slavery, 1870–1939*. Oxford: Clarendon Press, 1982.

Brown, Elsa Barkley, and Gregg Kimball. "Mapping the Terrain of Black Richmond." *Journal of Urban History* 3 (March 1995): 296–346.

Brown, Henry Collins. *Brownstone Fronts and Saratoga Trunks*. New York: E. P. Dutton, 1935.

Brown, Vincent. *The Reaper's Garden: Death and Power in the World of Atlantic Slavery*. Cambridge, MA: Harvard University Press, 2010.

Buckner, Timothy R., and Peter Caster. *Fathers, Preachers, Rebels, Men: Black Masculinity in U.S. History and Literature, 1820–1945*. Columbus: Ohio State University Press, 2011.

Caddoo, Cara. *Envisioning Freedom: Cinema and the Building of Modern Black Life*. Cambridge, MA: Harvard University Press, 2014.

Callow, Alexander B. "The Crusade Against the Tweed Ring." In *American Urban History: An Interpretive Reader with Commentaries*, 191–209. New York: Oxford University Press, 1982.

Campbell, James. "African Americans and Parole in Depression-Era New York." *The Historical Journal* 54 (December 2011): 1065–86.

———. *Crime and Punishment in African American History*. New York: Palgrave Macmillan, 2013.

———. "'You Needn't Be Afraid Here: You're in a Civilized Country': Region, Racial Violence and Law Enforcement in Early Twentieth-Century New Jersey, New York and Pennsylvania." *Social History* 35 (August 2010): 253–67.

Carby, Hazel V. "Policing the Black Woman's Body in an Urban Context." *Critical Inquiry* 18 (Summer 1992): 738–55.

Carnes, Mark C., and Clyde Griffen. *Meanings for Manhood: Constructions of Masculinity in Victorian America*. Chicago: University of Chicago Press, 1990.

Carter, Michael J., and Celene Fuller. "Symbols, Meaning, and Action: The Past, Present, and Future of Symbolic Interactionism." *Current Sociology* 64 (2016): 931–61.

Celik, Zeynep, Diane Favro, and Richard Ingersoll, eds. *Streets: Critical Perspectives on Public Space*. Berkeley: University of California Press, 1994.

Chauncey, George. *Gay New York: Gender, Urban Culture, and the Making of the Gay Male World, 1890–1940*. New York: Basic Books, 1994.

Chesney-Lind, Meda. *The Female Offender: Girls, Women, and Crime*. Thousand Oaks, CA: Sage, 2004.

Chesney-Lind, Meda, and Randall G. Shelden. *Girls, Delinquency, and Juvenile Justice*. Chichester, UK: John Wiley & Sons, 2014.

Clark, Kenneth, and Gunnar Myrdal. *Dark Ghetto: Dilemmas of Social Power.* New York: Harper & Row, 1965.

Clement, Elizabeth Alice. *Love for Sale: Courting, Treating, and Prostitution in New York City, 1900–1945.* Chapel Hill: University of North Carolina Press, 2006.

Cohen, Michael M. "Jim Crow's Drug War: Race, Coca Cola, and the Southern Origins of Drug Prohibition." *Southern Cultures* 12 (Fall 2006): 55–79.

Colvin, Mark. *Penitentiaries, Reformatories, and Chain Gangs: Social Theory and the History of Punishment in Nineteenth-Century America.* New York: St. Martin's, 1997.

Connolly, Harold X. *Blacks in Brooklyn from 1900–1960.* New York: New York University Press, 1977.

Connelly, Mark Thomas. *The Response to Prostitution in the Progressive Era.* Chapel Hill: University of North Carolina Press, 1980.

Cook, Will Marion, Jesse A. Shipp, and Paul Laurence Dunbar. *In Dahomey: A Negro Musical Comedy.* London: Keith, Prowse & Co., 1903.

Corbould, Clare. "Streets, Sounds and Identity in Interwar Harlem." *Journal of Social History* 40 (Summer 2007): 859–94.

Courtwright, David T. "The First American Cocaine Epidemic." *OAH Magazine of History* 6 (Fall 1991): 20–21.

———. "The Hidden Epidemic: Opiate Addiction and Cocaine Use in the South, 1860–1920." *The Journal of Southern History* 49 (February 1983): 57–72.

Cullen, Francis T. *Rethinking Crime and Deviance: The Emergence of a Structuring Tradition.* Totowa, NJ: Rowman & Allanheld, 1984.

Cullen, Francis T., and Robert Agnew. *Criminological Theory: Past to Present: Essential Readings.* New York: Oxford University Press, 2006.

Cullen, James, and Ames Grawert. "Fact Sheet: Stop and Frisk's Effect on Crime in New York City." Brennan Center for Justice (October 2016).

Currie, Elliott. *Confronting Crime: An American Challenge.* New York: Pantheon Books, 1985.

Czitrom, Daniel. "The Politics of Performance: From Theatre Licensing to Movie Censorship in Turn-of-the-Century New York." *American Quarterly* 44 (December 1992): 525–53.

Dabel, Jane. *A Respectable Woman: The Public Roles of African American Women in 19th-Century New York.* New York: New York University Press, 2008.

D'Emilio, John, and Estelle B. Freedman. *Intimate Matters: A History of Sexuality in America.* Chicago: University of Chicago Press, 1988.

Derrick, Scott S. *Monumental Anxieties: Homoerotic Desire and Feminine Influence in 19th-Century U.S. Literature.* New Brunswick, NJ: Rutgers University Press, 1997.

De Young, Mary. "Help! I'm Being Held Captive!: The White Slavery Fairy Tale of the Progressive Era." *Journal of American Culture* 6 (1983): 96–99.

Doezema, Jo. "Loose Women or Lost Women?: The Re-Emergence of the Myth of White Slavery in Contemporary Discourses of Trafficking in Women." *Gender Issues* 18 (2000): 23–50.

Donovan, Brian. *White Slave Crusades: Race, Gender, and Anti-Vice Activism, 1887–1917.* Urbana: University of Illinois Press, 2006.

Dormon, James H. "Shaping the Popular Image of Post-Reconstruction American Blacks: The 'Coon Song' Phenomenon of the Gilded Age." *American Quarterly* 40 (December 1988): 450–71.

Dorsey, Allison. *To Build Our Lives Together: Community Formation in Black Atlanta, 1875–1906.* Athens: University of Georgia Press, 2004.

Douglas, Ann. *Terrible Honesty: Mongrel Manhattan in the 1920s.* New York: Farrar, Straus and Giroux, 1995.

Dowling, R. M. *Slumming in New York: From the Waterfront to Mythic Harlem.* Urbana: University of Illinois Press, 2007.

Duis, Perry R. *The Saloon and the Public City: Chicago and Boston, 1880–1920.* Urbana: University of Illinois Press, 1980.

Dumenil, Lynn. *The Modern Temper: American Culture and Society in the 1920s.* New York: Hill & Wang, 1995.

Eberhart, George M. "Stack Lee: The Man, the Music, and the Myth." In *A Question of Manhood: A Reader in U.S. Black Men's History and Masculinity,* edited by Darlene Clark Hine and Earnestine Jenkins, 387–440. Bloomington: Indiana University Press, 1999.

Ellis, Edward Robb. *The Epic of New York City: A Narrative History.* New York: Coward-McCann, 1966.

Erenberg, Lewis A. *Steppin' Out: New York Nightlife and the Transformation of American Culture, 1890–1930.* Westport, CT: Greenwood Press, 1981.

Fainstein, Susan S., and Scott Campbell, eds. *Readings in Urban Theory.* Malden, MA: Blackwell Publishers, 2002.

Fanon, Frantz. *The Wretched of the Earth.* New York: Grove Press, 2004.

Farr, Finis. *Black Champion: The Life and Times of Jack Johnson.* Greenwich, CT: Fawcett Publishing, 1969.

Feimster, Crystal N. *Southern Horrors: Women and the Politics of Rape and Lynching.* Cambridge, MA: Harvard University Press, 2011.

Flagg, Earnest. "The New York Tenement-House Evil and Its Cure." *Scribner's Magazine* (July 1894): 108–17.

Fletcher, Tony. *All Hopped Up and Ready to Go: Music From the Streets of New York, 1927–1977.* New York: W. W. Norton, 2009.

Forman, James. *Locking Up Our Own: Crime and Punishment in Black America.* New York: Farrar, Straus and Giroux, 2018.

Fosdick, Raymond. *John D. Rockefeller, Jr.: A Portrait.* New York: Harper and Brothers, 1956.

Franklin, John Hope, and Alfred A. Moss Jr. *From Slavery to Freedom: A History of Negro Americans.* New York: McGraw-Hill, 1993.

Frazier, E. Franklin. "The Changing Status of the Negro Family." *Social Forces* 9 (March 1931): 386–93.

———. *The Negro Family in the United States.* Chicago: University of Chicago Press, 1966.

———. "Negro Harlem: An Ecological Study." *American Journal of Sociology* 43 (July 1937): 72–88.

Freedman, Estelle B. *Their Sister's Keepers: Women's Prison Reform in America, 1830–1930.* Ann Arbor: University of Michigan Press, 1981.

Friedman, Andrea. *Prurient Interests: Gender, Democracy, and Obscenity in New York City, 1909–1945*. New York: Columbia University Press, 2000.

Friedman, Lawrence M. *Crime and Punishment in American History*. New York: Basic Books, 1993.

Fronc, Jennifer. "The Horns of the Dilemma: Race Mixing and the Enforcement of Jim Crow in New York City." *Journal of Urban History* (October 2006): 3–25.

———. *New York Undercover: Private Surveillance in the Progressive Era*. Chicago: University of Chicago Press, 2009.

Fuentes, Marisa J. *Dispossessed Lives: Enslaved Women, Violence, and the Archive*. Philadelphia: University of Pennsylvania Press, 2018.

Gaines, Kevin. *Uplifting the Race: Black Leadership, Politics, and Culture in the Twentieth Century*. Chapel Hill: University of North Carolina Press, 1996.

Gardiner, Judith Keegan. "Theorizing Age with Gender: Bly's Boys, Feminism, and Maturity Masculinity." In *Masculinity Studies and Feminist Theory*, 60–89. New York: Columbia University Press, 2002.

Gates, Henry Louis, Jr., and Gene Andrew Jarrett, eds. *The New Negro: Readings on Race, Representation, and African American Culture, 1892–1938*. Princeton: Princeton University Press, 2007.

Gatewood, Willard B. "Booker T. Washington and the Ulrich Affair." *Journal of Negro History* 55 (January 1970): 29–44.

Genovese, Eugene D. *Roll, Jordan, Roll: The World the Slaves Made*. New York: Pantheon Books, 1974.

Gibson, Mary. *Born to Crime: Cesare Lombroso and the Origins of Biological Criminology*. Westport, CT: Praeger, 2002.

Gilfoyle, Timothy. *City of Eros: New York City, Prostitution, and the Commercialization of Sex, 1790–1920*. New York: W. W. Norton, 1992.

———. *A Pickpocket's Tale: The Underworld of Nineteenth-Century New York*. New York: W. W. Norton, 2006.

———. "White Cities, Linguistic Turns, and Disneylands: The New Paradigms of Urban History." *Reviews in American History* 26 (March 1998): 175–204.

Gilmore, Al-Tony. *Bad Nigger! The National Impact of Jack Johnson*. Port Washington, NY: Kennikat Press, 1975.

———. "Jack Johnson and White Women: The National Impact." *Journal of Negro History* 58 (January 1973): 18–38.

Gordon, David M. "Capitalism, Class, and Crime in America." *Crime and Delinquency* 19 (April 1973): 163–86.

Green, Adam. *Selling the Race: Culture, Community, and Black Chicago, 1940–1955*. Chicago: University of Chicago Press, 2007.

Greenberg, David F. *Crime and Capitalism: Readings in Marxist Criminology*. Philadelphia, PA: Temple University Press, 1993.

Greer, Brenna Wynn. *Represented: The Black Imagemakers Who Reimagined African American Citizenship*. Philadelphia: University of Pennsylvania Press, 2019.

Griffin, Farah Jasmine. *"Who Set You Flowin'?": The African American Migration Narrative*. New York: Oxford University Press, 1995.

Grittner, Frederick K. *White Slavery: Myth, Ideology, and American Law*. New York: Garland, 1990.

Gross, Kali. *Colored Amazons: Crime, Violence, and Black Women in the City of Brotherly Love, 1880–1910*. Durham, NC: Duke University Press, 2006.

———. "Exploring Crime and Violence in Early-Twentieth-Century Black Women's History." In *Contesting Archives: Finding Women in the Sources*, edited by Nupur Chadhuri, Sherry J. Katz, and Mary Elizabeth Perry, 56–74. Urbana: University of Illinois Press, 2010.

Grossman, James R. *Land of Hope: Chicago, Black Southerners, and the Great Migration*. Chicago: University of Chicago Press, 1989.

Gussow, Adam. *Seems Like Murder Here: Sothern Violence and the Blues Tradition*. Chicago: University of Chicago Press, 2002.

———. "'Shoot Myself a Cop': Mamie Smith's 'Crazy Blues' as Social Text." *Callaloo* 25 (Winter 2002): 8–44.

Guterl, Mattew Pratt. *The Color of Race in America, 1900–1940*. Cambridge, MA: Harvard University Press, 2001.

Gutman, Herbert G. *The Black Family in Slavery and Freedom, 1750–1925*. New York: Pantheon Books, 1976.

Guy-Sheftall, Beverly. *Daughters of Sorrow: Attitudes Toward Black Women, 1880–1920*. Brooklyn, NY: Carlson Publishing, 1990.

Hahn, Steven. *A Nation Under Our Feet: Black Political Struggles in the Rural South from Slavery to the Great Migration*. Cambridge, MA: Harvard University Press, 2003.

Haley, Sarah. *No Mercy Here: Gender, Punishment, and the Making of Jim Crow Modernity*. Chapel Hill: University of North Carolina Press, 2016.

Harold, Claudrena N. *New Negro Politics in the Jim Crow South*. Athens: University of Georgia Press, 2016.

Harris, LaShawn. *Sex Workers, Psychics, and Numbers Runners: Black Women in New York City's Underground Economy*. Urbana: University of Illinois Press, 2016.

Harris, Leslie M. *In the Shadow of Slavery: African Americans in New York City, 1626–1863*. Chicago: University of Chicago Press, 2003.

Hartman, Saidiya. *Wayward Lives, Beautiful Experiments: Intimate Histories of Social Upheaval*. New York: W. W. Norton, 2019.

Haywood, D'Weston. *Let Us Make Men: The Twentieth-Century Black Press and a Manly Vision for Racial Advancement*. Chapel Hill: University of North Carolina Press, 2018.

Hazzard-Gordon, Katrina. *Jookin': The Rise of Social Dance Formations in African American Culture*. Philadelphia, PA: Temple University Press, 1990.

Heap, Chad. *Slumming: Sexual and Racial Encounters in American Nightlife, 1885–1940*. Chicago: University of Chicago Press, 2009.

Henri, Florette. *Black Migration: Movement North, 1900–1920*. Garden City, NY: Anchor Press, 1975.

Hicks, Cheryl. *Talk with You Like a Woman: African American Women, Justice, and Reform in New York, 1890–1935*. Chapel Hill: University of North Carolina Press, 2010.

Higginbotham, Evelyn Brooks. *Righteous Discontent: The Women's Movement in the Black Baptist Church, 1880–1920*. Cambridge, MA: Harvard University Press, 1994.

Hine, Darlene Clark. "Rape and the Inner Lives of Black Women in the Middle West." *Signs* 14 (Summer 1989): 912–20.

————, and Earnestine Jenkins, eds. *A Question of Manhood: A Reader in U.S. Black Men's History and Masculinity*, Vol. 1, "'Manhood Rights': The Construction of Black Male History and Manhood, 1750–1870." Bloomington: Indiana University Press, 1999.

Hinton, Elizabeth. *From the War on Poverty to the War on Crime: The Making of Mass Incarceration in America*. Cambridge, MA: Harvard University Press, 2016.

Hirschi, Travis. *Causes of Delinquency*. Berkeley: University of California Press, 1969.

Hobson, Barbara Meil. *Uneasy Virtue: The Politics of Prostitution and the American Reform Tradition*. Chicago: University of Chicago Press, 1997.

Hoch, Paul. *White Hero Black Beast*. London: Pluto Press, 1979.

Hodes, Martha. *White Women, Black Men: Illicit Sex in the Nineteenth-Century South*. New Haven, CT: Yale University Press, 1999.

————. *Sex, Love, Race: Crossing Boundaries in North American History*. New York: New York University Press, 1999.

Hodges, Graham Russell Gao. *Root and Branch: African Americans in New York and East Jersey, 1613–1863*. Chapel Hill: University of North Carolina Press, 1999.

Hoffman, Frederick L. *Race Traits and Tendencies of the American Negro*. New York: American Economic Association, 1896.

Homberger, Eric. *The Historical Atlas of New York City: A Visual Celebration of Nearly 400 Years of New York City's History*. New York: H. Holt, 1998.

Horn, David G. *The Criminal Body: Lombroso and the Anatomy of Deviance*. London: Routledge, 2003.

Hornsby-Gutting, Angela. *Black Manhood and Community Building in North Carolina, 1900–1930*. Gainesville: University of Florida Press, 2009.

Horowitz, Helen L., and Kathy Lee Peiss. *Love Across the Color Line: The Letters of Alice Hanley to Channing Lewis*. Amherst: University of Massachusetts Press, 1996.

Hudson, Larry E. *To Have and to Hold: Slave Work and Family Life in Antebellum South Carolina*. Athens: University of Georgia Press, 1997.

Hunt, Alan. "Regulating Heterosocial Space: Sexual Politics in the Early Twentieth Century." *Journal of Historical Sociology* 15 (March 2002): 1–34.

Hunter, Tera. *Bound in Wedlock, Slave and Free Black Marriage in the Nineteenth Century*. Cambridge, MA: Harvard University Press, 2017.

————. *To 'Joy My Freedom: Southern Black Women's Lives and Labors after the Civil War*. Cambridge, MA: Harvard University Press, 1998.

Ikard, David. *Breaking the Silence: Toward a Black Male Feminist Criticism*. Baton Rouge: Louisiana State University Press, 2007.

Israels, Belle Lindner. "The Way of the Girl." *Survey* 22 (1909): 486–97.

Jackson, Kenneth, and David Dunbar, eds. *Empire City: New York through the Centuries*. New York: Columbia University Press, 2002.

Johnson, Marilyn. *Street Justice: A History of Police Violence in New York City*. Boston: Beacon Press, 2003.

Jones, Jacqueline. *Labor of Love, Labor of Sorrow: Black Women, Work, and the Family from Slavery to the Present*. New York: Basic Books, 1985.

Katz, Jack. *Seductions of Crime: A Chilling Exploration of the Criminal Mind—From Juvenile Delinquency to Cold-Blooded Murder*. New York: Basic Books, 1988.

Keire, Mara L. "The Vice Trust: A Reinterpretation of the White Slavery Scare in the United States, 1907–1917." *Journal of Social History* 35 (2001): 5–41.

Kelley, Robin D. G. *Race Rebels: Culture, Politics, and the Black Working Class.* New York: Free Press, 1994.

———. "'We Are Not What We Seem': Rethinking Black Working-Class Opposition in the Jim Crow South." *Journal of American History* 80 (June 1993): 75–112.

Kendi, Ibram X. *Stamped from the Beginning: The Definitive History of Racist Ideas.* New York: Nation Books, 2016.

Keve, Paul W. *Prisons and the American Conscience: A History of U.S. Federal Corrections.* Carbondale: Southern Illinois University Press, 1991.

Kimmel, Michael. *Manhood in America: A Cultural History.* New York: Oxford University Press, 2012.

King, Shannon. "'Ready to Shoot and Do Shoot': Black Working-Class Self-Defense and Community Politics in Harlem, New York, During the 1920s." *Journal of Urban History* 37 (2011): 757.

———. *Whose Harlem Is This, Anyway?: Community Politics and Grassroots Activism during the New Negro Era.* New York: New York University Press, 2015.

Kiser, Clyde Vernon. *Sea Island to City: A Study of St. Helena Islanders in Harlem and Other Urban Centers.* New York: Atheneum, 1969.

Kisseloff, Jeff. *You Must Remember This: An Oral History of Manhattan from the 1890s to World War II.* San Diego, CA: Harcourt Brace Jovanovich, 1989.

Kramer, Steve. "Uplifting Our 'Downtrodden Sisterhood': Victoria Earle Matthews and New York City's White Rose Mission, 1897–1907." *Journal of African American History* 91 (Summer 2006): 243–66.

Kuhn, Manford H. "Major Trends in Symbolic Interaction Theory in the Past Twenty-Five Years." *The Sociological Quarterly* 5 (1964): 61–84.

Kusmer, Kenneth L. "African Americans in the City Since World War II: From the Industrial to the Post-Industrial Era." *Journal of Urban History* 21 (1995): 458–504.

Lane, Roger. *Roots of Violence in Black Philadelphia, 1860–1900.* Cambridge, MA: Harvard University Press, 1986.

Lankevich, George. *A Brief History of New York City.* Port Washington, NY: Associated Faculty Press, 1984.

Leab, Daniel J. "Women and the Mann Act." *Amerikastuden/American Studies* 21 (1976): 55–65.

Lears, Jackson. *No Place of Grace: Antimodernism and the Transformation of American Culture, 1880–1920.* Chicago: University of Chicago Press, 1981.

———. *Rebirth of a Nation: The Making of Modern America, 1877–1920.* New York: HarperCollins, 2009.

LeFlouria, Talitha. *Chained in Silence: Black Women and Convict Labor in the New South.* Chapel Hill: University of North Carolina Press, 2015.

Leiter, Andrew B. *In the Shadow of the Black Beast: African American Masculinity in the Harlem and Southern Renaissances.* Baton Rouge: Louisiana State University Press, 2010.

Lemann, Nicolas. *The Promised Land: The Great Black Migration and How It Changed America.* New York: Alfred A. Knopf, 1991.

Lemelle, Anthony J. *Black Masculinity and Sexual Politics.* New York: Routledge, 2010.

Lepore, Jill. *New York Burning: Liberty, Slavery, and Conspiracy in Eighteenth-Century Manhattan.* New York: Alfred A. Knopf, 2005.

Levine, Lawrence. *Black Culture and Black Consciousness: Afro-American Folk Thought from Slavery to Freedom.* New York: Oxford University Press, 1977.

Lewinson, Edwin R. *Black Politics in New York City.* New York: Twayne Publishers, 1974.

Lewis, David Levering. *When Harlem Was in Vogue.* New York: Penguin Books, 1997.

Lewis, Earl. *In Their Own Interests: Race, Class and Power in Twentieth-Century Norfolk, Virginia.* Berkeley: University of California Press, 1991.

Liebow, Elliot. *Tally's Corner: A Study of Negro Streetcorner Men.* Boston: Little, Brown, 1967.

Light, Ivan. "The Ethnic Vice Industry, 1880–1944." *American Sociological Review* 42 (June 1977): 464–79.

Lindsey, Linda. *Gender Roles: A Sociological Perspective.* Upper Saddle River, NJ: Prentice Hall, 2005.

Linton, Ralph. *The Study of Man.* New York: Appleton-Century-Crofts, 1936.

Litwack, Leon F. "Jim Crow Blues." *OAH Magazine of History* 18 (January 2004): 7–11.

Lubove, Roy. "The Progressives and the Prostitute." *Historian* 24 (May 1962): 308–30.

Madhubuti, Haki R. *Black Men: Obsolete, Single, Dangerous? Afrikan American Families in Transition: Essays in Discovery, Solution, and Hope.* Chicago: Third World Press, 1990.

Majors, Richard, and Janet Mancini Billson. *Cool Pose: The Dilemmas of Black Manhood in America.* New York: Lexington Books, 1992.

Makalani, Minkah. "Internationalizing the Third International: The African Blood Brotherhood, Asian Radicals, and Race, 1919–1922." *Journal of African American History* 96 (Spring 2011): 151–78.

Marcus, Irwin. "Hubert Harrison: Negro Advocate." *Negro History Bulletin* 34 (January 1971): 18–19.

May, Elaine Tyler. *Great Expectations: Marriage and Divorce in Post-Victorian America.* Chicago: University of Chicago Press, 1980.

McBride, David. "Fourteenth Amendment Idealism: The New York State Civil Rights Law, 1873–1918." *New York History* 71 (April 1990): 207–33.

McDermott, M. Joan, and Sarah Blackstone. "White Slavery Plays of the 1910s: Fear of Victimization and the Social Control of Sexuality." *Theatre History Studies* 16 (1996): 141–56.

McFarland, Gerald W. *Inside Greenwich Village: A New York City Neighborhood, 1898–1918.* Amherst: University of Massachusetts Press, 2001.

McGerr, Michael. *A Fierce Discontent: The Rise and Fall of the Progressive Movement in America.* New York: Oxford University Press, 2003.

McGirr, Lisa. *The War on Alcohol: Prohibition and the Rise of the American State.* New York: W. W. Norton, 2016.

McKay, Nellie Y. *Jean Toomer, Artist: A Study of His Literary Life and Work, 1894–1936*. Chapel Hill: University of North Carolina Press, 1984.

McKee, Margaret, and Fred Chisenhall. *Beale Black and Blue: Life and Music on Black America's Main Street*. Baton Rouge: Louisiana University Press, 1993.

McKelvey, Blake. *American Prisons: A History of Good Intentions*. Montclair, NJ: Patterson Smith Publications, 1977.

McLennan, Rebecca M. *The Crisis of Imprisonment: Protest, Politics, and the Making of the American Penal State, 1776–1941*. New York: Cambridge University Press, 2008.

McManus, Edgar J. *A History of Negro Slavery in New York*. Syracuse, NY: Syracuse University Press, 1966.

Mead, George Herbert. *Mind, Self, and Society from the Standpoint of a Social Behaviorist*. Chicago: University of Chicago Press, 1934.

Mercer, Kobena, and Isaac Julien. "True Confessions." In *Black Male: Representations of Masculinity in Contemporary Art*, edited by Thelma Golden. New York: Whitney Museum of Art, 1995.

Merton, Robert K. "Social Structure and Anomie." *American Sociological Review* 3 (October 1938): 672–82.

Messner, Steven F. "Merton's 'Social Structure and Anomie': The Road Not Taken." *Deviant Behavior* 9 (1988): 33–52.

Meyerowitz, Joanne J. *Women Adrift: Independent Wage Earners in Chicago, 1880–1930*. Chicago: University of Chicago Press, 1988.

Mintz, Steven, and Susan Kellogg. *Domestic Revolutions: A Social History of American Family Life*. New York: Free Press, 1988.

Mitchell, Michele. *Righteous Propagation: African Americans and the Politics of Racial Destiny after Reconstruction*. Chapel Hill: University of North Carolina Press, 2004.

Moore, Louis. *I Fight for a Living: Boxing and the Battle for Black Manhood, 1880–1915*. Urbana: University of Illinois Press, 2017.

Muhammad, Khalil Gibran. *The Condemnation of Blackness: Race, Crime, and the Making of Modern Urban America*. Cambridge, MA: Harvard University Press, 2010.

Mumford, Kevin. *Interzones: Black/White Sex Districts in Chicago and New York in the Early Twentieth Century*. New York: Columbia University Press, 1997.

Mustakeem, Sowande. *Slavery at Sea: Terror, Sex, and Sickness in the Middle Passage*. Urbana: University of Illinois Press, 2016.

Musto, David. *The American Disease: Origins of Narcotic Control*. New York: Oxford University Press, 1999.

Muth, William R., and Thom Gehring. "The Correctional Education/Prison Reform Link: 1913–1940." *Journal of Correctional Education* 37 (March 1986): 14–17.

Mutua, Athena D., ed. *Progressive Black Masculinities*. New York: Routledge, 2006.

Myrdal, Gunnar. *An American Dilemma: The Negro Problem and Modern Democracy*. New York: Harper & Row, 1962.

Odum, Howard Washington. *Negro Workaday Songs*. Chapel Hill: University of North Carolina Press, 1926.

Okrent, Daniel. *Last Call: The Rise and Fall of Prohibition*. New York: Scribner, 2010.

Osofsky, Gilbert. *Harlem: The Making of a Ghetto: Negro New York, 1890–1930*. New York: Harper & Row, 1963.

———. "Race Riot, 1900: A Study of Ethnic Violence." *Journal of Negro Education* 32 (Winter 1963): 16–24.

Ottley, Roi. *New World A-Coming*. New York: World Publishing, 1943.

Parker, Tracy. *Department Stores and the Black Freedom Movement: Workers, Consumers, and Civil Rights from the 1930s to the 1980s*. Chapel Hill: University of North Carolina Press, 2019.

Patchay, Sheena. "Transgressing Boundaries: Marginality, Complicity and Subversion in 'Nervous Conditions.'" *English in Africa* 30 (May 2003): 145–55.

Pegram, Thomas R. *Battling Demon Rum: The Struggle for a Dry America, 1800–1933*. Chicago: Ivan R. Dee, 1998.

———. "The Dry Machine: The Formation of the Anti-Saloon League in Illinois." *Illinois Historical Journal* 83 (Autumn 1990): 173–86.

Peiss, Cathy. *Cheap Amusements: Working Women and Leisure in the Turn-of-the-Century New York*. Philadelphia, PA: Temple University Press, 1986.

Peterson, Carla L. *Black Gotham: A Family History of African Americans in Nineteenth-Century New York City*. New Haven, CT: Yale University Press, 2012.

Pinar, William F. "The 'Crisis' of White Masculinity." *Counterpoints* 163 (2001): 321–416.

———. *The Gender of Racial Politics and Violence in America: Lynching, Prison Rape, and the Crisis of Masculinity*. New York: Peter Lang, 2001.

Pochmara, Anna. *The Making of the New Negro: Black Authorship, Masculinity, and Sexuality in the Harlem Renaissance*. Amsterdam: Amsterdam University Press, 2011.

Powers, Madelon. *Faces along the Bar: Lore and Order in the Workingman's Saloon, 1870–1920*. Chicago: University of Chicago Press, 1999.

———. "The 'Poor Man's Friend': Saloonkeepers, Workers, and the Code of Reciprocity in U.S. Barrooms, 1870–1920." *International Labor and Working-Class History* 45 (1994): 1–15.

Pritchett, Wendell E. *Brownsville, Brooklyn: Blacks, Jews, and the Changing Face of the Ghetto*. Chicago: University of Chicago Press, 2002.

Provine, Doris Marie. *Unequal Under Law: Race in the War on Drugs*. Chicago: University of Chicago Press, 2007.

Quinney, Richard. *Class, State, and Crime*. New York: Longman, 1980.

Richardson, James F. *The New York Police, Colonial Times to 1901*. New York: Oxford University Press, 1970.

Richardson, Riche. *Black Masculinity and the U.S. South: From Uncle Tom to Gangsta*. Athens: University of Georgia Press, 2007.

Riesman, David. *The Lonely Crowd: A Study of the Changing American Character*. New Haven, CT: Yale University Press, 1962.

Roberts, Leonard H. "The Historic Roots of American Prison Reform: A Story of Progress and Failure." *Journal of Correctional Education* 36 (September 1985): 106–9.

Roberts, Randy. *Papa Jack: Jack Johnson and the Era of White Hopes*. New York: Free Press, 1983.

Robertson, Stephen, Stephen Garton, Shane White, and Graham White. "Disorderly Houses: Residences, Privacy, and the Surveillance of Sexuality in 1920s Harlem." *Journal of the History of Sexuality* 21 (September 2012): 443–66.

Roediger, David R. *The Wages of Whiteness: Race and the Making of the American Working Class*. New York: Verso, 1991.

———. *Working Toward Whiteness: How America's Immigrants Became White: The Strange Journal from Ellis Island to the Suburbs*. New York: Basic Books, 2006.

Rosen, Ruth. *The Lost Sisterhood: Prostitution in America, 1900–1918*. Baltimore, MD: Johns Hopkins University Press, 1982.

Rosenfeld, Richard. "Robert Merton's Contributions to the Sociology of Deviance." *Sociological Inquiry* 59 (October 1989): 453–66.

Roth, Randolph. *American Homicide*. Cambridge, MA: Harvard University Press, 2009.

Rothbart, Ron. "The Ethnic Saloon as a Form of Immigrant Enterprise." *International Migration Review* 27 (Summer 1993): 332–58.

Rothman, David J. *Conscience and Convenience: The Asylum and Its Alternatives in Progressive America*. Boston: Little, Brown, 1980.

Rothman, Sheila M. *Woman's Proper Place: A History of Changing Ideals and Practices, 1870 to the Present*. New York: Basic Books, 1978.

Rotundo, E. Anthony. *American Manhood: Transformations in Masculinity from the Revolution to the Modern Era*. New York: Basic Books, 1993.

Rudwick, Elliot M. "W. E. B. Du Bois in the Role of Crisis Editor." *Journal of Negro History* 43 (July 1958): 214–40.

Sacks, Marcy. *Before Harlem: The Black Experience in New York City Before World War I*. Philadelphia: University of Pennsylvania Press, 2006.

———. "Re-Creating Black New York at Century's End." In *Slavery in New York*, edited by Ira Berlin and Leslie Harris, 327–49. New York: W. W. Norton, 2005.

———. "'To Be a Man and Not a Lackey': Black Men, Work, and the Construction of Manhood in Gilded Age New York City." *American Studies* 45 (Spring 2004): 39–63.

———. "'To Show Who Was in Charge': Police Repression of New York City's Black Population at the Turn of the Century." *Journal of Urban History* 31 (September 2005): 799–819.

San Gupta, Gunja. "Black and 'Dangerous'? African American Working Poor Perspectives on Juvenile Reform and Welfare in Victorian New York, 1840–1890." *Journal of Negro History* 86 (Spring 2001): 99–131.

Schatzberg, Rufus, and Robert J. Kelly. *African American Organized Crime: A Social History*. New Brunswick, NJ: Rutgers University Press, 1997.

Scheiner, Seth M. *Negro Mecca: A History of the Negro in New York City, 1865–1920*. New York: New York University Press, 1965.

Schlesinger, Arthur. "The City in American History." *Mississippi Valley Historical Review* 27 (June 1940): 43–66.

Scott, James C. *Domination and the Arts of Resistance: Hidden Transcripts*. New Haven: Yale University Press, 1990.

Seidler, Victor J. *Rediscovering Masculinity: Reason, Language, and Sexuality*. New York: Routledge, 1989.

Shapiro, Herbert. *White Violence and Black Response: From Reconstruction to Montgomery.* Amherst: University of Massachusetts Press, 1988.

Shaw, Clifford R., and Henry D. McKay. *Juvenile Delinquency and Urban Areas: A Study of Rates of Delinquency in Relation to Differential Characteristics of Local Communities in American Cities.* Chicago: University of Chicago Press, 1942.

Simon, Rita James. *Women and Crime.* Lexington, MA: Lexington Books, 1975.

Sims, Kimberly Joyce. "Blacks, Italians, and the Progressive Interest in New York City Crime, 1900–1930." PhD diss., Harvard University, 2006.

Smallwood, Stephanie E. *Saltwater Slavery: A Middle Passage from Africa to American Diaspora.* Cambridge, MA: Harvard University Press, 2008.

Somé, Malidoma Patrice. *Of Water and the Spirit: Ritual, Magic, and Initiation in the Life of an African Shaman.* New York: Putnam, 1994.

Spillane, Joseph F. *Cocaine: From Medical Marvel to Modern Menace in the United States, 1884–1920.* Baltimore, MD: Johns Hopkins Press, 2002.

Sprague, Stuart. "Lure of the City: New York's Great Hotels in the Golden Age, 1873–1907." *Conspectus of History* 1 (1977): 73–84.

Staples, Robert. *Black Masculinity: The Black Male's Role in American Society.* San Francisco: Black Scholar Press, 1982.

Stansell, Christine. *City of Women: Sex and Class in New York, 1790–1860.* New York: Knopf, 1986.

Strausbaugh, John. *Black Like You: Blackface, Whiteface, Insult & Imitation in American Popular Culture.* New York: Jeremy P. Tarcher/Penguin, 2006.

Stryker, Sheldon. *Symbolic Interactionism: A Social Structural Version.* Menlo Park, CA: Benjamin Cummings, 1980.

Suddler, Carl. *Presumed Criminal: Black Youth and the Justice System in Postwar New York.* New York: New York University Press, 2019.

Sugrue, Thomas. *The Origins of the Urban Crisis: Race and Inequality in Postwar Detroit.* Princeton, NJ: Princeton University Press, 1996.

Sullivan, Larry E. *The Prison Reform Movement: Forlorn Hope.* Boston: Twayne, 1990.

Summers, Martin. *Manliness and Its Discontents: The Black Middle Class and the Transformation of Masculinity, 1900–1930.* Chapel Hill: University of North Carolina Press, 2004.

Sutherland, Edwin H., and Donald R. Cressey. *Principles of Criminology.* Chicago: Lippincott, 1960.

———. "A Theory of Differential Association." In *Criminological Theory*, edited by Francis T. Cullen and Robert Agnew, 122–25. New York: Oxford University Press, 2006.

Tannenbaum, Frank. *Crime and the Community.* New York: Columbia University Press, 1938.

Thompson, Heather Ann. *Blood in the Water: The Attica Prison Uprising of 1971 and Its Legacy.* New York: Vintage Books, 2016.

Thurman, Wallace. *Infants of the Spring.* New York: Macaulay Company, 1932.

Trotter, Joe William. *Black Milwaukee: The Making of an Industrial Proletariat, 1915–45.* Urbana: University of Illinois Press, 1985.

———. *The Great Migration in Historical Perspective: New Dimensions of Race, Class, and Gender.* Bloomington: Indiana University Press, 1991.

Turnbull, Charles W. *Casper A. Holstein: Unusual Humanitarian.* St. Thomas, VI: Dept. of Education, 1974.

Van Notten, Eleonore. *Wallace Thurman's Harlem Renaissance.* Atlanta, GA: Rodopi, 1994.

Vogel, Shane. *The Scene of Harlem Cabaret: Race, Sexuality, Performance.* Chicago: University of Chicago Press, 2009.

Wade, Wyn Craig. *The Fiery Cross: The Ku Klux Klan in America.* New York: Oxford University Press, 1998.

Wallace, Maurice O. *Constructing the Black Masculine: Identity and Ideality in African American Men's Literature and Culture, 1775–1995.* Durham, NC: Duke University Press, 2002.

Wallace, Michelle. *Black Macho and the Myth of the Superwoman.* New York: Verso Press, 2015.

Wallace, Mike. *Greater Gotham: A History of New York City from 1898–1919.* New York: Oxford University Press, 2017.

Wallace, Mike, and Edwin G. Burrows. *Gotham: A History of New York City to 1898.* New York: Oxford University Press, 1999.

Watkins-Owens, Irma. *Blood Relations: Caribbean Immigrants and the Harlem Community, 1900–1930.* Bloomington: Indiana University Press, 1996.

Weil, François. *A History of New York.* New York: Columbia University Press, 2004.

Welter, Barbara. "The Cult of True Womanhood: 1820–1860." *American Quarterly* 18 (Summer 1966): 151–74.

Whalan, Mark, ed. *The Letters of Jean Toomer, 1919–1924.* Knoxville: University of Tennessee Press, 2006.

White, Deborah Gray. *Ar'n't I a Woman?: Female Slaves in the Plantation South.* New York: W. W. Norton, 1999.

———. *Too Heavy a Load: Black Women in Defense of Themselves, 1894–1994.* New York: W. W. Norton, 1999.

White, Shane. *Somewhat More Independent: The End of Slavery in New York City, 1770–1810.* Athens: University of Georgia Press, 2004.

———. *Stories of Freedom in Black New York.* Cambridge, MA: Harvard University Press, 2007.

White, Shane, Stephen Garton, Stephen Robertson, and Graham White. *Playing the Numbers: Gambling in Harlem Between the Wars.* Cambridge, MA: Harvard University Press, 2010.

Wicker, Tom. *A Time to Die: The Attica Prison Revolt.* Chicago: Haymarket Books, 2011.

Wiebe, Robert H. *The Search for Order, 1877–1920.* New York: Hill and Wang, 1967.

Wilder, Craig Steven. *In the Company of Black Men: The African Influence on African American Culture in New York.* New York: New York University Press, 2001.

———. *A Covenant with Color: Race and Social Power in Brooklyn.* New York: Columbia University Press, 2001.

Wilkerson, Isabel. *The Warmth of Other Suns: The Epic Story of America's Great Migration.* New York: Random House, 2010.

Wilson, James Q. *Thinking About Crime*. New York: Basic Books, 1975.

Wilson, James Q., and George L. Kelling. "Broken Windows Theory." *The Atlantic Monthly* 249 (1982): 29–38.

Wilson, William Julius. *The Truly Disadvantaged: The Inner City, the Underclass, and Public Policy*. Chicago: University of Chicago Press, 1987.

Wolcott, Victoria W. "'Bible, Bath, and Broom': Nannie Helen Burrough's National Training School and African American Racial Uplift." *Journal of Women's History* 9 (Spring 1997): 88–110.

———. *Remaking Respectability: African American Women in Interwar Detroit*. Chapel Hill: University of North Carolina Press, 2001.

Wolgemuth, Kathleen L. "Woodrow Wilson and Federal Segregation." *Journal of Negro History* 44 (April 1959): 158–73.

Woodward, C. Vann. *The Strange Career of Jim Crow*. New York: Oxford University Press, 1955.

Zacks, Richard. *Island of Vice: Theodore Roosevelt's Doomed Quest to Clean Up Sin-Loving New York*. New York: Doubleday, 2012.

Index

Note: Illustrations are indicated by page numbers in *italics*.

Baldwin, Davarian, 232n13
Baldwin, James, 26, 58
Banks, William, 81–82, 84, 89
Barker, John Marshall, 67, 230n2
bars. *See* rent parties; saloons
Battle, Samuel, 52, 227n207
Beckert, Sven, 199n18
Bederman, Gail, 18, 204n79, 245n25
Bedford Hills, in general, 121, 176–77, 179,
    181, 183, 255n162, 261n80, 262n85,
    271n108, 272n114; intake, 117, 255n162;
    internment, 117, 139–40, 146, 181;
    interviews at, 135, 138–40, 262n85;
    investigators, 179, 183, 273n128;
    Laboratory of Social Hygiene at, 139;
    Parole Board at, 176–77. *See also*
    imprisonment, parole
Bedford-Stuyvesant (neighborhood), 35
Bell, Derrick, 14
Bellamy, Madge, 136
Benga, Ota, 191–92, 274n12
Bennett, Sallie, 257n184
Bertillon, Alphonse, 4
Big Flat Gang, 33
Billson, Janet Mancini, 14, 205n86
Binet-Simon intelligence test, 159
Birth of a Nation, The (film), 97, 246n29,
    248n67
Bishop, Hutchens C., 42, 130, 215n94,
    219n131
Black, Daniel P., 14
black and tans: and slumming, 61, 70, 75,
    104–6, 191; as a refuge, 55, 65, 74; as
    targets of scrutiny, 68–69, 230n3,
    235n62, 241n161, 249n83, 250n89; in
    general, 58, 60–70. *See also* saloons
Black Boy (Wright), 22–23
"black brute" stereotype, 97, 122
black businesses, 77, 83, 85, 130, 225n188,
    237n91, 240n144, 253n133
black codes, 18
black men: emasculation of, 50;
    employment prospects of, 44, 47; job
    insecurity of, 49; public space and, 27;
    saloons and, 64–65; surveillance and,
    74, 172; violence and, 62

black nationalism, 11, 56, 229n227, 231
blackness: criminality and, 9; as
    "problem," 20; Sharp trial and, 96;
    uncontrollable, 25, 194–95
Black Star Shipping, 48
black women: advocacy for, 131; and
    crucible of black criminality, 142;
    domesticity and, 127, 136; Du Bois and,
    132–33, 260n45; feminine conservation
    and, 132; gender norms and, 72;
    marriage and, 131, 221n147; paternalism
    and, 149; patriarchy and, 137; police
    and, 117; as proportion of population,
    44; as providers, 146; reformers and,
    133; respectability and, 128–29, 260n53;
    sexual violence and, 118, 247n54; in sex
    work, 52, 121, 247n53; in slavery, 102–3,
    248n62; violence performed by, 153;
    "white slavery" and, 102
Blair, Cynthia, 15
Blake, George, 268n42, 268n48
Blease, Cole, 113–14
blues: and antimodernism, 191–92; as
    cathartic, 21–22, 62; as retributive, 56,
    125, 230n232
boarders, 126; as large population, 45,
    145, 217n104–5, 107; as necessity in
    black households, 28, 40; and rape,
    140; as threat to privacy, 43. *See also*
    lodgers
bodily mutilation, 52, 103
Bolton, Sidney, 268n47
Bontemps, Arna, 55
Bottle Alley Gang, 33
Bowery (neighborhood), 33
Bowman, Jerome, 272n121
boxing, 112–14, *114*, 114–17, 253n133,
    254n141
Brace, Charles Loring, 244n13
Bradley, Cornelius, 185–86
Bradshaw, Adelaide, 170
Branch, Clinton, 90–91
Brewer, Jack, 26–28
"Broken Windows Theory," 190
Bronx, 34, 41, 85
Bronx Zoo, 191, 274n12

Committee of Fourteen (COF) (cont.)
general, 234n59, 235n60, 235n64,
interracial contact and, 78–79;
protests against, 231n4, 240n129,
race and, 68–69, 81, 83–84, 106,
240n129
Committee on Amusements and
Vacation Resources of Working-Class
Girls, 244n11
community: business and, 79; public
space and, 36; saloons and, 61; society
vs., 198n16
competition: in business, 84; crime and,
189; in employment, 28–29, 49–50; in
housing, 39; race and, 49
complaint letters, 51, 68, 74, 80–84, 141,
162, 164, 169–70, 174–85, 215n90,
235n63
complaints: police brutality, 35
conflict theory, 136
Connors Café, 76
Conrad, Joseph, 10
conscription, 33
control theory, 206n98
"coon songs," 21, 64, 69, 104, 191
Cooper, Anna Julia, 131, 137, 202n57
Copeland, Olivia, 129
Cop Remembers, A (Willemse), 104
Cotton Club, 75
Cotton States Exposition, 111
courting culture, 244n11
Cowing, Rufus B., 121, 201n46, 257n184
Cox, Sylvia, 179, 271n105
CPL. See Citizens' Protective League
(CPL)
Crane, Stephen, 87, 119, 242n162, 244n13
Crawford, Joan, 136
Crazy Blues (Smith), 125
crime(s): capitalism and, 19–20, 189;
categories of, 16–17; fines for, 162–63;
gangs and, 88, 201n46; job insecurity
and, 50; manhood and, 150–51;
patriarchal, 16–17, 128, 144–45, 153;
pleasure, 16, 30; policy, 190; race and,
161; saloons and, 63–64, 67–68, 88;
subsistence, 16–17, 145; Tammany Hall

and, 35, 79. See also imprisonment;
vice
Criminal Man (Lombroso), 4
criminology, 4–6, 15–16, 199n25, 207n110
Crisis (magazine), 56
critical criminological theory, 16, 19
critical race theory, 14
critical theory, 16
Crowder, Eugene, 168–69
crucible of black criminality, 17–20, 97,
145, 194
"culture of poverty," 9, 14, 205n85
Cunningham, Loretta, 149–50, 152–53

Daly, John, 74–75
dancehall, 26, 64, 81, 94, 118, 238n114,
249n74
Darkwater (Du Bois), 260n45
Davinne, Ford, 249n83
De Forest, Robert W., 214n81
Democratic Party, 35, 66, 79–80,
207n104, 213n71, 244n9. See also
Tammany Hall
Dewey, Annie, 213n76
Dewey, Melvil, 213n76
differential association, 206n98
Dike, Norman, 267n25
discrimination: economic solvency and,
144–45; imprisonment and, 156, 161;
job, 222n153, 225n188; Malby Equal
Rights Act and, 59; saloons and, 84.
See also racism
disease, 38, 214nn85–86, 215n87, 217n115,
216nn115, 117. See also health
disorderly conduct, 54–55, 63, 91, 138,
256n175
Dixon, Thomas, 243n29
domestic abuse, 141–42, 151–53, 176;
male-female rivalry and, 73; marriage
and, 153; masculinity and, 72; patriarchal crime and, 128; patriarchy and,
129, 148–49; saloons and, 67, 71
domestic authority, 72, 131, 134–35, 145
domesticity: masculinity and, 143;
women and, 95, 127, 135–37, 245n20,
259n42. See also family

Hughes, Langston, 44–45, 75
Hurley, R. F., 209n17

immigrants: Afro-Caribbean, 3; competition with white, 28, 44; German, 213n75; Irish, 2; Italian, 242n162; Jewish, 107, 213n70, 250n86; nativist policies on, 96; in Tenderloin, 34; urban spaces and, 7; whiteness and, 12; "white slavery" and, 94, 104–5, 108, 245n20
imprisonment, 156–58; discipline and, 165–66, 268n48; family and, 157–58, 168–70; growth of, 190–91; guilty pleas and, 161–62; health care and, 164–65, 268n47; Jim Crow and, 159; labor in, 158–59; life after, 170–76; "new penology" and, 163; parole and, 171–76, 267n38; racial disparities in, 160–61, 266n18; reform, 163–65; rehabilitation in, 172; of women, 176–85
In Dahomey (Dunbar), 192
infidelity, 24, 115, 126–27, 129, 140–42, 149, 151–53
intelligence testing, 159
interracial closeness, 59, 70
interracial communion, 241n161
interracial conflict, 22
interracial leisure, 60, 67–68, 78, 82, 85, 106
interracial marriage, 6, 20, 107, 113–14, 118
interracial prostitution, 100, 123
interracial rape, 96–97
interracial sex, criticism of, 5–6, 19, 20, 23, 67, 70, 95–98; prostitution, 94–109, 119–124; in general, 246n31, 248n67, 249n83; Jack Johnson and, 113–117
interracial violence, Amenia conference and, 36; and crucible of black criminality, 194; in general, 9, 18, 57, 58–60, 62–63, 70–72, 92, 109–112; in prison, 165–166, 167; interracial leisure and, 82; migration and, 29; police and, 27; race and, 103–4; retributive violence, 21–23; saloons and, 59; slavery and, 18; Washington attack and, 110–11

investigator(s): and prostitution, 250n89; parole, 173, 175, 179; police, 71, 107, 109, 262n94, 271n106; prison, 268n48; private, 39; in saloons, 61, 67–68, 76–80, 86, 238n97, 250n83
investigation(s): antivice, 61, 68; Lexow Committee, 35; and paradox of progressive thought, 6–7; parole, 173, 180; Property Owners' Protective Association of Harlem, 39; race and, 52–53; Rockefeller Grand Jury, 107–8; of saloons, 59, 67, 76, 79–80, 84–87, 215n90, 231n4, 234n59, 249n83; sex work and, 100, 215n90; Sharp trial, 118; Tenement Commission, 37
Irish immigrants, 2
Israels, Belle Lindner, 244n11

Jackson, Mabel, 168
jail. *See* imprisonment
Jamaica (Queens), 35, 189, 212n64
James, Monte, 71
Jameson, Jacob, 49–50
Jeffries, Jim, 2, 112–17
Jenkins, Earnestine, 14
Jenkins, Wallace, *47*
Jewish immigrants, 107, 213n70, 250n86
Jim Crow, 22, 55; imprisonment and, 159; interracial reproduction and, 98; migration to escape, 29; origin of term, 6; parole and, 171; respectability and, 129; violence and, 60; whites and, 98
job insecurity, 49–50, 128–29, 144, 271n108
Johnson, Jack, 2, 112–14, *114*, 114–17, 123–24, 253n133, 254n141, 255n152
Johnson, James Weldon, 29, 80
Johnson, Lyndon, 190
Johnson, Marilyn, 213n70, 226n199
Johnstone, Robert Zachariah, 230n3
Jones, Clifton, 144, 262n95–96
Jones, William H., 65
Julien, Isaac, 203n73
"Jump Jim Crow," 6

Katz, Jack, 62, 208n136, 233n19
Kelling, George L., 190–91

McDonough Amendment, 158–59
McKay, Claude, 35, 41, 56
McKinley, William, 3
McKinney, Susan, 219n126
Mercer, Kobena, 203n73
Merton, Robert K., 189, 273n1
Meyer, George, 27
middle class: African American, 28–29, 31, 36–37, 41–42, 153–54; domesticity and, 180; family and, 153–54; masculinity, 88–89, 145; respectability and, 139; saloons and, 64, 69–70; sexual correctness and, 54–55; whites, 109, 191–92
migrants, and achieved status, 203n72; and disease, 38; and seeking opportunity in New York, 3, 7, 29, 44, 46, 49–50, 55, 77, 127, 188; and seeking manhood, 12; criticism of, 21, 41–42, 134, 202n56, 203n62, 204n80, 209n20, 210n47, 217n113, 219n131, 222n156; in general, 1, 2, 10, 116, 198n13, 212n59, 212n64, 228n211; issues associated with, 128, 161, 216n101, 217n113, 225n188; women, 131–133, 143, 146
migration, and seeking manhood, 12; for freedom, 21, 127, 203n72; Great Migration, 198n13, 212n59; hardships of, 128, 134, 216n101; in general, 27, 107, 116, 212n64, 225n188, 228n220; intraurban, 34, 61,
Miles, Josie, 56
Miller, Frederick, 32–33, 35, 57, 211n49
Miller, Kelly, 10, 14, 30, 161
Miner, Maude, 105
Minettas district, 60, 87, 241n161
minstrel shows, 21, 64, 69, 191
Mitchel, John Purroy, 87
Mitchell, Michele, 258n10
modernity, 191
Moody, Henrietta, 148
Moore, Fred, 30, 80–81, 85, 106, 229n227, 240n129
Moore, Fred R., 80–81
Moretti, Sofia, 239n117

Morgan, John Tyler, 10
Moss, Belinda, 107
Moss, Frank, 51, 226n196
motherhood, single, 141–42
Mott, Hannah, 41
Moynihan Report, 205n85
Muhammad, Khalil Gibran, 15, 206n90
mulattoes, 2, 5, 60, 87–88, 98, 115, 200n31, 241n161, 242n162
Mumford, Kevin, 237n85
Munro, John J., 212n63
murder: intraracial, 42, 85–86, 89–92, 125–29, 168, 257n3; interracial, 26–28, 32–35, 58–60, 72–73, 118, 144, 150, 227n200, 262n94; in general, 2, 15–16, 22, 25, 141, 145, 155, 165, 198n9, 211n49, 268n47; intimate partner, 146–47, 148–50, 151–54, 247n57
Murphy, Harold, 43
music, 20–22, 64, 69, 104, 189, 191–93

National Association for the Advancement of Colored People (NAACP), 30–31, 55–56, 210n37
nationalism, black, 11, 56, 229nn227, 231
National League for the Protection of Colored Women, 100
National Negro Business League, 77
National Training School, 260n53
National Urban League (NUL), 43, 50, 225n188
"Negro Bohemia," 34
Negro Liquor Dealer's Association, 84
Negro Printer's Union, 222n156
New Jim Crow, The (Alexander), 14
Newman, Harriet, 39
"New Negro," 11–12, 26, 31, 55–56, 96, 203n73, 205n89
"new women," 96–97, 136–37, 245n21
New York: in black imagination, 188, 198n13
New York Amsterdam News, 37, 48, 52, 74, 84
New York House of Refuge, 1
New York Probation and Protective Association, 105

New York Sun, 87, 133, 143

New York Times, 200n41

New York Tribune, 118, 244n5, 246n40, 251n90, 252n123, 257n187

Nigger Heaven (Van Vechten), 192

nightlife, as an industry, 28, 55, 64, 85; as a refuge, 60, 64, 74; in general, 61, 101, 105–106, 176, 236n66; white participation in, 62, 69, 70, 84

Nixon, Richard, 190

Nott, Charles Cooper, 211n49

NUL. See National Urban League (NUL)

numbers (gambling), 47–48, 63, 175, 190, 228n220; unjust arrest, 162, 190–91

Obama, Barack, 187–88

O'Connor, John, 215n90

Odd Fellows, 37–38

Of Water and the Spirit (Somé), 1

Ogburn, William Fielding, 147, 212n61, 228n211, 263n114

Olympia Music Hall, 64

opium, 100

Oppenheim, David, 76

"other-directedness," 3, 198n16

Overton, Aida, 80

Ovington, Mary White, 146, 161, 163, 218n116, 222n156, 264n114

Parker, George, 175

Parker, John, 239n117

Parkerson, Florence, 272n120

Parkhurst, Charles, 5

parole: board and personnel, 13, 39, 158, 163, 167–68, 171–77, 179–83, 185–86; records, 13; releases, 1, 24, 34, 60, 141, 155–56, 160, 170–77, 179–83, 185–86; as system, 156, 158–60, 170–77, 179–83, 190, 270n73, 270n76; violations, 157, 166–67, 170, 175–76, 180, 182, 185, 269n54, 270n73, 272n115. See also imprisonment

paternalism, 5, 19, 21, 42, 134, 149, 236n66

paternity suits, 263n99

patriarchal crimes, 16–17, 128, 144–45, 153

patriarchy, as criminogenic, 129, 148, 207n110; in general, 18–19, 182, 205n89, 207n110; middle-class, 127, 153; loss of, 127, 137; white, 103, 109, 134,

Payton, Philip A., 215n94

Peabody, George, 251n107

pedestrians, 53–54. See also sidewalks

Perkins, Joseph, 182

Peters, Derry, 159

Philadelphia, Pennsylvania, 190

Philadelphia Negro (Du Bois), 10, 206n94

Philadelphia Tribune, 114

Pickett, Lizzie, 137–39

Pierce, Hattie, 54

Pierce, Shelton, 88

pimps, 16, 64, 67, 88–89, 100–101, 105–6, 120, 137, 184, 235n64, 247n44

Pitts, Adam, 176–80, 183–85, 271n105, 271n135

Pitts, Evelyn, 176–77, 178–81, 183–85, 272n116, 271n135

Plantation Negro as a Freeman, The (Bruce), 5

pleasure crimes, 16, 30

Plessy v. Ferguson, 6, 10, 55

police, 28, 32, 35–36, 50–54, 58–59, 190–91, 213n70, 225n193, 226n194; commentary about blacks by, 70, 74, 89, 102, 118; and corruption, 7, 63, 79–80, 82, 98, 101, 107–8, 123, 190, 245n20; and neglect of black citizens, 53, 91, 147, 228n211; and racial riots, 2, 6, 22, 25, 27–30, 49–53, 56, 58–60, 111, 225n193, 252n127

police brutality, 194, 209n14; Citizens' Protective League and, 226n199; criminality and, 25; investigation of, 35, 52; legacy of, 188; Miller trial and, 33; public space and, 23; racialization of, 213n70; resistance to, 89

policy shops, 63

political machines, 213n71. See also Tammany Hall

politics: black masculinity and, 203n73, 232n13; employment and, 44; housing and, 37; "New Negroes" and, 96; of respectability, 31; saloons and, 66–67; sexual, 74, 95, 97, 116, 118, 142; slavery and, 103; violence and, 27; Washington assault and, 112; "white slavery" and, 115

Poole, Joseph, 32–33, 36, 211n49

Pope, James, 162

population growth, African American, 33–34, 212n59

poverty: "Broken Windows" thesis and, 190; criminality and, 25, 195; and "culture of poverty" debate, 9, 14, 205n85; gangs and, 33; health and, 38; in Hell's Kitchen, 2; masculinity and, 151; parole and, 173; progressivism and, 131; race and, 19–20; sex work and, 123; and wealth, 20

Powell, Adam Clayton, 11–12, 110, 114, 229n224

Powers, Madelon, 233n19

precarity, employment, 50

pregnancy, 145–46, 260n57

Price, Thomas F., 96, 202n57

prison. *See* imprisonment

prison reform, 163–65

probation: documents, 13; New York Probation and Protective Association, 105; officer, 162; as system, 163

Progressives, 5; black, 36, 131–32, 217; courting culture and, 244n11; criminological views of, 9, 145; marriage and, 131–32; saloons and, 70, 76, 79, 234n58; sex work and, 105, 108, 122, 133; Sharp trial and, 94–95, 97, 101; women and, 134. *See also* reformers

Prohibition, 62

Property Owners' Protective Association of Harlem, 39

prostitution. *See* sex work

protest, 20, 25; of Civil War conscription, 33; crime as, 15; Du Bois and, 31

public houses, 58–63. *See also* saloons

public racial violence, against African Americans, 6, 22, 58–59, 109–112; as a term, 18–19, 21, 23, 25, 92, 103, 110, 167, 229n227, 231n5; black initiated, 9, 55–57, 61–62, 88; draft riots, 6; riots, 6, 27–29; police and, 27–29, 33–35, 50–51, 58–59, 194; segregation as, 188;

public space, 33, 36, 42–43, 54–55, 108, 211n48, 236n75

Queens, 34–35, 41, 223n167

queer men, 55, 73–74, 229n224

Question of Manhood, A (Clark & Jenkins, eds.), 14

race: competition and, 49; crime and, 161; health and, 40; homosexuality and, 73–74; imprisonment and, 160–61; poverty and, 19–20; reproduction and, 97; slumming and, 68–71; womanhood and, 136–37. *See also* African Americans; whites

Race, Racism, and American Law (Bell), 14

race riots: emancipation and, 6; gangs and, 33; in Hell's Kitchen, 2; Johnson-Jeffries match and, 112–13; as overshadowing everyday racial violence, 209n14; police in, 51

Race Traits (Hoffman), 9–10

racial destiny, 42, 122, 130–34, 201n49, 258n10, 259n26

racial uplift, 79, 127, 133–34

racism: capitalism and, 189; popular, 71; scientific, 96; uncontrollable blackness and, 25. *See also* discrimination

ragtime music, 64–65, 191–92

Railroad Bill, 21–22, 193

Raines Law, 100, 235n60

Rainsford, William S., 86, 238n97

rape, 96, 103–4, 245n17. *See also* sexual violence

Ray, Jacqueline, 182–83

Reagan, Ronald, 190

Redding, Montgomery, 164, 166–67, 268n44, 269nn254–55

Redman, Julius, 149–50

Red Summer, 6, 56, 230n236

Reed, Ruth, 221n147, 263n100

tenements, and prostitution, 100, 121, 137, 249n83; and black ownership, 215n94; conditions in, 28, 33, 37–38, 41–43, 214n81, 217n113, 218n116, 220n138, 230n2; in general, 16, 27–28, 68, 112, 252n127

Terman, Lewis, 159

Terrell, Mary Church, 30

Thatcher, Earl, 164

Thinking About Crime (Wilson), 190

Thomas, Will, 148

Thomas, William Hannibal, 217n126

Thorpe, Robert, 50–52, 227n200

Thurman, Wallace, 41

Tin Pan Alley, 64

Tönnies, Ferdinand, 198n16

Toomer, Jean, 46

"tough on crime" rhetoric, 9

Traffic in Souls (film), 95–96

"treating system," 95

trials: Branch, 90; Burns, 72; Harper, 42–43; Maxwell, 89–90; Miller, 32–33, 35, 57, 211n49; Rockefeller Grand Jury, 107–8; Sharp, 94–97, 99, 101, 104–6, 109, 116, 118–23, 244n6, 255n168, 256n175; Snow, 125–27, 129

tuberculosis, 40–41, 217n115, 217n115, 120. *See also* disease; health

Tupac. *See* Shakur, Tupac

Turner, George Kibbe, 105, 107–08

Ulrich, Albert, 109–12, 115, 251n102

unemployment, 28, 50, 93, 101. *See also* employment

United Negro Improvement Association (UNIA), 229n231

Urban League, 41, 43

Utopia Neighborhood Club, 220n141

vagrancy, 46, 54, 267n25; incidence of, 54

Van Vechten, Carl, 192

Veiller, Lawrence, 214n81

vice: African Americans and, 68; black progressives and, 131; Chinese and, 247n44; housing and, 230n2; interra-

cial sex as, 106; police corruption and, 108; as resistance, 232n17; saloons and, 84, 86, 88, 234n59; Sharp trial and, 121; Tenderloin and, 53. *See also* crime(s)

vice campaigns, 96–97

Vinegar Hill (neighborhood), 35

violence, 2; and crucible of black criminality, 17, 145; disease and, 214n85; of forced labor, 17–18; gangs and, 33, 242n171; imprisonment and, 156, 159, 165–66; interracial sex and, 96, 111–12; Johnson-Jeffries match and, 112–13; large-scale, 6; masculinity and, 19, 90–91; from police, 27, 51, 213n70, 226n199, 252n123; police refusal to investigate, 53; powerlessness and, 18; respect and, 15; retributive, 11, 21, 57, 149; saloons and, 93, 229; segregation and, 188–89; sexual, 40, 148–49, 247n54, 259n44; slavery and, 18; "white slavery" and, 98. *See also* domestic abuse; interracial violence

Voice from the South, A (Cooper), 131

Wade, Wyn Craig, 248n62

Walker, George, 80

Walker, John, 143–44, 161–62

Walsh, Edmund, 170

Waring, J. H. N., 203n66

War on Crime, 190

War on Drugs, 190

Washington, Booker T., and accommodationism, 11, 31, 200n34; and racial violence, 109–112, 116–117, 123–124, 229n227, 251n102, 251n107; criticism of Jack Johnson, 115; criticism of working class, 14, 42; death of, 31; in general, 77, 249n80; and National Negro Business League, 218n120

Washington, D.C., 34, 77, 138

Washington, Forrester B., 45

Waters, Ethel, 254n141

Watts, Helen, 94–95, 101, 118–19, 256n175

Weeksville (neighborhood), 35

Wells, Ida B., 56, 245n17
Wells, Liddy, 144–45, 262n94
Welter, Barbara, 259n42
What's Happening (television program),
245n23
Wheeler, Rebecca, 49
White, Deborah Gray, 259n44, 261n83
White, George Henry, 12
white gangs, 33, 112
Whitehead, Dell, 1–2, 5, 7, 200n32
white masculinity, 12, 19, 97–98, 205n86,
245n25
White Plains, New York, 138
White Rose Mission Society, 131, 134
whites: blackness as "problem" for, 20;
demographic change and, 188; and
fetishization of black saloons, 70, 76;
health of, 40–41, 215n86, 217n115;
Johnson/Jeffries match and, 112,
115–16; middle class, 109, 191–92;
migrants and, 210n47; migration of,
from cities, 188–89; mulattoes and,
200n31; police and, 28, 53–54; public
racial violence and, 103–4; regard for
black women by, 102; restrictive
covenants and, 29; sex work and, 105;
slumming and, 68–71; womanhood
and, 99–109. *See also* race
"white slavery," 94–96, 101–2, 104–5,
121–22, 245n17, 248n72, 249n86
White Slave Traffic Act, 96–97, 106,
249n81
white women: black men as menacing to,
52; Committee of Fourteen and, 84;
employment of married, 137; as
"fallen," 133; feminine conservation
and, 132; paternalism and, 149; saloons
and, 68, 80, 234n58; self-support by,
44; as slummers, 79; violence and,
70–71. *See also* "white slavery"
Whitin, Frederick, 230n4
Whyos (gang), 33
Wilcox, Ruby, 117, 138–40
Wilcox, Walter, 266n18
Wilder, Craig Steven, 203n70

Wilkins, Barron, 76–78, *78*, 79, 83–86,
126, 238n114
Wilkins, Leroy, 77, 80, 82–86
Wilks, Sonny, 269n62
Willemse, Cornelius, 54, 104, 209n12,
248n69
Williams, Bert (entertainer), 80
Williams, Bert (parolee), 175
Willis, Clarence, 152
Wilson, James Q., 190
Wilson, Woodrow, 6, 201n43
Winston, Devil, 21
Winters, Victoria, 139–40, 261n80
Witt, Jesse, 89–92
Wolcott, Victoria, 258n12, 260n53
womanhood: black, 17, 128, 154, 193; new,
136–37; saloons and, 73; white, 95,
99–109, 122
Woman's Christian Temperance
Union, 108
women: black, white regard for, 102;
black manhood and, 132–33;
domesticity and, 95, 127, 135–37,
245n20, 259n42; employment and, 117,
137; "fallen," 95–96; family and, 96,
136; imprisonment of, 176–85; and
imprisonment of men, 169; job
insecurity of, 128–29; Ku Klux Klan
and, 103; in marriage, 127–28, 135–36,
139–40, 181–82; masculine renewal
and, 134; masculinity and ownership
of, 95–96; "new," 96–97, 136–37,
245n21; in pregnancy, 145–46,
260n57; respectability and, 138–39,
258n12; saloons and, 71–72, 240n147.
See also black women; white women
work: avoiding toil, 133, 140–41, 184; in
general, 44, 57, 92, 143, 148, 151, 155,
168, 184; bad pay and, 28, 143;
commodification of, 3; competition
with whites, 29; criticism of the
unemployed, 42, 46, 162, 182;
dissatisfaction with, 8, 45–46, 48,
domestic, 135, 137–40, 163; imbalance
in male and female work, 128–29,

work (cont.)
146–47, 150; job loss, 40, 143–44; migrating for, 26, 29, 77; and prejudice, 44, 145; and reform, 5; restricting women from, 72–73, 130–31, 151, 183; seasonal, 44, 91, 144; unemployment drives men/women to crime, 43, 49–50, 142–41; work and leisure combined, 60–65, 136

work as rehabilitation, 163, 170–76, 179–81; work in prison, 166–67. *See also* sex work; employment

World War I, 11–12, 31, 96, 136, 205n89, 226n199

World War II, 189, 192

Wright, Richard, 22–23

Young Men's Industrial League, 225n188

www.ingramcontent.com/pod-product-compliance
Lightning Source LLC
Chambersburg PA
CBHW020457270326
41926CB00008B/636